AF573998

Sovereignty: Interpretations

Also by Jo-Anne Pemberton

GLOBAL METAPHORS
Modernity and the Quest for One World

Sovereignty: Interpretations

Jo-Anne Pemberton
Senior Lecturer
School of Social Sciences and International Studies
University of New South Wales, Australia

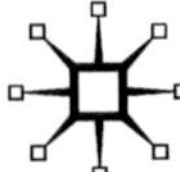

First published 2009 by
PALGRAVE MACMILLAN

Palgrave Macmillan in the UK is an imprint of Macmillan Publishers Limited, registered in England, company number 785998, of Houndmills, Basingstoke, Hampshire RG21 6XS.

Palgrave Macmillan in the US is a division of St Martin's Press LLC, 175 Fifth Avenue, New York, NY 10010.

Palgrave Macmillan is the global academic imprint of the above companies and has companies and representatives throughout the world.

Palgrave® and Macmillan® are registered trademarks in the United States, the United Kingdom, Europe and other countries.

ISBN-13: 978–1–4039–3582–3 hardback
ISBN-10: 1–4039–3582–3 hardback

This book is printed on paper suitable for recycling and made from fully managed and sustained forest sources. Logging, pulping and manufacturing processes are expected to conform to the environmental regulations of the country of origin.

A catalogue record for this book is available from the British Library.

Library of Congress Cataloging-in-Publication Data

Pemberton, Jo-Anne.
Sovereignty : interpretations / Jo-Anne Pemberton.
p. cm.
Includes bibliographical references and index.
ISBN 978–1–4039–3582–3 (alk. paper)
1. Sovereignty. I. Title.
JC327.P38 2008
320.1'5–dc22

2008025819

10 9 8 7 6 5 4 3 2 1
18 17 16 15 14 13 12 11 10 09

Printed and bound in Great Britain by
CPI Antony Rowe, Chippenham and Eastbourne

For my mother.

Contents

Preface

I am considerably indebted to a number of people who have supported me in preparing this manuscript. My colleague in Sydney, Helen Pringle has provided enormous encouragement and I have gained much enlightenment on the finer points of political theory from my extensive conversations with her. Helen has also been very generous in pointing me towards materials of interest. Ephraim Nimni, Preston King, Roderic Pitty and Mark Rolfe have also been an invaluable source of both emotional and intellectual support and I offer them my sincerest thanks. There are several others who have assisted me in the course of writing this book and whom I would like to thank: Jamie Roberts, Isabel Homrich da Jordanda and Sandrine de Castro all of whom have drawn my attention to literature of great relevance to this topic. There are several others who have assisted me in a variety of ways in writing this book to whom I wish to express my deepest thanks: Jens Boel, Mahmoud Ghander and Steve Nyong of the UNESCO Archives and Peter Carmen of the Paris American Academy. Many thanks also to Laetitia Thibaut and David Santoro who assisted me with a number of French translations. Finally, I would like to thank members of my family: Mark, Sally, Gail, Gregory and Christian Pemberton all of whom provided support in various ways.

The topic of sovereignty is a very broad one and relates to any number of issues. Inevitably, one has to be selective in choosing what materials and topics to include and in deciding on how much space one will accord them. Obviously, some readers will have a different view than I do of the choices I have made. Originally I intended to include a chapter on the status of humanitarian intervention when viewed through the prism of sovereignty, however, I came to the conclusion that as this topic has been extensively and very effectively addressed in recent years, its inclusion was unnecessary. Nonetheless, I have touched on this topic at certain points throughout the book.

The book is organised thematically. Chapters 2 and 3 address the internal and external dimensions of the question of sovereignty. Chapter 4 deals with the relation between sovereignty and imperialism as well as the role sovereignty plays in the post-colonial world. Chapter 5 continues this examination of the relation between sovereignty and colonialism, except its focus is specifically on the experience of those indigenous peoples who continue to live under a form of colonial rule and who are striving to establish their right of self-determination. The Chapter 6 looks at the question of where sovereignty lies, if it lies anywhere, in the context of the European Union while Chapter 7 returns to more general issues in examining the relationship between sovereignty, the state and war. At the same time, it is important to note that at certain points the individual chapters refer back to or flag certain topics raised in the other chapters.

All translations from the French texts listed in the bibliography are mine as is the translation of the 1909 edition of Pasquale Fiore's *Diritto Internazionale Codificato e la sua Sanzione Giruidica*. Where I have translated a quotation from the French appearing in an English language text this is indicated in the Notes section at the end of the book.

1
Introduction

During the closing decades of the twentieth century, there appeared a sizeable body of literature spun around the theme of globalisation with much of this literature heralding the decline or even demise of the sovereign state. Globalisation in its various forms – economic, cultural, environmental and so forth – had blurred the old lines of territorial demarcation. Social activity, and with it social problems, were beginning to spread profusely across borders. Territorial divisions were said to be melting away, merging into the almost seamless flux of late modernity. Viewed against this background, the sovereign state, as a legally and politically sealed unit, looked increasingly anachronistic: a remnant of a rapidly fading past in which territory defined almost everything. Thus, the question was posed: how are communities to organise themselves in an increasingly borderless world? Proposals centred on the notion of multi-level governance were prominent in this context, suggestive as they were of a world characterised by overlapping but complementary jurisdictions ranging from the local to the global.

Yet, despite this shift away from state-centric perspectives we were not always told to discard the term sovereignty itself. Rather, it was suggested that sovereignty needed to be reconceptualised so as to accommodate the increasing porosity of territorial borders and multi-dimensionality of world politics. Hence, we saw such adjectives as pooled, shared or divided attached to the word. The difficulty, however, is that such reconceptualisations would render sovereignty its own opposite, that is, the opposite of what it has been taken to mean since at least the late sixteenth century: supreme, absolute and indivisible authority. It is, of course, true that the meaning of the word 'sovereign' has shifted in the past. In medieval France, for example, the word *souverain* could stand for any authority 'which had no other authority above itself' and thus, France's 'highest courts' in that period were designated '*Cours Souverains*' (Oppenheim, 1912, p.111; see also Bluntschli, 2000, p.388). It was the French lawyer Jean Bodin who restricted the scope of the term, using it to refer to that supreme authority which is vested in the state and only in the state. This understanding was taken up and rendered more explicit by later authors in a context in which rulership was becoming increasingly depersonalised and even though, hand in hand with sovereignty's depersonalisation, state organs were multiplying.

Bodin's adaptation of the concept was well suited to a period in which the overall trend was in the direction of the centralisation of royal power, something which entailed anti-hegemonial struggle and a general consolidation of state borders. Now it may be that a world comprised of discrete and hierarchically organised entities is no longer an effective way of managing human affairs. The sovereign state form is, after all, only one way of organising social experience. If the sovereign state is indeed becoming a moribund institution then the term sovereignty will likely either fall into disuse or be redefined along the lines indicated above. However, it is not apparent that the sovereign state is as irrelevant as some have suggested. It is true that globalisation, the impact of which is highly uneven, raises important questions about the *de facto* enjoyment of this *de jure* condition. Further, to the extent that this phenomenon conduces to a strengthening of international co-operation and international institutions, it is to be welcomed. Even so, the state remains the basic unit of world politics and, whatever may be the fate of particular governments or regimes, there is little evidence that the institution of the state has become illegitimate in the eyes of people the world over. Certainly, there are many groups who are highly dissatisfied with the state in which they live, however, the response of such groups, where they cannot reach accommodation with the state which encircles them, is usually to engage in secessionist struggle with the ultimate aim of establishing a new and independent state.

That the rhetoric concerning the dilution of sovereignty in a globalised world became less intense in the early twenty-first century may be due to the added focus on military-territorial security in this period. In the first decade of the twenty-first century the power of the state, and the significance of the kind of power that it possesses, became more perceptible. Yet, talk of sovereignty's demise was in any case bound to die down given the palpable and continuing presence of an international system constructed around sovereign states. My view is that claims about the end of sovereignty in a shrinking world were often more hortatory than real, driven by the conviction (one that has been embraced in other periods of history and not without reason), that the sovereign state is a destructive institution which fosters oppression within the state and suspicion and conflict without.

Again, the preceding observations are not meant to suggest that the current system will or should remain with us for eternity. As I have indicated, the state system is only one way of managing the affairs of humanity and humanity may well decide one day that it is no longer adequate to the task. A survey of domestic and international conditions as regards conflict, extreme poverty, human rights abuses, and environmental degradation provides compelling evidence of the current failings of this system. However, as indicated, my assumption is that the institutions of the state and sovereignty will be with us for some time to come not only because of the absence of ready alternatives but also because these institutions continue to command widespread support. Independent statehood is currently seen as the principal means by which the security of a community can be achieved and its self-expression realised and this is even though the sovereign state remains, at the same time, the principal source of insecurity and too often serves as an obstacle to communal flourishing. Indeed, these two points are crucially inter-related: the qualities which render the sovereign state a useful instrument in some contexts, such as its law and order powers, render it a threatening institution in others.

Accepting these last points, a critical re-examination of the concept of sovereignty would seem to be in order and throughout this study I have sought to bring to light what I believe to be the ethical imperatives embedded in it, although in full recognition of the fact that the institutionalisation of the concept poses significant risks. I do not call what I have undertaken a reconceptualisation of sovereignty simply because my belief is that these imperatives, in a more or less developed form, are evident in most of the writings on sovereignty produced since at least the time of Bodin. That these imperatives have been neglected or only confusedly understood by some theorists can be explained in terms of a tendency to conflate sovereignty with political power and, related to this, to overlook the social context, whether internal or external, in which the idea of the sovereignty of the state is forged. However, it is in political life above all that infantile understandings, not to mention cynical manipulations, of the concept have been most in evidence. Political actors down through the centuries as well as in the present day have been conspicuous in their attempts, often successful, at personalising the power of the state even while claiming to be its servant. Yet, personalised power, whether in disguised or explicit form, is not sovereignty at all since by definition power that is merely personal has no constitutive base: it refers only to the will of the person or persons who assert some obscure right to wield it.

That the concept of sovereignty originally was developed in connection with theories of personal rule and the absolutist state should not be allowed to elide, as I argue in Chapter 2, the essentially democratic thrust of the concept. That sovereignty's origins can only lie with communal willing was well understood from the beginning. Authors such as Bodin and Thomas Hobbes, although associated with absolutist renditions of the theory of sovereignty, clearly appreciated that the authority of the state ultimately depended on a communal state of mind made manifest in constitutive acts and continuing acceptance of the state's authority. It was not difficult to go from here to arguing, as came to be widely accepted from the eighteenth century onwards, for a right of collective resistance to the commands of power and the institution of democratic political forms. The popularisation of sovereignty has thrown up its own problems such as the danger of ochlocracy, indeed, it was because of this danger that Bodin resisted what he called popular states or at least suggested that popular states should only be governed by the virtuous and wise. The response to the problem of ensuring that the people as a body is protected from itself generally takes the form of the constitutionalisation of rights and representative democracy. However, in seeking to distance the people from itself representation cannot avoid the problem, the problem that it is principally designed to ameliorate if not resolve, which is the gap between rulers and ruled.

It was because the existence of such a gap gave scope to abuses of power that Rousseau eschewed representation. Government by popular assemblies is not widely considered to be an option in modern democracies and thus attention must turn to ways of ensuring that the distance between rulers and ruled, while necessary for the business of government, is not such that access to the public sphere is unduly curtailed. The problem of the abuse of state power tends to be more pronounced in non-democratic states or states lacking institutions independent of the executive charged with enforcing constitutional rights and this last issue is addressed in relation to China in Chapter 4. Yet it is also a problem, to a greater or lesser degree, in democratic states where periodic electoral processes have proved to be an insufficient means of checking corruption and dictatorial uses of power and given this, and given the tendency of power to ignore or obscure its origins in communal attitudes, the idea that democracy has as its corollary a right of insurrection is something of which the public should be ever conscious and public officials ever wary. Yet, a radicalisation of contemporary democratic processes must extend beyond assertions of people power, as important as these can be, in the streets or elsewhere. Indeed, we need to ask of any given polity who comprises the people. A truly democratic polity, is one in which the sovereignty of the state is solidly and *widely* anchored to the community, such that the voices of the marginal and disempowered are ensured a hearing in the public sphere.

A sophisticated understanding of what sovereignty signified internationally took a long time to develop and this matter is traced in Chapter 3. Even though the beginnings of the sovereign state system were forged in a context of anti-imperial struggle, some members of this system proved more than willing to indulge in imperialist behaviour themselves. Part of the explanation for this kind of behaviour concerns another form of infantilism when it comes to thinking about sovereignty: the notion that sovereignty can somehow be asserted as a set of international rights while being virtually ignored as a set of international obligations. This way of thinking is depicted well in Freud's essay 'On Narcissism' wherein he sources the beginnings of the narcissistic personality to the projection onto the child of the parents' own narcissistic feelings. He writes in relation to this: 'Illness, death, renunciation of enjoyment, restrictions on his [the child's] own will, are not to touch him; the laws of nature, like those of society, are to be abrogated in his favour; he is really to be the centre and heart of creation, "His Majesty the Baby"' (Freud, 1957, p.48). Drawing an analogy between state-centric behaviour and childish narcissism is hardly new. Rousseau, for example, in his essay called *Considerations on the Government of Poland* noted that becoming a great power means being able to say like the Russians of the day, that is, like a child: 'When the whole world is mine, I shall eat a lot of candy' (Rousseau, 1762).

That said, it is also important to emphasise that there is more than stunted emotional development at stake here: a decentralised political and legal order gives rise to certain inconveniences and an interventionist policy has historically been seen as a way of addressing these. Although it would be wrong to suggest that there was no recognition of the incompatibility between state sovereignty and intervention prior to the nineteenth century, (Bodin and many theorists after him understood the necessary relation between sovereignty and non-intervention and in the early eighteenth century, the institution balance of power was conceived of as a means of preventing hegemonic behaviour), it was only in the period following the defeat of Napoleon Bonaparte that the relation between sovereignty and non-intervention really began to crystallise in state practice. Most notable in this context, was the Congress system. This system was instituted towards the end of the Napoleonic wars and involved meetings among the powers to discuss issues of common concern and declare on the public law of Europe. Efforts at placing relations in Europe on a sound legal footing accelerated in the second half of the nineteenth century. Especially after the Franco-German war of 1870–1871, there was a renewed push (renewed, because of the earlier efforts of Jeremy Bentham and the Abbé Henri Grégoire among others), to codify and extend international law, with the ultimate aim of abolishing war.

The twentieth century saw states significantly redefine their rights and responsibilities under international law and not only in relation to intervention and the use of force. States exercised their sovereignty to greatly add to their range of obligations, such that it is difficult today to maintain that the municipal realm remains a domain wholly reserved to states. My argument here is that the logic of sovereignty in the international sphere should lead to the entrenchment and extension of state obligations. Even though states have often tended to act as if there is only one sovereign in the world, the fact that states inevitably come into contact with and need each other means that they must find ways of managing their relations. Indeed, it is impossible for a state to maintain a solipsistic outlook since the rights of states only gain meaning in a social context: their existence depends on shared frameworks of understandings and, based on these, mutual recognition. It follows that sovereignty is not above international law but can only be thought of in relation to an international legal order. Relations between states are thus managed within a context of mutual recognition which must from the outset encompass such norms as respect for sovereignty and its corollary non-intervention (see Jackson, 1998, p.9n and Frost, 1996, p.152). Beyond this, and based on these basic principles as well as the emergence of certain shared values and interests, states can enter into any number of obligations. Indeed, one could argue that sovereign states, as sites of potentially ever thickening sets of mutual responsibilities, can serve as the instruments of their own transcendence, or at least as instruments by which international relations can move beyond its primitive, egoistic stage to a situation in which law is sovereign. In stating this last, I am not urging the appearance of international institutions equipped with a power of sanction comparable to that of the state, but only the widespread adoption or internalisation by states of a law-abiding attitude.

I have suggested that states have indefeasible obligations to one another by virtue of the fact, as argued by Mervyn Frost, that they are constituted, at least in part, through acts of mutual recognition. Each state is implicated in the constitution of the other. Yet, while *prima facie* these obligations concern interstate relations, in a fundamental sense they are obligations owed by one portion of humanity to another. This is even though they are carried out *via* the mechanism of the state. It is the idea of humanity obligations, and the idea of the sovereign state as a means, albeit contingent, of protecting the interests of humanity that leads us to the concept of humanitarian intervention. We owe duties to other states, such as respect for their territorial integrity, only because we owe duties to humanity and where those who wield power in a state are destructive of the interests of humanity then sovereignty loses its *raison d'être*. While sovereignty may serve as a license to kill in certain circumstances, it is not a license to murder, whether externally or internally. Although sadly it has been exploited and even invoked as such, it remains the case that the rights a state enjoys under this rubric are wholly a function of the rights we possess as human beings and states cannot be permitted to do that which is impermissible for human beings (Christopher, 2004, p.132).

It is on the natural rights of human beings that our obligations to the stateless also rest. Humanity, as the final author of the state system, in order to advance its ends, imposed on states an individual and collective duty of care towards the stateless. Summing up these points, one can say that there is an important sense in which the legitimacy of the state system is contingent upon its ability to advance the well-being of human beings irrespective of their nationality or legal status. Indeed, every effort to advance the interests of humanity *via* the mechanism of the state system, whether in the form of individual states or in the form of international institutions, is a reaffirmation of its value.

In Chapter 4, I further examine the relation between sovereignty and empire, addressing the argument that while sovereignty entails non-intervention in the context of a state system in which states mutually recognise each other, this rule need not apply to entities not recognised as sovereign. A prominent line of argument developed in defence of imperialism in the past was that the European law of nations did not apply to entities, regardless of whether these entities possessed developed state organs or not, deemed uncivilised by European standards. Intervention in such entities thus was not a violation of sovereign rights as they could not be said to be in possession of them. This argument was used to justify the swallowing up of large parts of the world by European powers. It also was used to justify interference within China's borders, causing the Chinese, in order to defend themselves against foreign incursions, to examine and embrace the European law of nations including the principle of sovereignty and this development is discussed in some detail. In any case, my response to this defence of imperialism echoes previous comments. Sovereignty is only of instrumental value: it is nothing more than a means of providing a secure space in which communities can grow and flourish. The crucial value at stake is thus autonomy and whether this autonomy is crowned by the concept and institutions of sovereignty is irrelevant when it comes to the question of intervention and conquest. Indeed, the preservation of a people's independence is important precisely because it affords them the opportunity to engage in a struggle to become sovereign and self-determining in the Kantian sense. For a long time, sovereignty allied itself with imperialism, giving justification to European domination of large parts of the globe. However, I argue that the relation between sovereignty and imperialism was superficial and bound to collapse in the light of the much more potent and intellectually inevitable relationship that grew between sovereignty and the principle of self-determination. Sovereignty's significance lies in the fact that it is both an articulation of the struggle for self-determination and a means, although not a necessary means, of furthering this never-ending struggle. Imperial domination, since it involves an explicit repudiation of the principle of self-determination, thus threatens the principle of sovereignty itself.

It could be argued that the post-World War II unravelling of colonial systems earlier established by European powers marked a further maturation in thinking about the concept of sovereignty. Indeed, this development can be seen as a direct legacy of an earlier maturation in thinking in the European context involving the popularisation and constitutionalisation of the sovereignty of the state. Decolonisation reflected recognition that the institution of sovereignty, if it is to be more than *de facto* mastery, must be based in legitimacy. Some maintain that the post-colonial sovereignty regime (under which the sovereignty of territories which were not self-governing was recognised, based on the idea that the peoples of these territories had a right to self-determination irrespective of their level of empirical preparedness), has failed the people of the post-colonial world. It is a regime which has fostered and allowed to flourish corrupt, inept and repressive governments, governments which deny their citizens genuine self-determination, reducing them to subject status or even worse. A widely held view is that the international sovereignty regime aids and abets such governments, shielding them from international criticism and interference.

It is true that the muscular rhetoric of sovereignty employed by some governments in the international context is merely a smoke-screen intended to divert attention away from the vicious reality that lies beyond. It is also true that the international recognition of the external sovereignty of the state, which as we have seen is in an important sense constitutive of it, can serve to legitimate tyrannical governments operating under its banner. Clearly also, external sovereignty is a significant obstacle to efforts to provide oppressed and suffering peoples with humanitarian assistance. Even so, the problem with the external sovereignty of certain states, is not a problem of sovereignty *per se*. First, there is nothing in the theory of sovereignty that says that states are immune from criticism or that the borders of a state can never be crossed in the name of humanity. In fact, as regards this last, historically most legal and political theorists have argued to the contrary. Second, the problem of external sovereignty, in this context, lies with the ongoing recognition of something which is internally absent. In principle, recognition of the sovereignty of the state is simply declaratory of what is assumed, by virtue of a state's constitution, to already exist: sovereignty. Thus, international recognition does not *give* a state sovereignty, although it certainly helps to preserve the sovereign independence of the state as well as *de facto* situations of power. The upshot of all this is that while one may speak of the failure of the post-colonial international sovereignty regime (to the extent that it has hindered the struggle for self-determination either through reinforcing the power of dictatorial governments through non-interference and, importantly, inappropriate interference), the issue internally speaking is not so much the failure of sovereignty as its non-existence.

Now one should not discount the significance of the achievement of sovereign independence by formally colonised peoples and the value that they continue to place on their independent status. However problematic its internal make-up may be, the external sovereignty of the state, in the sense of an internationally recognised right of independence and non-interference, may still be prized. The issue then becomes, not one of finding alternatives to sovereign statehood for certain parts of the world, but one of how to render states which are weak, ineffective and/or illegitimate properly sovereign within: as truly self-determining. Michael Walzer, following John Stuart Mill, points out that self-determination by definition, as is also the case with sovereignty, cannot be given to a people: self-determination can only be achieved by a community through its own 'efforts'. Indeed, following on from earlier remarks, external sovereignty may be valuable even where internal sovereignty is lacking in that it secures an area in which a people can strive to become authentically free, even though there may be many serious obstacles in their path and they may experience many setbacks along the way. Walzer acknowledges that a people may exist amidst circumstances so dire that any notion of them struggling for their freedom is inconceivable, yet he remains sympathetic to what he calls Mill's 'stern doctrine of self-help' and for this he has been criticised (Walzer, 1977, pp.87–90; see also Doppelt, 1978, p.10).

Jack Donnelly is similarly wary of intervention, stating that it is 'much easier to produce great harm than to provide major help'; intervention may unleash further violence through exacerbating rivalries and tensions and also, through forestalling organic struggle, hinder the development of the necessary psychological basis for free institutions. Rather than intervention, Donnelly recommends 'self-restraint'. By this he means that states, or more specifically powerful states, should avoid 'actions [military, economic or diplomatic] that actively support or encourage rights violating régimes' in order to 'return the fate of human rights to a national struggle between dictators and their citizens' (Donnelly, 1988, p.259). Yet, this rejection of international 'paternalism' in the form of intervention, which as we have seen can be traced back to Mill and Kant, obviously cannot be the last word on the question of human rights (Donnelly, 1988, p.259). The question of human rights concerns much more than the problem which is state repression: there is also the question of the economic blockages to their realisation and while these blockages may be an effect of dictatorial government they are also an effect of structural economic conditions of which the wealthy members of the state system are the architects. Removing economic blockages to the realisation of human rights might indeed entail self-restraint in some areas or circumstances, however, in others, especially when it comes to the very poor, a much more activist form of international policy-making is required. Economic action, whether in the form of aid or other types of assistance, should not be regarded as charity since, as already pointed out, each state is implicated in the construction of the other and thus in a fundamental sense we are each responsible for the other. That the state system is grounded in mutual obligations means that this system has never been and never can be a purely self-help system. Once we understand this point, we can then proceed to meditate on the kinds of obligations states owe each other.

Most importantly, as I have also suggested, when we speak of state obligations we are really speaking of the obligations of one part of humanity to another. To repeat, sovereignty is a status conferred by humanity for the advancement of individual communities and humanity as a whole. These points taken together suggest an obligation on the part of the economically privileged, by virtue of their very existence and as a part of their humanity obligations, to assist in the creation of the conditions of the good life for all. If this obligation is not fulfilled then the very poor and destitute, who like those rendered stateless through war or persecution effectively live in a state of nature, cannot but be expected to exercise their natural right of necessity. The assertion of such a right was widely criticised in the past as it served as a pretext for imperial conquest. Yet, despite its considerable abuse, there is a sense in which the articulation of such a natural right has merit. As Walzer suggests in discussing Thomas Hobbes's defence of a right of necessity, there are circumstances in which it is 'right to set aside any consideration of territorial integrity-as-ownership and to focus instead on life' (Walzer, 1977, p.57).

In Chapter 5, the concepts of sovereignty and self-determination are further explored in relation to the condition of indigenous peoples. The question of the relation between indigenous peoples and the states which enclose them has been to the fore in recent years in part because of the debates leading up to the passing of the UN's Universal Declaration on the Rights of Indigenous Peoples in September 2007. Controversy has surrounded the Declaration because of its assertion of a right of self-determination, in relation to political, economic and cultural matters, on the part of indigenous peoples. Even though it is quite clear that the Declaration only refers to a relative form of self-determination (that is, a limited right of self-determination within the constitutional framework of the sovereign state), some have objected to this document because of its alleged secessionist implications. The word sovereignty is sometimes used by indigenous groups, however, this is usually in order to refer to the form of internal self-determination described above. It is true that it is sometimes used by the same groups in its full legal sense, although claims to sovereignty of this nature can be seen as a means of venting anger at past and present injustices or as a means of moral suasion. Given that indigenous peoples typically live under conditions of continuing colonial domination, such claims are bound to be in most cases rhetorical (although this in itself is not without significance), rather than real. Some have urged indigenous groups to stop using the word sovereignty because its employment gives rise to the suspicion that behind the claims to a right of internal self-determination lies a more ambitious agenda. Others have argued that the assertion of a continuing indigenous sovereignty based on prior ownership should be avoided, simply because such an assertion is not convincing and is seen as merely a 'lever for concessions within the established constitutional framework' (Alfred, 2001, p.28). It is certainly true that claims to a continuing indigenous sovereignty are often intended to serve this rhetorical purpose, however, to the extent that such claims are successful in this regard, it is because they bring to mind important historical questions concerning the legitimacy of European conquest.

A good number of authors have explored the debates concerning the sovereign status and rights of indigenous peoples against a background of imperial conquest and domination. Such debates have been characterised by considerable ambiguity with authors such as Vitoria, Grotius and Vattel, to a greater and lesser degree, condemning colonial conquest while also providing pretexts for it, whether in the form of a right of civilisation or a right of necessity. These distinct but overlapping ideas gained increasing currency as imperialism accelerated, however they were also subject to considerable legal critique. The writings of Rousseau and Kant, with the latter seemingly ascribing a right of self-determination even to those he deemed to be in a state of lawless freedom, and the French revolution's elevation of the principle of equality, inspired nineteenth century continental publicists to critically analyse and challenge, wholly or in part, these two justifications of imperialism. Throughout the nineteenth century, the right of civilisation, as the most cited justification for imperial domination, was repeatedly denounced on the grounds that it was contrary to natural law, the law of nations, scientific reason and increasingly state practice. Attention also turned to the question of whether a lack of civilisation precluded a people from exercising sovereignty, with some arguing that the question of sovereignty should be treated separately from the question of civilisation: a people could be regarded as sovereign in respect to their internal arrangements even though they lacked European conventions and culture. Indeed, some argued that it did not really matter whether non-European peoples possessed the European concept of sovereignty or not in order for them to be treated as sovereign: the mere presence of a human society was enough to establish a right to external independence.

Appearing alongside this form of criticism, were denunciations of the criterion of civilisation itself, with some authors stating it was impossible to apply given that civilisation was a relative notion and that no civilisation was capable of objectively measuring itself. In addition to this, the concern was expressed that the putative right of civilisation could also be used to justify imperial conquest within Europe. Further, as critics of imperialism noted, those defending the right of civilisation or the broadened notion of *terrra nullius* typically acknowledged the sovereign rights of indigenous peoples in maintaining that the acquisition of their lands or a part of their lands should be undertaken by means of treaties rather than by force. In fact, much of the land acquired during the age of imperialism was acquired by the former rather than the latter means. Yet, this also raises the tantalising question of whether indigenous peoples could ever have ceded sovereignty through the instrument of the treaty. Some indigenous peoples claim today that such surrender was impossible in the light of their customary laws, a point that is more than a little reminiscent of the ancient and widely recognised principle that the one thing a sovereign can never do is annihilate its own sovereignty.

In terms of state practice, Chapter 5 examines the treatment of indigenous peoples in the United States, Canada, Australia and New Zealand in respect to the issue of indigenous rights, including the right of self-determination, in both the past and present. It examines the problem of indigenous groups insisting on a continuing sovereignty in a situation in which there is no domestic legal forum in which such a right can be asserted against the sovereignty of the state. As has been acknowledged by various state legal institutions in a number of instances, domestic legal forums are wholly creatures of the state's sovereignty. Nonetheless, as already suggested, even if claims to an ongoing sovereignty by indigenous representatives are not legally persuasive, the re-examination of the historical record that such claims invite may cause us to view indigenous rights less as a grant made at the discretion of the sovereign power than as a payment of a debt that is *owed*.

Chapter 6 of this study examines the European Union (EU) as its developing legal and political contours are held up as indicative of how a post-sovereignty world might be shaped. In this regard, the EU has been projected as an institutional hybrid: it is neither an interstate arrangement nor a supranational entity. The EU's ambiguous status is above all seen as being reflected in the fact that while it lacks some of the traditional marks of sovereignty, for example, military, policing and taxation powers, the doctrine of the supremacy of EU law (as laid down by the European Court of Justice in 1964), has been implicitly accepted by Member States. According to this doctrine, the effect of the obligations that Member States enter into in joining the EU is that any 'unilateral act incompatible with the concept of the community cannot prevail' (*Costa v. ENEL*, Case 6/64, 15 July 1964).

Closely related to the idea of the supremacy of EU law is the principle of direct effect: EU law is directly effective in the jurisdictions of Member States without the need for it to be subsequently enacted by national parliaments in order to take effect. This applies whether an EU norm precedes or follows a 'national provision' (Hartley, 1998, p.218). The mutually supporting notions of direct effect and the supremacy of EU law have led, in particular, to claims concerning the demise of the sovereignty of Member States, and it is worth recalling here that law-making power was for Bodin chief among all the marks of sovereignty. Yet, on close inspection it becomes clear that the sovereignty of Member States remains intact. Certainly, significant powers, including certain law-making powers, have been transferred to EU institutions. Nonetheless, sovereignty has not been limited. As indicated above, historically it has been considered impossible for a sovereign to extinguish its own sovereignty. To do so would be to destroy the ground on which it stands, thus rendering all its acts void. This recalls another crucial point: sovereignty is not personal power but is constituted power and it follows from this that its sphere of operation must be contained within certain constitutional boundaries. Action taken by those who wield the sovereign power which oversteps constitutional limits, while possible politically, can never be undertaken legitimately or be considered a sovereign act.

Some have argued that the British Parliament, in passing the European Communities Act of 1972, achieved what had hitherto been thought impossible under British constitutional law: that Parliament could bind future Parliaments. As I have mentioned, law-making power is considered to be the chief mark of sovereignty and supreme law-making power has always been understood by theorists to mean the power to make and unmake the law and it is precisely this that is meant by the old saying that the sovereign is above the law. Now if we accept the definition of sovereignty as the supreme power to make and unmake the law, then it would follow that Britain's submission to EU law is only by virtue of the 1972 Communities Act and that, at least from the perspective of the British constitution, (and it is important to note that domestic courts of Member States have upheld the view that EU law is not supreme in respect to all the provisions of their state constitutions), Parliament is free at any moment to pass legislation withdrawing Britain from the EU (Hartley, 1999, p.167). If the British Parliament enacted such legislation, then EU law would no longer prevail over national legislation and the courts would no longer be able to 'disapply' British law where it came into conflict with EU law. Viewed from this angle, EU law is supreme only as long as Member States choose to continue to be members of this legal order.

At the same time, the EU is obviously much more than an ordinary intergovernmental arrangement and this is especially because of the principle of direct effect. In this regard, it stands in contrast with international law in general which often requires, depending on a state's constitution, national legislation in order to come into effect. The so-called dualist doctrine, which is discussed in this Chapter, insists on this point: it is through their enactment in national legislation that international treaties become the law of the land. In desisting from passing such enabling legislation, possible given the decentralised nature of the international legal order, states are ignoring the international legal obligations that they have entered into with other states. Thus, it can be stated that in comparison with the wider international legal order, the EU legal order is highly organised and developed. In this regard, I agree with those who think that it provides a template for the wider international legal order: international law could make progress *via* 'the multiplication of specialized legal orders based upon constituent treaties...which may in the long term tend to provide the international order with the institutional and normative advances that are part of the [European] Community legal order' (Leben, 1998, p.298).

There is no logical reason why international law in general should not have direct effect. Indeed, as Hugo Krabbe points out, as a matter of logic it should: it does not make much sense that one can enter into international legal obligations and be bound by those obligations yet also be free not to carry them out (Krabbe, 1930, pp.244–5). That states can ignore their international legal obligations, whether under the guise of the dualist doctrine or not, is the price we pay for maintaining a high degree of legal and political decentralisation internationally. However, such a situation is logically incoherent and based on a primitive understanding of sovereignty: that the legal order of the sovereign state is superior to that of the international legal order.

Chapter 7 reflects in more depth on a question touched on in Chapter 3: the place of war in a sovereign state system and, in relation to that, the problematic relation between war and law. This Chapter begins with an examination of the view expressed by Rousseau that war, by which he means intense and sustained levels of violence, is a product of the state system: war springs not from nature but is a consequence of the appearance and replication of the state form. Once one state appears other states are bound to appear by virtue of the threat posed to segmented societies by peoples organised into states. Thus, a state system arises because states, in the absence of a law enforcer, confront each other as potential enemies. In one sense for Rousseau, the insecurity felt by states is a paranoid fantasy and the hostilities consequent upon that insecurity a form of madness, albeit a madness that has a certain method in it. Yet, Rousseau appreciated that war is an instrument of reason, an instrument deliberately chosen by states in the pursuit of their policy objectives and which, as a result, should be used in a disciplined way. The importance of this view is that it suggests that war can and should be guided by intelligence and this leaves open the possibility that more rational analysis may see this activity circumscribed in any number of ways. Rousseau, of course, went beyond this in exploring ways in which perpetual peace might be achieved, yet he is also noted for the case he mounts concerning the principle of distinction: only states can be enemies never human beings.

Following in the wake of Rousseau, Kant explored the morally problematic issue of deploying the bodies of others in dangerous and bloody contexts and demonstrated the absurdity of the notion that war could be considered a right of states. This notion, the most extreme expression of the view that the state's legal order is superior to the international legal order, was an absurdity because a claim to a right of war was simultaneously a complete and emphatic denial of the existence of any sovereign right at all. Kant was writing in a context in which the view of war as a policy tool was commonplace. It is a view that would gain especially stark expression in the work of Carl von Clausewitz, someone who would issue some highly instructive warnings concerning the mercurial nature of military conflict. Given the predominance of the political conception of war, and given the high level of political and legal decentralisation in Europe in the eighteenth and nineteenth centuries, it was hardly likely that states would agree to war's abolition. Yet, as discussed earlier, certain early nineteenth century developments point to a strong sense that in a multi-polar system recourse to war needed to be curbed.

The latter part of the nineteenth century would see attention turn to regulating war's effects, something that was impelled by the industrialisation of the means of war as well as by the fact that war was still not illegal. Vattel had argued in the eighteenth century that the just war doctrine, by then in a state of decline, was dangerous. States entering conflicts brandishing the sword of justice were likely to deny any rights to their adversary, the consequence of this being escalating levels of violence. The alternative Vattel proposed was that participants in war, or at least participants in ordinary wars, should typically be seen as moral equals and thus as in possession of the same belligerent rights. This view, or later versions of it, informed the push to codify international law in the late nineteenth century although, as discussed in Chapter 3, these legal efforts also overlapped with a simultaneous push to outlaw war as an instrument of policy, something which was achieved in stages between 1920 and 1945.

The general argument of this chapter, that war and sovereignty stand in contradiction, is then addressed specifically in relation to wars of anticipation – an issue that has become controversial in recent years particularly in the light of the 2003 invasion of Iraq. The broad conclusion reached in this context is that the assertion of a right of anticipation is the assertion of a privilege and not a right and as such is a denial of the principle of sovereign equality.

This study concludes with a brief chapter which seeks to isolate the major difficulties engendered by the institution of sovereignty which have been raised throughout, pointing to certain conceptual perspectives from which these difficulties might be addressed, albeit without necessarily abandoning the concept of sovereignty itself.

2
The Municipal Realm

Society and the state

In his very suggestive study of the concept sovereignty, F.H. Hinsley maintains that while the state may be only one way of arranging and systematising social power, once this form has established itself the concept of sovereignty is almost bound to emerge. When the machinery of the state begins to enclose and dominate society, controversies over who is entitled to wield this machinery and in whose name are inevitable (Hinsley, 1986, p.17). Initially, society encounters the state as a strange and unnatural form, the modes of which are foreign to traditional 'ways' and because of this, and because the state centres on the 'principle of dominance', the community resists its imposition. Such opposition, along with the fact that establishing the state is an arduous enterprise, explains why it has not always made its appearance. There is no 'desire' on the part of society to be dominated by the state, rather there is 'an urge in men', whether for reasons of private gain or public benefit, 'to possess its kind of power' (Hinsley, 1986, pp.10, 15–16). Going further than Hinsley, Jacques Derrida argues that all states originate in a form of violent capture, although the violence of which he speaks is both real and metaphorical in character.[1] He states:

> *All* Nation-States are born and found themselves in violence...the moment of foundation, the instituting moment, is anterior to the law or legitimacy which it founds. It is thus outside the law, and violent by that very fact.... Before the modern forms of what is called, in the strict sense, 'colonialism', all States.... have their origin in an aggression of the colonial type. This foundational violence is not only forgotten. The foundation is made in order to hide it; by its essence it tends to organise amnesia, sometimes under the celebration and sublimation of grand beginnings (Derrida, 2001, p.57).

The metaphorical dimension of Derrida's explanation of the violent origins of the state concerns its necessarily pre-legal basis and in this regard, his contention is simply tautologically true. That aside, and following on from Derrida's remarks, the question addressed in this chapter is whether sovereignty serves merely as a means of sublimating the state's violent beginnings as well as the forms of violence in which it continues to participate, through bathing the state in a lustrous glow (thus, recalling the divine and princely motifs that informed its early conception), or whether the logic of sovereignty can lead us down a radical democratic path. Even if the state were founded on the doctrine that might is right, which John Austin shrewdly described as either a 'truism affectedly and darkly expressed' or 'false and absurd', it is also the case that over time might must make right and in so doing acquire legitimacy (Austin, 1906, pp.186–7).[2]

It is argued below that the concept of sovereignty is an initial means of reconciling power with legitimacy or the state with community. The transmutation of might into right is no simple matter and it has universally required determined efforts. Yet it is through such exertions that the people emerge as something more than a loose collectivity, becoming instead *a people*. Obviously, there is power in this shared identity as it can issue in concrete and efficacious action, such that the rulership comes to appreciate or is compelled to appreciate that *l'union fait la force*. Etienne Balibar points out that it is at 'insurrectional' moments that the collective 'we' is at its most condensed and it is such moments that ideally result in a condition of 'democratic reciprocity' whereby the people grant each other rights as individuals, rights which are properly speaking 'transindividual' as they have been collectively seized (Balibar, 2004, pp.185–6).

The state's manifestation as an external and coercive machinery of command, stands in sharp contrast with the organic forms of rule in stateless societies where authority largely depends on 'psychological and moral coercion rather than on force' and where the 'structure of command invariably emanates directly from the community.' Even where there is 'final authority that is fully effective for...[a stateless society's]...purposes' it is an authority which is internal to the community and operates in accordance with its rules. The state, however, stands apart from and over the community and it is only with the emergence of this type of command structure that we find an institution in which the concept of sovereignty can be lodged (Hinsley, 1986, pp.15–17). Yet, if the institution of the state succeeds in establishing itself the concept of sovereignty may take a long time to emerge or may not emerge at all. Hinsley notes that the 'resistance of the customary society to the ways of the state, the disregard by the traditional ruler of the influence of the changing community, the persistence on both sides of the outlooks of the "segmentary state"' were striking characteristics of the development of the state in Europe and for some time forestalled that 'turning-point' which sees that meeting or association of state and society which is necessary for the appearance of sovereignty. He adds that these features were even more prominent in ancient Egypt, the Chinese Empire and Ottoman Turkey such that 'the advance of the mutual impact of government and, society ... [was] ... even more halting and slow' and hence 'the turning point ... [was] ... even longer delayed – if it was ever achieved' (Hinsley, 1986, pp.20–1).

Sovereignty needs the state: sovereignty cannot exist without the state because by virtue of it being supreme political authority it demands an institution distinct from the community in which it can locate itself and through which it can exercise dominance. Yet, as noted, the appearance of the state does not guarantee that the idea of sovereignty will emerge. The idea that there exists in the body politic a supreme authority only arises when the community no longer regards 'the state as alien to the society and have to some extent begun to identify the claims of the state with the needs of the community' (Hinsley, 1986, pp.17–18). However, irrespective of whether the community in some way needs the state or simply cannot fend it off, the state must be controlled. Equally, where resistant elements confront the state machinery, elements which it cannot eliminate, the state must come to some arrangement with the community. The state and community must negotiate between them a relationship and this relationship may take the form of sovereignty (Hinsley, 1986, pp.21–2).

To think of the state in terms of sovereignty is to think of the exercise state power as authoritative or to demand that it be so. The community through vesting sovereignty in the state frees the state to act but also seeks to discipline its actions. Thus, while one might agree that the state is the result of and perpetuates a kind of violence, this is not *prima facie* the case with sovereignty, even though it undoubtedly and endlessly entails the risk of violations of its terms. Sovereignty involves the incorporation of a people by the state, however this is by no means a passive process of absorption. For sovereignty to exist there must be a people conscious of itself as a people, conscious of its power as a people and collectively ready to believe and act as if sovereignty were vested in the state.

In his *Law of War and Peace* (1625) Hugo Grotius claimed that the act of submission to the sovereignty of the ruler was irrevocable since the sovereignty of the state arises from a pact and 'it is a rule of the law of nature to abide by pacts' as this is the best way the common good which lies at the base of the state is served, although Grotius added a number of important qualifications to this claim (Grotius, 1925, pp.14–15, 44).[3] In challenging Grotius's contention Rousseau stated: '"A people," says Grotius, "may give itself to a king." Therefore, according to Grotius a people are *a people* even before the gift to the king is made. The gift itself is a civil act; it presupposes public deliberation. Hence, before considering the act by which a people submits to a king, we ought to scrutinize the act by which people become *a* people' (Rousseau, 1968, p.59). Rousseau's point is that the constitutive moment, or the process through which the people 'take collectively the name of a *people'*, occurs at the time of a prior and original social contract (Rousseau, 1968, p.62). Yet, this act of association also presupposes public deliberation, and so it is better to say that the people both make and are made by the constitutive moment: they both create and are created by 'the institution of sovereignty' (Balibar, 2004, p.158).

Sovereignty thus emerges where state and society agree to render power as authority because they both need and fear each other. Yet, while the concept in a sense bridges the distance between society and state, it also defines and preserves it. Sovereignty has its source in the community but it is located in the state which rules over it. Sovereignty flows upwards through an act of collective will only to move downwards in the form of supreme authority and political power. Hinsley is surely right to argue that 'its fundamental aim, and ultimate achievement...[is]...to cover up' the inescapable 'dualism' between the rulership and people that the activity of government involves (Hinsley, 1986, p.130). The rulership usually would prefer that the sovereignty of the people slept undisturbed. As Alexis de Toqueville states, the notion of the sovereignty of the people, which lies 'more or less, at the bottom of almost all human institutions', generally remains concealed from view. It is 'obeyed without being recognized, or if for a moment it is brought to light, it is hastily cast back into the gloom of the sanctuary' (Toqueville, 1945, p.55).

It is precisely because of the inescapable dualism that the business of government entails and the sorts of dangers that it poses, that it is vital that we stay alive to the fact that the sovereignty of the state is only real to the extent that it is collectively imagined. Austin stated, following Jeremy Bentham, that the positive mark of sovereignty is that the '*bulk* of the given society is in a *habit* of obedience or submission to a *determinate* and *common* superior' (Austin, 1906, pp.96–7; Bentham, 1948, p.38).[4] This statement may conjure relations of repression and submission, yet for Austin what accounted for political obedience was a positive disposition toward government on the part of the mass of population rather than a fear of punishment. Austin knew that sovereignty rested on a general attitude of mind, specifically, a 'law-abiding' attitude, his fundamental contention being that 'authority is merely the reflex of habitual obedience, that in default of this all is vanity' (Manning, 1933, pp.202, 208).[5] For this reason, as the nineteenth century British idealist T.H. Green stated in discussing Austin, sovereignty must not be thought of 'in abstraction as the wielder of coercive force, but in connection with the whole complex of institutions of political society', that is, in connection with a general will. As he famously stated: 'Will, not force, is the basis of the state' (Green, 1999, pp.69, 84).

It is precisely because Austin understood that the sovereignty of the state was grounded in the will of the electorate that he regarded 'superiority' and 'inferiority' as entirely 'reciprocal' notions, such that it was possible to view the sovereign as 'inferior' to the people (Manning, 1933, p.223). There is nothing strange about the notion of sovereignty in Austin. Rather, as Charles W. Manning explains, it is simply a theoretical means of explaining and relating the ritual obedience of the population to the decrees and enactments of a range of empirical legal authorities (Manning, 1933, p.199). Further, Austin did not deny that the community might assert its sovereignty against the rule of the state as it is ultimately the community at whose discretion a political superior commands and the constitution survives unchanged (Manning, 1933, p.192).[6]

It is only when we have reached the point at which the community is seen as the ultimate authority behind the 'personified collectivity' or 'sovereign number', both of which could be more or less coextensive with the whole community, that the full implications of sovereignty concerning the domestic polity begin to be realised (Manning, 1933, pp.191, 199). A.V. Dicey criticised Austin for confusing sovereignty in its legal sense with sovereignty in its political sense, the former being 'the power of law-making unrestricted by any legal limit' and the latter that body the 'will of which is ultimately obeyed by the citizens of the state' (Dicey, 1908, pp.70–1).[7] Theorists, including those who insisted on the unchallengeable sovereignty of the prince, generally understood that the source of sovereignty lay in communal willing. However, as Rousseau indicated in his critique of Grotius, the idea that sovereignty ultimately was vested in the people seemed the logical conclusion of the understanding that it was a *kind* of gift passed from the community to the prince. Yet, even where the sovereign number becomes coextensive will the whole community, as it does most rigorously with Rousseau, the distinction between sovereign and subjects 'remains intact' (Manning, 1933, p.191). One should draw a distinction between the people in its sovereign capacity and the people or individuals that it commands. One can soften the dualism between community and state *via* the notion, admittedly problematic, of popular sovereignty. However, one cannot overcome it without imagining some plane on which minds melt into unity, a conceptualisation which would render the idea of sovereignty superfluous.

Doctrinal origins

We have seen that stateless societies, even where final and supreme authority is present, do not possess sovereignty in the strict sense because they lack administrative institutions sharply distinct and separate from the community (although certain complexities in relation to this matter are introduced in Chapter 5). That sovereignty can only be located in such institutions points to the impersonal nature of the sovereign power and this is something which further distinguishes this form of rule from systems in which authority is determined on the basis of tribal status or lineage. It is precisely because the ancient Greek city states, although complex organisations, had not established 'organs of a government authority...separate from the tribal community' that they cannot be thought of in terms of the principle of sovereignty. That they did not, according to Hinsley, is because the Greek *polis* was 'instinctively anti-monarchical' and further considered itself an element in a 'wider single but segmentary society' (Hinsley, 1986, pp.28–9).[8]

In the ancient world, it is only when Rome becomes an empire that the concept of sovereignty begins to be approached because it is only after the institution of the principate in 27 BCE that a form of state, that is, an institution of government separate from the whole community, starts to emerge. The *imperium*, an abstraction signifying the totality of the authority of the Roman Emperor, expanded to the point where the Emperor became in fact a supreme ruler with the Emperor's supremacy finding expression in his position, as declared by the jurist Ulpian in early years of the third century CE, as *legibus solutus* (Hinsley, 1986, pp.38–42). The formula *princeps legibus solutus est* approaches what would later be determined to be the core meaning of the word sovereignty: the supreme power to make and unmake the law (Bodin, 1967, p.44). Roman legal doctrine evolved under the empire to the point that laws were seen as commands and the Emperor's right to command was seen as inhering in his *imperium* and it was this which placed the Emperor '*above the law*' (Hinsley, 1986, pp.41–2). Due to the persistence of republican strains of thought, it continued to be disputed as to whether the source of the Emperor's *imperium* lay with the Roman populus (*imperium* or *maiestas populi Romani*), or lay with the semi-divine figure of the Emperor himself. However, what was not disputed was the belief that somewhere in the Roman body politic there existed a locus of supreme authority (Hinsley, 1986, pp.41–3; see also Passerin d'Entrèves 1967, p.93).[9]

With the passing of the Roman Empire, the concept of supreme legislative power faded from European political and legal thought, and it would take the break-up of Christendom for its renaissance progeny to begin to be clearly delineated. While the coherence of Christendom in the thirteenth and fourteenth centuries already was fracturing the bonds that united its members, these bonds were still too strong for entities which were effectively becoming independent to conceive of themselves as fully legally distinct from the two key institutions of *respublica christiana*: the empire and the papacy (James, 1986, p.4). Indeed, it was rather Christian authorities who most sharply outlined a doctrine of sovereignty in advancing the spiritual and political claims of the papacy. Medieval church lawyers claimed supreme legal authority for the papacy over *respublica christiana* in stating that the 'Roman Pontiff is considered to hold all the laws encompassed in his bosom' (Passerin d'Entrèves, 1967, p.97). Early in the fourteenth century Boniface VIII, foreshadowing Hobbes, dismissed the notion of the dual government of Christendom as an 'unworkable "monster"' (Passerin d'Entrèves, 1967, p.97).[10]

Feudal relations and the theory of government that explained and justified these relations also delayed the emergence of the concept of state sovereignty. The king was a superior without being a supreme authority. The king sat atop a chain of lords each with their own entitlements and concerns. According to the thirteenth century jurist Philippe de Beaumanoir, the 'king is "sovereign" in his kingdom, but so is an earl in his earldom, and even a baron in his barony. If the king's authority is greater than the earl's or the baron's, this is primarily because it is wider than theirs, not so much because it is higher in kind' (McIlwain, 1933, p.97).

While supporters of papal supremacy were the first to draw on Roman legal doctrines of *legibus solutus* and *plentiudo potestatis*, these were soon embraced by secular rulers (Vincent, 1987, p.48). Julian Franklin points out that in the medieval era Roman legal notions were well embedded in educated discourse and that as a result, the 'basic equation of the position of the king of France with that of the Roman *princeps* became the tacit starting point for all reflections.' Thus, one finds legal theorists in the closing years of the thirteenth century relying on this notion in order to give expression to the independence of the monarch in relation to the papacy and the Holy Roman Emperor, their celebrated prescription being: '*Rex Franciae in suo regno est imperator sui regni*' (Franklin, 1973, p.6). The expression 'a king is an emperor in his kingdom' gained currency and the language of empire continued to be drawn on by monarchs in order to assert their autonomy into the early modern era (Passerin d'Entrèves, 1967, p.98). For example Henry VIII, who had adopted the foreign designation 'His Majesty', declared in 1533 'this realm of England is an Empire' in order to express the notion 'of sovereignty within the body politic for which the technical language did not yet exist' (Hinsley, 1986, pp.118–19).[11]

Jean Bodin, who had studied Roman legal doctrine and was a supporter of *les Politiques*, a group which upheld the 'interests of the State above religious or personal considerations', was the first to state clearly and forcefully articulate the modern doctrine of sovereignty, a doctrine that would be radicalised by Rousseau but without being fundamentally altered (Merriam, 1900, p.13). Although he was not the first to use the term as it had been in circulation during the Middle Ages (albeit with a rather different meaning to the one accorded it by Bodin), Bodin claimed to be the first to properly define it in *Les six livres de la république* (1576) (Bodin, 1967, p.25).[12] Alexander Passerin d'Entrèves notes that it was because of his efforts that the word 'entered the vocabulary of law and politics', although its adoption by languages other than French took place sooner in some countries than it did in others (Passerin d'Entrèves, 1967, p.102). While it was enthusiastically received in England not long after the publication of Bodin's work and well before the work's appearance in English under the heading of *Six Bookes of a Commonweale* in 1606, in Germany the imported word *souveranetät* did not achieve acceptance until around the middle of the eighteenth century. Hinsley reports that it was not until the early nineteenth century that the meaning of *souveranetät* fully corresponded with French and English usage, a development which was consequent upon Napoleon Bonaparte's interventions in the region (Hinsley, 1986, pp.120, 137).

Bodin and law-making power

The immediate background to Bodin's theory concerns the civil and religious wars which broke out in France in the second half of the sixteenth century. These conflicts nearly tore the country apart and culminated in the St. Bartholomew Day's massacre which took place on the night of August 23–24 in 1572 and saw up to three thousand French Protestants slaughtered in Paris and between 10,000 and 20,000 deaths in total as anti-Huguenot hostility spread throughout the rest of the country (Elliott, 1968, pp.215, 220; King, 1974, p.51). Bodin was partly responding to those political realists who maintained that the state is founded on force. He pointedly condemned Machiavelli who, he stated, had 'been fashionable among the agents of tyrants' for having made 'the twin foundations of Commonweals impiety and injustice'. It was Machiavelli's thought, according to Bodin, which had influenced the political schemes of a key player in the political machinations leading up to the St. Bartholomew Day's massacre: Catherine de Medici (Bodin, 1606, pp. A69–A70).[13]

A consequence of this massacre was the emergence of sharply opposed doctrines concerning the French constitution (Franklin, 1973, p.vii). On the one side, there were the Huguenot *Monarchomaques* (as they were later styled by their opponents), who, informed by earlier conceptions of rulership, argued that the position of sovereign was an office occupied but not owned by the ruler. For the *Monarchomaques* the 'king in his office' was simply the 'first servant *of* the State' and thus was 'subject *to* the State'; on this view, popular resistance to tyranny could be justified (Vincent, 1987, pp.52, 62).[14] On the other side, there were those such as Bodin who sought to provide a coherent rationale for, while at the same time attempting to civilise, the doctrine of absolute royal authority (Franklin, 1973, pp.vii, 107). When Bodin developed his theory, absolutism was already on the rise in France, in both the political and intellectual domains, although the absolutist state down to the time of the French revolution would remain an aspiration rather than a real achievement of the French monarchy (Vincent, 1987, p.49; see also Mettam, 1988, pp.13–14).

Yet, while the concept of sovereignty may have lain at the crux of absolutist theory and rationalised moves in the direction of the absolutist state, its relationship with notions of personal rule was contingent rather than necessary, as Rousseau's radicalisation of the concept shows. This is also the case with sovereignty's early association with the old doctrine of divine right and the modern doctrine of *raison d'état* both of which provided justification for the total compliance of subjects and concomitantly the absolute authority of the ruler. Both of these notions were used to deflect constitutionalist arguments through representing the monarch as the embodiment of justice and reason. By definition, the monarch could do no wrong (Vincent, 1987, pp.50, 69, 70–2).

Andrew Vincent contends that one must be careful not to confuse absolutism with tyrannical government. This is because absolutist rulers saw themselves, and were generally seen by those they ruled, as promoters of 'order' and 'legality'; further, absolutist theory was not without constitutional principles (Vincent, 1987, p.46). In any case, despite this early marriage between sovereignty and notions of absolutist and personal rule, there are grounds for arguing that the logic of sovereignty takes us in contrary directions: towards the pole, as already indicated, of popular rule as well as the pole of the impersonal state. Indeed, absolutist theory was itself ambiguous on the question of the personal state. On the one hand, the state was identified with the monarch and the territory and population were regarded as the property of the monarch in line with developments in the theory of property, specifically the emergence of the concept of freehold property (Vincent, 1987, pp.50, 62). On the other hand, the acceptance of this identification depended upon the application of the Roman principle of legal personality (a principle which served, in the Roman private law context, as a means of rendering individuals and groups as legal persons and thus as bearers of rights and obligations it being based on the natural law understanding that 'in the beginning all men were born free'), to the state and monarch conceived as one and the same being (Remec, 1960, pp.167–8). The monarch was the incarnation of the collective personality of the state and was endowed with a sovereign will. Thus, the 'sovereign person *was* the State. The State *was* the person of the sovereign' (Vincent, 1987, pp.50, 73). It was only later when the absolutism of the French monarchy had reached its zenith that there was a shift, as Vincent adds:

> ...away from the fictional aspect of absolutism...theorists, impressed by absolute sovereignty, property theory, divine right and reason of state arguments, identified the State with the real person of the sovereign. However, neither the fictional, artificial character of legal personality nor the 'office' theory of kingship was totally forgotten (Vincent, 1987, pp.50–1).

Bodin did not subscribe to that version of divine right which maintained that the sovereign was obliged to establish the 'true religion' and which, in making of the prince a God on earth, seemed to render the state the monarch's personal property. Nonetheless, powerful religious themes inform the *République*. For example, the princely sovereignty depicted by Bodin perfectly mirrors the monotheistic government of heaven (Engster, 1996, pp.491–2; see also Bodin, 1967, pp.10–12).[15] Bodin preferred monarchical government, not only because it better reflected the structure of the cosmos, but also because he believed that aristocracies, and even more so 'popular states', were less 'united and knit together' than monarchies, this last being obviously incapable of dividing against itself (Bodin, 1967, p.212; Vincent, 1987, p.56). Thus, he writes that while:

> ...factions and seditions are dangerous to monarchies...Monarchs can preserve their authority...But if the people in a popular state are divided, there is no sovereign to appeal to, any more than there is when the governing class in an aristocracy splits up into cliques (Bodin, 1967, p.139).

Bodin does not preclude the possibility that the sovereign power could be wielded by a group of persons. As he states, 'law signifies the right command of that person, or those persons, who have absolute authority over all the rest without exception' (Bodin, 1967, p.43). While sovereignty may find expression in the person of the monarch, it is not reducible to the monarch since it ultimately inheres in the state and not in any particular person. For Bodin, a state without sovereignty is inconceivable and thus he defines a state as a 'lawfull government of many families...with a puissant soveraigntie'. He goes on to explain that 'Maiestie or Soveraigntie is the most high, absolute, and perpetuall power over the citizens and subjects in a commonweale...which neither lawyer nor politicall philosopher hath yet defined' (Bodin, 1606, pp.1, 84). Sovereignty is the most high or supreme power in the sense that it is not constrained by a higher power, hence 'none but he is absolute who holds nothing of another man' (quoted in Merriam, 1900, p.14).

Bodin did not accept that element of Roman doctrine which maintained that 'the *imperium* is inherent in the community and conferred by it on the ruler' (Tooley in Bodin, 1967, p.xxiv). Since the end of the thirteenth century, according to Otto Gierke, the idea that government found its justification in the 'voluntary submission of the community' had been an 'axiom of political theory' (quoted in Merriam, 1900, p.12). For Bodin however, this element of Roman thought seemed to detract from the absolute nature of sovereignty. Further, he would have been concerned that this idea was being used by Huguenot publicists to support a right of resistance against the ruler's commands (Tooley in Bodin, 1967, p.xxiv). The term absolute thus points to the legally unbounded condition that the sovereign enjoys and, very importantly, to the indivisible nature of sovereignty. As Bodin writes: 'Just as Almighty God cannot create another God equal with Himself, since He is infinite and two infinities cannot co-exist, so the sovereign prince, who is the image of God, cannot make a subject equal with himself without self-destruction' (Bodin, 1967, p.42).

To speak of divided sovereignty is to destroy the character of the conception: it is to render it as something which it is not. Of course, one could redefine the word so that it meant much the same thing as power but we would still need some term to convey that supreme and undivided legal authority that the word sovereignty is intended to signify. While the sovereign can delegate power, such a delegation is in itself an act of sovereignty and can always be revoked. Hence, Bodin insists that the 'power of being the source of the law is incommunicable. The sovereign may, of course, give certain persons the right to make laws, which will then have the same authority as if made by the sovereign himself' (Bodin, 1967, p.58). The notion that sovereignty is perpetual power reinforces the point that it is exercised at no person's behest bar the sovereign. As perpetual power sovereignty cannot be seen as being possessed 'in virtue of some office or commission, nor in the form of a revocable grant', although certain ambiguities in relation to this point are raised below. In any case, Bodin states in relation to his claim concerning sovereignty as perpetual power, that the 'people has renounced and alienated its sovereign power' permanently, irrevocably and without conditions. Bodin's argument as to the permanency of the communal alienation of its sovereignty draws on the divine and natural law precept that a 'true gift' cannot be 'burdened with obligations'(Bodin, 1967, pp.25–7). As we have seen, Rousseau would turn Grotius's version of this argument on its head in arguing that since sovereignty is a kind of gift passed on to the ruler by the community, the community must remain the original and continuing source of the sovereignty of the state.

However, in terms of the overall force of Bodin's argument it was important that sovereignty not be seen as a grant since he maintained that power which is 'given with restrictions', excluding those established by the 'law of God and nature...is neither absolute power nor, properly speaking sovereign' (Bodin in Jones, 1975, p.57). At one point, Bodin restricts the meaning of the word perpetual so that 'perpetual authority' means authority that 'lasts for the lifetime of him who exercises it' otherwise, as he states, only 'aristocracies and popular states, which never die' could only be considered truly sovereign. Yet it is also the case that this term hints at the impersonal nature of the sovereign power for even in the case of a monarchy, sovereignty and majesty (this last term signifying the dignity of the state which the monarch as the ultimate authority within the state personifies), is not extinguished on the death of the prince and indeed it cannot be since, as we have seen, there can be no state without sovereignty (Bodin, 1967, p.26; Passerin d'Entrèves, 1967, p.100).[16]

Above all, it is crucial to emphasise that while sovereignty is power it is a specific kind of power: law-making power. Bodin writes that the 'the first mark of a sovereign prince is the power of giving laws...without consent of any besides himself' and all the other marks of sovereignty, such as the power over taxation, judicial appointments and war and peace, while essential to its operation, 'are only aspects of, or derivations from, this primary right of giving laws' (Bodin in Jones, 1975, p.58).[17] Laws are commands issued by a sovereign and the 'distinguishing mark of the sovereign', and this is true by definition given what has just been referred to as the first mark, is 'that he cannot in any way be subject to the commands of another' (Bodin, 1967, pp.25, 28). It follows then that the sovereign is 'not bound by the laws of his predecessors, still less can he be bound by his own laws' and it is in these two respects that the sovereign can be said to be 'above the law' (Bodin, 1967, pp.2, 32).

The understanding of law as command marked a shift away from the old notion that law was discovered rather than created (Passerin d'Entrèves, 1967, p.89).[18] A changing society demanded a more dynamic approach to legal matters, something which was facilitated by a sharper appreciation that customary law was fashioned by society to serve communal purposes and therefore could be adapted should those purposes change. Passerin d'Entrèves notes that from 'being conceived as the expression of immemorial use and custom, law came gradually to be viewed as the expression of a consciously planned legislative act, adaptable to new situations and supplying them with suitable rules' (Passerin d'Entrèves, 1967, p.89; see also King, 1974, p.131).

Bodin's own work reflects this changed understanding of law for in his *Methodus ad Facilem Historiarum Cognitionem* (1566) he insists that it is essential that the state has supreme authority, an authority consisting in the control of the 'administration and interpretation of the law' rather than the discretionary authority to make, amend or unmake the law as is the case with the *République* (McIlwain, 1933, p.99). Thus in the *Methodus,* Bodin denies that princes are 'above the law' and describes as 'base' the notion that 'whatever pleases' the prince 'shall have the force of law' (Bodin, 1945, p.203). Arguably, such comments suggest a more limited understanding of the reach of public power than that which is elaborated in the *République*. Although Bodin never argues therein that the prince is above the law, in the sense that there are basic laws the prince cannot change, his attitude to customary law in the *République* differs from the attitude he expresses in the *Methodus* (King, 1974, p.301).[19]

In the *République* Bodin argues against the view of Demosthenes, Aristotle and Cicero that the first princes were selected for 'their justice and their virtue'. To the contrary, he insists, the 'origin and foundation' of states was in 'force and violence' as practised by those whose 'highest endeavour was to kill, torture, rob and enslave their fellows.' The fact that there were 'innumerable slaves' in the 'first commonwealths' demonstrates this, as slavery could not exist 'unless there had been some violent forcing of the laws of nature' (Bodin, 1967, p.19). The institution of sovereignty involves the transformation of the state of slavery into a state of freedom. In contrast with the slave who is not endowed with legal personality, Bodin defines the citizen as one who is 'free because he has certain rights and privileges';

thus being a free citizen is the obverse of subjection. At the same time, one is only a citizen because one has submitted oneself to 'the majesty of him to whom he owes obedience'; a citizen is free but only because his or her liberty has been constrained in contrast with those living in a state of nature who are completely free to do whatever they are capable of doing (Bodin in Jones, 1975, p.72 and Jones, 1975, p.73).

Thus, just as there can be no state without sovereignty there can be no citizenship without sovereignty. In the absence of sovereignty, the human condition is characterised by a lawless freedom, which soon transmogrifies into 'pure and complete servitude' (Bodin in Jones, 1975, p.72). In the commonwealth Bodin describes citizens do not all enjoy the same rights, yet there is nonetheless a basic equality among citizens insofar as each is equally subject, as they logically must be, if sovereignty is to be conceived as supreme power (see Jones, 1975, p.73). It is in this notional realm where all subjects kneel before the sovereign, heads equally bowed, that we glimpse the neutral, public gaze of the state. Thus, Bodin writes that while there may be in the state a 'diversity of laws, language, customs, religion, and race', and certainly an unequal distribution of rights, each are equally bound to a 'single sovereign' and it is such subjection that 'constitutes a commonwealth' (Bodin, 1967, p.20).

As we have seen, Bodin's sovereign in not directly answerable to the people. However, he emphasises that a commonwealth 'is a *lawful* government' and a lawful government is one which governs in accordance with divine and natural law; thus, a sovereign state is to be distinguished from the kind of supreme power exercised by gangs of robbers and pirates (Bodin, 1967, p.57). Here, we touch on Bodin's conception of an absolute sovereignty that is at the same time limited (Balibar, 2004, p.145).

Bodin's incorporation of limitations into his theory sovereignty was not merely a strategic concession to French tradition. Rather, without the limits that Bodin incorporates into his notion of sovereignty, the concept would be indistinguishable from coercive power. Bodin's sovereign is and must be bound by divine and natural laws which oblige the sovereign to respect the 'natural liberty and the natural right to property' of citizens and subjects, if sovereignty is to be the kind of normative power which Bodin envisaged. Presenting sovereignty as being bound in this fashion was not merely a cosmetic exercise as Bodin, along with many of his contemporaries, took very seriously the idea that natural law conditioned the exercise of power (Bodin, 1967, p.56; Tooley in Bodin, 1967, p.xxvii).[20] Indeed, Bodin states that as God's lieutenant the sovereign is 'more strictly bound [by divine and natural law] than any of his subjects', adding that those who claimed the prince was not bound by any law at all 'insult the majesty of God' (Bodin, 1967 p.33). One should also make the point that it was because so much existing law contravened divine and natural law, for example laws permitting slavery, and not only because the sovereign had to be able to adapt law to the needs of the hour, that the sovereign had to enjoy the prerogative of unmaking existing law (Engster, 1996, pp.493,496; Bodin, 1945, pp.254–5).[21]

The dictates of justice and faith were not the only limits that Bodin incorporated within his concept of sovereignty. The activities of the sovereign power were also restricted by the *leges imperii* (*lois royales*), or fundamental constitutional laws of the realm, among these being the Salic law which was found by jurists in the fourteenth century (Croxton, 1999, p.587). This law, in addition to ensuring 'regular succession of the royal power' and thus the 'perpetuity of the sovereign power', prohibited females from inheriting the throne of France (Engster, 1996, p.497; Bodin, 1967, p.31).[22] While its immediate origins concerned the question of succession, one reason given for this prohibition of 'gynecocracy', additional to it being contrary to the laws of God and nature, was the fear that were a female sovereign to marry a foreign prince France's independence could be imperilled (Bodin, 1967, 203).[23]

Derek Croxton notes that over time another constitutional law was established, one that forbade the French monarch from disposing of royal landholdings in order to 'prevent the monarchy from weakening itself'. By the time of Cardinal-Duc de Richelieu's ascendancy this injunction had evolved into the principle that the French state 'might not cede territory; a treaty that did so was invalid' (Croxton, 1999, p.587; see also Vincent, 1987, p.59). The *République* reflects this tendency of thought. Bodin was concerned that through alienating the royal estate the crown would bankrupt itself and thereby impose unacceptable costs on subjects or imperil the French state (Franklin, 1973, p.73). He counselled that monarchs 'should not be constrained to burden their subjects with imposts, or devise excuses for confiscating their possessions, all kings and people have taken it for a universal and unchallengeable rule that the public domain should be sacred, inviolable, and inalienable, either through contract or prescription' (Bodin, 1967, p.186).[24]

Such a constitutional restriction had its roots in classical Roman law, which insisted that 'the one thing a sovereign cannot do is destroy his own sovereignty' (Tooley in Bodin, 1967, p.xxiv). Peter N. Riesenberg notes that medieval philosophers, reflecting on the concept of *imperium*, similarly insisted that the ruler 'should not and could not diminish the effective scope of his office and pass on less than the sum of authority requisite for proper executive action' (Riesenberg, 1956, p.5). As this last point suggests, the notion of the inalienability of sovereignty does not solely concern questions of expediency: as a matter of reason it is simply impossible for sovereignty, given what it is, to alienate itself or any constituent part of itself. Sovereignty, as a legal condition, cannot tear up the ground on which it stands without simultaneously ceasing to be itself and rendering its acts void. In the medieval context, the theory of inalienability was closely allied with office theory: the idea that the prince occupied his position on trust and that it came laced with obligations (Riesenberg, 1956, p.3). As we have seen, Bodin was no adherent of office theory, especially the version outlined by the *Monarchomaques*, yet his analysis of sovereignty strongly suggests, as Preston King argues, that 'sovereignty was not merely a person but an office' (King, 1974, p.126). This point is supported by the fact that Bodin embraced the theory of inalienability (a theory which reflects an understanding of sovereignty as perpetual power and as such, despite Bodin's contention to the contrary, suggests that sovereignty is indeed an office), that the constitutional laws of commonwealth being 'annexed and united to the Crown, cannot be infringed by the prince' because the 'traditional form of the monarchy' is the foundation of and sustains 'his very claim to sovereign majesty' (Bodin, 1967, p.31; see also King, 1974, p.134).[25]

Thus, the question of the inalienability of sovereignty concerns matters of expediency, logic and legitimacy. Although its historical entanglement with monarchical government for a long time obscured its impersonal character (although the idea of office clearly entails a conception of sovereignty as impersonal power), it eventually became clear that sovereignty was vested in the state and that as such it was only a notion conjured by the political community in order to manage its affairs. It is hardly surprising, therefore, that the idea of the inalienability of sovereignty in connection with the notion of sovereignty as an office finds powerful restatement in the context of post-revolutionary France. The French legal publicist Gérard de Rayneval, for example, insisted in 1803 that it is a 'fundamental maxim, that the public domain is inalienable' for the strong reason that 'sovereignty...is an office, a magistrature, a dignity, a trust and anything done in contempt of this truth is a violation of the social pact' (Rayneval, 1803, pp.152–3).[26]

While Bodin could not possibly have expressed himself in those terms, he well understood that ongoing communal consent was essential to the continuing sovereignty of the state, something which is evidenced by his emphatic insistence on the unchallengeable sovereignty of the prince, emphatic because he knew that in a real sense sovereignty would always be vulnerable to challenge. For this reason, Bodin recommended that the sovereign incorporate into his sovereign power certain other limits which, while not imprescriptable, were advisable on pragmatic grounds. In a chapter called 'How Sedition May Be Avoided' he writes that if the religion of subjects differs from that of the prince, the latter 'should not, in my opinion, attempt to coerce them' as that would only make subjects more 'obstinate' and may end by their becoming 'atheists' who, having lost their 'fear of God', would no longer fear the law (Bodin, 1967, p.142).[27]

Further, in line with Bodin's reasoning in relation to the inalienable nature of the sovereign power, he insisted that taxes should be the last resort when it comes to raising revenues and should be imposed only when justice and necessity require it, such as when a state is faced with the exigencies of war (and preferably only on those luxuries that are likely to 'corrupt the subject'). In imposing taxes, as well as in allowing large economic inequalities to persist, a ruler may lose his 'reputation' as a king and acquire that of a 'tyrant' (Bodin, 1967, pp.188–9). It should be apparent that the absolute sovereignty of which Bodin writes, exists within the boundaries of constitutional law and beyond that natural justice and only makes sense *qua* sovereignty when it operates within those boundaries which determine and shape its being.[28]

Carl Schmitt claimed in his *Political Theology* that Bodin 'incorporated the decision into the concept of sovereignty' (Schmitt, 1985, p.8). As is well known, sovereignty for Schmitt is the power to decide when exceptional circumstances, such as when the order and security of the state are endangered, demand the suspension of the existing constitution and the development of a new one. As he puts it: 'Sovereign is he who decides on the exception', the only definition which, according to Schmitt, 'can do justice to a borderline concept', this being a concept which pertains 'to the outermost sphere' (Schmitt, 1985, p.5).

In the *République* Bodin maintains that the 'sovereign prince can set aside the laws which he has promised...to observe...without the consent of his subjects' and although this might seem to support Schmitt's position, it is important to underline that Bodin adds the qualification that the prince may do so only if the laws the prince has made 'no longer satisfy the requirements of justice' as dictated by the laws of God and nature. Also very important is the fact that while the prince is above customary and statute law he is not above the fundamental constitutional laws of the state (Bodin, 1967, p.30). Bodin's sovereignty cannot be framed in decisionist terms since, as Frederick A. Dessauer points out, a '*decision* is possibly only where a choice is given between various possibilities' and thus the notion denies any rules of 'eternal validity' (Dessauer, 1946, p.19). Schmitt is right to point out that it is impossible to conceive of a constitution that has the exception as its founding principle, such that it can issue in a sovereign power which can decide on the exception: while constitutions enable power they also always and already delimit it. However, Schmitt's sovereign is precisely the one who decides when limits need to be exceeded (Balibar, 2004, p.136).

Schmitt, who may be seen as trying to overcome the difficulty of conceptualising a power alleged to be absolute but which is also circumscribed or limited, seemed to believe that in removing all the qualifications with which Bodin surrounded the sovereign power he was engaged in a purification of Bodin's theory. For Schmitt sovereignty becomes most real, becomes truly what it is, in such moments where 'the state remains whereas law recedes', the resultant vacuum being filled by a unitary political will

(Schmitt, 1996, p.12). Indeed, since a person or a committee can only make the decision, what Schmitt calls sovereignty is really personal power. By contrast, one of the defining features of sovereign power is that, contrary to Schmitt, it is not 'personalistic' (Schmitt, 1996, pp.33, 47). It is not vested in a person or persons but is vested in the state and what this means is that there can be no sovereignty outside of a set of constitutional norms.

A decision which is 'above any rule', as François Rigaux also points out, cannot be a sovereign decision as it bespeaks a power existing outside of any norm and as such it is essentially 'anarchical' (Rigaux, 1998, p.328). Schmitt distinguishes the exception from 'anarchy and chaos' because the exception is presided over by the decision. Yet, Rigaux's point is correct to the extent that the decision, pushed to its logical conclusion, becomes a law, so to speak, unto itself. It is the sole determinant of where borders are located and of the dimensions of the outermost sphere and these are matters, and the same can be said of the question of who rules in a state of emergency, which can never be decided in advance (Schmitt, 1996, p.12; see also, Norris, 2000 and Eulau, 1942, p.17). As Balibar states, sovereignty in Schmitt's hands is an 'unlimited and purely self-referential competence to suspend the laws in order to re-establish the conditions of their effectiveness' (Balibar, 2004, p.136).[29]

Those who view Bodin's incorporation of natural law limits into his theory as an inconsistency and a legacy of medieval of thinking effectively join Schmitt in his interpretation of sovereignty. On this view, for the 'logic' of sovereignty to become 'cruelly complete', as Charles E. Merriam stated in relation to Thomas Hobbes's rendition of the concept, such theoretical restrictions must be removed (Merriam, 1900, p.27). Yet, this is to misconstrue the real significance of the concept and to miss what is at stake in its conception. While its origins lie outside the domain of positive law (that is, its origins lie with the needs and desires of society and the necessity of negotiating with power), it is a concept normatively defined and intended to promote the commonweal and thus there are necessarily limits internal to this notion (Vincent, 1987, p.59). Power is harnessed by law but is always presumed to be qualified by it. Without limits internal to it, the concept of sovereignty loses its normative character, the very thing that distinguishes sovereignty from *de facto* control. Bodin's theory can thus be seen as a deduction from natural law and this is why he could so liberally, and with no sense of inconsistency, incorporate natural law into it (McIlwain, 1933, p.98).[30] While Bodin might agree, if pushed, that law can recede and the state remain he might also add, again if pushed, that such a state would be bereft of sovereignty.

The main blockage in Bodin's theory is his absolute insistence on non-resistance to legitimate authority. A legitimate king, according to Bodin, rules according to the principles of 'natural justice, which he sees and recognizes clearly and distinctly like the brilliance of the sun' (Bodin in

Jones, 1975, p.60n). Yet, Bodin obviously understands that kings may behave unjustly, such as by enslaving subjects, the very phenomenon which sovereignty was designed to overcome and which Bodin rejected as cruel, unnatural and a cause of insurrection, civil disturbance and revolution (Bodin, 1967, p.16). Nonetheless, while tyrannicide is to be applauded, that is the slaying of one who has illegally seized power, the disposal of a legitimate prince is never permissible 'however evil and tyrannical he may be' (Bodin, 1967, p.68). This was a position which, as we have seen, the *Monarchomaques* challenged and which would continue to be repudiated in the early years of the following century by Catholic writers such as Francisco Suárez (Nys, 1896, p.230).[31]

Bodin offers the pragmatic advice that to assassinate a legitimate authority may bring about the 'ruin' of the kingdom. However, more important in terms of his theory, is the notion that it is impossible for a subject to 'proceed against his king by way of justice': the courts are entirely within the jurisdiction of the king. Again collapsing legality into right, Bodin poses a rhetorical question: 'if it be not lawful for subjects to proceed against their prince by way of justice, how should they proceed against him by way of fact?' (Bodin in Jones, 1975, p.68). Despite his acknowledgement of the communal beginnings of sovereignty he insists, because of the irrevocable nature of the communal alienation of its sovereign power, that 'the subject has no jurisdiction over his prince, for all power and authority to command derives from' the sovereign, a sovereign who is 'ordained' by God (Bodin, 1967, pp.67–8). Thus, there are no earthly limitations to the exercise of the sovereign's power internal to the state. I say internal because Bodin allows that a foreign prince may depose of a cruel king by 'force of arms' (Bodin, 1967, p.69). This is possible because the foreign ruler is not, and cannot be according to the principle of the non-alienability of the sovereign power, in a state of subjection to any other authority and thus owes no-one his obedience bar his Creator (Jones, 1975, p.70).

The theoretical strain caused by Bodin's refusal to countenance the idea of legitimate resistance to unjust laws is evident in his concession that should the sovereign issue a command contrary to the moral law, it is permissible for the subject to disobey, although he/she 'must then seek refuge in flight, go into hiding or suffer death' rather than in any way threaten the life or dignity of the king (Bodin, 1967, p.68). Bodin recognises that power may unbind itself from law and therefore, one might add from sovereignty itself. Nonetheless, his system effectively permits power to operate outside the bounds of justice and under the guise of the majesty or sovereignty of the state. To put it another way, the paradox that presents itself is that it is within the gift of sovereignty to become its own other. As Balibar writes, the 'most difficult problem' posed by Bodin, as exemplified by the analysis of Schmitt, is that 'of the *limitations* of a power that is nonetheless presented as being "unlimited"' (Balibar, 2004, pp.144–5).[32] As we have seen, for Bodin there cannot be law without there being a supreme will to command it and this will cannot be supreme unless it is responsible to no other but itself. Of course, sovereignty is perpetually responsible to God and natural law but, given the apparatus of power represented by what Bodin called the marks of sovereignty, (something which Antoine Pillet later described as the 'ensemble of exterior signs' by which we recognise the sovereign authority), the possibility that sovereignty might descend into what Austin called 'practical mastery' remains very real (Pillet, 1899, p.505; Manning, 1933, p.202).

If sovereignty should not be seen as pure political power nor should it be seen as a purely normative or juristic phenomenon. This is because control of coercive means is among the marks of sovereignty and this is necessarily so because while sovereignty finds its ideal expression in a relationship of command and willing obedience it also presupposes acts of disobedience. Certainly, these means are harnessed to law and are overseen by a sovereign will conceived in normative terms, yet force remains an elementary part of the sovereignty of the state. Force polices the distance between the rulership and the ruled and secures the highness of the state, coming into its own where the law-abiding attitude falters. Bodin's sovereign commands virtue but for precisely this reason it can also deliver punishment and punishment that tests the boundaries of virtue. 'Good government', he writes 'requires on occasion the use of force, and states are often ruined by the prince's mildness, while others are saved by cruelty' (Bodin in Jones, 1975, pp.67–8).

Further, as we have seen, such is the absolute nature of the power he accords the sovereign she/he can deliver punishment even where she/he ceases to command virtue. This was a necessary requirement of sovereignty as he saw it such was his concern with the alternatives to absolutist rule, a rule he knew would always and unavoidably be less than absolute because people would never all be thinking the sovereign's thoughts nor obeying the sovereign's will. As he knew, sovereignty is always in danger of dissolution which is precisely why it required coercive power, but this is also why sovereignty, on grounds of expediency and not just for reasons of morality, had to include within itself limitations. The evolution of the concept of sovereignty is in a sense about entrenching, enriching and securing of those limitations.

As we saw, Bodin preferred monarchies to aristocracies and popular states because of the tendency of these last two forms of government to resolve into factionalism. However, at least in regard to popular sovereignty, this was not Bodin's last word on the matter for he also depicts the popular state as the most absolute, if not the most disturbed, form of state. On the one hand, in popular states disputes over the location of sovereignty, inevitable whenever there is a separation between rulership and the ruled, are eliminated because in such states 'the people, rulers and ruled, form a single body'. Such a body is unquestionably above the law because the people 'cannot bind themselves by their own laws'. Yet, because nothing can bind the people as a body (not even, as Rousseau would later point out, a constitution), and because 'the true nature of a people is to seek unbridled liberty without restraint', popular states are potentially dangerous (Bodin, 1967, p.75).[33] Unless ruled by 'wise and virtuous men' popular states tend towards, if not faction, then the 'the worst tyranny there is' (Bodin, 1967, p.193). Bodin's preference for monarchy over popular states springs not only from his concern that there be some power to adjudicate between competing groups but also from his concern, strange as it may at first appear, that the sovereign power should not be abused, a problem which would see later writers set off in an opposite direction although without resolving it.[34]

The Hobbesian artifice

Hobbes viewed the marks of sovereignty in almost exactly the same way as Bodin: all the 'markes' of sovereignty, the right to 'make, and repeale Lawes' and to control money and militia, were 'incommunicable, and inseparable' from the rest. Laws, money and militia were essential to the operation of sovereignty, although Hobbes would add that since the 'Actions of men proceed from their Opinion' it is also imperative that the sovereign control 'Doctrines' (Hobbes, 1968, pp.233, 236, 313, 376–7).[35]

Hobbes also upheld the view that the one thing the sovereign cannot do is alienate any one of the instruments of sovereignty as these are 'inseparably annexed' or bound to the sovereignty of the state. As instruments intended to procure the safety of individuals these are the foundations on which the sovereignty of the state rests; to renounce any of these instruments or pass them to another would immediately entail renunciation or dissolution of the sovereign power. As Hobbes writes, in such cases, unless the 'name of Sovereign...[is]...no more given by the Grantees to him that Grants them', the 'Grant is voyd' (Hobbes, 1968, pp.237, 377). For Hobbes too, the idea of a state without sovereignty is inconceivable. Sovereignty is the essence of the body politic, it is a 'publique Soule' which endows the state with will or 'Motion'; should the sovereign expire the state is 'governed no more, than the carcase of a man, by his departed, (though Immortall) Soule' and all the rights of the sovereign power, along with all the obligations towards it, would be immediately extinguished (Hobbes, 1968, pp.375–6).[36] Yet, the impersonal nature of the state and the sheer artificiality of the institution of sovereignty is more striking in Hobbes than it is in Bodin. Sovereignty is referred to as an 'office' and he announces in his introduction to the *Leviathan*: 'I speak not of the men, but (in the Abstract) of the Seat of Power, (like to those simple and unpartiall creatures in the Roman Capitol, that with their noyse defended those within it, not because they were they, but there,)' (Hobbes, 1968, p.75).

We have seen that for Bodin popular states were the most absolute form of state because there is nothing beyond the people which can bind them. Popular sovereignty, conceived in the most severe terms, collapses the distinction between rulership and the ruled. For Bodin, popular states posed a moral problem because they eliminate all checks on political will, thus allowing for a lack of restraint. Yet for Hobbes, the fact that the people cannot bind the people meant not so much the idea that popular sovereignty was dangerous, but rather that it was conceptually impossible. The idea of popular sovereignty was impossible as it entailed the self-contradictory notion that 'the People must be superior to the People'; such a notion was as absurd as the idea that a person could command him or herself (Hinsley, 1986, p.142).[37]

Sovereignty denotes a relationship of command and obedience and in a truly popular state, at least if conceived in an ideal way, commands become meaningless for there is none to receive them.[38] In any case, Hobbes did not believe that the multitude could establish a consonance of wills since the multitude is by definition '*Many*' and not '*One*' in a qualitative and not just quantitative sense; the multitude is characterised by competing ideas and interests and thus popular assemblies, if they were not to fall silent from indecision, must treat the majority of voices as if it were the voice of all (Hobbes, 1968, pp.220–1). For Hobbes, the question of the form of government, that is, whether sovereignty was wielded by a 'man, or a Court', was less vital than that of how to render the multitude of wills as one (Hobbes, 1651, Chaps. VI, XI).[39] The answer to this question lay with the conceptualisation of a '*Feigned* or *Artifiicall person*' in which all public rights and powers are vested by means of covenant among individuals. The word person is significant in this context for, as Hobbes underlines, it is derived from the Latin *persona* which refers to the '*disguise*...of a man, counterfeited on the Stage' or more specifically to an actor's mask. Thus, a '*Person*' is like a stage character and, as he adds, to '*Personate*, is to *Act*' the part of or '*Represent*' another (Hobbes, 1968, p.217).

Sovereignty arises from a single decision on the part of individuals. Individuals come together, albeit only once, and agree among themselves to authorise the construction of a power in which all their rights will be consolidated. In stating that the '*Pacts* and *Covenants*, by which the parts of this Body Politique were at first made, set together, and united, resemble that *Fiat*, or the *Let us make man*, pronounced by God in the Creation', Hobbes makes it clear that sovereignty is constituted power (Hobbes, 1968, pp.81–2).[40] While on the one hand sovereignty is a kind of collectively willed self-delusion, on the other hand, to the extent that this delusion is maintained, such that an individual or individuals continue to be vested with all the authority and power of the state, its existence is real, palpable and potentially confronting. Thus, sovereignty is an unreality become real *via* representation and one of the overriding tasks of the sovereign impersonator, if sovereignty is to do its work, is to obscure through its words and deeds, and even through the way it characterises its silences, its arbitrary origins. This is a task that cannot be completed because the minds of individuals can never be wholly conquered and for this same reason, the sovereignty of the state is forever endangered.

Thus, sovereignty requires 'Power and Strength' of such a degree that it is able 'by terror thereof...to forme the wills of them all, to Peace at home, and mutuall ayd against their enemies abroad' (Hobbes, 1968, pp.227–8). Yet, here too, sovereignty should not be seen merely as coercive power. Sovereignty is meant to be exercised in accordance with divine and natural law, both of which are communicated to the sovereign *via* the faculty of reason, and to serve those ends which inspired the covenant which created it. Yet, as with Bodin, the limits which are integral to the concept of sovereignty, can in practice be ignored. Hobbes acknowledges that the sovereign may fail to procure the people's safety in which case, he warns, the sovereignty of the state will simply dissolve, although without ever being breached, and the multitude will return to that natural condition of every man for himself. Indeed, the placing of a subject's life in danger, even through the imposition of the death penalty for a crime of murder, gives rise to a natural right of resistance since '[s]ubjects have Liberty to defend their own bodies, even against them that lawfully invade them' (Hobbes, 1968, p.268).

Yet, the idea of resistance in Hobbes is applied only to individuals and as such, it does not generally dissolve the sovereignty of the state. Whatever fate befalls particular individuals, the sovereign authority remains intact. In any case, popular resistance was inconceivable in Hobbes's schema as the people are a 'union of wills only for the moment in which they surrendered all will to the state', after that moment, as we have seen, their unity could only be expressed through the institution of the sovereign (Hinsley, 1986, p.143). Further, since every individual is the author of the sovereign power every individual has willed, at the moment of the covenant, the possibility of being killed. Presaging Rousseau, Hobbes insisted that, guilty or innocent, a man is the 'author' of his own fate at the hands of the sovereign because he is '[a]uthor of all his Sovereign shall do' (Hobbes, 1968, p.229). Yet, one may nonetheless rightly refuse to die at one's own hands, just as one may rightly refuse to kill another if ordered to do so. This is because the promise made in covenanting was in the nature of *'[k]ill me, or my fellow, if you please'* but not *'I will kill my selfe, or my fellow'* (Hobbes, 1968, p.269).

Thus, the adjective '[a]rbitrary', which Hobbes applies to government by a sovereign power, can be said to point to the fact that sovereignty is not natural but is instituted power and that it is legally unfettered power, as a consequence of which the sovereign effectively may will whatever it pleases. This means that an air of unpredictability always surrounds sovereignty. Sovereignty is unavoidably arbitrary in this sense given the kind of power that it is and given that it can only ever be wielded by a limited number of volitional human beings whose minds we are not capable of reading. Sovereignty thus inevitably produces unexpected inconveniences, however, the alternative to this is no government at all and a return to perpetual war (Hobbes, 1968, p.169; see also Martel, 2004, §19, §26).[41] Indeed, it is not just knowing what the sovereign can do that keeps people quaking in fear, but that it is not possible to know what it might do and it is in this added sense that we can say the sovereign will is incommunicable (Martel, 2004, p.8, n126; see Martel, §16, n126).[42]

However, the state cannot unify wills simply through engendering fear without endangering its existence: fear might result in obedience but it might also lead to dissent. Indeed, while exacting obedience through engendering fear of punishment is certainly prominent among sovereignty's means, ultimately sovereignty depends for its existence on communal willing. Sovereignty is thus but a single idea shared among many minds and though the sword is real enough, the authority to wield it, if not always the capacity, rests on the persistence of the *idea*. Hobbes writes in *Behemoth* that 'the power of the mighty hath no foundation but in the opinion and belief of the people' and thus it would follow that a prudent ruler would realise that in undertaking activities that would endanger the state and nation he/she would risk losing his or her sovereign powers (Hobbes, 1682). Hobbes tells us that while the '[l]egislator' is not the one 'by whose authority the Lawes were first made' he is the one 'by whose authority they now continue to be Lawes' (Hobbes, 1968, p.315). However, just as Hobbes recognised that laws which are formally just can be 'pernicious', he also knew that there is an underlying sense in which the second part of the previous statement is untrue and that the consent of the governed must be continually renewed (Green, 1999, p.9). Indeed, one is struck by the fragility of and latent sense of anxiety surrounding this mythic-cum-mechanical contrivance, an anxiety which springs from an acute awareness that it can be, to borrow from Bodin, 'dispersed in a single breath' (Bodin, 1945, p.220).

That power springs from the thoughts of the people points to the importance of the educative role of the state, at least if the people are to not think thoughts that would interfere with the operation of the sovereignty of the state (Hanson, 1984, p.345).[43] Thus, while civil laws, which Hobbes appropriately described as '[a]rtificiall Chains', these being the laws of the sovereign and not of the community, were significantly upheld because of the 'danger...of breaking them', education could also play an important role in ensuring that people understood and appreciated the rights of the sovereign and remained in thrall to him, a sovereign so awesome, that when 'in his presence' all subjects, irrespective of their standing in relation to each other, 'shine no more than the Starres in the presence of the Sun' (Hobbes, 1968, pp.238, 263, 377).

Hobbes's instrumentalist justification of the state was seen in the early eighteenth century as giving encouragement to anarchistic and revolutionary sentiments and not without reason (Hinsley, 1986, p.147). Indeed, pluralist critics of the state would deploy the utilitarian test, in seeking to determine the basis of political obligation, to subversive ends in the early twentieth century. Harold J. Laski for example, embraced the idea of the experimental state according to which 'the reasonable satisfaction of my impulses... [is]...the test of institutional adequacy', the anarchistic implications of which he acknowledged even though he insisted that the word reasonable should be interpreted with the concept of the social good in mind (Laski, 1925, p.39; Pemberton, 1998, p.285). As the basis of political obligation, the test of whether the state satisfied public demands meant that it would always be surrounded by a 'penumbra of anarchy' and it is more than arguable that Hobbes was also highly conscious of this penumbra, even though he sought to obscure it by depicting the state in terms of the towering, superhuman figure of the Leviathan (Laski, 1925, p.250).

In Hobbes's wake the concept of sovereignty became entrenched in European political theory, even if political communities in Western Europe 'remained too backward or too disturbed' to appreciate its full significance until well into eighteenth century, in particular, its location in the impersonal abstraction which is the state (Hinsley, 1986, p.130).[44] Further, with the exception of German thinking on the topic due to its particular governmental arrangements, older notions of 'double majesty or divided sovereignty' were no longer propounded (Hinsley, 1986, p.144). Theorists might clearly separate the power of the state into legislature, executive and judiciary while continuing to conceive of the state as a legal unity with 'all three' of these institutions 'in their discordant concord' constituting the 'life of the state' (Passerin d'Entrèves, 1967, p.121). For Baron de Montesquieu it is in the coterminous actions of these three organs that we see sovereignty in operation: sovereignty flows through them and governs their movement. As Montesquieu writes, these three powers, since 'there is a necessity for movement in the course of human affairs...are forced to move, but still in concert' (Montesquieu, 1949, p.160).

The notion of divided sovereignty would be discussed later in the American context as a means of comprehending the distinctive powers awarded to state members of the union and the national government. Thus, James Madison argued that the constitution of the United States should be 'neither a national nor a federal constitution, but a composition of both' with the states forming the federation retaining a 'residuary and inviolable sovereignty' (Madison, 1788). Madison's application of the word sovereignty to individual states of the union seems confusing. As John C. Calhoun later pointed out in objecting to Madison's apparent division of the sovereign power, '[s]overeignty is an entire thing, to divide is – to destroy it', stating also that one 'might just as well speak of half a square, or half a triangle, as of half a sovereignty' (Calhoun, 1851; Calhoun, 1853, p.232) Calhoun's argument that sovereignty is 'not the sum of the various powers' but is rather the 'supreme power' of which the various powers are 'emanations or outgrowths', exposed as a chimera the idea of a sovereignty shared among the federal government and the states. Logically, there could be no compromise between the notion of a sovereignty vested in the nation and the notion that sovereignty was retained by individual states, although it would take a 'trial of arms', in the form of a Civil War, to definitively settle this issue (Merriam, 1900, p.171).

That aside, on close examination it would appear that Madison possessed a more subtle understanding of the principle of sovereignty than Calhoun suggests, one which approximates the thinking of Montesquieu who understood that '[a]s a legal structure the State is one, however divided its power' (Passerin d'Entrèves, 1967, p.121). This understanding is also reflected in the American Constitution which opens with the words 'We the People'; thus, as Passerin d'Entrèves notes, the 'strongest vindication of popular sovereignty goes hand in hand with the most forcible assertion of the division of power.' Passerin d'Entrèves also makes the point that the purpose which the 'division of power' (an expression which he thinks, following Madison, better reflects Montesquieu's thought than that of the division of powers), was designed to serve could not have been accomplished without a clear idea of the sovereignty of the state (Passerin d'Entrèves, 1967, pp.119, 121–2). According to Montesquieu, political freedom turns on 'tranquillity of mind' and this is only possible where the sovereign power is separated, thus quelling apprehensions about the imposition of 'tyrannical laws'; nonetheless, Montesquieu was in no doubt that under a republican system sovereignty sprang from a single source (Montesquieu, 1949, pp.151–2).[45]

Rousseau and the risk of casualties

Rousseau criticised those political theorists who viewed sovereignty as divided and distributed among the various organs of the state: the legislature, executive and judiciary. He joined Hobbes in emphasising the utter indivisibility of sovereignty: its necessary unity and singularity. Those who would divide sovereignty, he wrote in a sentence reminiscent of Hobbes, 'make the sovereign a creature of fantasy, a patch-work of separate pieces, rather as if they were to construct a man of several bodies – one with eyes, one with legs, the other with feet and nothing else' (Rousseau, 1968, p.71). Rousseau also took from Hobbes the idea that sovereignty is 'absolute power', although for Rousseau the sovereign power is vested in a gathering of persons conceiving of themselves as '*a people'*, which as we saw with

Hobbes, appears impossible because there is no people in the singular only a multitude (Rousseau, 1968, p.74).

For Rousseau, it is through a social contract that the 'multitude' is 'united in a single body', with members mutually obliging themselves to obey the commands of the 'single body' which they now form (Rousseau, 1968, p.63). Yet, the sovereign or body politic itself has no obligation to obey the laws that it creates. Rousseau argues, as did Hobbes, that the sovereign conceived as a single identity or will is incapable, just like the individual, of making a promise to her or himself. This shows Rousseau writes, that there 'neither is, nor can be, any kind of fundamental law binding on the people as a body, not even the social contract itself', a point which suggests that Rousseau conceived of the people, as functioning as both, although at different moments, as a pre-legal and legal sovereign (Rousseau, 1968, pp.62–3).[46]

Sovereignty means lawful government and lawful authority, according to Rousseau, cannot be based on anything but covenants. Since physical might cannot give rise to morality or right there is no 'duty of obedience' to illegitimate powers (Rousseau, 1968, pp.52–3). Tyranny can never be considered a right of a king or any rulership as, besides being contrary to natural law, it is a manifest absurdity that a person would contract to enslave him or herself or give his or her freedom for 'nothing' in return. He adds that to 'say the same of a whole people is to conjure up a nation of lunatics; and right cannot rest on madness' (Rousseau, 1968, p.54). Indeed, if a people consent to nothing but sheer obedience, it does not thereby create a sovereign power but rather creates a master and thus it simultaneously dissolves itself as a body politic (Rousseau, 1968, p.70).

Rousseau follows a Hobbesian line of reasoning in rejecting the idea that the institution of government involves a contract between the ruler and the ruled, as this conception also implies the subjection of a sovereign people to a superior. There is only one social contract: the social contract which creates the sovereign number and any other contract which violates the terms of the original contract must be rendered void. The same applies in relation to treaty making, such that the obligations that the body politic incurs as a result cannot violate the terms of the social contract. Thus, for example, the sovereign number cannot 'alienate a part of itself or submit to another sovereign'. It is impossible and 'self-contradictory' for the sovereign to either limit itself or alienate its power. It exists only by virtue of the contract and to 'violate the act which has given it existence would be to annihilate itself; and what is nothing can produce nothing'. The sovereign number cannot act outside of the social pact which gave it life without ceasing to be sovereign and returning individuals 'to absolute freedom' (Rousseau, 1968, pp.63, 144).[47]

Further to this, acts of sovereignty cannot exceed the terms of the 'general covenants' that have their basis in the social contract. Rousseau describes these covenants as 'equitable', because they bestow equal rights and obligations on citizens. From the sovereign perspective there exists only the people as 'a whole body', that is, there is 'no distinction' to be made among the individuals who compose the body politic and this means that the sovereign cannot, without impairing its competency, impose heavier duties on one citizen than another (Rousseau, 1968, pp.76–7). Given that sovereignty inheres in the whole body of the people, it is not necessary for the 'sovereign. to give guarantees to the subjects'; such a body would not wish to harm 'any particular member' since the relations of mutuality among members mean that in doing so it would only be harming itself (Rousseau, 1968, p.63). Rousseau thus presents us with a sovereignty that is 'wholly absolute, wholly sacred, wholly inviolable' on the one hand, but which is also limited on the other, by the end which is the common good as well as by the natural rights which individuals 'ought to enjoy as men' (Rousseau, 1968, pp.74, 77). Such limitations frame the sovereign power or rather are integral to it. Yet, they act as limits only to the extent that they are internalised by the sovereign power because there is nothing beyond this power, whether we are thinking of the people as the legal or pre-legal sovereign, except the dictates of justice. Rousseau states that 'when the people as a whole makes rules for the people as a whole, it is dealing only with itself', yet while this relation is in principle regulated by certain fundamental norms, as we have seen, a people is at liberty 'to alter its laws, even its best laws' (Rousseau, 1968, pp.81, 99; see also Merriam, 1900, pp.34–5).[48] Balibar writes in relation to Rousseau's conception of sovereignty:

> The jurists have neither been able purely and simply to avoid or accept the provocation contained within Rousseau's definition of sovereignty as a 'relation' that the body politic maintains 'with itself' whose effect is to unbind it from any form of obligation with respect to the form of government it has itself chosen and to render useless any formal guarantee of the right of subjects (that is, of citizens taken individually), since 'it is impossible for the body to want to harm all of its members' (Balibar, 2004, pp.149–50).[49]

If we imagine a sovereign body which is all-encompassing and on which there are no formal checks, then any guarantees of rights can be seen as wholly at the discretion of the sovereign. Rights exist to the extent that they please the sovereign. However, such is the power of the sovereign body it can decide that it will no longer tolerate such rights and such a withdrawal of toleration, since it is authorised by the sovereign, would be formally lawful. As we have seen, Rousseau's sovereign is bound by considerations of justice and equity, yet he constructs an absolute power on which there are not, and cannot be, any formal limitations but on which there would appear to be few practical limitations as the people, as Hobbes stated of the Roman populace, cannot overthrow the people.[50] Rousseau's resolution of the dilemma posed by his theory, a dilemma which as we have seen was touched on by Bodin in his discussion of popular states, lies with the general will, a will which is neither the will of the multitude nor the majority but which is 'always rightful and always tends to the public good' (Rousseau, 1968, p.72; Hinsley, 1986, p.155).[51]

However, from a juristic perspective constitutional guarantees of natural rights remain crucial precisely because the virtuous will is not necessarily general and the general will is not necessarily virtuous. Indeed, as Rousseau sees the construction of the sovereign body as a means of escaping slavery, such rights must be part of the sovereignty of the state: their promotion is what authorises the sovereignty of the state and derogation from them is what destroys it. They are fundamental and imprescriptible because they are the very stuff of the social contract and as we have seen it is impossible for the sovereign body to destroy the thing that gives it life. The people acting politically can dissolve the social contract, but the minute this happens their status as a sovereign body is extinguished. Yet, need this mean that the people revert to being a mere multitude? The response has to be in the negative for there must be a sense of *the people*, as Rousseau implicitly acknowledges, if the idea of sovereignty is to arise.[52]

We saw with Hobbes that the only way in which the wills of the multitude can be condensed into one is through representation or impersonation, although as we also saw this does not entail that there is a consonance between the wills of the many and that of their impersonator. Thus, for Hobbes, sovereignty is representation although the content of that representation can be prescribed only by the one or those who are given the authority and power to personate the rest. Rousseau, however, eschews representation (of legislative power) because, by definition, will cannot be represented: 'either it is the general will or it is something else; there is no intermediate possibility' (Rousseau, 1968, p.141). Another cannot represent will and any attempt at representing it will necessarily deform and particularise it. It cannot be impersonated without ceasing to be what it is, that is, without failing to faithfully misrepresent the *authentic* will of the people. For this reason, those deputies who occupy government positions are to be seen as 'agents' of the sovereign rather than the sovereign's representatives (Rousseau, 1968, p.141) Whereas the rulership in Hobbes consumes the state, in Rousseau the state, in the form of the body of the people, consumes the government. Thus, government is reduced to a 'mere commission' (Hinsley, 1986, pp.153–5; see also Merriam, 1900, p.37).

Rousseau seeks to forestall the development of substantial state organs in which power may insinuate itself and slowly accrete. He knew that citizens with money to spend and desirous of a life of ease, might cease to be active as a sovereign body and would instead pay representatives to govern the nation as well as mercenaries to fight for it. Through 'laziness and money' he warned, they would 'end up with soldiers to enslave the country and deputies to sell it' (Rousseau, 1968, p.140). Yet, while Rousseau identified the sovereign with the community and eschewed representation, he understood that it was nonetheless a contrivance. Rousseau's social contract resulted in the construction of a fictional person in the form of a collective body endowed with life, will, and a 'common *ego*' (Rousseau, 1968, p.61). Further, the unified will of this body was not necessarily identical on all occasions with the wills of all individual members. There could be some distance between the general will and particular wills. Again, if there were a perfect consonance of wills the concept of sovereignty would be redundant.

Rousseau points to such a perfect consonance when he notes that the 'words "subject" and "Sovereign" are correlates, the meanings of which are brought together in the single word "citizen"'; in the shape of the citizen we witness that seamless meeting of 'freedom and obedience' which Rousseau says is the 'essence of the political body' (Rousseau, 1968, p.138). Here, sovereignty reaches a vanishing point. Yet Rousseau expects no such perfect consonance of wills, but rather expects disobedience and resistance on the part of those who are subject to decisions of the general will. Since every individual has a 'private will' distinct from the general will, he or she will not remain committed to the general will 'unless means are found' by which to 'guarantee their fidelity' (Rousseau, 1968, p.63). Rousseau expects that some individuals, thinking that the 'artificial person which constitutes the state is a mere rational entity', may seek to evade their duties as subjects while enjoying the rights of citizenship and that in such situations they should be constrained by the 'whole body'; without such constraint the social contract would be an 'empty formula' (Rousseau, 1968, p.64).

Sovereignty is no pale abstraction in Rousseau as will or legislative power comes equipped, and must be so equipped in order that it subsist, with universal powers of compulsion: executive power (Rousseau, 1968, p.77; see also Bluntschli, 2000, p.341).[53] Rousseau addresses the question of why the state can inflict death on individuals when individuals do not possess the right to kill themselves. His response to this question is to point out that the end of the social pact is the self-preservation of those who initiated it. If one of the purposes of the pact was to 'avoid becoming the victim of a murderer' then it entails, according to Rousseau, consent to execution 'if one becomes a murderer oneself' (Rousseau, 1968, pp.78–9). The avoidance of murder does not have as its necessary corollary the institution of the death penalty but, leaving that matter aside, his more general point is as follows: 'Whoever wills the end wills also the means' (Rousseau, 1968, pp.78–9).[54]

Yet, it is not just be those who violate of the pact who may suffer harm. Rousseau confesses that the means we will for the end of self-preservation involve 'certain risks, even certain casualties'; the terms of the social contract entail that if the sovereign should say to a man: '"It is expedient for the state that you should die", then he should die' (Rousseau, 1968, p.78). In relation to this, it is important to note his admission that 'the sovereign alone is judge' of what is of communal 'concern' (Rousseau, 1968, p.74). This admission suggests that even in his schema, even with his insistence on anchoring sovereignty as tightly to the people as people, the distance between sovereignty and the people in their multitude remains as it must remain. The decisions of the general will are commands and there are individuals distinct from the general will who receive these commands. Thus, the general will cannot avoid, in a sense, merely representing or misrepresenting the will of some. Hence the need for constraints, which as we saw carries with it the risk of casualties which is why there is a continuing need for sovereignty, even at its most popular, to put itself in question.

An inescapable dualism

The state must inevitably wield sovereignty if there is to be government. Further, representation, in distancing the people from itself is a means by which the people controls itself. The people, being in a possession of a collective power which may do violence, must do a kind of violence to itself through imposing the sovereign state over and above itself. Again, this means there is always a gap between the state and the people it governs, this last being conceived inclusively and not simply as a majority. While this rupture notionally can be 'overcome in the ideal unity of the nation, the nation itself always divides back up into antithetical terms' (Balibar, 2004, p.151).

Emmerich de Vattel's *Law of Nations* (1758) well reflects the attempt to resolve the gap between state and society as well as the inevitable reappearance of this gap. The nation, he states, is a state, a body politic or society formed by a 'group of men' who have 'common interests and must act in concert'; for this reason, the community must establish a '*Public Authority*' the task of which is to 'order and direct what is to be done by each in relation to the end of the association. This political authority is the Sovereignty; and he or they who are invested with it are the *Sovereign*' and is subject to the fundamental laws or constitution of the state (Vattel, 1863, p.1).[55] As the constitution of the state, the laws of which are 'inviolable and sacred', is a creature of the nation it follows, as Vattel states, 'that the nation is superior to the sovereign'; it also follows that the constitution is subject to the will of the nation. The nation can change the constitution in accordance with its requirements and in order that the constitution best reflects the nation's character, assuming of course the nation observes the fundamental requirement '*to know itself*' (Vattel, 1863, pp.7, 14).

Yet, the division between the state and society or ruler and the ruled soon re-establishes itself in Vattel's narrative, as the perceptible sovereign appears to absorb the moral personality and will of the political community. Vattel writes that when the nation endows a person with sovereign power:

> A political society is a moral person inasmuch as it has an understanding and a will, of which it makes use for the conduct of its affairs, and is capable of obligations and rights. When, therefore, a people confer the sovereignty on any one person, they invest him with their understanding and will, and make over to him their obligations and rights, so far as relates to the administration of the state, and to the exercise of the public authority. The sovereign, or conductor of the state, thus becoming the depository of the obligations and rights relative to government, in him is found the moral person, who, without absolutely ceasing to exist in the nation, acts thenceforwards only in him and by him. Such is the origin of the representative character attributed to the sovereign. He represents the nation in all the affairs in which he may happen to be engaged as a sovereign. It does not debase the dignity of the greatest monarch to attribute to him this representative character; on the contrary, nothing sheds a greater lustre on it, since the monarch thus unites in his own person all the majesty that belongs to the entire body of the nation. The sovereign, thus clothed with the public authority, with every thing that constitutes the moral personality of the nation, of course becomes bound by the obligations of that nation, and invested with its rights...all these rights, I say, reside in the sovereign, who is therefore indifferently called the conductor of the society, superior, prince, &c. (Vattel, 1863, p.14).

Indeed, it is in recognition of the inevitability of this division and the perils to which it may lead, that Vattel reserves for the nation the right of revolution. He insists that this right is 'indisputable' and as the thing to which a 'powerful republic owes its birth.' He adds that the 'high attribute of sovereignty' does not bar the 'nation' from curbing an 'insupportable tyrant', pronouncing 'sentence on him' and withdrawing 'itself from his obedience' (Vattel, 1863, p.17).[56] Vattel's work reflects the gradual triumph of the doctrine of state sovereignty over the conception of sovereignty as, on the other hand, the personal possession of a prince and, on the other, popular sovereignty understood in a literal sense. Yet his work also recognises the problem that is state power by insisting on the people's undeniable right of resistance.

By the mid-nineteenth century, the word people no longer denoted the dispersed subjects of monarch. The appearance of novel social configurations and alliances had rendered '"Society" an element weighty enough to be bracketed with "State"' making it very difficult, even a 'pathetic travesty' to maintain, as shown by the revolutionary outbreaks of 1848 and 1849, that the sovereign was the repository of all power (Emerson, 1928, p.128). Hinsley argues that it had become clear that a further conceptual development concerning sovereignty was needed in order to overcome the breach between state and society which, while necessary for the purpose of government, risked damaging cooperation between them. Further, given the growing status of society and the growing importance, and competitiveness of international relations, such cooperation could no longer be avoided.[57] According to Hinsley, this development saw sovereignty located in 'the body politic of a state-personality which is neither the physical executive state nor the physical political community but a notional bearer of power' which finds expression, at different moments, in the various institutions of the state be it the legislature, the constitution or even the electorate (Hinsley, 1986, p.157). He adds that this conception was the only possible way in which the division between state and society could be eliminated, 'could indeed be replaced by correlation of their needs and rights, despite their continuing and unavoidable separate existence' (Hinsley, 1986, pp.156–7).

The theoretical path to this conception was smoothed by thinkers such as Georg Hegel. Hegel conceived of the state as an 'organic totality' endowed with personality and represented the monarch as simply the point of articulation of the sovereign 'I will': the wholly necessary point at which the state's personality, which otherwise exists only in the abstract, was actualised (Hegel, 1991, pp.317–19). Some have detected traces of decisionism in this 'I will'. Certainly, Hegel describes the 'moment of ultimate decision' as being among the powers of the sovereign and insists that that his 'absolute self-determination constitutes the distinguishing principle of the power of the sovereign.' Yet it is important to note that Hegel states in relation to the formula of the 'I will' that it 'does not imply that the monarch may act arbitrarily' (Hegel, 1991, pp.313, 321). Hegel acknowledges the 'common misunderstanding' which equates the 'ideality' of the state with 'mere power' and sovereignty with despotism. However as he notes, and this supports Rigaux's observation in relation to decisionism, despotism means a 'condition of lawlessness', a negative condition wholly in contrast with sovereignty which operates 'under lawful and constitutional conditions' (Hegel, 1991, p.316).

The organic conception of the state was also embraced by Johann Kaspar Bluntschli who denied that sovereignty could be located in the people, the monarch or an abstraction such as the general will. In relation to the notion of the general will, he argued that Rousseau had made the mistake of treating '[l]aw...as the product and not as the limitation of arbitrary will.' By contrast, Bluntschli insisted that while '[w]ill may animate and effect changes in it, it is not of itself Law...The Will of the Sovereign presupposes Sovereignty' (Bluntschli, 2000, p.390). For Bluntschli, sovereignty is 'not something before, nor outside nor above the State', rather it is to be understood as the very 'power and majesty of the state itself.' Sovereignty, he added, 'is the right of the whole, and as certainly as the whole is stronger than any of its parts, so certainly the sovereignty of the whole State is superior to the sovereignty of any member of the State' (Bluntschli, 2000, p.393). Thus, while Bluntschli did not discount monarchical sovereignty he insisted that the state must always be considered as being superior to 'even its most effective organ[s]' (Merriam, 1900, p.102). As to the sovereignty of the people, Bluntschli allowed that one could speak of it but only where the word people was understood to mean 'the politically organised whole' (Bluntschli, 2000, p.393).

It was the development of the concept of state sovereignty as opposed to ruler sovereignty, as well as the popularisation of state rule that saw sovereignty conveyed *via* constitutional mechanisms. Constitutionalisation of sovereignty was seen as necessary in order 'to guard against', not only anarchy, but also the arbitrary use of supreme power such that citizen's rights would be denied (Hinsley, 1986, p.156). In reference to this point and to Bluntschli's criticism of Rousseau, one should note that in France after the July Revolution of 1830, political discourse shifted from characterising sovereignty as the '*will* of the *people*' to treating it as the '*reason* of the *nation*' with the nation being understood, not as a pre-legal institution, but specifically as the people 'organized within the constitution or charter' (Merriam, 1900, pp.81–3). Explaining the thinking behind this shift, the Duc de Broglie stated in 1842 that: 'To appeal from the sovereignty founded and regulated by the charter to any other sovereignty, is to appeal to numbers, to brute force; it is to pretend to organize disorder, even; to bring nothingness into existence' (quoted in Merriam, 1900, p.82).

The constitutionalisation and democratisation of sovereignty, along with the growing complexity of the business of government, led to changes in the institutional form of the state. Further, as the organs of the state multiplied, so too did sovereignty come to acquire an 'impersonal, a legal, even a metaphysical connotation' (Hinsley, 1986, p.219). Yet as Vincent argues, the lineage of the 'impersonal' state of the contemporary period can be traced directly back to the 'personal State' of the renaissance. It is to this earlier personalisation of the state, first in the form of a natural person and then in the form of a fictional being, that the modern state owes its 'cohesive unity'. Diurnal political discourse in which the anthropomorphisation of the state has proved to be an almost irresistible feature, reflects this inheritance (Vincent, 1987, pp.51, 75).

The juristic theory of the state

By the early twentieth century sovereignty, once seen as the legal and political manifestation of the majesty and power of a supreme monarch, had come to encapsulate, condense and make sense of an intricate web of legal and political relations (Emerson, 1928, p.254). As an adjective, the word sovereign had ceased to meaningfully describe a particular person. At the same time, none of the empirical institutions of modern government was able to absorb it. This is why it came to be seen as purely an abstraction, an abstraction personified by the state and authorising the acts of the state, this last itself being a wholly notional entity whose 'personality...is exhausted in this attribute, since the state-person has no reality except as a juristic or political entity' (Sabine and Shepard in Krabbe, 1930, p.xxxii). What also emerged forcefully with the refinement and elaboration of the concept, was its legal or normative quality: sovereignty is not 'above, but within the law and is in fact constituted by the law' (Emerson, 1928, p.254).

The juristic theory of the state, that is, the conception of the state as a juristic personality, arose in late nineteenth century Germany although it was widely embraced throughout Europe. Under this theory, sovereignty was dissociated from the 'actual possession and exercise of political power' and was instead treated as a purely normative phenomenon (Emerson, 1928, p.254). The idea of the state as a juristic personality arose, as with those theories which conceived of the state as a 'living organism', partly because of the difficulty of finding a specific location in which the sovereign power inhered since it could no longer tenably be attributed to either the populace or to an absolute monarch (Merriam, 1900, pp.128–9; Eulau, 1942, p.8). It was also developed in order to realise the 'ideal of an authority which is more than the expression of an arbitrary will', the former being the original meaning of the term *Rechtsstaat*: a 'Kantian legal-state' (Sabine and Shepard in Krabbe, 1930, pp.xxxv–xxxvii; Merriam, 1900, pp.124, 128). Yet, the understanding of law as the will of the sovereign forever delimits and defeats the juristic conception of the state. Indeed, despite the good intentions behind the theory it effectively (especially as a result of the rise of the positivistic theory law which, in an effort to render the study of law a science, dismissed all discussion of 'value and content' instead insisting that 'the only justification of any legal system was to be "efficacy"'), lead to the idea that 'every State, in as far as it is a legal system can by definition be considered to be a *Rechtsstaat*' (Passerin d'Entrèves, 1967, p.146).

As Neil MacCormick writes, to treat the state and sovereignty in purely juristic terms holds out dangers because it gives rise to the idea that the state cannot be legally critiqued or constrained as the state itself is a creature of law (MacCormick, 1993, p.13). Because of his restriction of law to a command issued by a determinate superior, Austin had also argued that the power of the sovereign cannot be subject to 'legal limitation', although as we saw he did not deny recourse to resistance on the part of the community and was clearly aware that the state is subject to a range of normative expectations (Austin, 1906, p.156).[58] Rather than defining the state as a purely juristic phenomenon, and thus be caught in the perverse tautology to which this gives rise, MacCormick suggests that the state should be seen as a political phenomenon: as an instrument of political power. This, however, is only to vacate the field and leave sovereignty open to capture by decisionism. Much better, is his suggestion that one might view sovereignty as a 'politico-legal' notion since the administration of law requires political power and the exercise of political power usually involves appeals to 'normative power' (MacCormick, 1993, p.11).

Yet the conception of sovereignty as lying at a point where law and politics converge is inherently unstable. While sovereignty creates and to a degree is created by law, as theorists from Bodin to Schmitt have recognised, it cannot be 'conceived of without a bearer capable of making highest laws and of executing them', that is, it presumes a bearer with a 'real will' and this can only be a 'physical person or a group of persons' (Eulau, 1942, p.8). Yet, obviously this means that the compulsive powers of the state are ever open to corruption (MacCormick, 1993, p.14). This is of enormous moment given, as T.H. Green wrote, that the power of the state 'is compulsive in the sense that it operates on the individual in the last resort through fear of death' (Green, 1999, p.121). It is a mark of sovereignty that the state has a monopoly of the means of coercion, however, this feature of state sovereignty as Balibar remarks, is the least susceptible to democratic control (Balibar, 2004, p.202). Normative power is thus always at risk of being deformed and debased. For this reason, just as the state assumes disobedience on the part of subjects so must citizens assume disobedience on the part of the state. The citizenry must be relentless in making its expectations clear and relentless in insisting that 'the exercise of political power be confined within some normative order' in order that political power is used in a disciplined manner (MacCormick, 1993, p.14). While sovereignty frequently serves to reinforce the demands of political power, it can also be seen as a kind of leash which if pulled firmly and often enough, will teach power that it must restrain itself and render itself accountable (Hinsley, 1966, p.25). The imputation of grandeur to the sovereign state, in part a legacy of the theological and monarchical finery in which sovereignty was cloaked in its early years, makes no sense, indeed is infantile, unless this institution can demonstrate its moral adequacy and justify its acts (Passerin d'Entrèves, 1967, p.148).

The advent of democratic rule saw the state endowed with sufficient authority to override special interests. This allowed for a further secularisation of the state (although this also had as its corollary the 'sacralization of the *name*' of the nation-state), as well as state invasions of the economic sphere, leading ultimately to the construction of the social welfare state (Balibar, 2004, pp.152–3). As Balibar argues, if the sovereignty of the state is not to be merely an empty assertion guaranteed only by coercive means or threatened by insurrection, then the state must be constantly 'incorporating new kinds of loyalties and disciplines (such as patriotism or civic spirit, public education, health, good morals)', an incorporative effort which is always correlated with a parallel process by which civil society is placing pressure on and demanding the reconstitution of the state in line with public needs (Balibar, 2004, p.147).

However, the future of such efforts is in doubt. First, because the explosion of diversification in major centres puts into question the relationship between state and society in a context in which growing cultural transnationalism is eroding the state's universalist and transcendental claims, such that political or national identity has been '*particularized*' or rendered somewhat banal. Further, the relentless assaults of global capital on the social welfare state bring into question the capacity and willingness of the state to intercede in conflicts between economic groups (Balibar, 2004, pp.152–3). Some states may struggle to maintain their economic autonomy. Others may serve as an agent of the market in which case the dualism between society and state will sharpen. Indeed, in some instances, the state may become explicitly repressive in implementing market demands. The present condition of democracies, is one in which the state, as a set of bureaucratic institutions, typically stands aloof from the community with popular sovereignty becoming largely emblematic. Writing in relation to contemporary constitutional thought, Balibar notes a definite retreat from the principle of popular sovereignty and he explains that this is because the 'people' are 'both unavailable and undesirable.' They are unavailable because of the immense profusion of cultural and social multiplicity, such that the people can only be appealed to 'in an ideal way' (Balibar, 2004, p.184).

The reason for their unavailability helps explain their undesirability. The people are undesirable, not simply because the rulership prefers to rule with as few fetters as possible, but also because the people's representatives do not want or find it difficult to represent the conflictual differences which are part of what the people are. Balibar argues that separating out the idea of the people from the idea of democracy is deeply troublesome because it is of the essence that we view ourselves, and not the state, as the ultimate custodians and guarantors of democratic methods and processes. Democracy is inconceivable in the absence of a people because it involves more than a set of procedures or the formal guarantee of certain rights. Citizenship, he writes, should not be seen as 'merely a status granted by a pre-existent entity or authority' but should 'become once again a conquest or institution of autonomy' (Balibar, 2004, pp.184, 190). Kant argued in *Contest of the Faculties* (1798) that 'beings endowed with freedom cannot be content merely to enjoy the comforts of existence, which may well be provided by others', rather, what is crucial is the '*principle* which governs the provision of such comforts'; and the principle in question entails that one must 'demand for the people...nothing short of a government in which the people are co-legislators.' This demand however, is forestalled by an insidious form of propaganda that conceals from a people 'the true nature of its constitution'. To borrow Kant's observation regarding the contemporaneous British situation, the people are deceived 'with the illusion that...[the sovereignty of the state]...is *limited* by a law which emanates from them, while their representatives, won over by bribery, secretly subject them to an *absolute monarch'* (Kant, 1970a, pp.183, 186–7).

To demand that people become authentic co-legislators is not to insist on frequent resort to popular riots, although that may be necessary in some circumstances. Rather, it is to emphasise that while the concept of *the* people is an abstraction, as the people cannot be encountered as a singular personality, people's 'powers', as Rousseau stated, can be combined such that they are 'directed by a single motive' and 'act in concert.' This is imperative as the 'sum of forces' necessary to control existing forces 'can be produced only by the union of separate men' (Rousseau, 1968, p.60). The often fragile and fraught negotiations between the sovereignty of the people and the sovereignty of the state, in the course of which as Balibar points out, social conflicts have both been articulated and repressed, are still of great consequence precisely because of the social fracturing and economic constraints imposed on the state by globalisation. It is in the midst of such negotiations that the political significance of sovereignty finds expression: in the struggle on the part of people to assert their will through constituting power and the equally important imperative that they control it through the institution of the state (Balibar, 2004, pp.153–4).

As I have indicated, there are necessarily repressive features to this act of self-control yet, as Balibar argues, it is the only way in which the rule of law can be guaranteed outside of vesting power and authority in a transcendent figure or institution (see Balibar, 2004, p.196). The democratic state, at least in theory, avoids a sharp tension between society and rulership to the extent that the figures of sovereign and citizen, as we have seen with Austin, are wholly reversible. These figures are correlative ideas such that the citizen legislates sovereignty and sovereignty commands the citizen and this is why the history of these two concepts, from Bodin to Rousseau, is so closely linked (see also Balibar, 2004, p.196). While representative democracy grows out of the idea of popular sovereignty, it imposes limits on expressions of the popular will. That is, if sovereignty is not to degenerate into majoritarian domination or factional struggle it requires the institution of representation. Representative democracy is a means of disciplining expressions of the popular will. It places a 'distance "between the people and itself"' by subjecting the popular will to a set of protocols concerning its expression and conduct. The danger at issue is that of investing power in an independent and superior body which may be corrupted (Balibar, 2004, p.187).

However, performing this act of distancing is necessary because the identity of the people is not wholly singular but is multifarious and fractious. At the same time, if representation is to keep faith with itself and the term people to meaningfully signify the whole of the people, then social antipathies must be allowed a presence in the public sphere: they must be represented rather than repressed or displaced. In turn, it is through representation that social conflicts can be normalised or regularised, indeed, unless the '"We"....[is]

represented in its multiplicity' it will *'become once again a multiplicity* and be represented as such', presumably by the kind centralised authority proposed in theories of sovereignty written before the concept of the people became available (Balibar, 2004, pp.187–8).

Balibar argues that the choice facing us is between a form of rule in which the people are only symbolically present or the representation of 'social antagonisms' and this is because, as he also states: 'there can be no new "Leviathan" that would regulate beliefs and officialize knowledge…and there is even less possibility for a new "civic religion" that would relativize "traditional" or "revealed" religions and relegate them to private choice' (Balibar, 2004, pp.151–2, 201). The presence of and need to represent social conflicts should not simply be sourced to growing diversification or to disaffection resulting from the unequal distribution of the benefits of industrial development. Rather, it goes to the heart of the idea of the dēmos itself understood as a forum in which social cleavages are played out as well as a point at which concord, whether strained or harmonious, is forged (see Balibar, p.184). However, such an agonistic approach to democracy requires that tranquillity of mind of which Montesquieu wrote and, as William E. Connolly puts it, 'a certain *empathy* for what we…[are] not', whoever we may be (Connolly, 1993, p.195).

Balibar's response to these issues is that the process of making of a community should proceed not from any formal theory of communicative action since such theories may constrain as much as they open up discussion, but on the basis of the notion of a '"community of fate" in which individuals and groups can neither *separate nor get along at will'* and who are destined to share a history (Balibar, 2004, p.173).[59] Society is composed of individuals and collectivities that are bound to collide and clash with each other but who also need each other and are in a very basic sense, beyond even their concrete duties, responsible for each other. As members of a community (and if sovereignty is to genuinely give expression to the will of the people and not just a part of it), we all have a stake in and responsibility for ensuring that those who live on the margins, those who have no power to draw on except the combined power of the community, have the resources to be heard (Balibar, 2004, p.184).

Montesquieu observes that the liberty of 'every citizen constitutes a part of the public liberty, and in a democratic state is even a part of the sovereignty' and it follows from this that the less citizens enjoy freedom, whether positive or negative, the more the sovereignty of the state is diminished (Montesquieu, 1949, p.236). If one's voice is not heard, if one's will is not incorporated in the public will of the state because of one's marginal status, then one effectively ceases to be a citizen and one becomes a mere subject or even worse. As Rousseau insists, you are not a citizen unless you 'share in the sovereign power' (Rousseau, 1968, p.62).

3
The International Arena

An anti-hegemonic doctrine

In the case of imperial Rome, the external significance of sovereignty was not at all developed and nor did it need to be for the reason that Rome shifted directly from being a 'city state into a universal empire' (Hinsley, 1986, p.159). However, in the competitive environment of early modern Europe thinking about the exclusivity of territorial jurisdiction in relation to outside powers was inescapable. In this period, the anti-hegemonial implications of sovereignty were revealed by the fact that the institution of sovereignty, at the inter-state level, required nothing less than the dismantling of *respublica christiana*, even though resistance to hegemony was thought through in a self-regarding manner by states themselves (Passerin d'Entrèves, 1967, p.98).

There is considerable debate as to when the principle of sovereignty properly and generally crystallised as state practice. For a long time, the 1648 Peace of Westphalia has been seen as the turning point. A British barrister-at-law, John Hosack, wrote in 1882 in reference to it that 'the theory of equality among so many differing so widely in extent and resources should have been thus publicly acknowledged was an important step in progress of society' and although the general point Hosack makes concerning the significance of treating as legally equal the empirically unequal is very important, it cannot be said that this development was embraced immediately and unambiguously at the time of the Westphalian settlement (Hosack, 1882, p.226).

According to Croxton, even though what were in effect sovereign states participated in the Westphalian negotiations, appreciation of the notion of an international system comprising sovereign equals was weak and limited. Some rulers were reluctant to accord rulers in neighbouring states the same status they claimed for themselves. A sovereign state system would only become a reality when states became willing to apply the principle of sovereignty to other states and not only within their own domains. Although the concept of sovereignty was not a novelty at the time, the idea of constructing a state system on this basis was neither explicitly nor implicitly embraced during the Westphalian negotiations. While states were concerned to protect their own sovereignty, the question of whether sovereignty was to be 'multipolar' was another matter entirely. It was not just that appreciation of the fact that recognition of the sovereignty of one state was tied to the recognition of the sovereignty of other states was somewhat lacking, it was also the case that certain states, namely Spain and France, remained in a position to aspire to hegemony (Croxton, 1999, pp.570–1, 590).

It is also worth noting that the language and ideas contained within the Westphalian settlement were those current in the latter part of the middle ages and reflected the continuing grip of the notion of a christian *universitas* (Jackson, 1999, p.439). Thus, the Articles of the Treaty of the Peace signed at Münster in Westphalia between France, the Empire and the states forming the Empire opened with the words: 'By the Ambassadors Plenipotentiarys of the Sacred, Imperial, and Most Christian Majestys, and the Extraordinary Deputys, Electors, Princes and States of the Sacred Roman Empire' (Parry, 1969a, p.319). The text of the agreement was in Latin with expressions such as '*supremum dominium*' and '*superioritate supremque dominia*' being used to describe the jurisdictional powers recognised by the agreement in relation to France, expressions which were translated as '*Droit de Souveraineté*' in the 1651 French translation (Die Westfälischen Friedensverträge, 1648).[1] As to the estates of the Holy Roman Empire, under the terms of the settlement and in order to 'prevent for the future any Differences arising in the Politick State', these were 'confirmed in their *ancient* Rights, Prerogatives, Libertys, Privileges' and accorded 'free exercise of Territorial Right' (*Landeshoheit*) in ecclesiastical as much as in political matters in their respective areas of jurisdiction (Parry, 1969a, p.337).[2] Further, they were also now allowed to form alliances with foreign powers, although this was limited to alliances which were not targeted 'against the Empire' (Croxton, 1999, p.573).

Croxton argues that the estates did not see themselves as being accorded sovereignty under the terms of the agreement. To the contrary, he adds, they persisted in thinking of themselves as forming a 'single body', continued to accept the Emperor 'as their actual or nominal overlord' and, as prescribed by the Westphalian settlement, continued to enjoy voting rights at the imperial Diet, pay 'common taxes' as well as raise a 'joint army' (Croxton, 1999, p.574; see also Parry, 1969b, pp.337–8).[3] Although the estates disdainfully disregarded the Empire in later years, it was only with the dismantling of the Holy Roman Empire, under the Rhinebund Act of 1806, that German states which up until then had only been granted *Landshoheit*, were recognised as being in possession of the 'plénitude de la souveraineté' (Merriam, 1900, p.121). This is not to say nothing changed after 1648 or to deny that sovereignty-like themes are embedded in the text of the agreements. As Daniel Philpott observes, 'discernible behavioural changes' were consequent upon the agreement, notably the fact that after 1648 'only states exercised significant power, and they rarely forcibly interfered in one another's religious affairs' (Philpott, 2001, pp.23, 83).

This change in behaviour was reflected in a shift in the rhetorical appeals made by states, such that the invocation of 'Christian unity' became less common and was eventually replaced by an insistence on international pluralism 'based on a secular society of sovereign states' (Jackson, 1999, p.439). An attempt to unite the crowns of Spain and France, officially described as 'the great danger which threatened the liberty and safety of all Europe', gave rise to the War of the Spanish Succession which lasted from 1702–1713. The resultant Anglo-Spanish Treaty of Utrecht of July 13 1713, announced that the 'peace and tranquillity of Christendom' (it being the last treaty to invoke Christendom in its text), in the future would rest with 'an equal balance of power', something which was described in the Treaty as 'the best and most solid foundation of a mutual friendship, and of a concord that would be lasting on all sides' (Parry, 1969b, pp.325–6).[4] It is also important to emphasise that the balance of power system which began to take shape in the eighteenth century, was predicated on the idea that the various states of Europe had a shared interest in preventing hegemonial behaviour. That is, the idea of the balance of power presupposed an international society and reflected the understanding that the sovereignty of each state is valuable.[5] François Fénelon, a fierce critic of the wars of glory and punishment of Louis XIV because of the terrible price they exacted from the French people and hatred of France they engendered in its neighbours, wrote in 1720 of the balance:[6]

> Neighbouring states are not only obliged to observe towards each other the rules of justice and publick faith; but they are under a necessity, for the security of each, and the common interest of all, to maintain together a kind of society and general commonwealth; for the most powerful will certainly at length prevail and overthrow the rest, unless they unite together to preserve the balance (Fénelon, 1815, p.766).[7]

However, consciousness that the principle of sovereign equality should govern relations between European states and that this principle formed the necessary basis of a Europe conceived as a law governed space, remained partial and incomplete in the eighteenth century. Doctrines of intervention continued to be espoused. The French revolution, in terms of the international principles it articulated, was significant because here was a case of a whole nation, and not just philosophers or publicists, advancing the idea of the primacy of international law rather than the doctrine of reason of state (Mirkine-Guetzévitch, 1928, p.308). Thus, the French National

Assembly on May 22 1790 renounced all wars of conquest instead insisting on respect for the liberty of foreign nations. On April 13 1793, its successor, the National Convention, proclaimed the principle of non-intervention (Nussbaum, 1954, p.119; Mirkine-Guetzévitch, 1928, p.310).[8] However, the idea of 'international universalism' on which these principles were based when combined with the principle of nationality, (widely understood in France to mean in the manner of Rousseau that a nation is by definition a 'free' people), led to the unavoidable conclusion that revolutionary France was an ally of 'all peoples' and thus was opposed to 'all monarchs' (Mirkine-Guetzévitch, 1928, p.312).

On 19 November, 1792 the National Convention adopted a proposal, put forward by Louis-Marie de Larévellière-Lepeaux, called '*Le droit international et le droit politique*'. This proposal declared, 'in the name of the French nation', that France would accord 'fraternity and assistance to all people who would want to recover their liberty' and charged the executive power with 'giving to the generals the necessary orders in order to bring assistance to these peoples and to defend the citizens who have been or could be harassed in the cause of liberty' (Nys, 1896, p.385; see also Hornung, 1886, p.204). As Frabrice Brandli points out, such decrees placed France 'outside the "Westphalian" system of equilibrium which recognised States', not peoples, as the 'unique, legitimate actors' (Brandli, 2007).

George Friedrich von Martens of the University of Göttingen, writing in the preface to the 1796 German edition of his *Précis du droit des gens moderne de l'Europe fondé sur les traits et l'usage*, perceived in the French rejection of traditional diplomacy and the doctrine of revolutionary intervention grave dangers to the established political and legal order of Europe (Frey and Frey, 2006, p.3).[9] Similar concerns were expressed by statesmen, with the British foreign minister George Canning maintaining that revolutionary France's declarations concerning foreign affairs concealed French ambitions for 'universal oppression' and 'universal dominion' (quoted in Temperley, 1968, pp.41, 58; Frey and Frey, 2006, p.2).[10] Continental autocrats, in particular, were disturbed by the implications of France's effective denial of legitimacy, as expressed in the decree of 19 November 1792, to any 'authority which did not come from the nation'; not surprisingly, the doctrine of revolutionary intervention was soon met by a doctrine of counter-intervention (Mirkine-Guetzévitch, 1928, p.313). Nussbaum claims that when Martens pronounced that 'a state may intervene in domestic crises of a foreign nation if "called in to aid by the party which has justice on its side," and even without such call on the ground of a special right or simply on the ground of self-preservation', it was the interference by Austria and Prussia in the French revolution that was at the forefront of his thinking. Given this, he adds, it was a pronouncement which was clearly 'more political than legal' (Nussbaum, 1954, p.183).

It should also be noted that, as the observation of Fénelon cited above shows, while the principle of the balance of power was meant to stabilise boundaries and guard against intervention, in the eighteenth century its preservation was also cited as grounds for intervention and indeed this defence of intervention continued well into the nineteenth. As the Argentinean diplomat and historian Carlos Calvo noted in his 1868 *Droit international théorique et pratique: précédé d'un exposé historique des progress et la science du droit des gens*, 'all the coalitions formed against France from 1789 up until the treaties of 1812 and 1813' were driven, not only by fear for the future of the 'monarchical order' in Europe, but also in order to sustain the existing balance of power (Calvo, 1887, p.281). Indeed, in the context of the coalitions against France these two imperatives were entirely mutually informing: to conserve the balance was to conserve the monarchical order and vice versa. The coalitions against France well illustrate the limitless logic of the argument in favour of intervention in the name of the balance of power. As J.J.G. von Justi presciently pointed out in his *Die Chimäre des Gleichgewichts von Europea* in 1758, *reductio ad absurdum* this argument ended up in the proposition that a state could justifiably intervene in another state in order to prevent or overturn internal governmental reform insofar as this could be said to strengthen a state in its external dealings (Anderson, 1961, p.167).

The persistence of doctrines of intervention shows, according to Hinsley, that the full implications of sovereignty in the international sphere were only sketchily appreciated for a long time. What the idea meant for international practice was only really appreciated by all European states after the defeat of Bonaparte in 1815 and the triumph some years later, of 'Castlereigh's ideas over Alexander I's conception of the Holy Alliance and of the Congress system' (Hinsley, 1986, p.204). This Alliance, formed on 26 September 1815, was among the governments of Russia, Austria and Prussia. Within the Act of the Alliance, there was no reference to international law and its own legal status was uncertain. Rather, the Act amounted to a vague statement to the world at large that the sovereigns of Russia, Austria and Prussia would be guided by the religious principles of 'Justice Christian Charity, and Peace' in the 'administration of their respective States, and in their political relations with every other Government' (Holy Alliance, 2007). Nussbaum argues that the counter-revolutionary, interventionist implications of the Alliance become readily apparent when one considers that all the parties to it were believers in the divine right of monarchs (Nussbaum, 1954, p.188). However, others have pointed out that the Alliance was only rendered a political instrument, that is, an instrument of counter-revolutionary intervention, with the Protocol of Troppau in 1820. This happened under the guidance of Vienna's Prince Metternich and in reaction to the Spanish and Neapolitan revolutions (Seaman, 1964, pp.11, 15). In any case, as Sharon Korman writes, while the Congress system, understood as the public law of Europe (*droit public de l'Europe*), did not involve the outlawing of intervention and conquest, it nonetheless 'raised a strong presumption against unilateral changes in the status quo' (Korman, 1996, p.80).[11] At the Congress of Aix-la-Chapelle on 15 November, 1818 Europe's five major powers, including the members of the Holy Alliance, declared that:

> The sovereigns, in forming this august union, have considered as a fundamental basis their invariable resolution never to depart, either among themselves or in their relations with other states, from the most rigid observance of the principles of the law of nations, principles which, being applied to a permanent state of peace, can alone guarantee effectively the independence of each government and the stability of the general association (quoted in Fiore, 1918, p.95).

While disagreements continued thereafter concerning the fundamental principles on which the international system was built, as witnessed by the Protocol of Troppau, in the end, mutual recognition by states of each other's sovereignty proved irresistible. The recognition of the sovereignty of other states was an inescapable consequence of the assertion by any one state of its own sovereignty in relation to its territory and people: if a state insists on the value of its own sovereignty then it cannot but help admit its value to all. For this and other reasons, as the Russian publicist Friedrich Frommhold de Martens (who would head the 1899 Hague Convention) later noted, whereas at the beginning of the nineteenth century intervention was considered an 'uncontested' right by the second half it was considered 'an exception to the normal state of international relations', a change which he regarded as a great triumph for the law (Martens, 1883, pp.396–7).[12]

The development of the European law of nations

The application of the principle of sovereignty in the international sphere was essential to the development of a new legal order, one which began to form from the seventeenth century onwards, albeit in a 'piecemeal fashion'; importantly, it was of an international rather than cosmopolitan character (Keens-Soper, 1978, p.33). This new legal order did not involve a total rupture with the past as many traditional standards and customs would be a feature of it. However, in a Europe plagued by political and religious rifts and where traditional sources of authority were in decline, new grounds on which to base and a new justification for the legal order had to be found. The answer to this problem was, of course, the state (Bleckmann, 1994, p.80). While in the sixteenth and the seventeenth centuries, it was thought that the law of nations was 'personally binding upon sovereign princes' as well as other participants in international relations, this idea disappeared over time due to the increasing personification of the state. If the state itself were to be the new source of authority and justification for the legal order, then legal personality had to be vested in it. By means of personifying the state and treating it as a locus of 'reason and will', legal subjects were created who could serve as authors of the legal order while also being accountable to it (Remec, 1960, pp.23–4).[13]

Yet, a conceptual difficulty soon presented itself, one which concerned the grounds on which the law of nations could be said to be binding on its subjects. Clearly, the understanding that the sovereign state was the sole source of law, when combined with the insistence that no law issued by the sovereign could bind the sovereign, threatened to undermine the legal order that was gradually being constructed (Bleckmann, 1994, pp.80–1). In *De Iure Belli Tres* (1612) Alberico Gentile upheld the view that peace treaties based on 'deception' are 'not binding'; in this respect, he wrote, 'oaths are understood *rebus sic stantibus*': 'While circumstances remain as they are' (Gentile, 1933, p.151). Obviously, the casual application of such a principle would have had a profoundly destabilising effect in the international arena (Nussbaum, 1954, p. 96).[14] Nussbaum writes that Grotius, because he came from a trading nation, repudiated the principle of *rebus sic stantibus*, instead stressing the idea of keeping promises and upholding agreements (Nussbaum, 1954, p.112). Yet, Grotius also qualified his stance, insisting that a state could release itself from promises of assistance to allies that would prove 'burdensome and unbearable' (Grotius, 1925, p.426; see also Lauterpacht, 1927, p.102).

For Grotius, the notion of keeping faith with one's promises is both a pragmatic necessity and a matter of principle. It was a necessity since, as he states: 'There is no City so strong and of itself sufficient, but may sometimes stand in need of Foreign Aid....as soon as we recede from the Law, there is nothing we can certainly call ours' (quoted in Passerin D'Entrèves, 1967, p.126). In terms of the principle at stake, Grotius pointed out that individuals must act in good faith, not simply because they have consented to membership of a legal order so as to advance their interests, but because the 'authors' of the legal order 'are human beings having a share in the law of nature', a law which dictated that 'agreements must be kept' (Grotius, 1925, p.794). As the rulers of states are also human beings, they too remain bound by the law of nature in their dealings with other rulers. Thus, while international law has its basis in consent, the obligation to keep one's promises does not. The principle of good faith is a presumption of international law; it is a principle which international law must presume if there is to be any international legal order at all.[15]

Further, this principle is prior to and does not form a part of the law of nations. This is precisely because the obligation to conform to our agreements cannot be a matter of voluntary consent. To argue the latter case is to ignore the fact that the law of nations is ultimately guaranteed, and indeed can only be guaranteed, by right and not by will. At the same time,

Grotius understood that the warrant of natural law was not enough to ensure obedience to pacts. This is why he also grounded the obligation to observe them in 'legality' in the form of mutual consent (Hinsley, 1986, p.190). Thus, Grotius stated that the law of nations derives 'its obligatory force from the will of all nations, or of many nations'. Such a formulation was unsatisfactory according to Vattel as we shall see, nonetheless, it is a formulation which importantly acknowledges the social dimension of treaty-making and that, as a result, states cannot unbind themselves from their agreements in most instances save by their joint agreement (Grotius, 1925, p.44; see also Remec, 1960, p.73).[16]

Grotius understood that because sovereigns were not subject to any higher human power the gap between state practice and what the laws of nature required was likely to remain significant. In fact, his own writings were aimed at reducing this gap: through bringing 'about a greater coincidence between legality and justice' (Hinsley, 1986, p.190). Hinsley writes that Grotius's influence did not spread until the last decades of the seventeenth century, adding that even then it was limited to the realm legal theory. However, by the mid-eighteenth century it came to be widely appreciated by acute thinkers on the subject that, precisely because the international legal order lacked the coercive powers wielded by the state, it was imperative to conceive of the 'sovereign will of the single state' as being subject to 'some other higher restraint'. It was also at that time that the idea of Europe as comprising a system of independent sovereign states rather than the conception of it as a 'single *societas*', achieved clear expression, most notably, in Vattel's *Law of Nations* (Hinsley, 1986, pp.194–6, 200).

Vattel deduced from natural law, not the idea articulated by his contemporary the philosopher Christian Wolff of a 'great republic' (*civitatis maxima*) which Vattel dismissed as a 'fiction', but rather the idea of the sovereign equality of states and its corollary non-intervention irrespective of differences in national size and political capacity (Vattel, 1863, p.xiii; see also Hinsley, 1986, p.195).[17] Vattel wrote that nations could be 'considered as so many free persons living together in a state of nature' and as such they are 'naturally equal, and inherit from nature the same obligations and rights'; echoing Wolff (and also Bodin), he famously declared that just as a 'dwarf is as much a man as a giant' so too 'a small republic is no less a sovereign state than the most powerful kingdom' (Vattel, 1863, p.lxii; see also Butler, 1978, p.52).[18] Yet while Vattel dismissed the idea of a European-wide republic he nonetheless, and indeed for that very reason, conceived of sovereign states as existing in a social relationship with each other rather than in a vacuum. 'Each sovereign state' in Europe, Vattel noted, 'claims, and actually possesses an absolute independence of all the others', yet he added that Europe as a whole:

> 'still formed a political system...closely connected by the relations and different interests of the nations...It is not, as formerly, a confused heap

of detached pieces, each of which thought herself very little concerned in the fate of the others...[but]...a kind of republic, of which the members...unite for the maintenance of order and liberty' and which has its consequence in the 'equilibrium of power' which seeks to ensure that 'no one potentate' is in a position 'to predominate, and prescribe laws to the others' (Vattel, 1863, pp.xiii, 414).

Vattel makes it clear that under international law states are the sole bearers of rights and duties, the consequence of this being the near complete exclusion of individuals from the purview of international law. In line with this, Vattel adopts a more restrictionist approach to the question of intervention than did Grotius. The latter insisted that in the context of inter-state relations any free person, namely a prince, had a 'right of demanding punishments' for excessive violations 'of the law of nature or of nations in regard to any persons whatsoever', be they cannibals, pirates or 'arrogant despots' inflicting upon their 'subjects such treatment as no one is warranted in inflicting' (Grotius, 1925, pp.504–6).[19] A right of punishment was important to Grotius since it meant that natural law could be said to be real law, that is, law with the power of sanction (Christopher, 2004, p.73). By contrast, Vattel argued that the right of punishment existed only because a people had a 'right to provide for their own safety' and thus it could only be exercised against those 'by whom they have been injured.' Did Grotius not realise, he asked, that his views on punishment opened the 'door to all the ravages and enthusiasm and fanaticism, and furnishes ambition with numberless pretexts' (Vattel, 1863, p.137).

Grotius was aware that natural law might be abused by those seeking 'pretexts' for their 'own ends ', however, as he correctly pointed out, a 'right does not at once cease to exist in case it is to some extent abused by evil men' (Grotius, 1925, p.584). However, it is arguable that punishment by foreign princes took on more significance for Grotius because he was less in favour of domestic rebellions. Vattel however, as we have seen, invoked a right of popular resistance against tyranny and thus could simultaneously contract the grounds justifying outside intervention. The law of nature in Vattel's hands recommended non-intervention because it was a community's right to punish despots rather than other rulers. Yet, Vattel was not unyielding on the question of intervention, arguing that a coalition of states could intervene to halt persecution by fanatical tyrants of a people who shared their faith. He wrote that where such persecution 'becomes a case of manifest tyranny...all nations are allowed to assist an unhappy people', with such action also possibly serving to enhance the security of those intervening through arresting the power of a disturbed and untrustworthy nation (Vattel, 1863, p.159).[20] Vattel also maintained that where a ruler establishes an 'insupportable' tyranny, thus obliging 'the nation to rise in their own defence', every other 'foreign power has a right' to give aid should the people being oppressed 'implore their assistance' (Vattel, 1863, p.155).

Vattel's concessions to intervention are not such glaring exceptions to the rule of non-intervention as they first appear because of the way in which he constructs situations justifying intervention. His view is that in cases of evident tyranny, the 'bands of the political society are broken' and thus the 'sovereign and his people' are rendered as 'two distinct powers'; civil war similarly involves the rupture of social bonds, producing two 'independent parties' who see each other as 'enemies' (Vattel, 1863, pp.155, 424). Intervention in both these instances is thus equivalent to the 'intervention of a third state in the dispute between two sovereign nations' (Remec, 1960, p.233). Further, it should be emphasised that Vattel preferred that rulers facing civil conflict be offered 'good offices for the restoration of peace', rather than be subject to the sort of punitive measures proposed by Grotius, an approach which was less threatening to international order and more acceptable in an age in which the norm non-intervention was establishing itself (Vattel, 1863, p.427). Vattel also makes it clear that while in some instances there might be a right of and interest in intervention, it is not a duty of states. The duties of political societies to non-citizens, he insisted, are imperfect. Political societies, because of their shared origins in the wider human society, have a duty to do 'everything in...[their]...power for the preservation and happiness of others', however such duties are not absolute as they are conditioned by 'our duties towards ourselves' (Vattel, 1863, p.134).[21]

Hinsley argues that Vattel sought to close the distance between natural law and the law of nations by associating the former with the actual behaviour of states. The development of positivism reflected a similar desire to adapt legal theory to state practice, although such moves only became thinkable because the behaviour of states in Europe, at least in relation to each other, had shown some improvement (Hinsley, 1986, pp.197–8). Vattel's *Law of Nations*, perhaps in part because of its accessible style, found a wide audience among political actors and jurists in Europe and North America and was adopted as a manual by the foreign ministries of France, the United States and Britain (themselves newly minted institutions), in the latter part of the eighteenth century (Lesaffer, 2002, p.384; Hinsley, 1986, pp.200–1).[22] Its adoption in this regard points to the growing awareness on the part of European states of the need to normalise their relations with each other. This awareness stemmed from a growing apprehension of their intensifying interdependence and of the fact that they had gained increasing capacity to inflict harm on one another, all of this against a background in which the powers were 'approaching a condition of greater near-equality'. Even so, there would continue to be periods of retrogression with certain powers reverting to 'the primitive or imperial pattern', a pattern that would remain standard practice for European powers operating in the non-European parts of the world (Hinsley, 1986, pp.203, 213).[23]

Due to these factors, international law acquired increasing prominence in the conduct of diplomacy and, in relation to this, there was a growing demand for the modernisation of its content and of the manner in which it was communicated to audiences (Nussbaum, 1954, p.233). The updating of international law (the word having been introduced to political and legal discourse by Jeremy Bentham), was undertaken within an intellectual context which valorised the empirical methods of the natural sciences (Bentham, 1970, p.296).[24] Positivist legal thought was characterised by a rejection of the 'speculative' approach of the natural law school and by its efforts to ground its theoretical conclusions in the methods of the physical sciences: 'observation and painstaking research.' However, disregard for natural law thinking was a matter of political and not just intellectual prejudice. Nussbaum observes that natural law thinking, 'having furnished the conceptual weapons for the French revolution, became an easy target for the theorists of the counterrevolution' (Nussbaum, 1954, p.233).

Yet, it is important to note that the legal writings of Bentham (who dryly remarked that the law of nature always seemed to coincide with the views of right and wrong of its proponents), had been translated into French in 1789 for the benefit of members of the Constituent Assembly and that they exercised some influence in France concerning the reform and codification of the law of nations (Nussbaum, 1954, p.185).[25] Ernest Nys argues that it was Bentham's legal philosophy in particular, which inspired the *Déclaration du droit des gens* which was presented to the National Convention on the April 23 1795 (4 *floréal an* III), by one of its members: the constitutional Bishop of Blois, Abbé Henri Grégoire (Nys, 1911, p.876; Degan, 1989, p.99). This *Déclaration*, which drew on Vattel's *Droit des nations* and was intended to form part of the Constitution of year III, gave expression to Grégoire's belief that the 'law of sociability between nations is nothing other than natural law applied to the great corporations of the human race' (quoted in Nys, 1896, p.405). This *Déclaration* contained twenty-one articles with its first article affirming the 'state of nature' existing among nations and the 'universal morality' which binds them (quoted in Nys, 1896, p.395).[26] Article 6 stipulated that each nation has 'the right to organise and change the form of government' and for this reason Article 7 stipulated that, no nation has the right to 'interfere in the governments of other nations.' In Article 17, Grégoire insisted that nations have the right to 'undertake war' in defence of their 'sovereignty', which is inalienable, and their 'liberty' and 'property'. Indeed, other nations have a right to assist a state defending itself as challenging the independence of one nation, as specified in Article 15, is to be regarded as 'an outrage against the human family'. Yet, sovereignty was not presented by Grégoire as the supreme political good. He maintained in Article 5 that since sovereignty sprang from universal morality then the 'particular interests of a people' were 'subordinate to the general interests of the human family', thus showing an awareness, one that was continuous with previous natural law thinking on the subject, that while sovereign rights were inalienable they were not unlimited (quoted in Nys, 1896, pp.395–6).[27]

The Convention, although it paid 'homage to the purity of his intentions', did not put Grégoire's proposal to the vote in 1795 (Chevally, 1912, pp.1, 50). This was because, as Grégoire later recorded, aspects of the proclamation (such as its insistence that only governments founded on 'liberty and equality' were legitimate and that peoples had the 'right to organise and change the forms of its government'), would have annoyed those 'despots' with whom France was planning to 'enter into negotiations' (quoted in Nys, 1896, p.395 and Nys, 1911, p.893).[28]

The doctrine of revolutionary intervention, earlier articulated by the Girondins, had already been vigorously challenged by Robespierre, with Robespierre accusing the Girondins of setting the crowns of Europe against France and thus endangering the revolution (Mirkine-Guetzévitch, 1928, p.314).[29] However, it was Danton above all who, for reasons *realpolitik* and patriotism, sought to reconcile the 'new revolutionary exigencies with the old diplomatic traditions' and who thus sought to persuade the Convention to pronounce itself, as it did on April 13 1793, against intervention in the domestic affairs of other states (Mirkine-Guetzévitch, 1928, pp.315–16). Indeed, when Grégoire had first proposed his *Déclaration* on June 18 of that year (seeking to attach it to the year I Constitution), Bertrand Barère de Vieuzac, a member of the Jacobin Club, called on the Convention to not forget the 'position of France in the European milieu', underlining the fact that the Convention was a 'political' and not just a 'philosophical and legislative assembly' (quoted in Chevally, 1912, p.49). The Convention's declaration that France was the 'friend and natural ally of free peoples', he insisted, said 'enough to Europe concerning the difference between the governments' (quoted in Nys, 1896, p.394).

Given the forces of counter-revolution arrayed against the revolution and more generally the imperatives of *raison d'état*, it is not surprising that France quickly re-embraced the ways of the old diplomacy. It was able to do this by managing a 'synthesis between the State and the nation which permitted one to think of the relations between States in terms of "international relations"' (Brandli, 2007). Nonetheless as we have seen, both the Assembly and the Convention had already proclaimed 'some broad principles of natural-law pedigree' in renouncing wars of conquest and attacks on the freedom of other nations and these still stood (Nussbaum, 1954, p.119). According to B. Mirkine-Guetzévitch, the proclamation of these principles, along with the declaration of Grégoire and that of Constantin François Volney before him, bears testimony to the 'level of international juridical consciousness of the epoch': that the French revolution had achieved an 'exact comprehension of the primacy of international law' and 'international solidarity' (Mirkine-Guetzévitch, 1928, pp.308, 310).[30]

Martens acknowledged that aspects of Grégoire's proposal gave expression to universal truths, such as Article 1 concerning the state of nature existing among states, Article 2 which stated that states are 'sovereign and independent whatever be the number of individuals which compose them' and Article 10 which asserted that 'each people is master of his territory'. Such truths he pointed out, had not been lost on the theory and practice of the old diplomacy, although he also maintained that their mere restatement would not have any 'salutary effect' (Chevally, 1912, p.52; see also Frey and Frey, 2006, p.3). As for the remaining Articles, Martens dismissed them from a variety of angles. Some, he thought, offered no obvious advantage over the usages of the old diplomacy. Others, such as Article 3 which stipulated that a 'people must act with regard to others as they would like others to act with regard to them', he regarded as moral principles without force. As for the asserted right of humanity in Article 5, Martens thought that this 'consideration would never determine any people to sign an act contrary to its own interests' (Chevally, 1912, p.53).[31] Very worrying for Martens, and this is continuous with his views concerning French revolutionary doctrine, was the Declaration's Article 6 insistence on the right of peoples in regard to their form of government and the assertion in Article 8 that the only governments which 'conform with the rights of peoples' are those 'founded on equality and liberty' (quoted in Chevally, 1912, p.54). These Articles, Martens warned, constituted a 'menace to the standing order of things' as they justified not only the 'overthrow of existing governments' but also interference by one state in the government of another, not withstanding the fact that Article 7 of the Declaration expressly ruled out such a right of interference (Nys, 1911, p.893; see also Rayneval, 1803, pp.151–2; Chevally, 1912, pp.54, 60 and Hornung, 1886, p.204). Marten's overall conclusion was that the interests of nations would be much better served by preserving the old diplomacy with all its 'lacunae', disputations over the meaning of its terms and 'antique ornaments', rather than by embracing a code such as that of Grégoire the various aspects of which were either pointless or dangerous (quoted in Chevally, 1912, p.54). In any case, Martens thought it sheer fantasy to think that the peoples of Europe, as self-regarding and irrational as they were, would ever be able to undertake the codification of the law of nations, even assuming they were capable of seeing its advantages (Nys, 1911, p.893). As he explained:

> That the people of Europe will ever unite for the purpose of agreeing upon general and positive stipulations touching the laws of nations as a whole, or to sign a declaration of the law of nations enunciated by any one of them, and thus become agreed upon a positive code of international law, is something which appears to me to be stripped of all

> appearance of truth, and to fall into the category of a project of perpetual peace, the outcome of ancient theories, which although renewed and presented under forms more or less visionary, is at the outside nothing but a beautiful play of fancy which one may contemplate with pleasure in moments of ease, but which, as long as men are men who, in spite of the efforts made for their perfection remain dominated by their passions and blinded by their individual interests, will be nothing but a chimera, viewed either from the standpoint of its execution, or from that of the advantages which it may hold out (quoted in Nys, 1911, p.890).

Chevally argues that Martens concocted the 'aggressive character' he ascribed to Grégoire's *Déclaration* and that in doing so he had 'abused' his authorial 'superiority' (Chevally, 1912, p.54). She also points out that Martens had 'totally omitted' from his analysis a number of important Articles, including Article 21 which stated that treaties between states were 'sacred and inviolable' and Article 15 which, in asserting that attacks on the 'liberty of a people are an attack against all other peoples', implicitly condemned the partitioning of Poland which had recently taken place (Chevally, 1912, pp.54–5). Further, as Silvestre Pinheiro-Ferreira wrote in his 1831 critical excursus on Martens's *Précis*, the *Déclaration* was not intended as a code for the law of nations any more than Thomas Paine's *Declaration of the Rights of Man* was intended as a substitute for a 'civil code' (quoted in Chevally, 1912, p.56). He added:

> Never have people thought that it was sufficient to put this small number of general principles in place of...[the established]...body of doctrines, vicious in the view of the reformers, and that they intended to replace with another body of doctrines which seemed to them more in conformity with the truth (quoted in Chevally, 1912, p.56).

Following Pinheiro-Ferreira, Chevally argues that Grégoire's proposal was a 'profession of faith' rather than a code, a profession of faith that truth stood on the side of the rights of peoples and against the 'arbitrary wills of sovereigns' whether in the domestic or international arenas (Chevally, 1912, p.60). As such, it also reflected the idea that reform of the internal constitutions of states as well as of the laws which governed their relations was possible. Irrespective of Martens's scepticism and although conditions would remain for some time inhospitable to its reform, the nineteenth century would see a growing push, under the banner of science (understood in rationalist and not simply or always in purely empiricist terms) and greatly stimulated by the efforts of Kant, for the codification of international law along the lines suggested by Grégoire as well as by his contemporary Bentham (Klüber, 1874, p.23).[32]

Nineteenth century views: Austin to Treitschke

By no means all positivists eliminated natural law principles from their systems. Martens for example, while relying for the most part on positive law, 'turned to natural law when he could not rely on custom and treaties' (Frey and Frey, 2006, p.3).[33] Austin, by contrast, eliminated almost every trace of natural law from his system. Because of this and because he insisted that law was a command issued by a determinate human superior armed with sanctions, he was unable, unlike other positivists, to classify international law as law properly so-called. He stated

> ...the law obtaining between nations is not positive law: for every positive law is set by a given sovereign to a person or persons in a state of subjection to its author...[international law]...is law...set by general opinion. The duties which it imposes are enforced by moral sanctions: by fear on the part of nations....of provoking general hostility, and incurring its probable evils (Austin, 1906, p.102).

Austin did not set out to deny international law as he appreciated the merit and utility of regulations governing international behaviour. Further, he was very familiar with the English idea, expressed in Lord Talbot's ruling in 1737 but which can be traced back to Gentili, that the 'law of nations is "the law of the land"'. Thus, he admitted 'that international law becomes law properly so-called – namely, municipal law – to the extent that its rules have been adopted by the courts of legislatures of a given country' (Nussbaum, 1954, pp.137, 234). Even so, Austin's equation of international law with 'honor and fashion' was widely regarded as 'unsatisfactory' and thus was generally dismissed (Nussbaum 1954, p.234). Austin's way of classifying legal systems, while clearly reflecting the 'technical position' adopted by Bentham, ran counter to the 'spirit expressed' in a number of the latter's observations concerning international law: the need to organise and advance international law in order to maximise the 'happiness of the human race' (Jacobini, 1948, p.417).[34] Nonetheless, Austin's analysis at least had the virtue of highlighting the problem of how to render international law binding where the relationship between sovereignty or law and coercive power is over-emphasised and where natural law is taken out of the picture (Nussbaum, 1954, p.234).

Questions concerning the status of international law as law were also touched on by Hegel in his *Elements of the Philosophy of Right* (1820). Therein he explains that the state, since it is the 'power of reason actualizing itself as will', is the 'absolute power on *earth*' (Hegel, 1991, pp.279, 366). Only 'the spirit of the world', which emerges out of the 'dialectic' between the particular expressions of national spirits, sits in judgement on the state, its judgements being revealed through the unfolding of history (Hegel,

1991, pp.279, 366, 371). At first glance, such an account seems to point to what Hans Kelsen later called '[s]tate solipsism'. In order to explain this phenomenon, Kelsen pointed to the philosophy of subjectivism which 'seeks to understand things by proceeding "from the philosopher's own *ego*" and views the world as "the will and idea of the subject"; where the "sovereignty of the *ego*"' reigns, he argued, it becomes impossible to appreciate the other, that is the '*non-ego*'. In a similar fashion, the state subjectivist is incapable of 'comprehending other States as equal to' his or her own state; the 'sovereignty of the State-*ego*' is thus 'incompatible with the sovereignty of the State-*tu*' (Kelsen, 1946, pp.386–7).

The Hegelian state cannot be described as solipsistic in the sense given above, although this is not to say that Hegel's account of international relations is immune to solipsistic interpretations. To start with, Hegel had a deep understanding of the fact that states need each other and in a very fundamental way. For Hegel each state, as a 'substantial rationality' and thus an absolute power on earth, was entitled to be recognised as sovereign and independent '*in the eyes of others*' (Hegel, 1991, pp.366–7). However, the entitlement '*to be recognized*' by others only pertained to the state as an abstraction. Whether a state in its particular expression gains recognition hinges on whether it is *recognisably* a state. It hinges, that is, on its 'content' by which is meant its 'constitution' and current 'condition' (Hegel, 1991, p.367). However, it is not just the content of the state that is of significance here, as an act of recognition 'also depends on the perception and will of the other state' (Hegel, 1991, p.367). Here Hegel shifts away from the understanding that recognition is purely declaratory to an understanding of it as constitutive. Hegel perfectly illustrates the former understanding in citing Bonaparte's statement before the Peace of Campo Formio that: 'the French Republic is no more in need of recognition than the sun is', a statement which, Hegel adds, points to that 'strength of existence [*Existenz*] which itself carries with it a guarantee of recognition' (Hegel, 1991, p.367). In relation to the latter approach to recognition Hegel explains:

> Without relations [*Verhältnis*] with other states, the state can no more be an actual individual [*Individuum*] than an individual [*der Einzelne*] can be an actual person without a relationship [*Relation*] with other persons... On the other hand, the legitimacy of a state, and more precisely...of the power of its sovereign, is a purely *internal* matter (one state should not interfere in the internal affairs of another). On the other hand, it is equally essential that this legitimacy should be *supplemented* by recognition on the part of other states. But this recognition requires a guarantee that the state will likewise recognize those other states which are supposed to recognize it i.e. that it will respect their independence; accordingly, these other states cannot be indifferent to its internal affairs. – In the case of a nomadic people, for example, or any people at a low level of culture,

> the question even arises of how far this people can be regarded as a state (Hegel, 1991, p.367).

Hegel's point is that since states, in some measure, co-create each other a recognising state needs to be assured that the entity it is recognising can reciprocate this recognition and this, in turn, requires assurances that the entity in question is so constituted that it can enter into and maintain relations of mutuality. An entity which is not so constituted that it can give rise to a sovereign voice, can be denied recognition because such an entity cannot embrace reciprocal obligations. As the last lines of the quotation indicate, constitutive theory can serve as part of the rhetorical armoury of imperialism as indeed it did in the nineteenth century.[35] At the same time, the constitutive account of recognition shows that recognition of their independent status is something that each state *owes* to other states. Recognition of the independence or sovereignty of each state is owed, and from the very outset, precisely because states in a sense co-create each other. Such an account, in positing a fundamental and inescapable condition of mutuality among states, is also highly suggestive as regards the enrichment of the rights and obligations of states. However, I want to leave aside the first of these two implications of constitutive theory for the present as they are addressed in the next chapter. Rather, what needs to be noted here is Hegel's acknowledgement that statehood is realised only in a social context and it is this that leads to or necessitates the law of nations. In developing the international implications of Hegel's theory of constitutive recognition, Frost shows that the rights borne by states in the international arena are, as with individual rights, collective achievements and that they presuppose certain 'constraining' conditions (Frost, 1996, p.139).

Beyond this, Hegel also acknowledges that international law is founded on the principle, one which has 'validity in and for itself', that the treaties 'on which the mutual obligations of states depend, *should be observed*'. However, while Hegel believes that the relations between states should be 'inherently governed by right', since in 'worldly affairs' there exists no power to determine and institute what is inherently right, adherence to international 'remains only an *obligation*'. Thus, it is only natural to expect 'relations governed by treaties to alternate with the suspension [*Aufhebung*] of such relations' (Hegel, 1991, pp.366, 368). International law is always provisional from the point of view of states since although states 'make mutual stipulations' they also 'stand above these stipulations' (Hegel, 1991, p.366).

This is necessarily the case if the state is to maintain its own '*welfare*', this being the 'supreme law' in the context of the state's 'relations with others'. The state must seek its own welfare if its 'abstract freedom' is to be actualised and if, in relation to this, it is to gain the recognition of other states

(Hegel, 1991, p.369). However, the way in which the state comprehends threats to its well being is '*inherently*...indeterminable'. This is because of the state of nature among states and because the state as 'Idea' can only subsist in the world, that is, interact with others, as a concrete or particular will. Thus, states are not works of 'art' and the will which they project onto the world is shaped by such internal determinations as 'passions, interests...talents and virtues, violence...and vices' (Hegel, 1991, pp.279, 371). It follows from this that the external relations among states are indelibly marked by 'arbitrariness, contingency, and error' (Hegel, 1991, p.279).

Critics of Hegel's treatment of international law generally concede, that while certain 'neo-Hegelian' thinkers may have denied the existence of international law, Hegel himself did not. However, critics also maintain that in labelling his discussion of international law as '"External Public Law" (*Äusseres Staatsrecht*)', an expression which has municipal connotations, and in representing the state as the 'embodiment of the Moral Idea', Hegel seriously weakened international law's foundations (Nussbaum, 1954, pp.176, 237).[36] Simply put, some argue that the Hegelian state, equipped with absolute sovereignty and invested with divine powers, is incapable of recognising any law as being 'higher' than its own. International law, rather than being a jointly binding set of limiting conditions, is thus rendered an expression of the will of the state, a will which can change at any moment (Remec, 1960, pp.22–3).

In response to this critique, it should be noted that Hegel, in addition to using the expression 'External Public Law', also used the expression *Völkerrecht* or law of nations even though he did not define it (Hegel, 1991, p.368; Nussbaum, 1954, p.237). Further, as Vincent points out, when Hegel writes of the state in spiritual terms he is not contending that the state is on 'some kind of divine mission' but rather that it is 'explicable as a product of Mind or Spirit' (Vincent, 1987, p.145). As to the question of the binding nature of international law, we have seen that Hegel admits that treaties, because of the indeterminate nature of the external relations of states, may be subject to change or even suspended. This condition of indeterminacy also explains why the possibility of war is ever present (Hegel, 1991, pp.368–70).

However, in relation to the conduct of war, Hegel points to certain fundamental norms such as the inviolability of envoys and the principle that war must not be waged against 'internal institutions' including peaceable families and 'private individuals.' He noted with approval that modern wars in Europe were 'waged in a humane manner' because the states of Europe formed 'a family' in terms of the 'universal principle of their legislation, customs, and culture' (Hegel, 1991, pp.370–1). Most importantly, he emphasised that even when in a state of belligerency, a state characterised by 'rightlessness...force and contingency', states still recognise each other as states and indeed, the state of belligerency as a legal relationship between states would not be possible otherwise. Implicit in such reciprocal recognition, Hegel insists, is an understanding that each state retains 'its validity for each other in their being in and for themselves' and that war 'ought to come to an end' (Hegel, 1991, p.370).

Based on the above qualifications Christian Tomuschat argues that Hegel did not in fact make the 'bindingness of international law dependent on the actual will of each individual State' (Tomuschat, 1999, p.167). Tomuschat points out that 'in his [Hegel's] time his writings were never understood as a call for subverting the edifice of international law' and adds that 'no publicist in nineteenth-century Germany called into question the concept of international legal order'. Tomuschat acknowledges the state-centrism of Hegel's analysis, however he explains that this simply reflected prevailing historical conditions. Thus, he states: 'Hegel's analysis reflected the realities of a world where indeed a legislative, and executive and a judicial function at the international level were totally unheard of. The point from which Hegel focused on foreign relations was the State as the principal power centre of its epoch' (Tomuschat, 1999, p.168). Tomuschat's observation suggests that Hegel's account of international relations, given its historicity, was informed by that same element of contingency which Hegel saw as permeating actually existing inter-state relations. As we saw, contingency arises, at least in part, because Spirit can only ever be articulated through finite wills and will in its finitude is ever open to being expressed in misguided and defective ways (Hegel, 1991, pp.279, 361, 368). As a result, international relations is an uncertain and fearful sphere, and how much more so it would have appeared at a time when there were no international institutions consecrated to safeguarding the sovereignty of states. That said, Hegel's theory of constitutive recognition *could* have taken him down the Kantian path towards perpetual peace. However, after having countenanced this possibility, Hegel advised that since the federation of states which Kant recommended presupposed 'an *agreement* between states... [it]...would always be dependent on particular sovereign wills, and would therefore continue to be dependent on contingency' (Hegel, 1991, p.368). Nonetheless, in support of the pacific possibilities contained within Hegel, it is worth noting that the Hegelian T.H. Green, who similarly understood that powers only become rights through 'social recognition', forcefully advocated the abolition of war. Green thought the underlying causes of war lay with the 'deficient organisation' of states and that improvements in the way in which states were internally constituted would advance humanity towards 'the dream of an international court with authority resting on the consent of independent states' (Green, 1999, p.135). Although Hegelian philosophy, or at least a perverted version of it, was often blamed for the First World War in English-speaking circles especially, there were also those who saw the League of Nations as consisting in, to express it in Hegelian terms, 'the march of God in the world' (Hegel, 1991, p.279; see Follett, 1918, pp.266–7, 360).

It was political rather than legal publicists such as Treitschke who drove Hegelian thinking on international law to its most negative conclusion in the latter part of the nineteenth century. Treitschke was also was no denier of international law. He insisted that a state, in order that it be treated in kind, should act with reason and conscience in relation to other states and he maintained that civilised advances were being made and could continue to be made in this area. Nonetheless, international law in his account rested on rather fragile foundations as he embraced the view that international law would only be adhered to where it served the security interests of the state. He wrote that 'every treaty is a voluntary curb upon the power of each, and all international agreements are prefaced by the clause "*Rebus sic stantibus*"' (Treitschke, 1970, p.328). Treitschke's approach was not solipsistic in the strict sense of the term in that he acknowledged that just 'as in individual life the ego implies the existence of the non-ego, so it does in the State.' However, what he deduced from the 'necessary...multiplicity of States' was not any prescription concerning perpetual peace or the sovereign equality of states, but rather that the 'State is power'. The state is power he wrote, 'precisely in order to asset itself against other powers', in particular by means of war (Treitschke, 1970, p.326). For Treitschke, 'self-preservation...is the highest duty of a State' and it was out of this duty of self-preservation, in the midst of a world of 'perpetual conflict' in which the 'weak and cowardly perish', that sprang the imperative for war, something which he thought international law would never be able to curb (Treitschke quoted in Sorley, 1916, pp.43, 54). In fact, Treitschke maintained that war furthered 'the great civilizing mission of mankind' (Treitschke, 1970, p.327).[37]

Towards a new legal order

The belief that international law emanated from an act of self-limitation (a case of the state willing not to will), and that a state was at liberty to withdraw from it was not a mainstream view in either Germany or elsewhere. Indeed, what the second half of the nineteenth century mainly witnessed was a significant push to codify international law and, ultimately, abolish war. For example, Louis Bara, a Belgian jurist, in his *La Science de la Paix* (1852), remarked on how sovereignty, which rendered states 'so proud', was seen by individual states as 'elevating them above all' (Bara, 1972, p.12). He endorsed the view of a colleague concerning the formulas of some in the positivist school which, although superficially scientific, left the law of nations *'aux misères de l'empirisme'*, that is, 'servile to the facts and to the gestures of the dominant diplomacy of which success has crowned the efforts' (quoted in Bara, 1972, pp.41–2). Bara thought the process of eliminating war would take some time and because of this he supported, unlike many in the growing peace movement, the codification of the laws of war (Cooper, 1972, pp.15–16). Nonetheless Bara's ultimate aim, guided by the strictures of justice and science, was the abolition of war and to this end he called for a universal charter addressing 'the rights of men and a massive inquiry into the principles which civilized peoples had developed and would accept regarding those rights' (Bara, 1972, pp.10–13, 39, 214; Cooper, 1972, p.16; see also Nys, 1911, p.884).[38]

Martti Koskenniemi points out that it was in the late nineteenth century, spurred by the 'political ascendancy of liberalism', the shock engendered by the violence of the Franco-Prussian war of 1870–1 and concern about the brutal treatment of colonised peoples, that international law in its modern form appeared (Koskenniemi, 2005, pp.2–3, 10; see also Ott in Klüber, 1874, pp.v–vii).[39] A significant development in this regard was the founding of the *Institut du Droit International* in Ghent in Belgium on September 11 1873. The *Institut*, according to its founder the Belgian publicist Gustave Rolin-Jaequmyns, was to be a 'permanent scientific body which undertook the mission of paying particular attention to the progress of international law, of defining the principles thereof, and of assuring the practical efficacy thereof.' Its membership comprised scholars from different parts of the world and included in its life, alongside Rolin-Jaequmyns, noted legal publicists such as Pasquale Stanislao Mancini (its first president), Carlos Calvo, Johann Kaspar Bluntschli, W.E. Hall and John Westlake (Nys, 1911, pp.888–9; Bara, 1972, p.10).[40]

The push to codify and develop international law was furthered by numerous other institutions, including the American Peace Society which was founded in 1828, the Association for the Reform and Codification of the Law of Nations (which had its origin in a proposal submitted to the English Association for the Advancement of Science in 1866 to draft a code of international law but which was founded in 1873 and renamed the International Law Association in 1894), and *l'Union Interparlementaire* which held its first conference in Paris in 1889. Peace congresses dating from the *Congrès des Amis de la Paix* in 1848 in Brussels through to the Hague Peace Conferences of 1899 and 1907 and the Universal Peace Congress at Stockholm in August 1910, also played an important role especially in terms of the codification of the laws of war (Nys, 1911, pp.888, 891; Renault, 1879, pp.52–3; Bara, 1972, pp.15–16). The Italian jurist Pasquale Fiore regarded such peace conferences as landmark developments heralding the coming of the day when, as Honoré Mirabeau had earlier put it, law will be '*le souverain du monde*' (quoted in Fiore, 1918, pp.i, 727).[41] Such initiatives, Fiore believed, were assisted by notable social developments in the second half of the nineteenth century such as the growing impact of public opinion on governments and 'the extraordinary development of commercial relations and means of communication between the different countries', all of which were facilitating the spread of the 'sentiment of solidarity of interests' (Fiore, 1918, p.9).

The First World War was a devastating blow to efforts to develop international legislation, most especially efforts to establish international arbitration of interstate conflict. Many in Britain blamed the war on monistic theories of the state, condemning in particular a 'certain grim Hegelianism' which in the hands of figures such as Treitschke had given rise to the political exaltation of the state (Laski, 1968, p.6; Laski, 1919, pp.302–4). Lauterpacht argued along these lines stating that:

> A political doctrine based on the omnicompetence and glorification of the state as an end in itself will naturally result, and has usually resulted, in the negation of the law of nations as a body of rules which, both in its binding force and in its creation is independent of the state. The present, still rudimentary, stage of international law is not in a small degree due to the prevalence of this type of doctrine (Lauterpacht, 1927, p.91).[42]

Many such criticisms reflected anti-German sentiment since their targets were typically German authors (Koskenniemi, 2005, p.35). However, it should be added that Laski, the most prominent British critic of the sovereign state in that period, condemned the theory of sovereignty in its entirety, chastising it for fostering oppression within the state and aggression without. Laski further argued that the adjective sovereign, when applied to the state, was increasingly empirically inadequate since the state's position was less than absolute; its operations were increasingly inhibited by the complex of wills, including both individual and group wills, which comprised modern society as well as by the growth of supranational institutions (Laski, 1925, pp.50–1, 64–5, 67). In the field of international law, pre-war exaltation of state sovereignty and the impoverished appreciation of international law that accompanied it, gave way to forms of legal monism which posited a necessary harmony between municipal and international law.

Hugo von Krabbe objected to the equation of sovereignty with the status of the state as a '*free personality* in international law' as this had led states to ground the 'binding force of law upon the very thing which should be the object of control, namely, the will' (Krabbe, 1930, pp.234–5). He described as fictional the idea of a 'self-supporting sovereign authority', adding that domestic law could not obtain its 'binding force from such a source'; both domestic and international law obtained their binding force from the same source: their 'spiritual nature'. Both were products of 'men's sense of right'. Thus, the distinction between national and international law did not rest on their origins or foundations but rather concerned the 'extent of the community to which…[their]..commands apply'. It is because international law expresses the sense of right of the entire world society, and not simply one particular community, that international law has priority over municipal law. To the extent that international law remains imperfect, this is not because it is 'rooted in the will of these states'; its incompleteness is a result of the current 'defective organization of the sense of right' (Krabbe, 1930, p.236). International law would remain imperfect as long as states remained sovereign, that is, until the international community began to *'pass through the phase of the idea of sovereignty'* (Krabbe, 1930, p.271). Krabbe believed that ultimately the sovereignty of individual states would be supplanted by the 'dominion of *spiritually* compelling norms, that is, by the "sovereignty of the law"' (Nussbaum, 1954, pp.278–9).

Kelsen similarly asserted the primacy of international law although in his hands legal monism was rendered as a science of the law, in contrast with the explicitly ethical construction developed by Krabbe (Nussbaum, 1954, p.280; Eulau, 1942, p.9).[43] The opposite view, namely that of the primacy of national law, maintains that international law gains its validity by virtue of being 'part of national law'. This view is often referred to as dualism or '*parallélisme*' (Kelsen, 1946, p.382; Mirkine-Guetzévitch, 1928, p.318). Yet dualism, as Kelsen points out, is really another form of monism. It is simply an inversion of the idea that international law is 'superordinate'. For Kelsen, either kind of monism could be upheld without contradiction. What could not be upheld was the genuinely dualist view that the national and international orders were 'two different, mutually independent, isolated norm systems, based on two different norms...if both the norms of international law and those of the national legal orders are to be considered simultaneously valid legal norms'. As Kelsen specifies, it is impossible in the field of normative thought to assert that 'norm: "*a* ought to be" and at the same time "*a* ought not to be"' (Kelsen, 1967, p.328). A situation where there was an irresolvable 'conflict' between an international and a national norm, if we were to adopt a strictly dualistic perspective and assume that the municipal legal order consists of valid legal norms, could only lead to the view that the international law was not a 'binding, normative order, valid simultaneously with national law'. In such situations, the validity of both the national and international legal orders can only be reconciled, according to Kelsen, by adopting either the national or international legal monistic position (Kelsen, 1967, p.329).

Kelsen maintains that national legal norms remain simultaneously valid with international legal norms even while being contrary to them to the extent that 'international law provides no procedure in which the norm can be abolished', his assumption being that a norm prescribed by a competent legal organ is valid. This applies even though it has been 'created by an act which as the character of a delict' and the norm in question invites a sanction: the norm remains valid until it is 'abolished by a legal act' or even if it is not abolished at all (Kelsen, 1967, pp.330–1). Given that international law generally does not have procedures by which the norms of the domestic legal order can be rendered invalid, it can be said that the fact that national legal orders may generate norms which are *prima facie* contrary to international law is a structural principle: international law delegates to states the discretionary power to interpret the content of international law. Thus, it can be said that there can be norms 'contrary to international law' so to speak, without international law itself being contradicted nor 'the assumption of a unity of international and national law' being destroyed (Kelsen, 1967, p.331).

Further to this, where a higher norm and an inferior norm do not conform with each other one cannot say, according to Kelsen, that the national legal norm is 'null' but only that it is 'annullable' and one can only say this 'if international law or national themselves are providing for a procedure in which this norm may be annulled' (Kelsen, 1967, p.342). While some states do have such legal procedures, international law itself generally does not because its judicial and enforcement mechanisms are largely decentralised, although Kelsen urged that there was nothing in his analysis to prevent it from becoming more centralised in the future.[44] On this matter, Kelsen stated in 1932 that it was in fact more important for states to accept the compulsory jurisdiction of international judicial bodies, thereby ceasing to decide themselves if one of their acts constituted a delict, 'than to abolish the right [of states] to exact justice themselves' (quoted in Leben, 1998, pp.289–90).

Yet, Kelsen also acknowledges that just as the primacy of international law perspective is quite compatible with a high degree of state autonomy, so too is the national perspective quite compatible with an 'effective' international legal order: provided that the state conceptualises sovereignty as the 'highest legal authority' rather than as 'unlimited freedom of action' (Kelsen, 1967, pp.343, 346). On the question as to whether the state's sphere of action is significantly restricted or not, Kelsen says the pure theory of law is 'indifferent'; the degree to which states are restricted by international law is a matter for politics not law, as is the question of whether we accept either the primacy of international or of national law (Kelsen, 1967, pp.343–4, 346–7).[45] Nonetheless, Kelsen suggests that the notion of the primacy of the national legal order is more likely to be abused than its opposite. This is because the former gives rise to the solipsistic conclusion that there is only 'one national legal order only, and therefore one State only, can be conceived as sovereign', this being the ideology of imperialism (Kelsen, 1946, p.385; Kelsen, 1967, p.343). The notion of the primacy of national law is problematic in the sense that it cannot logically comprehend the idea of the equality of states, the possible consequence of this being the denial of the existence of legal relations among states (Kelsen, 1946, p.386).

For Kelsen, the principle of the legal equality of states is only possible where we conceive of the international legal order as superior to the national legal order and thus cease to think of the state as sovereign (Kelsen, 1946, p.387).[46]

The possibility of legally binding relations among states can only be based on an objective world-view which acknowledges the existence of many states, and not just one state, and that these states are regulated by a hierarchy or pyramid of norms such that the international legal order is superior to the national legal order. Law, both municipal and international, derives its binding force in Kelsen's system from what he first called an '*Ursprungsnorm* (originary norm)' and then a *Grundnorm* or basic norm which is the premise on which the legal system is based (Rigaux, 1998, p.327).[47] This norm is immanent to the system and 'cannot be subjected to further analysis'; the question as to why the *Grundnorm* is binding is not addressed and cannot be addressed without going outside of the legal domain and into the realms politics and ethics (Nussbaum, 1954, pp.280–1).[48] Norbetto Bobbio claims that the *Grundnorm* serves as a form of '"logical" closure of his system'; it is a 'closure of convenience', but it is also a means of 'removing the legal system from the arbitrariness of political power, of asserting the primacy of law and of rights and freedoms over *raisons d'état*' (Bobbio in Zolo and Bobbio, 1998, p.358).[49] In terms of international law, Kelsen considered the *Grundnorm* to be *pacta sunt servanda*, although he later modified that position insisting that the 'basic norm of international law...must be a norm which countenances custom as a norm-creating fact', that is, 'states ought to behave as they have customarily behaved', abiding by agreements being the most significant of these customary behaviours (quoted in Rigaux, p.328; see also Kelsen, 1946, p.370).

Kelsen is well known for his conception of the legal order as a coercive order and his insistence that the international legal order is of a coercive character, its sanctions taking the form of war and reprisals (Kelsen, 1967, pp.320–2). In this regard, the international legal order is not different from the domestic legal order except for the fact that its power of sanction is decentralised. It is this that renders the international legal order 'imperfect' or 'primitive' (Bull, 1986, p.325).[50] Nonetheless, the collective security systems established by the League of Nations and then the United Nations, both of which Kelsen strongly favoured, marked something of a shift towards the centralisation of international enforcement mechanisms (Bull, 1986, p.328). At the same time, the idea of the basic norm is a departure from the Austinian equation of law with the presence of legal and political sanctions since it is from this norm, rather than from the presence of sanctions, that international legal obligations spring (see also Bull, 1986, p.124). This also underlines the fact that despite Kelsen's otherwise rigorous positivism, as Danilo Zolo has commented, the 'summit of the formalist self-reference of the pure theory of law...coincide[s] with the ancient theological idea of *civitias maxima*' which upholds the idea of the 'universal legal community of human beings' (Zolo, 1998, pp.309–10).[51]

For Kelsen the state is not sovereign, or at least its sovereignty is relative rather than absolute, precisely because national legal orders are inferior to the international legal order (Kelsen, 1946, pp.370, 385). Despite the mind's tendency to conceive of it in terms of the 'human ego', the state is only a medium through which international law is conveyed to individuals; the state is in reality a 'system of legal norms' which itself is authorised by the norms of international law (Nussbaum, 1954, p.280). This statement gives rise to two points. First, while the relation between the individual and international law is typically a mediated relation there is nothing 'inherent to international law' which renders it impossible, as the prosecution of war crimes by international tribunals shows, for it to touch individuals directly. As Kelsen stated in 1932: 'International law has, as a general rule, has states as its subjects, that is to say, individuals in a mediate way...and exceptionally too individuals in an immediate way. *It is not contrary to the nature of international law that what is today an exception should one day become the rule*' (quoted in Leben, 1998, p.295).[52] Second, if we accept the primacy of international law, it follows that ideally there should be no inconsistency between customary international law and municipal law; what is correct, normatively speaking, from its point of view must also be correct from the point of view of municipal law and it follows from this that international norms should have direct effect in an individual state's legal order.

Yet, as we saw, the fact that the international legal order is decentralised means that states are given scope to interpret international legal norms at will. While this would appear at present to be an existential condition of the functioning of international law, it is also what generates normative inconsistencies between the two legal spheres. As we also saw, Kelsen attempted to reconcile this 'legal reality' with his 'desire to construct a logically coherent model of legal systems' through treating as valid all norms created within the system by competent legal authorities until such a time as they are abolished by a legal act (Weyland, 1986, p.249). Kelsen believed that one can objectively assess the conformity of norms with higher norms and thereby their validity. Yet as Weyland argues, if any norm 'declared by a competent organ' is by definition valid, then the notion that norms derive their validity from their 'conformity with norms of higher levels' becomes 'meaningless' and the same can be said of the notion of validity: one cannot speak of a criterion of legal validity in a situation in which both A and not A can be considered equally valid legal norms. In place of objective legal criteria, one is left with the 'subjective judgements of officials' something which Weyland states 'brings him uncomfortably close' to the 'decisionist' position of 'American Realists' (Weyland 1986, pp.250, 252–3). Weyland concludes that Kelsen effectively removes 'the distinction between norm and no-norm, between validity and invalidity, and one is only left with the conception of a prescription declared to be valid or invalid' (Weyland, 1986, pp.254–5). For this reason, Weyland prefers to refer to those norms which are prescribed by those purporting to be 'acting in the capacity of legal organs' but which do not meet the criteria of validity as laid down by Kelsen, as 'norms in force': in order to distinguish them from norms which are objectively valid (Weyland, 1986, p.268).

Legal monism, in its emphasis on the primacy of international law, made an important contribution to our thinking about international law in relation to both the individual and the state. It highlighted the fact that the real subjects of international law are individuals, thus showing that international law is 'not confined to relations among states' but can 'encompass all human activities', most especially the way in which nationals are treated within their own state (Rigaux, 1998, p.332). As Lauterpacht stated, international monism had shown that:

> The dogmatic affirmation that the rights of...[individuals].....are the rights of the State and not those of individuals is nothing less that a restatement, in a generalised form, of the existing situation concerning the inability of the individual to undertake proceedings in the international domain (Lauterpacht, 1937, p.231).

Contrary to this dogma he asserted:

> The individual is the ultimate unit not only of international obligations, but also of international rights. In no other matter, does the monistic ideal express itself more forcefully than in this postulate that the final end of the international order must be the protection of the individual human being (Lauterpacht 1937, pp.231–2).

Further, in inverting the somewhat destructive pattern of thinking on international law that emerged in the nineteenth century, it contributed to and reinforced the view that war must be outlawed. Indeed, according to Bobbio and Zolo, Kelsen thought that international law must have as its culminating point the dissolution of the sovereignty of the state, as he believed that it is only this basis that a stable peace can be achieved (Zolo and Bobbio, 1998, pp.362–3; see also Kelsen, 1967, p.328).[53] Zolo points out that Kelsen indicated that the division of humanity into sovereign states might be only a temporary measure to be superseded by the emergence of a pacifist legal order, an order he described as the 'inverted image of imperialism' (Zolo, 1998, p.358).[54] Developing these points further, albeit slightly differently, one might say that the absence of a consistently law abiding attitude among the peoples of the world, means that there is need for a mechanism for ensuring virtue at home and peace abroad and sovereignty has been for some time the chosen mechanism. In this regard we might view the sovereign state as a way-station on the road to perpetual peace, and thus containing within itself the ultimate aim of self-transcendence and the attainment of the 'Idea' which is, as Kant described it, 'the civic union of the human race' (Kant, 1963, p.23). To the extent that the sovereignty of the state is crudely conceived, that is in a solipsistic fashion, it will remain an obstacle to peace and the unity of law. However, where the sovereignty of the state is meaningfully understood to be subject to and qualified by a range of higher norms, then such a cosmopolitical state may remain an ethical ideal rather than a political necessity. The crucial issue, concerning this second option, is the extent to which the element of contingency, to borrow from Hegel, prevails.

The constitution of sovereignty

Monism has been criticised for its view that the powers exercised by states are not original powers but are rather conferred on them by international law. Albert Bleckmann argues that however logically attractive this view might be it leads ultimately to a legally and politically unsustainable conclusion: the idea of the sovereignty of international law. As he correctly points out, while sovereignty implies the rule of law it also implies the power to enforce whatever rules issue from it and since the commands of the international legal community are generally not accompanied by the power of sanction, in contrast with the commands issued by states, it cannot be regarded as sovereign (Bleckmann, 1994, p.87). In response to this it can be argued that in speaking of the sovereignty of the law, one is simply referring to a situation in which a law-abiding attitude has been significantly and widely internalised by states. One might also object in relation to monism that to treat sovereignty as a mere emanation of international law is to discount the original and constitutive role of specific communities in the construction of their state, such that states and the communities they house are regarded as mere emanations or moments in the life of a larger, objective legal order. This is certainly an important consideration, touching as it does on the question of political legitimacy, although a monist might respond that since international legal monism can come in either relatively thin or thick forms it is quite compatible with the idea of states possessing considerable degrees of autonomy.

Leaving aside these arguments, it should be noted that in terms of positive international law, sovereignty cannot be regarded as delegated or derived power. Sovereignty is not, as Alan James points out, a requirement of international law which a state must fulfil in order to be regarded as sovereign. Rather, as he puts it, sovereignty 'concerns a state's situation in the light of its constitutional law', the possession of a constitution, written or unwritten, being the defining feature of a sovereign state (James, 1986, p.40).[55] From the perspective of international law, a state is sovereign if it can demonstrate that by virtue of its constitution it is 'constitutionally apart', that is, it is not part of a 'wider constitutional scheme' (James, 1986, pp.61–2). Thus, while international law endows the sovereign state with certain rights it does so on the basis of a sovereignty that has already been achieved or is assumed to have been achieved *via* a constitutional process. Hence, international law does not grant sovereignty to the state but rather 'presupposes' it (James, 1986, p.40).

Yet, even though sovereignty is not a formal provision of international law, politically speaking the internal sovereignty of the state would be hard to sustain in the absence of those rights which are consequent upon international recognition. If sovereignty is to be enjoyed as a legal status and not merely on the basis that one has the power to deter aggressors, then an international guarantee of non-intervention is an essential rather than contingent matter (Bleckmann, 1994, p.80).[56] International law helps to secure the existence of states through the formal guarantees of independence that it offers. While the world appears to be comprised of separate, discrete and 'self-generating' states, as reflected in the formal position that sovereignty comes from within, beyond this appearance is a tissue of shared perceptions and indeed it is only on this basis that the social institutions of statehood and sovereignty can arise and be 'stabilised' (Blaney and Inayatullah, 1996, pp.94–5). Thus, the international society of states should be seen, not as mechanism for upholding rights that are anterior to that society but rather as the institutional context in which statehood and the rights which accompany it are forged. States, as Jackson points out citing Frost's constitutive theory of recognition which in turn is derived from Hegel, '"reciprocally constitute one another" [through] mutual recognition and by subjecting themselves to a common *norm* of state sovereignty and non-intervention' (Jackson, 1998, p.9n; Frost, 1996, p.152).[57]

For Frost, the most important 'task is to make explicit the moral dimension that is already implicit in the simultaneous acceptance of the state and sovereignty norms' (Frost, 1996, p.141). This moral dimension encompasses the centrality of the principle of autonomy and, as a corollary, the prohibition against colonial domination (Frost, 1996, p.152). The value placed on autonomy is what gives rise to the obligation to recognise organised communities as states provided, they 'meet certain specific requirements' among which is the requirement that the citizens of the state claiming to be autonomous 'experience the well-being of the state as fundamental to their own well-being' (Frost, 1996, pp.152–3) Again, the state is merely an instrument of human happiness and not an end in itself and thus the autonomy of the state has no value should citizens be enslaved. Yet, it is not just autonomy which is valorised in Frost's theory of constitutive recognition. The idea of constitutive recognition also implies that we are each of us, beyond even our concrete duties, deeply *responsible* for each other both in an existential and ethical sense. Through acknowledging our mutually constitutive relations we may be able to invigorate a solidarist ethic of international responsibility.

A responsibility to humanity

The promotion of such an ethic is paramount if we wish to preserve the web of intersubjective meanings that sustains our communal existence. Respect for the social institutions of territorial borders cannot be expected to loom as large in the thinking of those who are effectively relegated, however much they are surrounded by all the formal markers of sovereignty, to a state of nature. As Kant observed, 'no-one originally has any greater right than anyone else to occupy any particular potion of the earth' and for this reason all individuals have a '*right to the earth's surface* which the human race shares in common' (Kant, 1970b, p.106). For Kant, the institution and hardening of the idea of the territorial state, never entirely eliminated the primordial notion of the earth as common surface to which all people had an equal right. However, Kant also circumscribed this right, its modern day residue being universal hospitality by which is meant 'the right of a stranger not to be treated with hostility when he arrives on someone else's territory', although not the right to be a permanent guest (Kant, 1970b, pp.105–6). In limiting the cosmopolitan law of universal hospitality, Kant was mindful of the fact that it was being used to justify imperial conquest. Nonetheless, he qualified the right of the host state to expel the visitor by adding that this could only be done as long as it did not cause the visitor's 'death', again underlining the point that the many of the conventions of the state system rightly melt away for those, such as the stateless, who are cast into the insecurity of the state of nature (Kant, 1970b, p.106).

Both Derrida and Balibar have spoken of the need to extend both the duty and right of refuge and hospitality beyond the limited scope set for them by international refugee law and current state policy so as to come closer to the 'the medieval principle of *quid est in territorio est de territorio*' (Derrida, 2001, pp.5–7, 11).[58] This requires a considerable change in the way territorial borders are conceptualised since, as Derrida points out, the division of the earth is so encrusted with tradition, so weighed down with significance that the soil upon which we found states and their structures 'is no longer soil pure and simple' (Derrida, 2001, p.21). Yet, while the partitioning of the earth and the sacralisation of borders has greatly compromised the right to a common surface, it has not eliminated it entirely and we might say that the respect for that right, in appropriate circumstances, is a condition implicitly imposed on the sovereign state system by the wider human society out of which it is formed. That is, to use Vattel's words, the obligation to provide asylum can be thought of as part of our 'duties of humanity', duties which condition the use of the 'right of domain' (Vattel, 1863, p.171; see also pp.74, 183).[59] As Vattel further states:

> The *universal society* of the human race being an institution of nature herself, that is to say, a necessary consequence of the nature of man, – all men, in whatever stations they are placed, *are bound to cultivate it, and to discharge its duties*. They cannot liberate themselves from the obligation by any convention, by any private association...they remain

> still bound to the performance of *their duties towards the rest of mankind* (Vattel, 1863, p.lx).

States have obligations not just to other states but also to individuals as members of the wider human community which has authorised the state system. The state system is just one way of managing the common affairs of humanity and it is only at the discretion of humanity that the state system subsists. In relation to the question of asylum, the specific argument that the previous points suggest is that humanity, in willing the sovereignty of its various parts, does so on the proviso that those human beings forced into a stateless condition will be found refuge. It can thus be argued that the provision of refuge is a fundamental responsibility of the state system: the obligation to provide asylum, where warranted, can be said to lie at the very foundation of international society. Thus, while borders generally advertise to strangers where they must not go, they also, under certain conditions, signal where sanctuary may in principle be found. Derrida knows, just as Kant did, that political pragmatism means 'universal hospitality...*without limit*' is a fantasy and that the sovereign state will always seek to limit the capacity of people to traverse state borders and frontiers whether by political or legal means (Derrida, 2001, p.20). Nor is this without justice given that borders are instituted precisely in order to seal off spaces in which a communities can exercise and enjoy their autonomy. Universal hospitality without limit would obviously endanger communal autonomy. As Rousseau 'resignedly accepted', the rupture between what justice requires and what states will, both singularly and jointly, is probably irresolvable (Butler, 1978, p.58). Yet at the same time, as Rousseau also appreciated, it is only *via* the mechanism of positive law that the 'laws of natural justice' can find expression and extravagant and dangerous readings of it be contained (Rousseau, 1968, pp.80–1). Concerning this point Derrida writes:

> It is a question of knowing how to transform and improve the law, and of knowing if this improvement is possible within an historical space which takes place *between* the Law of an unconditional hospitality, offered *a priori* to every other, to all newcomers, *whoever they may be*, and the conditional laws of a right to hospitality, without which *The* unconditional Law of hospitality would be in danger of remaining a pious and irresponsible desire, without form and without potency, and of even being perverted at any moment (Derrida, 2001, pp.22–3).

We have seen that Vattel thought the duty of punishment of crimes against natural law, as elaborated by Grotius, to be one such dangerous reading which is why he sought to circumscribe the rules of intervention and pragmatically tie the law of nations, in this respect, to the concern for the security of one's own state. Yet, Vattel himself, as is discussed in Chapter 5, offered a version of a natural law right that was highly vulnerable to abuse by would-be conquerors: the right of necessity. As we saw, Kant was acutely aware that the right to a common surface held out imperialist dangers. Yet, even though he went on to limit this right, it remained an ideal that he wanted us to keep in mind. If we keep in mind the original condition whereby the earth being held by no-one was jointly held by all, even while translating this ideal into practice in a limited or reductive fashion, we may go some way to loosening and undermining overly rigid, defensive and mystical conceptions of territorial borders.[60] Such a way of imagining our world may make us more appreciative of the claims on us of the world's destitute and persecuted and more open to the notion, foreshadowed by both Vattel and Kant, of a 'universal right of *circulation* and *residency*' with a view to extending and deepening cultural exchanges between societies and civilisations (Balibar, 2004, pp.176–7).

4
From Imperial to Post-Imperial Sovereignty

Imperial sovereignty

Jackson defines 'imperial sovereignty' as the practice of exercising 'supreme authority over a foreign territory' (Jackson, 1999, p.441). It is a description that well captures the scale and tone of the European engagement with the non-European world during the age of imperialism. Yet, it is also paradoxical for just as a system predicated upon multiple sovereignties should be averse to aggressive war, so too it should be averse to imperial conquest. Of course, if we think about sovereignty simply in terms of the principle of legal supremacy we should have no trouble with the notion of imperial sovereignty, as this last notion does not say anything about limits on the extent of territorial control. Yet, in a multipolar system the sovereignty of states can only be legally upheld where members of that system agree to desist from conquest. Viewed from this perspective, there is no imperial sovereignty only hegemony or empire, this last term being defined by Michael Doyle as 'a relationship, formal or informal, in which one state controls the effective political sovereignty of another political society' (Doyle, 1986, p.45). It is worth recalling that the struggle to establish the sovereign state system in Europe was an anti-imperial struggle, even if states in Europe took until at least the eighteenth century to begin to concede to each other the sovereign rights they claimed for themselves (see Bull and Watson, 1985, p.6). Drawing out the anti-imperial implications of the principle, Vattel argued that in alienating the sovereignty of a nation one was denying the state's reason for being:

> A nation becomes incorporated into a society, to labour for the common welfare as it shall think proper, and to live according to its own laws. With this view it establishes a public authority...the individuals who have formed this society, entered into it in order to live in an independent state, and not under a foreign yoke. Let not any other source of this right be all for the purpose of living in an independent State and by no

means with the intention of submitting to a foreign yoke (Vattel, 1863, p.30).

In stating this, Vattel was anticipating Kant who well appreciated that sovereignty and aggression formed an unnatural union in principle and not just a monstrous one in fact. Kant insisted that the autonomy of a 'nation which legitimately sees itself...as an independent state should not be ruled by another' (Williams, 1983, p.250). China and Japan saw themselves as independent states and for this reason Kant defended their autonomy, commending their governments for 'wisely' limiting their dealings with outsiders to 'contact, but not settlement' (Kant, 1987, p.78). While Kant gave no definite criteria for determining the existence of a sovereign state, and even suggested that a 'subjective element' is involved in 'determining which state can be regarded as "existing in itself" (*für sich bestenender Staat*)', he appeared to treat the presence of sovereignty as the objective test of statehood (Williams, 1983, pp.250–1).

However, it is arguable that while a sovereign state system must necessarily be anti-imperialist within its own confines, the rule of non-intervention does not apply to communities that are not organised in a sovereign fashion. It might seem that the internal logic of sovereignty does not prevent states from dividing among themselves the supposedly non-sovereign parts of the world. However, if sovereignty is a deduction from more general principles, namely that aggression is wrong because communal flourishing is valuable, then in order to stay true to its fundamental basis sovereignty must desist from conquest in all cases. As regards those who do not pass the test of sovereignty, Kant stated that 'even though such savages for their own part may regard themselves as superior on account of the lawless freedom they have chosen. The latter likewise constitute national groups, but they do not constitute states' (Kant, 1970c, p.164). Nonetheless, even this lawless condition did not justify outside interference and entailed only limited rights of settlement:

> But one might ask whether a nation may establish a *settlement alongside another nation (accolatus)* in newly discovered regions, or whether it may take possession of land in the vicinity of a nation which has already settled in the same area, even without the latter's consent. The answer is that the right to do so is incontestable, so long as such settlements are established sufficiently far away from the territory of the original nation for neither party to interfere with the other in their use of the land. But if the nations involved are pastoral or hunting peoples (like the Hottentots, the Tunguses, and most native American nations) who rely upon large tracts of wasteland for their sustenance, settlements should not be established by violence, but only by treaty; and even then, there

> must be no attempt to exploit the ignorance of the natives in persuading them to give up their territories (Kant, 1970c, pp.172–3).

Kant acknowledged the argument that conquest could serve 'the best interests of the world as a whole', such as by civilising the uncivilised or by purging a country of 'depraved characters, at the same time affording the hope that they or their offspring will become reformed in another continent (as in New Holland)'. However, he insisted that such 'supposedly good intentions cannot wash away the stain of injustice from the means which are used to implement them': violence and aggression (Kant, 1970c, p.173). Kant confessed to looking with 'deep aversion' upon the preference for a 'wild freedom' instead of a 'reasonable one'. Yet, his dialectical treatment of historical development suggests that he saw this condition as a necessary prelude to subjection to 'the restraint of law' (Kant, 1987, p.74). It was an historically, but also more importantly a morally necessary precondition because, as John Stuart Mill later put it, 'it is during arduous struggle to become free by their own efforts' that a people are most likely to acquire those 'feelings and virtues' which are conducive to the maintenance of freedom (Mill, 1963, p.382).[1]

War was wrong because the struggle for autonomy was impossible amidst outside attacks, as was interference in such struggles on whichever side. For foreigners to interfere in a state characterised by undecided 'inner strife...would be a trespass on the rights of an independent people struggling only with its own inner weakness' (Kant, 1987, p.69). If a people have a right to fight for their freedom, without hindrance or *assistance*, then it follows that not only must sovereignty defer to the principle of non-aggression it must also defer to the principle of self-determination which can be regarded as the 'supreme political good' (Kedourie, 1966, p.29). In *Religion Within the Limits of Reason Alone* (1793) Kant sought to respond to the argument that a people 'engaged in a struggle for civil freedom' were by definition undeserving of liberty (Kant, 1960, p.176n). Kant pointed to the absurdity of this argument: it implied that 'freedom...[could]..never arrive' for a people in bondage since it effectively maintained that people could only '*ripen* to freedom' where they were 'first of all placed therein.' More importantly, he went on to state that justice required that a people must be in an external sense free in order that through struggle they could make themselves free internally (Kant, 1960, p.176n). A people must have freedom in the negative sense in order that they can show themselves to be, in the words of Mill, 'fit for freedom' (Mill, 1963, p.381). Kant further stated in relation to this issue:

> The first attempts will indeed be crude and usually will be attended by a more painful and more dangerous state than that in which we are still under the orders and also the care of others; yet we never ripen with

respect to reason except through *our own* efforts...which we can make only when we are free (Kant, 1960, p.176n).

That the principle of self-determination should apply to non-sovereign peoples and not just sovereign states is underlined by the fact that Kant wrote of stateless societies *choosing* to be attached to their supposedly lawless freedom. Thus, all societies are engaged in the struggle for autonomy and generally should be left alone in order to persist in that struggle no matter what stage of this endless process they have reached, or in what way self-determination manifests itself.[2] The institution of sovereignty is one particular, albeit very momentous, expression of this struggle. Indeed, the value of sovereignty is that it provides a defined space in which individuals and communities can strive for freedom and self-expression. Thus, while we might say that sovereignty needs and promotes social homogeneity it also assumes, and to an extent esteems, conflictual social differences at the level of state. In any case, when the premises from which sovereignty, at least on the Kantian interpretation, are brought to light, the expression imperial sovereignty is rendered a contradiction in terms.

While the concept of national self-determination only began to animate the idea of sovereignty two centuries after the latter's initial development, traces of it are discernible in sovereignty's early formulations. Sovereignty is predicated on the principle of independence and even the more absolutist theories of sovereignty acknowledged that its ultimate source lay with the community and that it should be exercised for the benefit of the community. The relation between sovereignty and self-determination, however nascent and undeveloped, helps explain why the historic partnership between sovereignty and imperialism was always prone to implosion even though it took a long time for sovereignty's emancipatory significance to manifest itself. For the same reason, the claim that colonialism rendered sovereignty a global phenomenon is also ambiguous. Indeed, it is rather post-Second World War decolonisation which saw sovereignty become a global phenomenon and I would suggest also that decolonisation, along with the renunciation of aggressive war as discussed in Chapter 7, can be seen as another expression of the maturation of that principle.

The non-European world which expansionist European powers confronted was not without borders or lines of authority. While the precise concept of sovereignty may not have existed outside of Europe in the age of imperialism, it cannot be said that notions of hierarchy and territorial lines of demarcation were absent from contemporaneous social arrangements, (whether in Sub-Saharan Africa, Hindu kingdoms, the Arab-Islamic world, the Mexican and Peruvians empires in the Americas or the stateless political societies of Australasia) (Bull and Watson, 1985, p.2). European colonialism certainly involved the organisation of the 'world's exploitation' but it is not wholly accurate to say that it also involved the exportation of the '"border form" to the periphery' (Balibar, 2004, p.7).[3] Within the sphere of the so-called periphery there were territorial makers and lines of authority, more or less firm and more or less fiercely defended, which in many instances persisted after occupation, whether underneath, on the fringes of or amidst imperialist structures. European territorialisation of the earth thus involved an initial moment of deterritorialisation, not simply in the sense that the 'abstract signs' of the state were substituted for the 'signs of the earth', but also in respect to already pre-existing orders of belonging (Patton, 2000, p.92).

In most areas, the signs of the earth had been written over repeatedly, even if such writing were mysterious or almost indiscernible to the uninitiated. To the extent that we can speak of conquest taking place in countries 'that belonged to nobody' it was because in many instances the inhabitants, as Kant said in relation to the Americas, Africa and elsewhere, 'counted for nothing' (Kant, 1987, p.78). From the time of the Spanish seizure of the Americas to the Berlin Congress of 1884–1885, European powers competed ruthlessly against each other for colonial possessions due to the perceived economic and strategic advantages that such possessions brought. Concurrent with this, they sought to develop a treaty-governed public space in Europe (Balibar, 2004, p.138).[4]

Jackson writes that invocations of sovereignty played two distinct but related functions in the context of European imperial expansion. Sovereignty was invoked as a source of authority for the acquisition of territories and as a means of asserting a continuing legal title to peoples and lands as against the aspirations or claims of others (Jackson, 1999, p.442). Initially, as was the case with the 'mandate' of the conquistadors, conquest was seen as being authorised 'within the unitary scheme of Christendom' (Mayall, 1978, p.129). However, just as the idea that war could be sanctioned by any other authority than the sovereign prince evaporated, so too did the idea that the seizure of territory could be sanctioned by authorities other than the sovereign state disappear. Jackson notes that when the East India Company and the Hudson's Bay Company claimed 'territories in South Asia and North America they did so by reference to royal charter that they had obtained from the British Crown' (Jackson, 1999, p.442). Further, he adds that because imperialism was a competitive affair, the imperial powers wanted 'recognized title to foreign territory' rather than be faced with a situation whereby their colonial possessions were ever vulnerable to takeover. Thus, the powers effectively entered an agreement to mutually recognise their colonial holdings 'while agreeing not to recognize non-European political authorities' (Jackson, 1999, p.442).

While the decision not to recognise non-European systems of authority, at least not fully, was made for reasons of mutual advantage such non-recognition was considered as legitimate from the perspective of many European authorities who appealed to and were influenced by Roman legal doctrine and practices including occupation, *terra nullius* and conquest (Jackson, 1999, p.442). In theory, the principle of cession is compatible with an anti-imperial reading of sovereignty because it involves the willing surrender of territory to another party rather than its forced occupation, although we know in practice the distinction between the former and the latter was extremely slippery. The supposed right of conquest however, as has been stated of the putative right of war, reflected one of those gaps between what principle demanded and what the law of nations permitted, although as we have seen principle itself could supply numerous rationales for aggression. For Rousseau, conquest could never be a means of gaining title to a territory since submission to 'force is an act of necessity, not of will' and thus cannot give rise to a right (Rousseau, 1968, p.52).[5] While accepting the general force of Rousseau's point, Korman points out that conquest, 'in the technical sense', did not signify 'mere force' but rather denoted:

> ...a legal institution subject to rules...from which, by convention, legal rights could arise. When we say of a conqueror that it has acquired a piece of territory 'by right of conquest', we imply that some ingredient other than the power of the conqueror was involved in the transaction. We imply, first of all, that the action takes place within the context of a society...which grants rights to its members and which somehow *permits* the acquisition. And since the notion of permission implies the possibility of restriction, it becomes meaningful to speak of the conqueror's right as a 'right' and not merely a power (Korman, 1996, p.95).

Although Grotius listed wars of imperial expansion as among the unjust causes of war and Vattel condemned conquest on moral grounds, they also understood that as long as conquest was an accepted feature of state practice there was a need to legally institutionalise it. Institutionalisation was necessary in order to regulate the practice of seizing territory, temper the violence entailed by this practice, facilitate the cession of hostilities and confirm and stabilise the borders of acquired territories (Korman, 1990, pp.18–20, 25–6).[6] However, Korman's argument concerning the sense in which one could speak, without contradiction, of a right by conquest is only relevant within the context of the European international law of the day. From the perspective of non-European peoples, peoples who played no part in the formation of the European law of nations, conquest could only have looked like violent usurpation.

The extension of the European law of nations to the non-European world was important as a means of securing colonial claims and thus moderating intra-European colonial competition. Yet what is also relevant is that it served as a means of regulating relations between European and non-European peoples. As Charles Alexandrowicz notes, the evidence drawn from state practice from the sixteenth century down to the nineteenth century strongly indicates that many non-European powers were 'endowed with legal personality' and regarded as participants in the 'universal community of the law of nations' (Alexandrowicz, 1969, pp.468; see also Crawford, 1979, p.176).[7] Alexandrowicz highlights the treaties with Asian powers, but as Anthony Anghie notes, African kingdoms were also 'treated with all the respect due to sovereigns' by the European states with whom they entered into relations (Anghie, 1999, p.27).[8] These points indicate that European legal concepts and diplomatic practices were not alien to the conceptual framework and experience of non-European societies. Equally, they indicate that European rulers were capable of recognising, if only in an imperfect way, non-European rulers as equals.

In drawing attention to these points, I am not supposing that the precise concept of sovereignty was always present in the non-European world or even, in some contexts, the existence of concepts which remotely resembled it. Nor am I assuming that the perspectives on diplomatic relations and treaties between European and non-European nations were understood in the same way by all parties concerned. Yet what these points do suggest is that translation from one experience to the other was possible, even if there remained aspects which were untranslatable and even though this very fact would lead to the conclusion that European international law could only be extended in its entirety to Europeans themselves. The noted English legal publicist W.E. Hall wrote that international law, as a 'product of the special civilisation of modern Europe' and forming 'a highly artificial system', could not 'be supposed to be understood or recognised by countries differently civilised'. Differently civilised countries, Hall added, in order to be recognised as states 'must do something with the acquiescence' of European civilisation: accept European international law 'in its entirety' (Hall, 1924, p.47).[9]

What Martin Wight refers to as the 'orthodox' account of the relation between international law and non-Europeans, was upheld in the nineteenth century by positivists and natural law thinkers as well as by those such as Hall who incorporated elements of both approaches (Wight, 1977, p.156). (This is not to deny the existence of heterodox legal treatments of the subject and indeed, some of these are discussed in the next chapter). For example, the Scottish law professor James Lorimer, a natural law exponent, argued that full recognition should be extended to the states of Europe along with their 'colonial dependences' whereas partial recognition was to be extended to recognition to 'barbarous' communities such as Turkey, China, Siam and Japan. As regards 'the residue of mankind' or 'savage humanity', these were to be accorded 'natural or mere human recognition' (quoted in Wight, 1977, pp.116–17; see also Rougier, 1910, p.469). It was partly against the background of this division of humanity that the 'theory of intervention for humanity' was developed, it being embraced, to a greater or lesser degree, by figures such as Bluntschli, Calvo, Pasquale Fiore, Rolin-Jaequemyns and Wheaton. Antoine Rougier maintained that in the nineteenth century it was simply accepted by European peoples that they had 'not only a right' but also a duty to 'bring a germ of civilisation to barbarous lands' (Rougier, 1910, pp.468–9). However, as discussed in the next chapter, the right of civilisation and humanitarian intervention were also viewed by legal scholars with great scepticism. Numerous European legal scholars denounced intervention in the name of either civilisation or humanity, noting the horrors that had been visited upon non-European peoples in their names and out of concern that it was a recipe for universal empire (Renault, 1879, p.23). And it was for same reasons that advocates such as the Swiss jurist Joseph Hornung, insisted that any such interventions must be '*désinteréssée*': they must be undertaken as far as possible on a collective basis and with a view to the full emancipation of those being instructed in the ways of civilisation (Hornung, 1886, pp.188, 200, 205).[10]

Sovereignty's emergence in China

In her study of Chinese conceptions of the state, sovereignty and international law Suzanne Ogden points out that the general belief is that China, up until its encounters with the west in the nineteenth century, conceptualised the state differently and possessed no notion 'at all of "national sovereignty,"' even though the notion of '"equality of states" had at times appeared in Chinese international relations' (Ogden, 1975, pp.1–2). While China possessed a concept of suzerainty, it had a more supple understanding of hierarchy and borders than that entertained by European theorists of sovereignty. As Alan M. Wachman notes, the imperial Chinese state comprised a loosely joined tributary system in which the sovereignty of the Emperor was 'potential, not actual, control' and where the extent to which any such control was accepted varied according to time and place (Wachman, 2002, p.705).[11]

The Emperor in imperial China was conceived as the 'supreme authority under heaven' and all that was 'under Heaven' was conceived as the 'realm of the emperor'. Clearly, there could be only one supreme authority under Heaven and it was 'taken for granted that the emperor should be one of the Middle Kingdom'; for this very reason 'there was no such word as the "Chinese emperor"' (Onuma, 2000, p.12; see also Donnelly, 1998, p.2). The Emperor was thus not in a relation of equality with other rulers within the empire but instead ruled over them as an elder sibling or patriarch, although it is important to add that this form of rulership was conceived in cultural rather than political terms. As Suzanne Ogden explains, Chinese international relations was based on a universal 'morality' established by 'one entity and imposed on all others' by, at least in theory, 'moral suasion and cultural superiority' with conformity to this morality being demonstrated by adherence to Chinese customs and rules as well as by the performance of 'certain rites' (Ogden, 1975, pp.26, 28–9).[12] Thus, the imperial Chinese system was not properly speaking an international system but was rather a Sinocentric civilisation with the perpetuation of this civilisation being one of the chief concerns of successive dynasties (Onuma, 2000, pp.10–12).[13] Individual kingdoms within the empire were left to run their day-to-day affairs with considerable freedom as long as they paid tribute to the Emperor and abided by established codes of conduct.[14]

Statehood in imperial China meant membership of the Chinese 'family of states'. States outside this grouping, at least those who were yet to embrace Chinese culture, were not viewed as 'equals' but were regarded as 'barbarian' entities. The restricted nature of the Chinese system of civilisation was reflected in the fact that while 'armed struggle between equals was called war', when such struggles took place between a member of the Chinese family of nations and barbarian peoples it was merely regarded as a 'drive' (Ogden, 1975, p.22). Nonetheless, tributary policy was extended to all groups with whom China engaged diplomatically. For China, the key to security lay with keeping itself distant from international relations. In instances where foreigners wished to conduct international relations with China, Chinese security demanded that they had to do so as a 'vassal' of China , that is, by deferring to the Emperor and acknowledging his right to rule (Ogden, 1975, p.28).[15] Yet such a system was not aimed at imperial expansion or world empire: it made no demands on those foreigners who preferred to live outside the Chinese orbit (Ogden, 1975, p.28).

Nussbaum maintains that the view of outsiders as inferiors come to pay homage to China's superior civilisation allowed China to reconcile the authority of the Chinese state with the Portuguese settlement of Macau in 1557 which the Chinese saw as being grounded in tolerance (Nussbaum, 1954, p.65). Such a conception of the relationship with Europeans was by no means implausible at that stage. The same applies to the Chinese view that the demand that China defer to European international legal and diplomatic practices, as made by Lord McCartney when visiting China in 1793 on a trade mission on behalf of George III, was some kind of barbarian 'joke' based on an ignorance 'of the long established "universal" rules and rituals through which all nations must behave themselves' (Onuma, 2000, p.29).[16]

Yet, in subsequent decades Sinocentrism was increasingly contradicted by the reality of growing European power. However, the erosion of this worldview was slow to occur and this helps explains why the Chinese rulership misunderstood the institution of the 'unequal treaty' beginning with the Treaty of Nanjing in 1842. This treaty, along with the subsequent treaties of Wangxia in 1844 and Tianjin in 1858, gave formal expression to China's forced entry into the international system (Ogden, 1975, p.4; Ho, 1967, p.190).[17] Rather than seeing this and subsequent treaties as incursions on its sovereignty, the rulership viewed them as either defensive measures taken to manage and control foreigners in China or simply as concessions. For example, Ogden writes that extraterritoriality was at first seen as a means of excluding Europeans 'from participation in Chinese culture', the complexity of which the Europeans could not possibly be expected to understand (Ogden, 1974, pp.4–5).[18] Touching on the same issue, Yasuaki Onuma maintains that the Qing dynasty saw extraterritorial juridical competence as a grant to the foreign 'barbarians' in order that they could resolve their own disagreements. He adds that in a similar fashion, 'most favoured nation treatment' was seen, not as an international obligation, but 'as a benevolent policy of the emperor to treat all subjects under Heaven as equal' (Onuma, 2000, p.31).

However, from the European perspective, the unequal treaties were precisely a denial of the sovereignty of the Chinese state. They marked the beginning of a series of moves by which the independence of China was eroded, a process involving not only extraterritoriality but also 'treaty ports, spheres of influence and missions' (Ogden, 1975, p.4). As I have indicated, the Chinese characterisation of its relation with European powers was not for a long time implausible, and it is important to note that capitulations, seen by positivists as marks of inferiority, were in fact a feature of the 'ancient Asian tradition' and were not seen as derogating from the sovereignty of those communities hosting foreigners (Alexandrowicz, 1969, p.470).[19] Nonetheless, this characterisation ultimately ran up against the fact that by the nineteenth century, certain foreigners had acquired the capacity to coerce China and believed they had the right to do so.[20]

Thus, when westerners asserted their extraterritorial rights in China, having decided that the application of Chinese municipal law to them was unacceptable, they insisted that '[r]espect for sovereignty and territorial integrity was not an issue because China, lacking the rights of a civilized state under international law, was not considered a sovereign entity' (Ogden, 1975, p.39). Such a justification might ring hollow given that business with China, as with states in the rest of Asia, had earlier been conducted 'on the basis of moral and legal equality' (Bull and Watson, 1985, p.5). However, in the nineteenth century the notional equality that had characterised earlier relations between European states and various parts of the non-European world, as European powers grew in strength and 'notions of European superiority' became entrenched, gave way to all-out subjection or discriminatory treatment under an international law applied and interpreted by Europeans alone (Bull and Watson, 1985, pp.5, 426; see also Mayall, 1978, p.128).[21]

Gerrit W. Gong writes that the European incursion into East Asia amounted to more than a political and military confrontation as it involved a clash between two quite different cultures each with their distinctive standards of civilisation (Gong, 1985, p.172). This point requires qualification as the depiction of European penetration of the globe in terms of a clash or civilisations is rather misleading. As Brett Bowden underlines, the European 'expansion was largely an aggressive act..[often]...involving...violent conquest and suppression' (Bowden, 2005, p.2). However, irrespective of the nature of European incursions into the non-European world, it was the European standard of civilisation, elaborated first in treaties and then by legal publicists in the nineteenth century, which supplied the warrant for them (Gong, 1985, p.179). In essence, the so-called standard of civilisation required that non-European states or communities observe European standards of conduct in areas such as 'domestic law and order, administrative integrity, protection of the rights of foreign citizens...[and]...the fulfilment of contracts' (Bull and Watson, 1985, p.427; see also Gong, 1985, p.179).

Unsurprisingly, many non-European states and communities were deemed as having failed to meet these criteria. Even the Ottoman Empire, which at the end of the Crimean war was admitted to the 'Family of Nations' and allowed to 'participate in the advantages of the public law and Concert of Europe' (as specified in Article 7 of the Peace Treaty of Paris in 1856), still was not accorded equal treatment thereafter (Parry, 1969c, p.414; see also Bull and Watson, 1985, p.427).[22] The Treaty specified that the states of Britain, Austria, Prussia, Russia and Sardinia would respect the 'independence and integrity of the Ottoman Empire' (Parry, 1969c, p.414). However, due to the supposed 'inferiority of its civilisation' the Ottoman Empire's 'position remained ambiguous' as reflected in the 'régime of capitulations' imposed on it (Alexandrowicz, 1969, p.466).

That the European law of nations had been redefined as the law of civilised nations, reflected the belief that European civilisation was the only true civilisation in existence. At the same time, and despite it being loaded with Christian and Eurocentric connotations, this redefinition commenced a process whereby international law slowly evolved into a more religiously and culturally 'neutral' instrument. Since full international legal status now hinged, to a significant extent, on the ability of a given state 'to protect, life, freedom and the property of aliens', a door was open to the granting of this status to not only states outside of Europe but also non-Christian states (Onuma, 2000, pp.38–9; see also Tomuschat, 1999, pp.30–1).

It was inevitable that the Chinese empire, after having been coerced into joining the international system, would happen upon and embrace the idea of sovereignty (Fitzgerald, 1995, p.92). While the concept of the sovereign state was problematic for the Chinese given the 'universalist' worldview it had traditionally embraced, it was a concept which they could not afford to ignore (Fitzgerald, 1995, p.91). The principle of sovereignty and the various norms of international law associated with it were obvious means by which China could reassert its independence. Indeed, as early as 1839 a translation into Chinese of a section of Vattel's *Law of Nations* dealing with 'the rights of states in regard to contraband', had the effect of emboldening the Chinese in their stand against the English in respect to the opium trade (Ogden, 1974, p.5; Ogden, 1975, p.37).[23]

However, the realisation of the full significance of international legal thought for China was late in coming. Ogden writes that it was only twenty to thirty years subsequent to the Opium War that the Chinese understood the real meaning of their 'concessions to foreigners' (Ogden, 1975, p.43). The Chinese transition from its traditional one world philosophy only came in the latter part of the nineteenth century when it was widely feared in China that the future of the country was at stake. As John Fitzgerald points out, the Chinese state could not possibly continue to assume its 'centrality' in the face of 'Western gunboats and militia' (Fitzgerald, 1995, pp.92–3; see also Gong, 1985, p.179 and Onuma, 2000, p.53).

Ogden maintains that having appreciated the significance of their concessions, the Chinese at first felt a measure of shame, blaming China's weakness in foreign affairs on its lack of internal order. Chinese leaders continued to preoccupy themselves with the question of political and national unity well into the twentieth century in part for this same reason (Ogden, 1975, p.43). However, when the Chinese arrived at an appreciation of the concept of sovereignty as well as the international legal rights and obligations of states, 'their fear and shame turned to anger and resentment which welled up in a nationalistic movement', a movement which only became possible when the Chinese had shaken off their cultural universalism and begun to think of themselves as one state among others (Ogden, 1975, pp.44, 52; see also Gong, 1985, p.179 and Onuma, 2000, p.53).[24]

It was the introduction of the concept of sovereignty into the Chinese system of thought that rendered what had earlier been less remarkable from the Chinese perspective, namely the presence of 'alien forces' within China, so anomalous (Ogden, 1975, p.54; see also Gong, 1985, pp.172–3). The demise of the Qing dynasty, following a series of popular uprisings stirred by the dynasty's failure to protect Chinese dignity and the state's territorial integrity, marked the triumph of the nationalist movement and saw the establishment of the Republic of China in 1911 (Metzger and Myers, 1998, pp.32–3). The new Chinese state had two major and mutually informing objectives: eliminating the unequal treaties without and ordering the country within (Hsü, 1995, pp.8–9). Thus, Chinese international legal publicists sought to mould understandings of the significance of extraterritoriality and other rights enjoyed by foreigners in China, in a way that favoured the ongoing sovereignty of the Chinese state. It was claimed that extraterritoriality was merely a means of managing relations between 'peoples with unlike laws and moral codes'; further, the privileges extended under the principle were said to be 'purely personal to the subjects of the treaty powers'. As to such rights as the right of residence or to control of certain areas in China, these were simply 'independent grants from China' and in no way impaired China's 'territorial integrity' (Ogden, 1975, p.68).

The nationalist reform movement in China in the late nineteenth and early twentieth centuries well appreciated that internal unification of the country was a prerequisite for stronger assertions of Chinese independence internationally. It was this in particular, that led them to contemplate the relation between the Chinese people and state. The result was the adoption of two mutually informing western ideas: that of the political nation and of the state as the locus of sovereignty. It might be thought that the Emperor's position of supreme authority might have facilitated the assimilation of the idea of state sovereignty. Indeed, the position of the Emperor in Confucian tradition was in some ways similar to that of the sovereign described by Bodin: the Emperor ruled by virtue of a mandate from heaven and related to his subjects in the manner of a father ruling over a large family. Further, the Emperor had a duty to provide his subjects with physical and spiritual nourishment in return for which the subjects owed him loyalty, duty and obedience. Yet, traditional understandings hindered the flowering of the concept of state sovereignty, much as they did in Europe for a long period. One reason is that the idea of the supremacy of the person of the Emperor overshadowed the idea of the supremacy of the state and this explains why publicists of the movement for reform sought to personify the state, with Liang Qichao, the most prominent among these, describing it as the '"parents" of the people' (Ogden, 1975, pp.60–1).

Further, under Confucianism's hierarchical conception of government the state was the 'concern' of the Emperor and his ministers and not a direct concern of the people. This conception inhibited the development of the idea of the political nation and that identification with the state which is necessary, as we saw in Chapter 2, if the idea of state sovereignty is to properly take root. For the Chinese nationalists, strengthening the Chinese state meant that the state had to become the people's concern, both in the sense that the people came to see the state's affairs as their 'own affairs' and, related to this, in the sense that they felt they bore a responsibility for its government (Ogden, 1975, pp.58–9). Such a development entailed, as also discussed in Chapter 2, an erosion of the distinction between the rulership and the ruled, although it should be noted that many nationalists only embraced a limited form of democracy believing that political conditions in China were not hospitable to its full-blown adoption. This is true of Liang who, some suggest, considered the Chinese people 'too politically immature' to enjoy complete democracy and who expressed the concern that democracy could hinder the administration of the state. More importantly, he argued, drawing on Bluntschli and other western theorists, that sovereignty had to be vested in the state alone: sovereignty was the defining characteristic of the state and the state should be conceptualised as a 'separate and independent person' standing 'over and above the people and (even) the sovereign' (Ogden, 1975, pp.60–2; Ogden, 1974, p.5n; see also Howard, 1969, p.11).

The Chinese reformists thus sought to transmute the notional sovereignty of the emperor into the actual sovereignty of the state, elevate the position of the state and inspire a mutually informing sense of national consciousness and feeling of attachment to the state. The revolutionary republicans continued down this path such that the establishment of constitutional government under the Republic, as Jerome Ch'en writes, was partly intended to substitute 'Confucian orthodoxy which had hitherto been the fundamental principle of the state with a new concept, legitimacy', although they would quickly face the problem, amidst conditions of political instability, of how to reconcile democracy with the business of government (quoted in Gong, 1985, p.179).

China's efforts to escape foreign domination had also seen it deepen its acquaintance with European international law and diplomacy. Legal works, such as Wheaton's *Elements of International Law* (1836) (which was published in Chinese in 1864 at the request of the Qing dynasty under the heading *Wanguo Gong Fa* or *Public Law of Nations* and invoked in Chinese diplomatic correspondence), were closely studied and Chinese representatives participated, from as early as 1878, in international legal symposiums among these being the Hague Peace Conferences of 1899 and 1907 (Jianming, 2000, p.30; Renault; 1879, p.20n; Gong, 1985, pp.180–1; Onuma, 2000, p.32).[25] On the inauguration of the Republic and the creation of the Provisional government Sun Yat-sen stated: 'we will try our best to carry out the duties of a civilized nation so as to obtain the rights of a civilized nation' (quoted in Gong, 1985, p.181). Thereafter, China even more vigorously asserted its right to sovereign equality under international law, albeit sometimes in a manner that implicitly endorsed earlier European subjugation. For example, the Chinese government cited the principle of *rebus sic stantibus*, maintaining that the creation of the Republic was a sign of a 'change in circumstances.' In terms of its internal arrangements, it was argued, China was no longer the 'old, decrepit empire' which had signed the unequal treaties but was fast becoming an effective state and one which had already gained international recognition through its involvement in international legal affairs (Ogden, 1975, pp.69–70).

China's domestic reforms in conjunction with its embrace of international law in order to win back its independence meant that Chinese practices were increasingly consonant with the so-called standard of civilisation. Bull and Watson argue that it would be 'shallow' to view this standard as nothing more than a pretext for European domination of the non-European world. The standard of civilisation, they write, eventually 'came to be recognized' by the non-Europeans to whom it was applied and thus they themselves, albeit 'often at the urging of the Europeans', began to make efforts 'to close the gap' (Bull and Watson, 1985, p.427). However, this again does not answer the Kantian point concerning the injustice of external interference in the first place, let alone address the cruelties perpetrated by European powers under the banner of civilisation (see also Onuma, 2000, p.30n).[26]

The period following the establishment of the Republic was plagued by chaotic military conditions and considerable political disruption (Wakeman, 1995, pp.xvi–xvii). For these reasons, and despite China's efforts to close the aforementioned gap, the foreign powers exercising extraterritorial rights continued to question its ability to ensure the life, freedom and property of foreigners living in China and its capacity for organised government. Even in the 1920s, when the question of extraterritoriality began to be renegotiated, these powers continued to cling to their entitlements and negotiations over this issue continued until January 11 1942 only to be cut short by war (Gong, 1985, p.182).[27] This was despite the fact that China had full membership of the League and that its plenipotentiaries were participating in a wide range League activities as well as, in other contexts, the development of international law (Heuser, 2002, p.147).

Nonetheless, as a result of China's vigorous diplomatic efforts there were significant breakthroughs in the negotiations between 1928 and 1931 so that by the beginning of the 1930s control 'over maritime customs, tariffs, postal communications and almost two-thirds of the foreign concessions' had been returned to China (Kirby, 1994, p.18). These diplomatic successes encouraged China in its growing assertiveness in the field of foreign relations, an assertiveness no less embraced by the Chinese Communist Party (CCP) after the establishment of the People's Republic of China (PRC) in 1949, with the CCP decrying the application of 'criteria such as the "level of civilization" or the type of internal government' in determinations of statehood as 'pretexts to conceal relationships of power' (Ogden, 1977, p.316).

Rules of recognition

The standard of civilisation was part of the process of making explicit the criteria for recognition. Before the mid-eighteenth century, there were no explicit criteria in this regard as until then the question of recognition was dealt with only sporadically and thus it did not form a distinct part of international law (Crawford, 1978, p.96). A reason for this was the widely accepted and commonsensical understanding that sovereignty, as 'supreme power within a particular territorial unit', is not obtained from without but 'necessarily came from within' (Crawford, 1978, p.96). Pufendorf well illustrated the logical force of this understanding in stating:

> And so a people...desires thereafter to be under a king, by the act of conferring upon one person, sovereignty over itself also gives him the right

> to bear the name and title of king, and to represent his exalted position by fitting insignia. And just as such a king owes his sovereignty and majesty to no one outside his realm, so he need not obtain the consent and approval of other kings or states, before he may carry himself like a king and be regarded as such. But, in the same way, as it would entail an injury for the sovereignty of such a king to be called in question by a foreigner, so it would be an injury to deny him the royal title (Pufendorf, 1934, p.1009).

Even early positivist writers, despite their emphasis on the consensual nature of international law, maintained that for the sovereignty of a state to be, as Friedrich Saalfeld put it, 'complete in the Law of Nations', it did not require recognition by other states or rulers because while the 'latter may appear useful, the *de facto* existence of sovereignty is sufficient' (quoted in Crawford, 1978, p.97). What such views also touch on is the fact that the sovereign claims of European powers generally could be taken for granted. Sovereignty could be presumed of states in Europe without significant controversy since the most of the states claiming this status were palpably effective and could function in the international system without being formally recognised by every other member of the system (see Sørensen, 1999, p.596).

To the extent that the sovereignty was seen as thrusting outwards, the social context in which the sovereignty of states was constituted was obscured. Yet the notion that the sovereignty of the state was simply a factual issue, could not have remained uncritically accepted forever. First, during the life of the international system there have always been weak and even marginal states whose existence has very much depended on the support of larger powers, a fact which shows that there has always been more to international recognition than the possession of empirical power (Clapham, 1998, p.144). Second, encounters with non-European communities in which the marks of statehood were absent or obscure were bound to raise the question as to whether different social structures and systems of law should be conceptualised in terms of sovereignty. Recognition of small states in Europe and non-recognition of numerous states and communities outside of that region, irrespective of whether they were effective or not, demonstrates that the question of whether sovereignty was present or absent was not a straightforward factual matter but also involved an element of identification, deliberation and political choice.

In the nineteenth century, legal thinking on statehood took a constitutive turn, a development which some suggest reveals the influence of Hegel's legal thought (Raič, 2002, p.29). Oppenheim explained that the constitutive approach in the context of international law means that the state became ' an International Person and a subject of International Law' through 'recognition only and exclusively'. It followed from this that 'no new State has by International Law a right to demand recognition', although Oppenheim conceded that there are strong pragmatic reasons as to why recognition of a new state cannot be denied indefinitely (Oppenheim, 1912, pp.116–18; see also Alexandrowicz, 1969, p.467). Indeed, according to Crawford the 'predominant' nineteenth-century view, as a consequence of the extension of positivist thinking further into this field, was that 'there were no rules determining what were "States" for the purposes of other international law rules; the matter was within the discretion of existing recognized States' (Crawford, 1978, pp.95–6; see also Grant, 1999, p.3).[28]

Statehood was thus dependent upon a somewhat arbitrary policy of diplomatic recognition and this meant, according to Crawford, that the international law of the time, which was then of a highly decentralised nature, manifested 'a formal incoherence', a condition that could only be overcome by the 'development of an international law of territorial status independent of recognition' (Crawford, 1978, pp.95–6). One important consequence of constitutive recognition, as Kelsen points out , is that the 'legal existence of a state' comes to acquire a 'relative character.' That is, as Kelsen states, a 'state exists legally only in its relations to other states. There is no such thing as absolute existence' (Kelsen, 1941, p.609).[29] An appreciation of this point is crucial if we are to avoid state solipsism, however, *reductio ad absurdum*, it also holds out the danger of making a state's existence wholly dependent on the passing whims of other states, at least aside from such recognition that can be compelled by force. Where the will to recognise is the determinant of statehood one can hardly regard it as a legal condition; a state's personality would simply exist and 'not exist according to the expressed mental dispositions of the governing authorities of other States' (Williams, 1929 p.58). Showing an understanding of this problem, Bluntschli restated the earlier position that sovereignty emanates from within:

> The new State has the right to enter into the international association of States and to be recognized by other Powers, when its existence cannot be put in doubt and is assured. It has this right because it exists, and because International Law unites the States which exist in the world by common rules and principles, based on justice and humanity (Bluntschli, 1874, p.75).

The constitutive approach to statehood, where it makes that status wholly dependent on political acts of recognition, may do an injustice to those whose existence is denied and may also place unwanted burdens on the rest of the international community. The unrecognised state remains outside the 'pale of those rights and duties which', as Lord Canning argued in urging the recognition of the states of Latin America in March 1825, 'civilised nations are bound mutually to respect, and are entitled reciprocally to claim from each other' (quoted in Williams, 1929, pp.57–8). Yet, positivists were also correct in arguing that statehood could not merely be a declaratory matter whereby recognition is simply an 'acknowledgement of statehood already achieved' and, by virtue of this already achieved statehood, a duty on the part of the recognising state (Grant, 1999, p.4). This is because for every new state that emerges and becomes a subject of international 'new legal obligations...[are]...created for existing States'. This is the reason why it was considered necessary that there be 'consent – either to the creation of the State itself or to its being subject to international law with respect to the States affected' (Crawford, 1978, p.97).

Despite the prevalence of the constitutive position in the nineteenth century, the positivist position on what recognition entailed remained 'ambiguous' in that it encompassed both declaratory and constitutive approaches. Recognition was seen by positivists 'as either as a practical codification of established status, or as an expression of a political act which created this status' (Österud, 1997, p.172). This ambiguity could not be avoided. While there is an important sense in which recognition of the sovereignty of a state is an effect of intersubjective understandings among members of international society, at the same time, to make a very basic point, sovereignty cannot exist weightlessly: one cannot begin to conceive of an entity as sovereign in the absence of a population inhabiting a more or less determinate piece of territory. And as indicated, the sheer presence of a people and territory, irrespective of whether recognition is withheld or not, may have implications for international relations. For this reason, those states which were not recognised as sovereign equals, as well as 'native peoples with some form of regular government', were in the nineteenth century routinely 'given the benefit of, and thought to be obliged by, the whole *corpus* of international law', something which was by implication a significant concession to the declaratory school (Crawford, 1978, p.97). At the same time, even though it might seem that the recognition of effective entities is seamless, since effectiveness is so perceptually and politically compelling, there is always a constitutive dimension to the process of recognition. This is because effectiveness, at least as a legal criterion for statehood, amounts to more than brute presence. The status of effectiveness as a criterion for statehood depends on a common understanding that effectiveness has legal significance and that it is a condition which is considered *prima facie* worthy of respect. Indeed, if effectiveness were purely a factual matter its legal significance would be irrelevant.

Further, the presence in Europe of states which were considerably smaller and less powerful than, for example, Britain or France, showed that the notion of statehood was not in the nineteenth century reduced to mere power. Effectiveness, to the extent that it was the central criterion for statehood, could denote anything from the capacity to deter or fend off attacks to possession of a stable government happily independent of others. It was well understood in the nineteenth century that, assuming some measure of effectiveness, states had a right to autonomy irrespective of their differing capacities to defend that autonomy. The institution of the balance of power reflected this understanding: it reflected an appreciation of the fact that a legal structure ascribing formal equality to actors with differing levels of strength, could never be purely a self-help system if it were to stay intact and guarantee the legal rights of its members. This is not to deny the balance of power operated in an ambiguous way. As Cobban notes, it could serve to protect the national independence of small states but it could also serve as a pretext for eliminating small states, as exemplified by the decisions made at the Congress of Vienna concerning the partitioning of Poland and the annexation of Genoa (Cobban, 1969, p.188).[30] The fact that such decisions contravened an important element in the thinking behind the balance of power was reflected in a speech in the House of Commons by Sir James Mackintosh in April 1815 in which he stated in relation to the Genoan annexation, that to 'destroy independent nations in order to strengthen the balance of power, is a most extravagant sacrifice of the end to the means' (quoted Cobban, 1969, p.189).

Since there were no formal rules of recognition in the nineteenth century effectiveness was more of a political than a legal criterion for statehood: not all entities which were arguably effective were routinely recognised. Nor could we say that the alternative criterion of the standard of civilisation was a legal criterion given that its application was selective and given the conflicting and often confused definitions of it, as discussed in the next chapter. However, what the notion of the standard of civilisation did reveal was that it was possible to think about the criteria for statehood in ways other than effectiveness. This point is reinforced by the fact that the Treaty of Berlin, issuing from the Berlin Conference in 1878, in its articles concerning the recognition of Montenegro, Serbia and Romania as well as the autonomy of Bulgaria, declared that 'differences of religious belief or denomination should not be a reason for excluding or disqualifying any person from the enjoyment of civil and political rights' (Bentwich, 1933, pp.76–7).[31] Although decried as discriminatory by some, both critics and supporters saw these particular articles as expressions of the doctrine of *intervention humanitaire*, as elaborated by Bluntschli and others, and setting a precedent for the further intrusion of international law into the internal affairs of states (Renault, 1879, pp.22–5).

The concept of self-determination

According to Gilbert Murray, the expression self-determination in the sense of national self-determination only made its appearance in the context of mid-nineteenth century radical politics in Germany. However, the general idea of self-determination was already in the air in the latter part of the eighteenth century, some two centuries after the concept of state sovereignty was first developed.[32] Whereas sovereignty was a response to the problem of domestic and inter-state disorder, self-determination concerned the idea of the people or nation as the source of the sovereignty of the state. Of course, the notion of sovereignty in philosophical writings and commentaries had always been anchored to the idea of communal flourishing. Yet, the notion of sovereignty as an instrument of virtuous order, has a rather bloodless air about it and it is really only with the concept of self-determination that sovereignty finds its emotional ground. It was through its meeting with the concept of self-determination that this stately abstraction acquired flesh and heat. Indeed, there was almost an inevitability about the encounter between self-determination and sovereignty from the moment when theorists in the sixteenth and seventeenth centuries began to depersonalise and demystify rulership.

With the American Declaration of Independence of 1776 we see an early institutionalisation, at least at the municipal level, of the idea of self-determination as it states that when government becomes 'destructive of...[the]...ends' for which it is instituted, the people have a 'right', and indeed a 'duty', 'to alter or abolish it' (Declaration of Independence, 1776). The legal expression of the concept by the French revolutionaries was broadly similar with the French constitution of 1793 stating in Article 35 that: 'When the government violates the rights of the people, insurrection is for the people, and for every portion of the people, the most sacred of rights and the most indispensable of duties' (quoted in Merriam, 1900, pp.35–6).

As these statements on the rights of peoples or nations highlight, unlike the concept of sovereignty, the concept of self-determination was at the outset associated with internal opposition to and struggle against the established order. Yet, as American and French history (as well as the post-colonial experience of the second half of the twentieth century) shows, once an illegitimate regime is overthrown self-determination and the state quickly align. The state becomes to all effects and purposes the only unit of self-determination. Alfred Cobban notes that the French and the Americans, following their own revolutions, were 'among the strongest opponents of...the right of secession' with the French decreeing on December 16 1792 the 'penalty of death' for 'anyone who attempted to break the unity of the French Republic' and the Americans eventually finding themselves involved in a bitter 'war to keep the Southern States in the Union against their will' (Cobban, 1969, p.136).

In addition to emphasising the internal right of national self-determination, the French revolutionaries placed an emphasis on a nation's right to control its political destiny without interference by foreign powers, not surprisingly given the potential for counter-revolutionary intervention against the new French state (Doehring, 1994, pp.58–9). It was precisely the norm of non-intervention that the National Assembly was giving expression to in stating in its war declaration of April 20 1792 that: 'Every nation has alone the power of making its laws and the inalienable right of changing them' (quoted in Bluntschli, 2000, p.392). This norm continued to harden in the nineteenth century, a process which was aided by the incorporation of Latin American states into the international system during the first quarter of that century (Jianming, 2000, p.23). In their struggle to throw off the Spanish yoke Latin American leaders, like the French revolutionaries before them, drew inspiration from the legal thought of the anti-imperialist Bentham (Bentham, 1968, p.16).[33] After having achieved their liberation and following President Monroe's enunciation of the Monroe Doctrine opposing any European interventions in America's region in 1823, Latin American states would go on to endorse 'the principle of non-intervention at international meetings in 1826 and 1848' (Krasner, 1999, p.21). Also worth recalling in this context, is the publication of Calvo's highly regarded study of the theory and practice of international law in 1868 in which he proclaimed, having warned like Bentham before him that foreign dependencies came at too great a cost to colonial powers, that the 'acquisition of colonies and territories situated at a distance more or less great' from a metropolitan power could no longer be considered a justification for intervention' (Calvo, 1887, p.208).

Despite Calvo's urging, it would be a long time before the colonial powers came to accept that colonial intervention was illegitimate. However, when it came to international relations in Europe itself, there was growing acceptance of the principle of non-intervention. Indeed, acceptance of this principle was implied by the institution of the Congress system, a system which was premised on the principle sovereign equality (something which had been strongly championed at the Congress of Vienna), and, as already indicated, the mechanism of the balance of power.

Self-determination and the League of Nations

With the French Revolution, the notion of the 'nation unified in a state' gained clarity and form. It was a notion that greatly stirred movements aimed at overcoming political separation as well as overthrowing old regimes, inspiring in particular the movement for Italian unification. In was in his lecture at Turin in 1851 entitled '*Della nazionalità come fondamento del diritto delle genti*' ('Nationality as the Basis of the Law of Nations') that Mancini articulated the principle of nationality and 'justified the ethos of self-determination by associating it with the Declaration of Independence, the "*Déclaration des droits de l'homme et du citoyen*" and the works of Locke, Rousseau and Kant' (Weissberg, 1965, p.181). For Mancini, a people 'politically united by natural and historical factors' or who possessed 'the consciousness of common nationality' had a right under the law of nations to form an independent state. Although acquiring much fame, Mancini's doctrine failed to win legal acceptance because of the 'impossibility', political, practical and definitional, 'of accepting nations' or peoples 'rather than states as subjects of international relations' (Nussbaum, 1954, p.240; see also Bluntschli, 1874, p.70).[34] Even so, there was a growing tendency in the nineteenth century to view nations as representing 'a natural structure' of humankind, an idea which complemented and reinforced the notion of sovereignty as being vested in the state or nation rather than in a monarchical person (Doehring, 1994, p.59).

The political understanding of the word nation had prevailed in France since the eighteenth century and as late as 1878 the Dictionary of the *Academie Française* was giving as its primary definition of the nation, 'the totality of persons borne or naturalised in a country and living under a single government' (quoted in Cobban, 1969, p.30). However, in the latter part of the nineteenth century there was a general shift away from defining the national self politically towards defining it in ethno-cultural terms.[35] In his renowned 1882 lecture '*Qu'est-ce qu'une nation?*', Ernest Renan warned that the tendency to confound 'race with nation' and to attribute to 'ethnographic or rather linguistic groups a sovereignty analogous to the one of actually existing peoples' was a 'fatal' error (Renan, 2007, p.1).[36] Nonetheless, such an error in thinking won significant adherents among national minorities within the Ottoman, Austro-Hungarian and Russian empires. At first, this lead to demands for enhanced independence. However, these were soon followed, against a background of harsher and 'increasingly assimilationist' measures and in a context in which these empires were beginning 'to weaken militarily and politically', by calls for complete autonomy (Hannum, 1990, p.27).

President Woodrow Wilson viewed nationalist agitation and its suppression, as well as the race for colonies, as among the major causes of the First World War. Wilson's Fourteen Points, which provided the basis of the Covenant of the League of Nations, tentatively endorsed the principle of self-determination in stating therein that the 'world is to be made fit and safe...for every peace-loving nation which, like our own, wishes to live its own life...and...determine its own institutions' (quoted in Murray, 1922, p.6).[37] However, while the principle was current at the end of the First World War and was mentioned in the initial American version of the Covenant, no consensus could be reached on its meaning at the Paris Peace Conference and so it was not included in the final draft (Crawford, 1978, p.149n). Further, as stated in 1920 in the Report of the International Committee of Jurists appointed by the Council of the League to address the question of whether the Aland Islands could legitimately secede from Finland, its 'recognition in a certain number of international treaties' was not considered 'sufficient to put it upon the same footing as a positive rule of international law' (quoted in Hannum, 1990, p.29). As Hurst Hannum notes, in the period immediately after the First World War self-determination was 'considered only for "nations" which were within the territory of the defeated empires' and it was never considered to 'apply to overseas colonies' (Hannum, 1990, p.28).

However, there was a very limited attempt at decolonisation under the League of Nations. Under Article 22 of the League Covenant the colonies of Germany and some Ottoman territories, because their inhabitants were as yet unready 'to stand by themselves under the strenuous conditions of the modern world', were to be brought under the 'tutelage' of 'advanced nations'. In other words, the colonies and territories in question were to be made Mandates of the League of Nations with tutelage being exercised on behalf of the League by those states which were willing to act as Mandatories. Article 22 further specified that the 'well-being and development' of the peoples in Mandate territories was a 'sacred trust of civilisation and that securities for the performance of this trust should be embodied' (First World War.com). Mandate, a term derived from Roman private law signifying delegation, was a new instrument of international law and was designed to replace the traditional way of dealing with the colonies of defeated powers: annexation. Annexation was a solution which President Wilson could not accept and one which was also vigorously denounced by the Russian Bolsheviks (Nussbaum, 1954, pp.254–5; Korman, 1996, pp.136–8).[38] However, Nussbaum argues that while in principle the mandate system involved 'delegation of power by the League' to the mandatory state, in effect 'the mandate gave such a state full political dominance'. Thus, he claims it 'differed only from annexation by an obligation to render annual reports and by a number of duties or prohibitions, the observance of which was practically left to the discretion of the mandatory' (Nussbaum, 1954, p.255).

The Mandate territories were divided into three categories: A, B and C. These categories were applied to the various Mandates depending on a people's level of social and economic progress and other factors such as their 'geographical situation' (United Nations Library of Geneva, 1996, p.134). The authors of the Mandate regime believed that middle-eastern Mandates which formed the A category would be able, within a short period of time, to 'stand alone', as was the case with Iraq which achieved statehood under this system in 1932 to be followed by Syria and Lebanon in 1944 and Jordan in 1946 (Louis, 1985, p.201).[39] However, concerning the 'peoples of tropical Africa' in the B category, it was believed that it would take an extended period for them to achieve a level of progress which would warrant their independence. As for the 'primitive' peoples of the Pacific and the Hottentots of South West Africa in the C category, it was expected that their acquisition of statehood would take 'a period of centuries' if it were to be achieved at all (Louis, 1985, p.201).

Crawford argues that the Mandate system, like the UN's International Trusteeship System which succeeded it, was an 'assertion of international interest at a much earlier stage in the process towards independence than international law at the time allowed', noting in particular that the system made available to Mandates the principle of self-determination (Crawford, 1978, p.153). Wm. Roger Louis concurs with this view, stating that the system marked to some degree a 'triumph of internationalism of over nationalism, humanitarianism over slavery and self-determination over imperialism' and thus he refers to the period between 1919 and 1945 as one of 'enlightened imperialism' (Louis, 1985, p.204). Yet he too concludes, even though acknowledging that the Mandate system was innovative in terms of its insistence on the international accountability of mandatory states, that the Mandate territories were, as was stated at the time, 'colonies in all but name' and that the system continued to be underscored by colonial era assumptions about race (Louis, 1985, pp.202–3).

Since after the First World War there has been controversy over whether self-determination implies merely national self-determination or democratic self-determination. For some, rule by 'kith and kin' is a sufficient condition for self-determination (Neuberger, 1995, p.300). However, while one might agree that national self-rule might be preferable to alien rule, the idea of national self-determination, understood narrowly, elides the democratic origins of the concept. If we accept that self-determination is not simply a one-off consent to a form of government but involves its continuous affirmation, then it seems hard to escape the conclusion that it entails genuine involvement in the activity of government (Hannum, 1990, p.30).[40] Renan famously encapsulated this way of thinking about self-determination in stating that the existence of a nation is a *'plebiscite de tous les jours'* (Renan, 1882, p.58; see also Cobban, 1969, p.131). The only way of overcoming the dangers posed by separating self-determination from popular sovereignty, as Mayall puts it, is by a 'collectivist sleight of hand' whereby we assume the complete identification of the ruled with the rulership (Mayall, 1999, p.483). Such an assumption is not well founded given that there exists in all states a gap between the rulership and the ruled and that all states exhibit degrees of social heterogeneity aspects of which the state may seek to suppress. As Michla Pomerance argues, when it comes to the application of the principle of self-determination, one cannot avoid asking the crucial question: 'who is the "self" to whom' this right is attached. Nor can one avoid reaching the conclusion that 'recognition of the rights of one "self" entails a denial of the rights of a competing "self"' (Pomerance, 1982, p.2).

It was the understanding of self-determination as democratic self-determination that Woodrow Wilson (who tried unsuccessfully to make democracy a qualification for the League), and Lloyd George sought to apply in Eastern Europe after the Versailles negotiations. However, Kedourie points out that this principle was misunderstood in Eastern Europe where nationally based self-determination rather than the principle of popular self-government was emphasised (Kedourie, 1966, p.133; see also Neuberger, 1995, p.300 and Herman, 1996, p.50).[41] In the Balkans too, where the redrawing of national boundaries had also seen the emergence of state formations containing 'compact masses of foreign populations' whose own dreams of self-government lay unfulfilled, self-determination meant determination by the dominant national group (Hrissimova, 1996, p.45). Partly due to his consciousness of the international repercussions of minority agitation and its suppression in the Balkans at the close of the nineteenth century and at the beginning of the twentieth century, Wilson sought to persuade 'his allies to set up a programme of ethnic minority protection' in the newly founded as well as some already established states (Herman, 1996, p.50; see also Thornberry, 1989, p.869). The Minorities Treaties, most of which were executed in the years 1919 to 1921, were the chief instruments of this programme. The Treaties contained provisions concerning the right of minorities to 'nationality, to life, personal freedom, freedom of religion, equality before the laws of the host countries, equal civic, political and cultural rights, and freedom to use the mother tongue' (Hrissimova, 1996, p.46).[42]

Albert Geouffre de Lapradelle, in commenting on the Minorities Treaties in 1925, noted that their precedent was the Treaty of Berlin of 1878. As we saw, this Treaty recognised certain states 'under the condition that they undertook certain obligations', something which de Lapradelle regarded as 'an initial case of intervention in the cause of humanity'. As regards the minorities regime, de Lapradelle stated that is was a 'further exemplification of this same principle, only in a more complete, fully developed and better organised form' (quoted in Heyking, 1927, p.36n). Certainly, the countries in question resented what they saw as an incursion on their sovereignty and were indignant over the fact that not all states were required to commit themselves to the same human rights regime. Thus, they had to be compelled to sign the treaties 'under threat of being denied international recognition of their independence', something which rendered the Minorities regime according to Joost Herman a 'unique experiment in international law' (Herman, 1996, p.51).

William Rappard, the former head of the Mandates Section of the League Secretariat, took a more cynical view of the Treaties stating that they were 'palliative' given in 'lieu of self-determination' (quoted in Heyking, 1927, p.34n; Herman, 1996, p.49). Rappard was correct to the extent that the treaties only accorded a limited right of self-determination to peoples who were petitioning for complete independence from their state (Hannum, 1990, p.31).[43] The Minorities Commission which oversaw the regime certainly did not see the Treaties as entailing a right of unilateral secession. The Commission, in addressing the question of the Aland Islands in 1921, proclaimed that should minorities have a right of withdrawal from a functioning state 'order and stability within States' would be destroyed and 'anarchy in international life' would be inaugurated. The idea of a right of secession the Commission added, was 'incompatible with the very idea of the State as a territorial and political unity', a view which continues to be defended strongly by states today (quoted in Hannum, 1990, p.30).

In his 1914 discussion of 'The Right of Nations to Self-Determination' Lenin forcefully asserted that self-determination meant the 'political separation' of a nation from 'alien national bodies, and the formation of an independent state.' He dismissed the understanding of self-determination, as propagated by Otto Bauer and Rosa Luxembourg among others, as 'cultural-national autonomy' within the confines of the state as merely 'psychological' and historically backward (Lenin, 1972, pp.2–5; see also Neuberger, 1995, p.310). However, it was precisely this second, relativised understanding of self-determination, rather than Lenin's early understanding of self-determination as a right of secession, that was applied by the League's Minority Section in Eastern Europe and the Balkans. Baron A. Heyking told a meeting of the Grotius Society in 1924, that the need for a minorities' regime revealed the 'bankruptcy of the principle of national self-determination' as its effect was to turn the state in which it was applied into a racial unit rather than a purely 'juridic organism.' Nonetheless, Heyking applauded the extension of the principle of self-determination to minority groups within states, noting that in according it to these groups one preserved self-determination's moral force in relation to nations as a whole. Heyking's main concern lay with the weakness of the regime: with its enforcement mechanisms. For this reason, he argued that minorities should be given the legal status of *'personnes morales'* not only within their state but also without, thus permitting them to 'approach the Council of the League of Nations on equal terms with the representatives of Governments' (Heyking, 1924, pp.144–5, 150).[44]

It is not surprising that with the formation of new states under the Mandate system, the application of the principle of self-determination and the imposition of human rights obligations on states subject to the Minorities regime, attention turned to the question of whether international recognition had a 'creative efficacy' (Williams, 1929, p.54). These developments cast a clearer light on the role played by international society in the construction and maintenance of state identity. After World War One, legal opinion tended to the view, as stated by Paul Fauchille, that recognition 'is declaratory and does not constitute, create or attribute international personality', a position supported by jurists in the Aland Islands case and the German-Polish Mixed Arbitral Tribunal in 1929 (quoted in Williams, 1929, p.54n).[45] Sir John Fischer Williams, in discussing this 'new doctrine of recognition', agreed that recognition was not a '"creative" or "constitutive" act' when it came to the recognition of either new states or new governments, although he added that it could have a 'preservative' effect (Williams, 1929, pp.63, 75; see also Crawford, 1979, p.74). Further, he suggested in relation to new governments, that it was not always necessary to recognise every seemingly 'stable situation of fact' (Williams, 1932, p.115). While stable situations of fact generally should be recognised, it may be necessary on occasion to 'subordinate' recognition to the 'general present purposes of International Law – the maintenance of civilisation as a whole' (Williams, 1929, p.76; Williams, 1932, pp.115–16). At the same time, Williams added, for reasons of fairness and equity determinations as to when the general rule might be overridden should be made by an international body rather than left to the discretion of individual states (Williams, 1929, p.76; Williams, 1932, p.116).

The shift away from the nineteenth century emphasis on political recognition as constitutive of statehood to recognition based on 'empirical prerequisites' was exemplified by the adoption in 1933 of the *Convention on the Rights and Duties of States*, otherwise known as the Montevideo Convention (Crawford, 1978, p.111).[46] Implicit in the Montevideo Convention was that 'actual independence' was the key criterion for statehood and that where such an effective situation existed recognition was a legal obligation on the part of existing states (Österud, 1997, p.175). At the same time, a constitutive element was implied by the Convention in that effectiveness could only be rendered a legal criterion where there was a shared understanding that it should be. Further, as Williams' observations indicate and as exemplified by the Minorities Treaties, interwar thinking on the issue of recognition did not rule out the possibility that grounds other than effectiveness might be applicable in certain cases. Indeed, by the late twentieth century in international relations discourse it was widely accepted that compliance with internationally recognised human rights norms was necessary to achieving 'international legitimacy and full membership in international society', although post-Cold War state practice in this regard has not lived up to the rhetoric (Donnelly, 1998, p.21; Österud, 1997, pp.183–4).

Self-determination and the United Nations

The attitude towards colonial peoples at the end of World War II was much the same as it had been in 1919 with the fifth Marquess of Salisbury referring at the San Francisco Conference to the '"colonial ladder" which colonial peoples would climb at their own time and pace' (Louis, 1985, p.203). The League's Mandate System was transformed into the UN Trusteeship system, a system which was based on the same paternalistic premise: that it was the sacred trust of civilisation 'to promote the political, economic, social, and educational advancement of the inhabitants of trust territories and their progressive development towards self-government or independence as may be appropriate in the particular circumstances of each territory and its people' (UN Charter Articles 73 [b] and 76[b]). However this system, one which left the ultimate decision as to a people's preparedness for statehood with certain 'civilised' countries, could not remain in place for too long given the other historical forces at work. Cold War political imperatives, the increasing cost of sustaining colonies and local resistance were all factors which favoured the dismantling of empires. Domestic civil rights movements in western states aimed at ending minority oppression further strengthened anti-colonial thinking. However, the main reason why decolonisation took place so rapidly according to Jackson, is that there had been a change in norms: from criteria for statehood which emphasised empirical capacity to criteria centred on the principle of self-determination (Jackson, 1990, pp.15–16).

In order to undermine the moral authority of western countries the Soviet Union had pushed for self-determination to be included in the Charter: as a right of peoples under imperial domination. However, this was rejected in the course of the Charter's drafting. Obviously, imperial interests would not have favoured such an inclusion. Yet, this was not the only reason for its exclusion. Hannum points that one reason why the principle of self-determination did not 'rise to the level of a rule of international law' in the context of drafting the UN Charter was because of the experience of national self-determination after World War One (Hannum, 1990, p.33). The two references to the principle of self-determination in the Charter are contained in Articles 1(2) and 55 and speak of self-determination in relation to the development of 'friendly relations among nations' and in connection with the 'equal rights...of peoples' (Hannum, 1990, p.33).[47] However, while at the outset the word peoples was generally considered interchangeable with the word states, in midst of the 'moral and political imperative of decolonization' this restrictionist interpretation was overtaken. Thus, the 'vague "principle" of self-determination soon evolved into the "right" of self-determination' (Hannum, 1990, p.33).

The UN General Assembly's Declaration on the Granting of Independence to Colonial Countries and Peoples of 14 December 1960 proclaimed, in a clear repudiation of the racialist premises that underlay the imperialist system, 'the necessity of bringing to a speedy and unconditional end colonialism in all its forms and manifestations', that 'all peoples have the right to self-determination' and that '[i]nadequacy of political, economic, social or educational preparedness should never serve as a pretext for delaying independence' (Declaration on the Granting of Independence to Colonial Countries and Peoples, 1960). The relevant subject of this right to self-determination now included those 'territories whose peoples have not yet attained a full measure of self-government' as described in Chapter XI of the Charter, that is, colonial peoples (quoted in Crawford, 1978, p.153). The day after the Colonial Declaration was issued, and in an effort to clarify the meaning of the expression non-self-governing territories, the General Assembly passed Resolution 1541. This Resolution limited such territories to 'those "which were then known to be of the colonial type"'; self-determination was 'to apply only to colonies, not to nations or regions within existing states or within the territory of colonies once they became independent' (Philpott, 2001, p.156). Effectively, this meant that the subjects of this right were people living in 'colonial situations' as well as the peoples, taken as a whole, of existing states (Hannum, 1990, p.46).

Crawford maintains that self-determination continues to be less a right under international law than a legal principle. That is, self-determination, as with sovereignty, is 'not a right applicable directly to any group of people desiring political independence....[as]...it applies only as a matter of right only after the unit of self-determination has been determined by the application of appropriate rules' (Crawford, 1978, p.160).[48] For decolonisation to take place, non self-governing territories had to be determined to be self-determination units. This process of determination was, at least in an informal sense, more or less declaratory, more or less constitutive depending on the circumstances. In any case, while the principle was undeniably emancipatory for a period it quickly aligned itself with the sovereignty of the post-colonial state and the new boundaries quickly became as 'sacred, and consequently as unnegotiable, as the old' (Mayall, 1999, p.487). These new boundaries were challenged by secessionist groups who, taking the idea of self-determination to heart and concluding that self-determination was in fact a 'fundamental human right', insisted that 'it should apply to them' (Mayall, 1999, p.482). Such a conclusion is not surprising given that the term people was never clearly defined, yet however comprehensible was this conclusion, it is not one that finds support among states (Peang-Meth, 2002, p.110). 'No State', as Pomerance notes, 'has accepted the right of *all* peoples to self-determination. Only the States which acknowledged the "colonial" nature of their rule may arguably have conceded the right of self-determination as applicable against *themselves*' (Pomerance, 1982, p.46).

The 1960 Colonial Declaration, while supporting the right of 'self-determination of all peoples' in the context of decolonisation, nonetheless cautioned that 'any attempt at the partial or total disruption of the national unity and territorial integrity of a country' would stand in contradiction to the principles and purposes of the UN Charter (Declaration on the Granting of Independence to Colonial Countries and Peoples, 1960). The 1970 UN Declaration of Friendly Relations and Cooperation Among States continued in the same vein insisting that nothing should be done that 'that would dismember or impair, totally or in part, the territorial integrity or political unity of sovereign and independent States' (Declaration on Principles of International Law, Friendly Relations and Co-operation Among States in Accordance with the Charter of the United Nations, 1970). It would thus seem that in the post-colonial context, the distinction between self-determination units and sovereign states has been significantly erased. Hannum suggests that African states 'may simply be more honest' than other states in conceding that 'self-determination *of the state*' has triumphed over the notional 'self-determination of peoples that, if taken to its logical conclusion could result in some instances of secession' (Hannum, 1990, p.47).

The obverse of the conflation of the self-determination of peoples with the self-determination of states is the denial of a right to unilateral secession. The problem with according sub-national groups a right of self-determination and thus of unilateral secession is both conceptual and pragmatic. The conceptual problem is this: for a right to exist we must be able to identify the subject of this right and, as things stand, it is impossible to determine *a priori* who might be the recipient of such a right. As Crawford writes, the political understanding of self-determination 'is too vague and ill-defined to constitute a legal principle, much less a positive legal rule applying of its own force to particular "peoples" or to "peoples" in general.' In fact, as a legal principle self-determination is highly limited in scope: it applies to sovereign states and those entities which for a period may be designated units of self-determination by the international community (Crawford, 1978, p.149). On the more practical side, as Cobban observes, the idea of a right of secession is resisted, not simply because governments want to retain their grip on the country's population and territory, but also because secession is often a destructive enterprise and because the acquisition of statehood by a political entity imposes new obligations, possibly burdensome, on the international community. In any case, Cobban argues that the rights which really matter to human beings concern their freedoms and welfare and the protection of these need not require the formation of an independent state. Nonetheless, as he concedes, in certain extreme situations, where antagonisms are such that the people cannot constitute themselves as *a people*, or where the state acts in ways in respect to a portion of its population that gives the latter no choice but to resort to self-help, then unilateral secession may be the only answer (Cobban, 1969, pp.144–5; see also Hannum, 1990, p.4). The principle of territorial integrity must yield in extreme situations to the right of self-determination, understood here as a right of peoples and not simply as a principle applied to already recognised states. Where self-determination is interpreted in such a way that the principle of territorial integrity constantly triumphs over human rights considerations, the expression is emptied of all value and significance: the external self-determination of the state has value only if it facilitates and protects the internal self-determination of peoples (Raič, 2002, p.312). What follows from that, especially given that the international system offers little in the way of support to peoples or groups whose human rights are being abused, is that international law should recognise, under certain circumstances, 'the right of a people to unilaterally separate from the parent State' and it is arguable that contemporary international law, precisely because it recognises a right of internal self-determination, recognises a qualified right of secession (Raič, 2002, pp.312–13, 397).

Sovereignty and contemporary China

Patrick Thornberry notes that during the drafting of the Covenant on Civil and Political rights China, like many other states, insisted that self-determination belongs to 'national majorities and not minorities' and has consistently denied that minorities possess secessionist rights (Thornberry, 1989, p.880; Neuberger, 1995, p.310).[49] China has also taken a leading role in speaking out against western political actors and intellectuals who promote the idea that the traditional understanding of state sovereignty is unable to comprehend the phenomenon of globalisation and is an inappropriate means of dealing with a range of other issues of international concern (Qian, 1995, pp.138–40).

Of course, as with all states, the Chinese state has a naked self-interest in maintaining as much room to manoeuvre as is possible and can be seen as cynically deploying sovereignist, and even exceptionalist, arguments in defending actions which may breach international norms of conduct, such as its military aggression against Taiwan in response to its 1996 democratic elections and before that the state's violent suppression of the 1989 Tiananmen Square protests (Ong, 2004, pp.86–9). As Shambaugh argues, the CCP has a 'vested interest in playing up the history of weakness in the face of Western imperialism' during what it refers to as the 'century of shame and humiliation', as fuelling anti-foreign sentiment and nationalist passion engenders support for the state's foreign policy stance and shores up the legitimacy of the CCP as the ultimate guarantor of the state's security (Shambaugh, 1996, p.204; see also Wu, 2007, p.305 and Hughes, 1997, p.106). Nonetheless, what Edward Wu refers to as China's 'extremely strong, unconditional defense' of state sovereignty is clearly related to a genuine sense of historic grievance (Wu, 2002, p.364). Chinese memories of its hard-fought struggle against imperialism, as described in the opening paragraph of the Preamble to the Chinese Constitution, in the nineteenth and the twentieth centuries are not easily forgotten, and concessions on the issue of the unity and sovereignty of the state still invite accusations of treachery against the state (Fitzgerald, 1995, p.101; see also Chang, 1998, p.85 and Wu, 2007, p.301). Thus, China's experience of imperial intervention helps explain its insistence on the state's unconditional sovereignty over Hong Kong, irrespective of the 'one country, two systems' arrangement, as well as its push for national reunification as regards Taiwan (Wu, 2007, p.304).

China's sensitivity on the question of sovereignty, along with its concerns in relation to the current distribution of global power which it sees as 'structurally biased in favour of the West and against China', also helps explain its unease with human rights internationalism (Shambaugh, 1996, p.187). While China has ratified a number of important human rights conventions it has made reservations to them concerning 'the implementation mechanisms that could influence its national jurisdiction over human rights issues' (Wu, 2002, p.352). China vigorously insists that human rights 'issues fall, by and large, within the domestic jurisdiction' of each state and maintains that accusations of human rights abuses amount to foreign intervention in the sense of a violation of state sovereignty. (Wu, 2002, p.364; see also Wu, 2007, p.305). In addition, China's experience of international inequality from the nineteenth century up until the present inclines it to suspect, although its rhetoric is exaggerated in this regard, that the international human rights agenda, especially where this extends to humanitarian intervention, is a neo-imperialist enterprise (Wu, 2007, p.305; see also Carlson, 2004, p.16).

Concerns in relation to neo-imperialism were reflected in the Bangkok Declaration on human rights by Asian leaders which issued from a meeting of Asian governmental representatives preparatory to the United Nations World Conference on Human Rights in Vienna in 1993 and into which China had considerable input (Wu, 2002, p.357). The Declaration affirmed the principles of 'respect for national sovereignty, territorial integrity as well as non-interference' in a states' internal affairs and insisted that human rights should not be used as an 'instrument of political pressure' (Loh, 1995, p.155). While the Declaration did not deny the need to protect human rights, it nonetheless challenged the notion that there were '"universal standards" of human rights in Asia' (Wu, 2002, p.357). As Wu notes, Asian states adopted a 'relativist position' as regards human rights, emphasising the importance of history, culture and economics to their definition (Wu, 2002, p.357).[50]

Such considerations are raised by the Chinese government in justifying China's communitarian approach to human rights and more specifically, its privileging of 'subsistence' and 'development' rights over that of individual civil and political rights (Wu, 2002, p.367). Article 51 of the 1982 Chinese Constitution stipulates that the 'exercise by citizens of the People's Republic of China of their freedoms and rights may not infringe upon the interests of the state, of society and of the collective, or upon the lawful freedoms and rights of other citizens' (Constitution of the People's Republic of China, 1982). Liu Huaqiu, the leader of the Chinese delegation at the Vienna Conference, echoed this clause in the Constitution in stating that it was a 'universal principle of all civilised societies' that no individual should 'place his own rights and interests above those of the state and society'. He added that 'if the sovereignty of a state is not safeguarded, the human rights of its citizens are out of the question, like a castle in the air' (quoted in Davis, 1995, p.17). Liu is correct to the extent that there is nothing culturally particular about communitarian interpretations of the relation between the individual and society as a whole. All societies organised into states embrace collectivist principles since sovereignty itself is a collective right, whether in the form of a collective right of punishment, taxation or conscription. It is a collective right we impose on ourselves in order to promote individual well being. It is for this reason that the collective rights exercised on our behalf by the state in the form of sovereignty have, as Cobban states, their 'own natural limits', most prominently, 'the duty of respecting the liberties...of the individual'. Yet, precisely because the state is charged with protecting the well being of all, such liberties are not 'absolute' and are 'only to be asserted in the degree in which...[they are]...compatible with organised social life' (Cobban, 1969, p.139).

The crucial issue thus concerns the substance these two considerations are given and the way they are balanced against each other. In this regard, much may hinge on the constitutional form of the state. Wu writes that the 1954 Chinese Constitution (which was superseded by the Constitutions of 1975, 1978 and 1982), failed to 'establish constitutionalism', where that is understood to involve limitations on 'government powers in the interest of individual rights' and instead sought to facilitate the implementation of 'government policy under the absolute leadership of the Communist Party' (Wu, 2002, p.338). The problem here, as Chinese theorists of sovereignty dating back as far as Liang have noted in line with many past and present western critics, while in theory the purpose served by state sovereignty is to protect and promote the freedom of citizens, too often its effective purpose 'becomes the maintenance national sovereignty itself', such that the rights of citizens are subordinated to the claims of the state or rather those who dominate this mechanism (Ogden, 1975, p.221).

As was discussed in relation to Rousseau, in allowing the state to gather up our rights in order to preserve them, we place a powerful instrument in the state's hands and this entails certain risks. The favoured means among western theorists since the eighteenth century of reducing this element of risk has involved the popularisation of sovereignty and the division of power, however, at this stage the Chinese government would support neither of these policies. Chinese leaders have frequently reiterated that China 'will not practise western-style democracy' and have 'shunned the idea of a separation of power among the Communist Party, government and legislature' (Choi, 2007, p.A6). Nonetheless, Wu argues that the 1982 Constitution marks an improvement in the relations between state and society since it obliges the Communist party to act 'within the scope of the Constitution and the law', thus restricting the Party's previously 'unlimited' control over the Chinese state and Chinese people. Chapter 2 of the Constitution spells out the rights and duties of Chinese citizens and in this regard, it is considerably 'more detailed and elaborate than the corresponding parts of the three previous State constitutions' (Wu, 2002, p.341). Among the rights listed are nearly all those rights that one would expect a citizen to enjoy in a liberal-democratic state including, under Article 33 the principle of 'equality before the law', something which had been earlier rejected as a 'bourgeois' notion (Wu, 2002, pp.341–2). This Article was amended in

March 2004 with the inclusion of a third paragraph reading: 'The State respects and preserves human rights' (Constitution of the People's Republic of China, 1982).

Of course, many of the rights listed in the 1982 Constitution exist largely in a formal sense at this stage. Further, there are other inclusions in the 1982 Constitution that are continuous with the idea that Chinese citizens remain in many ways, 'subjects under the state's supreme sovereignty' (Wu, 2007, p.298). Louis Henkin, while conceding that the PRC has advanced beyond the 'hierarchism of traditional China' notes that the Constitution, 'does not claim to be a contract among the people establishing the state' but is rather a 'manifesto, by the leaders to the people'. Although the Constitution in its preamble is asserted to be the 'fundamental law' of the Chinese state, the unfortunate fact is that there are no independent institutions to determine its meaning and 'enforce it against high political authority' (Henkin, 1986, pp.26–7). At the same time, economic reform in China has lead to much greater levels of complexity in Chinese society and to the formation of national and transnational linkages of both an economic and cultural kind and these developments in turn have important implications for civil society and political identity. As Fitzgerald argues, changes in the Chinese economy and society mean that the Chinese Communist 'party-state' no longer has the stage to itself and that its leaders are increasingly less able to do 'just as they please without bringing their own identity and legitimacy into question' (Fitzgerald, 1995, pp.101–2; see also Waldren, 1995, pp.22–3).[51]

While any radical makeover of the Chinese state is at present out of the question, it is likely that it will have to reach further accommodations with Chinese society. As some officials are recognising, accommodation could be reached through giving further substance to the Chinese citizen's constitutionally enshrined rights and might also involve greater governmental transparency and accountability, especially through democratisation of the Communist Party and the awarding of important governmental roles to leaders from outside the party (Choi, 2007, p.A6).

Assuming a greater role in the international arena may also render the Chinese state more dependent on the goodwill and support of its citizenry. It may become less defensive about its sovereignty and more willing to embrace an international society approach to international relations. Some argue that as China's confidence has increased (through the recognition it has received due to its participation in international institutions such as the World Trade Organisation, and through improvements in certain bilateral relations, notably with the EU), it has shown a greater willingness to constructively engage with the outside world, not least because there is an appreciation that this is a means of enhancing China's sovereignty (Garrison, 2005, p.29). Fitzgerald argues that China's adoption of an international society approach would be consistent with modern Chinese history since, as we have seen, Chinese nationalists called upon international law, both before and after China's entry into the League of Nations, in seeking to liberate China from foreign domination. For this as well as other reasons, the rule of international law, as is also reflected in the Preamble to the Constitution of 1982, has assumed a great importance in Chinese thinking (Fitzgerald, 1995, p.103; see also Carlson, 2003, p.697 and Hughes, 1997, p.116). Further to this, he points out that an international society approach would also be consonant with China's 'One World' ethical tradition (Fitzgerald, 1995, p.103).[52]

Becoming sovereign

As Clapham observes, post-colonial and less developed states have been among the 'most strident defenders of Westphalian sovereignty', something which is hardly surprising given their history and their vulnerability to international pressures (Clapham, 1999, pp.522–3). However, he contends that the invocation of sovereignty in the post-colonial context, similar to its invocation in early modern Europe, is less often a defence against an unjust world than a means by which rulers 'assert...unfettered control...over their own domestic populations' (Clapham, 1999, pp.525–6). Clapham is referring, in particular to those states which Jackson has named 'quasi-states', that is, states which possess juridical sovereignty, in the sense that they have obtained external recognition, but which lack 'substantial and credible statehood by the empirical criteria of classical positive international law' (Jackson, 1990, pp.21–2; see also Clapham, 1998, p.144 and Clapham, 1999, pp.524–5).

While Jackson acknowledges that 'international inequality' is not new, he argues that it is far more substantial than in the past. The reason for this is that in the past 'small and weak states had to survive as best they could by their own efforts and those of whatever allies' they could muster. Indeed, the international struggle for survival was part of the reason why states sought in the nineteenth century to renegotiate their relation with society and win its support. In any case, according to Jackson the contemporary context is one in which 'insubstantial states', instead of having to rely on self-help, are 'exempted from the power contest at least in part and treated as international protectorates' (Jackson, 1990, pp.22–3). To the extent that it does not emanate from within but is merely a gift of the international community, the sovereignty of quasi-states can be regarded as inauthentic. As Daniel L. Blaney and Naeem Inayatullah put it in their gloss on Jackson, the sovereignty of quasi-states is 'legitimated and supported only as artefacts of the constitutive principles of international society' (Blaney and Inayatullah, 1996, p.86). Accepting this, it can be argued that it is the post-colonial sovereignty regime, through effectively according not insignificant powers to governments prone to incompetence, tyranny and corruption and then effectively protecting those governments by guaranteeing their borders, that has failed many of the people living in post-colonial states. The sovereignty regime can thus be seen as an a powerful obstacle to the expression of authentic self-determination in many parts of the post-colonial world.

Clapham argues that even though in all probability the sovereign state system will continue to fail in many parts of the world, its formal structure is likely to be left intact by larger players. This is not so much out of respect for the principle of sovereignty but through indifference, because of the costs involved in external management or intervention in 'delinquent Third World states' as well as the likelihood that any such intervention will fail (Clapham, 1999, p.535). A restoration of the Mandate system is not to be expected, although we might say that in relation to some states it continues to function except in an informal and less restrictive fashion (Jackson, 1990, p.187). Thus, apart from those states located in parts of the world where large interests are at stake, weak states 'are likely to be left to sink or swim on their own', with some returning to the pre-imperial situation where local potentates and 'warlords make deals with intermediaries of the global economy' (Clapham, 1999, pp.535, 537).[53]

In contrast with Jackson, Blaney and Inayatullah, while not dismissing depictions of 'corrupt, incompetent and repressive rulers, emptied treasuries and full prisons', emphasise the fact that judicial statehood independence remains an important achievement for former colonial peoples. This is so even if their sovereignty, in the sense of collective self-determination, is yet to be 'fully' realised (Blaney and Inayatullah, 1996, p.86). In this regard, the problem is not so much the failure of sovereignty (although one may well point to failures as regards the implementation of the post-colonial sovereignty regime), but rather its complete absence. Mark E. Denham and Mark Owen Lombardi acknowledge the problem of granting international personality to entities which, although formally sovereign, have been unable to 'inculcate and socialize their widely disparate populations into a universal, sovereign source of identity and authority' (Denham and Lombardi, 1996, p.3). The fact that, as they explain, the concept of sovereignty did not establish itself in many post-colonial states was not simply because official action was deficient. It was also because the necessary props of sovereignty, namely communal identification and a shared sense of belonging, were lacking in many post-colonial states to the extent that these states were not historically grounded (Denham and Lombardi, 1996, p.3).

The sovereignty-less internal condition may place communities in the South at the forefront of efforts to find alternative modes of political organisation to that of the sovereign state (Denham and Lombardi, 1996, p.8). However, this is unlikely given that sovereignty has been enthusiastically accepted in the post-colonial world and is jealously defended by it. Blaney and Inayatullah maintain that sovereignty is valued because it places 'limits on outside interference', although by no means absolute limits. They argue that of the uppermost importance is the 'dignity of the people' in terms of its 'right to rule itself' and that modes of political and social organisation 'must be worked out over time, primarily by the citizens themselves'. Rather than being a dead concept sovereignty remains, they insist, an 'unfulfilled promise for the Third World' (Blaney and Inayatullah, 1996, pp.83, 86–7).

What is at stake then is the becoming sovereign of states which are, internally speaking, incomplete in this regard. International personality alone cannot create sovereignty, as fundamentally it must come from within. As indicated, the basis of sovereignty is fragile in many post-colonial states because there is a lack of identification between state and society or a weak sense of communal belonging. In addition to these issues, there is also the difficulty of achieving the level of economic capacity that is necessary to sustain their juridical independence. This economic incapacity is held up as the defining feature of the quasi-state, however, it should not be seen as a purely internal condition as it also clearly concerns the organisation of the international economy (Blaney and Inayatullah, 1996, pp.85, 91).

One response to these problems combines elements of the ethical idealist and new liberal streams of thought which were current in late nineteenth century and early twentieth century Britain. These streams of thought ultimately fed through to the concept of the social welfare state and were based on the idea that the state had positive role to play, as T.H. Green put it, in removing those 'obstacles', whether economic, educational or medical, 'to the realisation of the capacity for beneficial exercise of rights' (Green, 1999, p.160). Indeed, Green thought this role formed the basis of political obligation, not only of the 'citizens towards the state' but also of 'individuals to each other' (Green 1999, p.5). In a similar way, it is argued that it is the role of international society to assist its members to construct authentic and flourishing sovereign selves through greater economic assistance. There are historical precedents for this given that the sovereign state system has never been fully predicated on self-help. Nor can it be since sovereignty is not the mere physical power to assert oneself but is a legal status that can only be preserved by virtue of mutual recognition, and it is the appreciation of this that forms the basis of a range of inter-state obligations. More specifically, we have seen that the collective institution of the balance of power in Europe was considered in the eighteenth and nineteenth centuries as a means of securing the rights of states, small states in particular. The understanding that larger powers had a responsibility to maintain the integrity of smaller powers was further institutionalised with the collective security system of the League of Nations and then United Nations. Now, a noted feature of the international discourse of post-colonial states and economically weak states in general is the argument that collective security should be extended:

> ... from its original Wilsonian military guarantee into a demand for collective economic security, on the very realistic ground that political independence is not enough to achieve sovereignty and that the economically powerful states also have an obligation to guarantee economic standards which the weak cannot provide unaided' (Bull and Watson, 1985, p.434).

The acknowledgement of a 'right to wealth', that is a human right to be free from extreme poverty, would no more stand in contradiction to the sovereignty of the state than does the existing system of collective security (Blaney and Inayatullah, 1996, p.97; see also Pogge, 2007). Its acknowledgement would denote a tacit admission, as discussed in the previous chapter in relation to Frost, of the context of social interdependence in which sovereignty and the rights attendant upon it is forged and preserved. Nor is there anything objectionable to the principle of sovereign equality in according special treatment to the world's very poor. Domestic redistributionist policies do not impair the notion of equal citizenship as long as welfare entitlements are in principle available to all.

That the commitment to freeing people from poverty is weak at the international level is due partly to a conception of international relations that elides the historical contingencies and structural inequalities on which the sovereign state system is inscribed. As Blaney and Inayatullah argue, where theories of sovereignty intersect with the traditional liberal thought they tend to treat states as unitary actors endowed with broadly similar capacities and all enjoying the same right to compete with each other on a level 'playing field' on which they have arrived all at the same time and in the same fashion (Blaney and Inayatullah, 1996, p.95). The liberal picture of states as self-producing entities, one which is significantly sustained and naturalised in political and legal discourse, is neither wholly fictitious nor lacking in value as it conduces to respect for communal autonomy, yet it also has a tendency towards an exclusionary 'asociality' (Blaney and Inayatullah, 1996, p.95).

Where the historical and social contexts surrounding state formation are ignored, states beset by multiple political and economic problems can be seen simply as defective and undeserving of assistance. Such an understanding is reflected in expressions such as quasi-states or failed states both of which suggest lack and deficiency (Blaney and Inayatullah, 1996, p.85). Related to this, is the tendency of international liberalism to obscure our mutually constitutive relations, that is, the fact that sovereignty is not wholly self-produced but relies in part on the cognitive acts of others. Indeed sovereignty is unthinkable without a community which can recognise and identify others as being like themselves. The dialectic between the becoming self and the becoming other means we are all of us deeply implicated in the construction of each other, something which applies to the empirically powerful and the empirically weak alike. Ideally, this responsibility for the being of others should translate into a greater sense of responsibility for the well-being of others, such that the more privileged members of international society would come to regard it as a sacred trust, to adapt Green, to 'give reality to...[the]...capacities' of those less well-endowed so as to enable 'them to be really exercised' (Green, 1999, p.8). The continuing legitimacy of the current international order and respect for the territorial borders that have been inscribed on the planet, borders which are at the same time both real and illusory, may well hinge on the fulfilment of this obligation.

5
Sovereignty, Self-Determination and the Rights of Indigenous Peoples

Historical and social conditions

In the last chapter I suggested that the right of self-determination, with the exception of the period of post-war decolonisation when this right was attached to former European colonies, has largely returned to its sovereign mooring. Yet while at one level the gap between the notions of self-determination and sovereignty has closed, at another level that gap has begun to open up again. Increasingly, the world's indigenous peoples are asserting a right of self-government, a right which is gaining international legal recognition. In this context, self-determination generally refers to something other than the sovereignty of existing states or the decolonisation of overseas territories.[1] It is often conceived, just as it was conceived in relation to minorities in the interwar period, in terms of internal self-determination. Yet the recognition of indigenous self-determination has a significance rather different from the recognition of minority rights as what is at stake is not simply cultural distinctiveness. What is additionally at stake in the case of the recognition of indigenous self-determination is the partial decolonisation of a people 'on the basis of "ancestral" occupation' (O'Sullivan, 2006, p.2). It is the matter of prior occupation which distinguishes indigenous people from minorities, this last being a label which indigenous peoples refuse to apply to themselves (Mayall, 1999, p.498; see also Haunani-Kay Trask, 2002, §21). As Douglas Sanders writes, indigenous peoples 'became minorities as a result of a history of colonialism or state expansion. If their positions are argued purely as minority rights, the colonial origins of their situation becomes unimportant' (Sanders, 1993, p.75).

Indigenous peoples comprise between 4 and 6 per cent of the world's population. Spread across a significant proportion of the world's countries, they exhibit a high degree of diversity in terms of culture and life-style (Zinsser, 2004, p.77; Hitchcock, 1994, p.2).[2] In addition to cultural distinctiveness and prior occupation, indigenous peoples are usually defined in relation to two other qualities: 'non-dominance' and 'self-identification as indigenous' (Hitchcock, 1994, p.2). All these qualities are summed up by the UN's Working Group on Indigenous populations, established in 1982 by the UN's Commission on Human Rights under the Sub-Commission on Prevention of Discrimination and Protection of Minorities, in its statement that indigenous people are:

> ...the existing descendants of the peoples who inhabited the present territory of a country wholly or partially at the time when persons of a different culture or ethnic origin arrived there...overcame them and, by conquest, settlement or other means, reduced them to a non-dominant or colonial situation (quoted in Maiguashca, 1994, p.357)

This definition has been controversial with some states in Africa and Asia denying that they house specifically indigenous groups and arguing that the description should be restricted to those non-European populations living in territories that were colonised by Europeans and continue to be dominated by their descendants (Lâm, 2000, pp.2–3). India, for example, argues that 'centuries of migration, absorption, and differentiation [have made it]...impossible to say who came first' (quoted in Keal, 2007). Hannum argues against such attempts to limit the reach of the definition, stating that there is little doubt that the notion of indigenous peoples should encompass tribal peoples of Asian, Arabic and African origin who continue 'pre-modern or pre-industrial lifestyles, including a communally oriented economic system' (Hannum, 1990, pp.89–90).[3] That aside, the concern of many multinational or multiethnic states of Asia and Africa is that according self-determination to national minorities, especially states long riven by ethnic conflicts, could lead to the dismemberment of the state. However, it should also be noted that developed countries with a long history of internal stability, such as the United States, Australia and New Zealand, have expressed the same concern in relation to indigenous self-determination.

The fact that indigenous groups and their supporters use the word sovereignty as well as insist on their inherent right of self-determination, may help us further understand why some states may be anxious about the developing international norms regarding the rights of indigenous peoples (Sanders, 1993, p.75). That the powerful term sovereignty is invoked alongside the potentially less explosive term self-determination, is explained by the injustices which indigenous peoples have suffered and continue to suffer (Sharp, 1997, p.264).[4] At the same time, there are also examples of state recognition of indigenous autonomy, albeit in varying degrees, such as in the United States, Canada, New Zealand and Nicaragua.[5]

The development of international norms concerning the rights of indigenous peoples is a further extension of the body of human rights law which emerged in the second half of the twentieth century. Bice Maiguashca writes that international human rights law, in particular the International Covenant on Economic, Social and Cultural Rights of 1966 with its stipulations concerning the right of self-determination and non-discrimination, undoubtedly facilitated the 'internationalization of the indigenous movement' (Maiguashca, 1994, pp.362–3). Yet there also emerged a growing sense that existing human rights instruments did not adequately address the special needs of indigenous peoples, in particular, their 'collective rights' (Pitty, 2001, p.57).

The first international instrument explicitly dealing with indigenous rights in the post-Second World War era was the 1957 International Labour Convention 107 Concerning the Protection and Integration of Indigenous and other Tribal and Semi-Tribal Populations in Independent Countries which recognised 'the right of collective and individual indigenous land ownership, indigenous customary laws, and the right of compensation for land taken by the government' (Hannum, 1990, p.77; see also Anaya, 1996, p.44).

However, the Convention was assimilative in thrust, favouring the integration of indigenous peoples into the wider society which enclosed them (Hitchcock, 1994, pp.9–10). In the late 1980s the Convention was revised, in part due to the efforts of indigenous peoples who, since the 1970s, had become increasingly active at the UN not least because of their deprivation of rights at home (Anaya, 1996, p.45). The intention behind the revision was to accord 'greater recognition' of indigenous peoples's 'social, economic, and cultural rights and particularly for the right of self-determination' (Hitchcock, 1994, p.10; see also Anaya, 1996, p.47). The resultant ILO Convention 169 Concerning Indigenous and Tribal peoples in Independent Countries, which came into force on 5 September 1991, sought to avoid the paternalism and integrationist tendencies of Convention 107 instead emphasising cultural rights as well as the 'the rights of people to maintain their social and political integrity' (Hitchcock, 1994, p.10; see also Hannum, 1990, p.78). Discussions in the course of revising Convention 107 also focussed on how international and local development programs had resulted in indigenous populations being deprived of their land and resources and thus the Convention also stressed the 'significance of indigenous peoples' land rights and ownership and control of natural resources' (Hitchcock, 1994, p.11). Some of the principles of ILO Convention 169 appear in the UN's Universal Declaration on the Rights of Indigenous Peoples which was developed in consultation with indigenous groups by the Working Group on Indigenous Populations and finally adopted by the UN General Assembly on 13 September 2007 (Hitchcock, 1994, p.11). While draft of this Declaration was completed as long ago as July 1993, for a long time it encountered opposition one important reason for this being its provisions relating to indigenous peoples' right of self-determination. It was only after the inclusion of a revised Article 46(1), under which any interpretation of the

Declaration which could be seen as authorising the dismemberment or impairment of a state's territorial integrity is ruled out, that a number of countries, including Japan, India and the United Kingdom, agreed to adopt it. In regard to self-determination, Articles 3, 4 and 5 of the Declaration state respectively:

> Indigenous peoples have the right of self-determination. By virtue of that right, they freely determine their political status and freely pursue their economic, social and cultural development.
>
> Indigenous peoples, in exercising their right to self-determination have the right to autonomy or self-government in matters relating to their internal and local affairs, as well as ways and means for financing their autonomous functions.
>
> Indigenous peoples have the right to maintain and strengthen their distinct political, economic, social and cultural institutions, while retaining their right to participate fully, if they so choose, in the political, economic, social and cultural life of the State (United Nations General Assembly, 2007).[6]

In the context of colonisation, indigenous peoples almost everywhere were subject to military attack or experienced genocide (Hannum, 1990, pp.74–5). Surviving generations were dispossessed of their lands, had their culture obliterated or gravely disrupted and were socially marginalised because of their indigenous status. The expansion of the physical and legal dimensions of the state in both the developed and developing world has further corroded traditional ways of life (Maiguashca, 1994, p.361). The type of rights being demanded by indigenous groups, including a right to cultural survival and autonomy as well as 'permanent sovereignty' over their land and resources, are only explicable against this background of physical colonisation, dispossession and cultural destruction (Daes, 2004, p.7)

The other matter to underline is that the rights indigenous groups claim, such as the right to cultural survival, are identified as collective and not just individual rights. Without doubt, the idea of group rights, such as the collective right to engage in traditional cultural practices, is problematic as it may serve to legitimise the oppression of individuals. The Native Women's Association of Canada, for example, 'has forcefully challenged the idea that Indian self-government must be based primarily on collective rights' as this has resulted in their subjugation 'to a century of patriarchal rule' (Maiguascha, 1994, p.372). This issue of individual versus group rights also proved contentious in relation to the Declaration, although it should be noted that the Declaration explicitly highlights its conformity with other international human rights instruments under Article 46(2). It is an issue that cannot be minimised by simply claiming that individuals have 'the freedom to leave the community if they do not wish to submit to the majority consensus', as this exit option in many circumstances may be psychologically unreal and practically impossible (Maiguashca, 1994, p.372). Governments, even in the most accountable of political systems, are routinely criticised for oppressing individuals and minorities in the name of the state as a whole and there is no reason why a group, in exercising its collective rights, could not be as despotic as any state. At the same time, if we accept that the state can exercise collective rights on behalf of and for the benefit of individuals the way is open to accepting that groups may exercise collective rights as well. This points again to the artificiality of the distinction between individual and collective rights. As Hannum argues:

> ...few rights can be thought of as purely 'individual'...rights to religion, education, and language generally have meaning only if they can be exercised in concert with others. 'Political' rights, such as the right to participate in government and to self-determination, presume the existence of a collectivity. Conversely, many so-called 'collective' rights...have little meaning unless individual members of the collectivity ultimately benefit from them (Hannum, 1990, p.109).

It is perhaps in recognition of the correlation between individual human rights and communal independence that the principle of self-determination is invoked in Article 1 of the International Covenant on Civil and Political Rights and the International Covenant on Economic, Social and Cultural Rights, and indeed, it is this same thinking that in theory underpins the institution of the sovereign state (Doehring, 1994, p.65). That aside, just as we regard it as unexceptional that individual liberties may be curtailed in the interests of the wider society it should not be controversial that group rights may be curtailed in the interest of the wider society and in order to preserve individual liberties. As the New Zealand constitutional lawyer Paul McHugh states of the relation between the U.S. state and the Indian tribes: 'The communal or group rights of aboriginal nations had to be reconciled with the constitutional values of the state itself, particularly those of equality, non-discrimination and due process' (McHugh, 2004, p.98). At the same time as Hannum argues, the reason why certain groups petition for autonomy is simply because they want to live apart and government should take seriously such demands out of respect for the principle of self-determination, a principle which states are ever ready to apply to themselves (Hannum, 1990, p.469).

An additional factor that has been critical in the development of international norms governing the rights of indigenous peoples is the writings of early publicists and historical documents relating to the practice of colonisation as these 'provide authority and theoretical roots' (Doubleday, 1989, p.384). Arguments grounded in law and history are important because they add moral ballast to the indigenous cause and, although not in all jurisdictions, 'allow litigation, by invoking prior state practice and prior state recognition of rights' (Sanders, 1993, p.75). Much discussion in relation to historical-legal materials has revolved around the question of whether they support the notion that indigenous peoples possessed sovereignty before colonisation, a sovereignty which many contemporary indigenous groups maintain is continuing. In one respect, this debate may seem unnecessary. Whether indigenous societies before contact possessed the concept of sovereignty is irrelevant to the question of the injustice of foreigners invading and seizing their lands. The mere fact of their independent existence as well as the value placed on it as evidenced by their resistance to state capture, should have been enough to establish their entitlement to be left alone. Rousseau alerts us to the moral significance of the basic and spontaneous desire for freedom of all living creatures in stating:

> ...when I see animals born free and hating captivity, breaking their heads against the bars of their prison; when I see multitudes of naked savages scorn European pleasures and brave hunger, fire, the sword and death, simply to preserve their freedom, I feel that it is not for slaves to argue about liberty (Rousseau, 1984, p.126)

One could hardly expect that communities which lacked developed state organs and were not in regular and explosive contact with other territorial entities, would develop the European concept of sovereignty.[7] Yet nor could such peoples have been seen, in good faith, as mere numerical quantities, bereft of social organisation and recognisable interests. Indeed, it is clear that Europeans over the centuries were quite capable of viewing indigenous communities as sovereign peoples or in a sovereignty-like situation, even if the Europeans did not act in accordance with this framework of understanding in numerous instances. Treaties between the European colonizers and, for example, the native inhabitants of North America and New Zealand show that there was an appreciation of the continuities between indigenous and European concepts of law and authority. As Miguel Alfonso Martínez, Special Rapporteur to the Sub-Committee on Prevention of Discrimination and Protection of Minorities, concluded: 'A critical historiography of international relations' demonstrates a 'widespread recognition of "overseas peoples" – including indigenous peoples in the current sense of the term – as sovereign entities by European powers and their successors, at least during the era of the Law of Nations' (Martínez, 1999, §§102, 104)

The era of the law of nations

Numerous studies have given an account of the opinions of early legal publicists on the question of the rights of indigenous peoples in the wake of encounters between Christian Europe and overseas peoples. The violence perpetrated against indigenous communities in the course of seizing their lands was bound to pose serious questions for Europeans schooled in Christian ethics and the natural law tradition. Debate among theologians and jurists concerning the liberty of indigenous people in the context of Spanish conquest of the new world had been underway since the late fifteenth century.[8] Writing in the 1912 edition of his *Manuel de Droit International Public*, Henry Bonfils noted that the predominant view among authors in that era and in the sixteenth century was that indigenous communities possessed 'neither the right of property' and nor '*a fortiori* right of sovereignty' a position, he adds, that would be refuted by the scholar and missionary Bartolomé de Las Casas and the University of Salamanca's Francisco de Vitoria (Bonfils, 1912, p.358; see also Despagnet, 1910, p.596).

In 1519, in front of King Charles, Las Casas challenged the view of the Bishop of Darien, Jean de Quevedo, that 'nature destined the Indians for servitude' (Nys, 1896, p.227).[9] Las Casas responded that there was little difference between the Bishop's argument and that advanced by Aristotle at the beginning of his *Politics*, adding that in a matter such as this, it would be more appropriate to rely on Christian doctrine rather than on the ideas of an 'idolater' (quoted in Nys, 1896, p.227). He stated: 'Our religion is one of equality; it adapts itself to all governments; it is suitable to all nations; it deprives people neither of their liberty nor their rulers, in order to reduce them to slavery under the pretext that nature has made them for this condition' (quoted in Nys, 1896, p.227).

Nys points out that Las Casas's intervention did not result in the strong measures on behalf of the Amerinidans for which he hoped and so the controversy concerning the status of the Amerindians continued. He writes that it was only with the publication *De Indis et de Iure Belli Relectiones* in 1532 by Vitoria that debate in the 'domain of theory' could be 'considered exhausted'; thereafter, he adds, 'authors were agreed on resolving the question in a humanitarian sense' (Nys, 1896, p.242). Vitoria commenced with the argument (one which he later revisits), that the Amerindians, since they were not mad but rather exercised reason, as shown by the fact that they had 'some order in their affairs', 'undoubtedly possessed as true dominion, both public and private, as any Christian', adding that they 'could not be robbed of their property, either as private citizens or as princes, on the grounds that they were not true masters' (Vitoria, 1991, pp.250–1).

Vitoria denied the right of the Spanish crown to claim title over the New World based on the crown's claim to mastery of the entire world, papal authority, rejection of the Christian faith or because of the moral sins committed by its inhabitants (Vitoria, 1991, Section II). At the same time, he also laid out the just causes for waging war against the Amerindians and the legitimate grounds on which the Spanish 'could have' acquired jurisdiction over the New World. These included violations of the principle of hospitality by the Amerindians in response to the Spanish exercise of their natural right to circulation and commercial exchange and where the Amerindians prevented the Spanish from spreading the teachings of Christianity (Vitoria, 1991, Section III). He went on to state that were the Amerindians in fact incapable of self-government due to their 'mental incapacity', this being the central question, then Spanish rule over them would be just, albeit provided that it was 'done *for the benefit and good of the barbarians, and not merely for the profit of the Spaniards*' (Vitoria, 1991, pp.290–1; see also Gibson, 1948, p.107). Of this last 'possible title' Vitoria states that it is 'mentioned for the sake of argument' since it could not be asserted 'with confidence' that the 'barbarians were in fact all mad' (Vitoria, 1991, p.290).

Las Casas argued that Vitoria, when discussing the possible titles by which the Amerindians 'could come under the jurisdiction of the Spaniards', mostly assumed that 'certain reasons for judging this war to be just are very false' and that these false reasons had been 'appealed to by...plunderers'. However, he added that at certain points in this discussion Vitoria was somewhat 'careless' and that this was because he wanted to 'moderate what seemed to the Emperor's party to have been rather harshly put'. That Vitoria's attempts at moderation were strategic was evidenced, according to Las Casas, by the fact that they were expressed 'hesitantly' and 'conditionally', something, which arose from Vitoria's fear 'that he might suppose or make false statements instead of true ones' (Las Casas, 1974, pp.340–1).[10]

Contemporary scholars do not see Vitoria's contribution in quite the same light. Many note that his discussion of the possible titles by which the Amerindians might come under Spanish jurisdiction foreshadows later justifications, namely the right of civilization (Anaya, 1996, p.12; see also Korman, 1996, p.56; Anghie, 1996, p.332; Bowden, 2005, p.11). Indeed, that the reasons given in justification of colonial conquest remained relatively continuous over the centuries Peter Fitzpatrick argues, suggests that the distinction between the universalising natural law phase and the regionally circumscribed positivist phase of international legal thought is not as sharp as has been supposed (Fitzpatrick, 2001, p.13). In this regard, one might add that however humane and progressive was Vitoria's application of the *jus gentium* (which for Vitoria was based in natural law and signified law '*inter homines*' and not a law among states), to non-European peoples this was unavoidably an act of conceptual subjugation (Nussbaum, 1954, p.81).[11]

Incorporating the Amerindians in the framework of the *jus gentium* meant they could be regarded as being in possession of certain natural rights, however, it did not follow from this that they and their rulers were held to be the equals of their Christian counterparts. As Nussbaum asserts, 'admission of non-Christian missionaries in Spain was, of course, unthinkable' (Nussbaum,

1954, p.81). That the Amerindians were relegated to an inferior position under the *jus gentium* was inevitable given the theological assumptions which underpinned this notion. That is, as Fitzpatrick explains, the reason why Vitoria countenanced the idea that Spain might have just title to the New World was doctrinal and not simply political. He points out that according to Vitoria's Thomistic premises 'secondary precepts' of natural law, such as the attribution of '*dominium*' attributed 'to all "men"', were conditioned by '"primary precepts" more intimate to the divinity' from which natural law issues (Fitzpatrick, 2001, p.10). Under such a conceptual regime, it was inevitable that non-Christians would be accorded discriminatory treatment: placed in a subordinate position in relation to a universalising Christianity (Fitzpatrick, 2001, p.11; see also Onuma, 2000, p.26). Vitoria was obviously discomforted by the violence inflicted on the Amerindians by the *conquistadores*. However, as Paul Keal points out following Anthony Pagden, his intention was not to persuade the Spanish to renounce their New World possessions (something which was also unthinkable), but rather to ensure that the Spanish exercised their sovereign rights in a way that respected the '*natural* rights' of the Amerindians, including their right of 'ownership of the lands occupied by them' (Keal, 2003, p.93).

Despite the legally inferior position they were accorded under the European *jus gentium*, Vitoria's reflections show that it was possible for a sixteenth century European Christian to conceive of non-European communities as independent political societies rather than as a lawless mass, even if these societies engaged in cultural practices which were repugnant to Christian beliefs (Vitoria, 1991, p.273).[12] Grotius's *Freedom of the Seas* (1633) provides further evidence of this pattern of thinking. Therein Grotius, drawing on Vitoria, accords 'infidels' the rights of sovereignty, stating that it would be 'heresy':

> ...to believe that infidels are not masters of their own property; consequently, to take from their possessions on account of their religious beliefs is no less theft and robbery than it would be in the case of Christians. Vitoria then is right in saying that the Spaniards have no more legal right over the East Indians because of their religion, than the East Indians would have had over the Spaniards if they had happened to be the first foreigners to come to Spain. Nor are the East Indians stupid and unthinking; on the contrary they are intelligent and shrewd so that the pretext for subduing them on the ground of their character could not be sustained. Such a pretext on its very face is an injustice. Plutarch said long ago that the civilizing of barbarians had been made the pretext for aggression, which is to say that a greedy longing for the property of another often hides itself behind such a pretext. And now that well known pretext of forcing nations into a higher state of civilization against their will...is considered by all theologians...to be unjust and unholy...They

> are not to be deprived of sovereignty over their possessions because of their unbelief, since sovereignty is a matter of positive law, and unbelief a matter of divine law, which cannot annul positive law. In fact I know of no law against such unbelievers as regards their temporal possessions. Against them no King, no Emperor, not even the Roman Church can declare war for the purpose of occupying their lands, or of subjecting them to temporal sway (Grotius, 1916, pp.13, 19).

Grotius's argument concerning the rights of unbelievers, however, had one significant loophole. Grotius insisted, after noting that on this particular topic a 'contrary view' was held by Vitoria, that foreign rulers had a right to punish those who gravely 'sin against nature'; war against such sinners, he added, was no less just than a war against 'savage beasts' (Grotius, 1925, p.506). Yet, it is important to note that Grotius acknowledged that this right of punishment could be exercised by non-Christian rulers. For example, he wrote that the Incas, by compelling 'neighbouring peoples, who did not listen to a warning to abstain from incest, from the intercourse of male persons, from the eating of human flesh...[had]...won for themselves an empire', an empire which was the 'most just of all... except in its religion' (Grotius, 1925, p.506n). Further, Grotius was mindful of the abuses to which this right of punishment was subject. Hence, he added the qualification that the 'law of nature must be distinguished from widely current national customs' and here too he cites Plutarch's view: that the desire 'to impose civilization upon uncivilised peoples is a pretext which may serve to conceal greed for what is another's' (Grotius, 1925, pp.505–7).

As was noted in the last chapter, in the age of imperialism the three main bases for acquiring sovereignty, based on Roman legal doctrine, were conquest, cession and occupation (Simpson, 1993, p.203). According to Sir William Blackstone, conquest and cession were the means of acquiring title to land that was 'already cultivated' whereas occupation was only applicable in lands which were *terra nullius* which Blackstone defined as land 'desert and uncultivated' (Simpson, 1993, p.199) Gerry Simpson contrasts Blackstone's strict definition of *terra nullius*, a definition which led him to question the justice of the invasion and occupation of native lands, with the 'general international law' view which held that the description *terra nullius* was also applicable to lands which were 'inhabited by uncivilized or disorganized groups' (Simpson, 1993, p.203).[13]

James Mayall highlights Vattel's role in extending the 'legal right of annexation of *terratoria nullius*' such that it could be applied to 'predatory peoples, hunting and gathering tribes and nomadic herdsmen who were a danger to their neighbours or pursued an '"idle mode of life" and occupied "more land than they would need under an honest system of labour"' (Mayall, 1978, p.128; see Vattel, 1863, pp.35–6). Vattel certainly argues that those who disdained to cultivate their lands and instead lived 'by plunder' should be 'extirpated as savage and pernicious beasts', however it is arguable that he did not expand the concept of *terra nullius* to the degree that some have suggested. Even though Vattel did not attribute sovereignty to groups he regarded as politically disorganised, he nonetheless argued that such groups had a right to autonomy in the lands they actually occupied, although much hinges on what the word occupied means (Vattel, 1863, pp.35–6).

Vattel dismissed as a 'notorious usurpation' the Spanish conquest of the 'civlized empires' of Mexico and Peru and their subjection to Spain's 'greedy dominion under the pretence of civilising them and instructing them in the 'true religion'. As these American nations had caused no injury to Spain, it was wrong for the Spanish to coerce them inside their borders and interfere in their internal affairs (Vattel, 1863, pp.36, 136). He stated in relation to this:

> The Spaniards violated all rules when they set themselves up as judges of the Inca Athualpa. If that prince had violated the law of nations with respect to them, they would have had a right to punish him. But they accused him of having put some of his subjects to death, of having had several wives, &c. – things, for which he was not at all accountable to them; and, to fill up the measure of their extravagant injustice, they condemned him by the laws of Spain (Vattel, 1863, p.155).

Vattel's argument is reminiscent of the one Grotius advanced in relation to the same topic, at the same time however, Vattel sharply dismissed the Grotian assertion of a right 'to chastise nations which are guilty of enormous transgressions of the law of nature' (Vattel, 1863, p.136). On this score, Vattel was influenced by his contemporary Wolff who, in his *Law of Nations* (1750), had rejected the view of Grotius that '[b]arbarism and uncultivated manners' were a just pretext for waging war against both nations and separate families. While Wolff conceded that the latter group lived without 'civil sovereignty' and could well find their welfare improved by subjection to a civil authority, he maintained that this did not justify any denial of the 'liberty…of those who are unwilling' (Wolff, 1934, pp.89, 159–60). For Wolff a nation, 'properly speaking', is a group of individuals subject to a civil sovereignty, yet the absence of civil sovereignty did not mean that separate families could be said to not own their lands. They did so, according to Wolff, in the form of a 'mixed community-holding' and even if these separate families wandered 'hither and thither' this did not impair their continuing ownership of the lands they intended to use 'only in alternation'; indeed for Wolff, an investigation into 'the reason' which impelled such families 'to wander through uncultivated places' could only demonstrate why possession of lands not permanently in use was necessary (Wolff, 1934, p.159).[14]

Vattel pointed to the natural duty of all nations to cultivate the earth based on the earth's destiny of feeding all its inhabitants (Vattel, 1863, p.35). Given this, and given that the earth ultimately belongs to all humankind, no nation has the right to claim for itself vast tracts of land which it cannot possibly hope to occupy and cultivate. Thus, Vattel stated of the 'erratic nations' of North America, that they had no 'right appropriate the whole of that vast continent to themselves', a continent through which they 'ranged' rather than 'inhabited' (Vattel, 1863, pp.36, 99, 170). He added that if European peoples, suffering under the pressure of population growth, came across 'land of which the savages stood in no particular need, and of which they made no actual and constant use', they were 'lawfully entitled to take possession of it, and settle it with colonies' (Vattel, 1863, p.100).

However according to Vattel, peoples who do not form a 'political society', such as families living independently of each other whether sedentary or 'wandering', while not possessing sovereignty nonetheless possess 'free domain' (Vattel, 1863, p.170). M.F. Lindley reasons in *The Acquisition and Government of Backward Territory in International Law* (1926) that Vattel accorded independent families mere property rights and that in respect of sovereignty their 'country would be *territorium nullius'* (Lindley, 1926, p.23). That is, when it came to independent families Vattel drew a distinction between jurisdiction and property. According to Jean Barbeyrac in his 1738 commentary on Grotius's *Law of War and Peace*, this distinction was based on false reasoning. In criticising the Grotian separation of the right of *imperium* from the right of *dominium* he stated: 'All the land within the compass of each respective country is really occupied, though every part of it is not cultivated or assigned to anyone in particular. It all belongs to the body of the people' (quoted in Manisty, 1926, pp.1–2). Vattel explicitly denies sovereignty (*empire*) to families living independently of each other due to their lack of political organisation. However, Lindley's point seems difficult to square with Vattel's insistence that while one can occupy land surplus to the needs of such families, no-one is 'entitled to seize the empire' (*empire*) of the country, not simply out of respect for property rights, but because 'no man has a right to command men who are born free' unless they 'voluntarily submit to him' (Vattel, 1863, p.170).[15] Vattel reiterates this line of argument in stating that the right of occupation of lands which independent families are incapable, due to their small number, of inhabiting is subject to the proviso that the occupiers leave 'the natives a sufficiency of land' and allow them to 'subsist in their full...absolute independence' (Vattel, 1863, p.170). Vattel's argument appears to be that while families living independently of each other cannot be said to be internally organised along sovereign lines, this does not mean they lack territorial integrity: although lacking internal sovereignty, there is a sense in which such families possess it in an external sense.

Clearly however, the right of territorial integrity of independent families is a lesser right than that of a politically organised society of which, one assumes, there would be no question of occupying parts of its territory, even if such parts had the appearance of being surplus to the needs of its inhabitants. Further, Vattel must have been aware that it was highly optimistic to think that those seizing part of a territory occupied by independent families might confine themselves to land surplus to indigenous requirements. It is also to be expected that Vattel's understanding of occupation and what rendered land surplus to requirements was coloured by Eurocentric understandings of occupation, habitation and use (see Keal, 2003, pp.100–2). Yet, there was at least a minimal recognition of cultural difference in these respects on the part of Vattel. For example, while Vattel suggested that the pastoral Arabs might need less land were they to 'carefully' cultivate the soil, he also stated of them that they 'possess their country...make use of it after their manner...[and]...reap from it an advantage suitable to their manner of life', adding that for this reason 'no other nation has a right to narrow their boundaries, unless she be under an absolute want of land' (Vattel, 1863, p.170). Based on the foregoing, one could argue that while Vattel expanded the meaning of *terra nullius* this expansion, theoretically at least, was somewhat limited. As Charles Salomon pointed out in his *De l'Occupation des Territoires sans maître* (1889), Vattel's argument in defence of the so-called 'right of necessity', a right grounded in the obligation to cultivate the earth, is not precise. His argument (presaged by Grotius and Hobbes), stands in contradiction to his otherwise insistence that pastoral and wandering families possess their country to the exclusion of all others (Salomon, 1889, pp.203–4).[16] Even so, Salomon would seem to agree that Vattel did not provide explicit justification for the forced appropriation of inhabited lands or the colonial domination of peoples who had caused injury to no-one (Salomon, 1889, p.204; see also Jèze, 1896, p.111 and Reynolds, 1996, p.53). It would be publicists following in Vattel's wake who would explicitly deny tribal societies, particularly non-sedentary societies, independent status because they were not sovereign states (Anaya, 1996, pp.16, 18).

Nineteenth century debates

To elaborate on the previous point it should be noted that one explanation as to why earlier publicists were more likely to vest sovereignty in non-European entities than were their successors was because of the initial identification by some authorities, as exemplified by the comments of Vitoria and Grotius, of sovereignty with a natural person: the person of the prince. Where sovereignty was conceived in natural or personalistic terms, it was not difficult to go from vesting it in the person of European princes to vesting it in the rulers of non-European communities be they emperors or tribal chiefs. However, from the mid-eighteenth century onwards, the understanding that sovereignty was vested in the institution of the state and as such was impersonal power spread and deepened. This development, coupled with the positivist identification of law with the presence of physical sanctions, encouraged the view that communities in which the institution of government was not sharply separate from the community and in which law-abiding behaviour largely rested on the internalisation of community norms could not be regarded as sovereign.

Not surprisingly, Austin was among those who discounted the sovereignty of what he considered politically disorganised societies, referring to these as natural societies and contrasting them with so-called independent political societies. Although certainly independent, natural societies, not being subject to a determinate human superior, could not be considered sovereign. As he put it, while members of such societies were 'connected by mutual intercourse' they were not in a 'state of subjection'. That is, the 'generality or bulk' of their 'members...[were]...not in a habit of obedience to one and the same superior'. Such societies, Austin maintained, echoing John Locke, took on a hierarchical form, in the sense of submitting themselves to 'one leader, or to one body of leaders', only in order to attack or repel an 'external enemy'. However, once the emergency was over this military machine dissolved and society reverted to its 'ordinary', segmentary condition (Austin, 1906, pp.101, 108–9).[17] Independent political societies were similarly not parts of a larger political arrangement, however, they were to be seen as sovereign precisely because their members were in a state of subjection. As he clear-sightedly observed, in a sovereign state it is only the sovereign element of the state that can truly be classed as being independent, a point which chimes well with Rousseau's suggestion that it is rather impertinent of those in a state of subjection, as Rousseau considered many of his European contemporaries to be, to lecture others on the virtue of freedom (Austin, 1906, p.97).

For Austin, since independent societies were not in a state of subjection to a determinate superior they did not possess, properly speaking, a system of laws. As with Austin's insistence that international law was not law 'strictly so styled', this was more a matter of classification rather than anything else (Austin, 1906, p.106). Austin followed Bodin in defining sovereignty as the freedom to make and unmake the law and Hobbes in insisting that law properly so-called must be accompanied by a power of sanction. Austin was not denying that independent natural societies were rule governed. Indeed, such societies could be seen as more tightly and inflexibly bound than contemporaneous societies in Europe. As Edward John Eyre observed in 1845 of the indigenous peoples of Central Australia: 'Through custom's irresistible sway has been forged the chain that binds in iron fetters a people, who might otherwise be said to be without government or restraint' (Eyre, 1845, p.384). However, the matter at stake for Austin is that natural societies generally are governed by the self-enforcing laws of the community rather than the enforceable commands of a superior who could change the law at will. He stated that the 'so-called' laws 'which are common to the bulk of the community' living in a state of nature 'are purely and properly customary laws: that is to say, laws which are set or imposed by the general opinion of the community, but which are not enforced by legal or political sanctions' (Austin, 1906, pp.108–9).

Lindley later challenged the Austinian way of framing the question of the sovereignty of tribal societies, arguing it was possible for sovereignty to 'reside in the community as a whole' and not just in a superior armed with the power to punish breaches of the rules it laid down (Lindley, 1926, p.21). He maintained that it was not necessary that indigenous societies possess the complex institutional arrangements of the modern state or even the concept of sovereignty itself for sovereign status to be ascribed to them. All that was required was recognition of the actual powers they exercised, powers which they doubtlessly understood. Further, Lindley argued that it did not matter whether the community conformed to the law through fear of punishment, by 'force of custom or from fear of supernatural consequences'. As long as a community displayed a law-abiding attitude then it could be viewed as a political society (Lindley, 1926, pp.21–2) Indeed, Austin himself opened the way to the recognition of the sovereignty of so-called natural societies. After citing as natural societies peoples living 'on the coasts of New Holland' and the 'North American continent', Austin went on to momentarily acknowledge that where such peoples rendered 'habitual obedience' to their 'own peculiar chief' they could be seen as 'congeries of independent political communities however small' (Austin, 1906, p.109). Lindley's argument finds further support in Austin if we consider his admission that, as a jurist, he did not feel the need to investigate into the actual basis of the community's habitual obedience to commands but was content to merely note the outward manifestations of such obedience. This was even though he otherwise insisted that legal commands, to qualify as such, must be backed by political and legal means of coercion.[18]

While Austin's focus was on the issue of political organisation and factual evidence of such organisation, later legal publicists tended to subsume the question of political organisation to the question of civilisation or collapse these two considerations into each other. For John Westlake the relevant criterion when determining whether tribal sovereignty exists, is not merely the presence or absence of government, but the presence or absence of a government under which Europeans can live. He stated:

> When people of the European race encountered American or African tribes, the prime necessity is a government under the protection of which the former may carry on the complex life to which they have been

> accustomed in their homes. Can the natives furnish such a government, or can it be looked for from Europeans alone? In answer to that question lies, for international law, the difference between civilisation and want of it (quoted in Anaya, 1996, p.20).

For Westlake, the question of the sovereignty of indigenous peoples was a wholly constitutive matter, hinging on determinations by established states as to their level of civilization, this last being explicitly defined in European terms. Thus, if indigenous peoples were incapable of ceding sovereignty this was because, in his view, sovereignty 'could only belong to "a native government capable of controlling white men under which white civilization can exist"' (Simpson, 1993, p.201n). As Westlake's Portuguese contemporary the jurist Martens Ferrão expressed it: '...international title to territory cannot be based on "cessions made by native chiefs, half or wholly savage, to the chance comer who gives them the most", because they do not themselves "possess any constituted sovereignty, that being a political right derived from civilisation"' (quoted in Westlake, 1910, p.141).

This last observation might seem to contradict Westlake's assertion, made in lamenting the fact that 'too often force is the first means employed against the indigenous population', that it was 'always desirable and generally possible' for governments to establish colonial protectorates through agreements with 'native chiefs' rather than by coercive means. However, Westlake went on to state that such agreements should confine themselves to those things which the 'native intelligence' could comprehend and this certainly did not include complex matters concerning the organisation and administration of the state (Westlake, 1910, p.123). What this intelligence could comprehend, according to Westlake, was property. He stated in this regard:

> Because a native tribe is unable to supply a government suited to white men, and therefore cannot be credited with sovereignty, it does not follow that it is not to be credited with rights of a simpler kind. Property is within the range of native intelligence, and at the moment when white sovereignty is acquired property may be held by natives or by whites to whom they have transferred it with full knowledge of what they were doing (Westlake, 1910, p.109).

This view was not especially remarkable for, as Frantz Despagnet wrote, whatever divisions their existed as regards the so-called right of civilisation, all were agreed that indigenous peoples were capable of exercising property rights (Despagnet, 1910, p.597). Citing Grotius, Westlake drew a distinction between the property rights of indigenous peoples and their right to sovereignty. Thus, Westlake insisted, along with other authors, that the continuation of native title was completely consistent with the establishment of

European sovereignty over a particular territory (Westlake, 1910, pp.109, 126–8; see also Simpson, 1993, pp.204–5).[19]

However, while the property rights of native peoples that had not been ceded were in principle not automatically extinguished on the acquisition of sovereignty by a European power, in practice these rights were bound to be considerably eroded if not denied altogether (Balkin, 1988, p.29). Certainly, Westlake did not believe international law could protect the interests of indigenous peoples since international society only concerned itself with 'regulating the mutual conduct of its members' and indigenous peoples were not subjects of international law once they were incorporated into the sovereignty of a European power (quoted in Anaya, 1996, p.21). Not withstanding the debate concerning whether indigenous communities possessed a right of sovereignty under international law or simply property rights, it remained the case that once they became 'municipal unit[s] within a larger State', even where the formation of this larger state was executed by treaty or treaties, such matters were rendered non-justiciable within the context of the international legal system as defined by Europeans (Crawford, 1979, pp.182–3). How indigenous peoples were treated following by their colonial overlords was, according to Westlake, simply up 'to the conscience of the state to which the sovereignty is awarded (quoted in Donnelly, 1998, p.4).

Although Lindley observes it reflected the broad outlook in Britain, Simpson argues that the position embraced by Westlake 'tended to be' in the 'minority' (Lindley, 1926, p.18; Simpson, 1993, p.201n). There were a good number of continental writers (including Bluntschli, de Martens and Pinheiro Ferreira), who denied, to a greater and lesser degree, sovereign rights to indigenous peoples, classifying the territories they inhabited as *res nullius* and insisting on such peoples' lack of civilisation. However, a significant number of nineteenth century continental publicists rejected this position on the grounds that it violated the principle of equality among both individuals and nations. In France in particular, where the *Déclaration des droits de l'homme et du citoyen* had from the outset been understood by figures such as Mirabeau and the Abbé Grégoire as applicable to 'the people of colour of a free condition as much as to the whites' and where there was a post-revolutionary tradition of thinking strongly hostile to conquest, a body of opinion sympathetic to the natural rights of indigenous societies was in evidence almost throughout the whole of the nineteenth century (Nys, 1896, p.272).[20]

The philosophy of Kant, with its emphasis on the individual and 'weakness for small nationalities even the barbarous' was also influential, in this regard, in France and elsewhere (Hornung, 1885, p.469; see also Klüber, 1874, p.22 and Jèze, 1896, pp.104–5). Continental writers following in Kant's wake in the first part of the nineteenth century included the French publicists Gérard de Rayneval and Eugène Ortolan and the German publicist Johann

Louis Klüber. De Rayneval conceded a right of occupation of the lands of 'errant hordes' to whom 'any idea of conservation' was foreign, provided the 'rights or interest' of persons were not injured (Rayneval, 1803, p.153). Yet, as regards the manner of the European conquest of the Indies, Africa and North America, he claimed that the 'tribunal of reason' for a long time had judged it as being in violation of 'all the principles of natural law and the law of nations on which is founded the social order of Europe' (Rayneval, 1803, p.lxxx; see also Jèze, 1896, pp.104–5). Ortolan's argument was that since science does not distinguish between men, even those who have not established a state equipped with the powers of a civilised state have a right to their territory, something which he insisted was then being recognised in state practice (Jèze, 1896, p.106). Klüber, in his *Droit des gens moderne de l'Europe* (1819) argued similarly, stating that that no nation is 'authorised by its qualities, whatever they be, notably by a high degree of culture, to rob another nation of its property'; however, he went further than both de Rayneval and Ortolan in decrying as illegitimate the seizing of the property of nomads on the grounds of either necessity or civilisation (Klüber, 1874, p.175n; see also Jèze, 1896, p.106 and Salomon, 1889, p.202).

Critics of the *mission civiliatrice* writing in the late nineteenth century continued in much the same vein. For example, the Swiss jurist Joseph Hornung, citing the influence of Rousseau and Kant, stated in relation to the treatment of the '*barbares*' that 'every individual or collective soul, however uncultivated and humble it be, must be respected in its dignity and liberty' (Hornung, 1885, p.469). However, what is also striking about the output of colonialist critics in this period is the attention given to the question of whether it was possible to be lacking in *civilisation* yet still in possession of a state and sovereignty. For example, Fiore in his *Diritto Internazionale Codificato* (1890), a tract unashamedly theoretical and philosophical in its thrust, begins his discussion of the status of tribal societies by treating government and culture as the two constitutive elements of civilisation. Thus, Fiore writes that a '*tribú selvaggie*' (uncivilised tribe), was a tribe 'lacking any form of political organization and which has neither the laws nor the customs of civilised peoples' (Fiore, 1909, p.123). However, Fiore then goes on to separate the question of government from the question of civilisation in maintaining that not all tribal peoples were to be classed as uncivilised in the full sense of his initial definition as there existed independent tribes who, despite their lack of European manners, possessed some form of government, a 'political constitution…and common law' (Fiore, 1918, p.115). Indeed, Fiore maintained that even uncivilised tribes 'living in their manner' were not 'outside of the law of humanity' and for this they could not be violently deprived of the lands they occupied (Fiore, 1909, p.126). He argued that the rights of peoples to the lands they occupy should not be contingent 'upon the level of the owner's civilization or culture' (quoted in Reynolds, 1996, p.56). His inevitable conclusion being that conquest, in order to diffuse civilization as well as for any other purpose (leaving aside those instances where collective intervention is justified by violations of fundamental principles of the common law of humanity), must be considered as 'illegal according to modern international law' (Fiore, 1918, pp.430–1; Fiore, 1909, p.269).[21]

Some of Fiore's French contemporaries, while adopting a similar argument in some respects, refused to accept the broad definition of *territorium nullius* embraced by Fiore and others. Fiore permitted the occupation of territories inhabited by a people not in possession of any sovereignty: a people not living, juridically speaking, in a civil state, although it should be added that like Vattel, he limited this right of occupation to those lands from which the 'indigenes do not profit' and which they cannot properly cultivate due to a lack of appropriate means (Fiore, 1909, p.416). Salomon challenged this definition, arguing that while determining what exactly is a state is possible in theory, it is much more difficult in practice. He further noted that few political communities conformed perfectly to the idea of the state (Salomon, 1889, p.207). Salomon's criticism in this regard was directed against Bluntschli who classed as *territorium nullius* any '*country which does not form part of any State* and [is] possessed by some barbarous tribes', a position seen as analogous to the one held by Fiore (Jèze, 1896, pp.121–2). As Salomon pointed out, it was rather difficult to see how something could be characterised on the one hand as *nullius* and on the other as being possessed by someone and the same objection could be made in relation to Fiore's classification as *nullius* lands which he nonetheless described as inhabited. Indeed, the fact that Bluntschli, and this is also true of Fiore, insisted that colonised lands could only legitimately be acquired by peaceful means (through obtaining the consent of the indigenous inhabitants, letting these inhabitants emigrate in peace and paying them adequate compensation), showed that he recognised that the rights of indigenous peoples were well-founded (Salomon, 1889, p.207; see also Jèze, 1896, pp.112, 115–16, 121–2; Fiore, 1909, p.416). Salomon, citing the opinion offered by Louis Renault a decade earlier, argued that the presence of a human society on a definite piece of territory was sufficient to establish certain essential rights: rights of possession, property and sovereignty, each of which remained sacred whoever be their holder. In relation to this last point Salomon stated, 'skin-colour or a state of civilisation little advanced does not prevent barbarous or savage peoples from exercising the rights of sovereignty...sufficient to render any violent occupation of their country contrary to law', although it should be recalled that this was also the view of Fiore (Salomon, 1889, p.206; see also Renault, 1879, p.21).[22]

Despagnet argued similarly to Salomon in his *Cours de droit international public* (1910), stating that 'every sovereignty', however 'rudimentary', should be respected including even the sovereignty of the uncivilised. He added that while a lack of civilisation might be considered a 'misfortune' for 'savage people' it could hardly be regarded as their 'downfall' (Despagnet, 1910, p.598). Indeed, Despagnet went on to maintain that civilization is an 'eminently relative' thing and that it cannot possibly 'measure itself'. The notion that only one's own society possessed 'a true civilization' gave rise to the idea that one had the 'right to impose it on others' and, Despagnet warned, this idea was a danger to the independence of not only overseas peoples but also to that of peoples in Europe. He asked rhetorically: 'What say, if we accept this theory, of the germanic race wanting to submit the latin races to the *Deutsche Kultur*?' (Despagnet, 1910, pp.596–7; see also Salomon, 1889, pp.204n–5n and Jèze, 1896, p.111n). Nonetheless and despite his reservations, Despagnet conceded that land inhabited by some '*peuplades*', (by which he meant small tribes of primitive peoples lacking in 'appreciable political organization' and not 'even having a conception of sovereignty', and as an example he mentions the Indian tribes of North America), was 'susceptible to occupation' (Despagnet, 1910, p.598).

Two other French commentators deserve mention in this context: Gaston Jèze, and Bonfils. Like Salomon, Jèze denounced the right of civilisation, a version of which he discerned in Vitoria's *De Indis*, declaring that the 'territories of savages' who 'energetically' refused the 'assistance of the more instructed' must be considered 'inviolable' and 'closed to all even to civilization.' To argue the contrary, he continued, was to yield to the 'maxim [that] "Force surpasses Right"' and to violate the 'fundamental rule of the equality of the races.' In addition, Jèze denounced the closely related notion of the 'right of necessity', the development of which he too sourced to Vattel and which continued to be promoted in the nineteenth century by commentators such as Ortolan and Antonin Deloume. These last two authors both maintained that in failing to properly cultivate the soil, errant or nomadic peoples were 'wasting a part of the common patrimony' of human kind and thus their land was liable to occupation (Jèze, 1896, pp.106–10, 112–13).

As for Bonfils, he rejected the thesis, one which he ascribed to Vattel, Marshall CJ, Bluntschli and Westlake, that 'savage peoples can only pretend to a sovereignty limited by the rights of colonization', because while they possess 'private property' they cannot be said to possess sovereignty since it is a concept 'they cannot understand'. Due to their supposed 'superior sovereignty', he noted, Europeans felt themselves duty bound to bring the 'benefits of civilization' to tribal peoples. Bonfils had little time for this line of argument counselling readers not to 'look too closely at this pretended civilization brought to these peoples' as it is 'always the law of the most strong that Europe, and above all England, bring' to them. Rather than the position which denied independence to tribal peoples, Bonfils recommended the view he associated with Georg Friedrich von Martens, August Wilhelm Heffter and Salomon and, one could add, Moser: that 'an absolute respect is owed to the independence of savage or barbarous tribes' and that they had an 'equal right to liberty' (Bonfils, 1912, pp.358–61; see also Jèze, 1896, pp.105–8).[23] Bonfils, sensitive to the issues of both cultural cleavage and commonality, added that while indigenous societies may not comprehend sovereignty in the same manner as the people of Europe (although in this regard he noted that the contemporary European understanding was not the same as it was in the tenth century), they nonetheless had a 'certain notion' of it, as evidenced by their 'treaties, truces, alliances and even in the protection that their rulers had offered peaceful explorers'. As with Fiore, however, he accepted that sovereignty could be acquired through voluntary cession, as long as any such cession was not a disguised form of occupation (Bonfils, 1912, pp.358–60).

Even W.E. Hall, who argued that a territory which had not been appropriated by a 'civilised or semi-civilised state' could be treated as *terra nullius* conceded that those who lacked so-called civilization could be viewed as sovereign (Lindley, 1926, p.18; see also Hall, 1895, p.21). For example, he stated that in the abstract there is nothing to prevent 'even a wandering tribe' from being deemed a subject under international law, that is, there is 'nothing...to render the possession of a fixed seat an absolute condition of admission to its benefits'. He further pointed out that the notion of 'tribal or national sovereignty' had been universally accepted after the fall of Rome. However, he added that this notion was lost in the medieval period because of the 'feudal idea which united the right of control with the possession of a determinate portion of land', an association that was reinforced by the replacement of feudal with Roman legal doctrine in the sixteenth century. Thus, what prevented wandering tribes from being deemed subjects was the requirement, wholly contingent and wholly Eurocentric as he implicitly acknowledged, that international law associated sovereignty, in the sense of 'exclusive control, over the members of a specific society' with 'territorial property' (Hall, 1895, pp.20–1). In addition to this, Hall was willing to concede, unlike Westlake, to 'barbarous or imperfectly civilised countries... powers of internal sovereignty' which could be 'surrendered by treaty' (Hall, 1895, p.130; see also Lindley, 1926, p.18).[24]

It was noted earlier that when it comes to the issue of the rights of indigenous peoples there is a significant continuity between the universalising natural law phase and the later regionally confined positivist phase of international legal thought: the former and not only the latter broached the idea of the right of civilisation. Yet the previous section illustrates that there is a continuity between both phases of legal thought in another and quite opposed sense: commentators writing during both phases were able to view indigenous peoples as being in possession of sovereignty, although it should be noted that nineteenth century legal publicists arguing in favour of this position did so with reference to the natural rights of man as well as, in many cases, to the actual law of nations. While acknowledging the relatively recent appearance of a doctrine which would deny 'any rights to primitive peoples to the territory they inhabit' (a doctrine grounded in the positivist notion that membership of the international legal order was contingent upon a capacity to understand and consent to international law as well as in the overlapping idea that only civilised communities were capable of exercising sovereignty), Lindsay pointed out that in fact the predominant view for over three centuries was that territories housing societies with a measure of political order should not be treated as uninhabited (Lindley, 1926, p.20). Further, as he noted, state practice over the centuries generally had reflected this legally predominant position, with European powers basing their title upon cession and conquest and not upon the occupation of '*territorium nullius*', a practice which applied even in the context of the fierce colonialism of the nineteenth century (Lindley, 1926, p.43).[25]

This last point is evidenced by the proceedings and aftermath of the Berlin Africa Conference which ran from 1884–1885. The Conference was designed to ease the competitive pressures amongst European powers regarding the future of the Congo Basin, and the continent of Africa in general, by reaching an agreement on what manner of acquiring territory should be undertaken in order to 'establish legitimate title to territory' in the African region (Onuma, 2000, p.40). At the meeting of January 31 1885, the American plenipotentiary at the Conference, John A. Kasson, suggested that the Conference's Declaration, which only provided for minimal requirements concerning the acquisition of tracts of land on the coasts of Africa, should explicitly address the rights of native rulers (Westlake, 1910, p.108). He stated:

> Modern international law follows closely a line which leads to the recognition of the rights of native tribes to dispose freely of themselves and of their hereditary territory. In conformity with this principle, my Government would gladly adhere to a more extended rule based on a principle which should aim at the voluntary consent of natives whose country is taken possession of in all cases where they have not provoked aggression...[The Declaration] only points out the minimum of the conditions which must necessarily be fulfilled...[I]t is reserved for the respective signatory powers to determine all the other conditions which must be fulfilled before an occupation can be recognized as valid (quoted in Crawford, 1979, pp.178–9).[26]

Anghie notes that according to Westlake, Conference delegates (among whom there were no African representatives), were cautious in their appraisal of Kasson's proposition and that scholarly opinion was divided as to whether Kasson's proposal 'reflected the practice of states', although Crawford argues that Kasson's proposal in fact did represent the stance of international law at the time (Anghie, 1999, p.59; Crawford, 1979, p.179). Indeed, Lindley regards it as significant that the Conference did not 'repudiate'

Kasson's proposal and he notes that the sovereignty of African princes was acknowledged in the course of the conference (Lindley, 1926, p.33). Lindley's contention finds support in observations concerning the Conference made by Salomon, Despagnet and Bonfils. For example, Salomon noted that despite the lack of success of Kasson's proposition it could still be said that the 'diplomats on diverse occasions implicitly approved of an approach consisting of passing treaties with indigenous chiefs' (Salomon, 1889, p.127; see also Despagnet, 1910, p.598 and Bonfils, 1912, p.360).[27] That aside, Anghie argues that the proposal was problematic from the point of view of the powers because formal adoption of rigorous criteria as regards the consent of native rulers to European occupation, would have entailed unacceptable restrictions on the actions of the colonists. However, if the proposal had been adopted unaccompanied by such criteria, it could only have encouraged 'European adventurers' to enter 'into more treaties with African states, claiming that such treaties conformed with the scheme Kasson outlined', a concern voiced by Westlake who called the scheme 'impractical and dangerous' (Anghie, 1999, pp.58–60). Nonetheless, as Anghie points out, it was Kasson's proposition that later served as the basis of '*any* remotely legal explanation for the partition of Africa', even if such an explanation simultaneously elided the violent and intimidating conditions surrounding the treaty-making process in Africa (Anghie, 1999, p.61).

In relation to the matter of treaties, it is worth recalling here that Roman legal doctrine held that the only thing a sovereign cannot do is extinguish its own sovereignty. This insight has been embraced by European theorists of sovereignty from Bodin through to Dicey. It is the idea that sovereignty as constituent power cannot be exercised in a manner that contradicts the grounds of its being. Thus, a sovereign authority renouncing its sovereignty simultaneously renounces its authority to act. Sovereignty can be renounced politically but it cannot be renounced *qua* sovereignty, at least in any formal sense. The point has often been made that obtaining colonies by means of treaties of cession was an admission of the fact that the communities ceding their powers were in fact sovereign since treaty-making assumes the presence of two or more states standing in a relation of legal equality (see Jèze, 1896, p.118). However, the issue I want to raise here concerns the theoretical impossibility of ceding sovereignty by means of a treaty. Now some contemporary indigenous groups strongly reject the notion that the legal compacts reached between indigenous peoples and the Europeans seeking to settle in their lands entailed the surrender of their 'international juridical status as nations'. This is not simply because they may have been deceived in the course of treaty negotiations, misunderstood or were ignorant of the actual terms of the agreements they ratified or only submitted to them under duress. Indeed, the argument here is that any such surrender by indigenous rulers, even if a knowing and willing surrender, was impossible because 'ancestral traditions and culture simply would not allow them to relinquish' their supremacy in relation to 'lands and governance' (Martínez, 1999, §§270–1). Is there not in this more than a trace of the argument that the bearer of the sovereign power is constitutionally incapable of alienating the sovereignty of the state and its corollary that any treaty purporting to do so is void?

Indigenous rights in the U.S.

The treatment meted out to indigenous peoples by their colonisers has ranged from limited recognition of prior rights to land and self-government to outright denial of them. The Royal Proclamation issued by George III at the conclusion of the French and Indian War in October 1763 formally acknowledged 'Indian Rights of occupation' and established a 'set of rules to govern treaty making with the Aboriginal peoples of North America' (Report of the Royal Commission, 1996, 2.1.1) The Proclamation, seen as a template for the 1840 Treaty of Waitangi between the British Crown and the Māori of New Zealand, granted Indian peoples a degree of independence, although it remains a subject of political and scholarly controversy as to 'whether... [it]...recognized or undermined tribal sovereignty' (Calloway, 2006, p.96). The Proclamation stated that the Indians 'with whom We are connected, and who live under our Protection, should not be molested or disturbed in the Possession of such Parts of Our Dominions and Territories as, not having been ceded or purchased by Us, are reserved to them...as their Hunting Grounds' (Royal Proclamation of October 7, 1763).[28]

With the conclusion of the American War of Independence in 1783, the Royal Proclamation ceased to have force in the United States (although it is still a feature of the Canadian Constitution). Nonetheless, the distinctiveness of the Indians as a people is recognised in the Constitution of the United States, Article 8 of which gives Congress the power 'to regulate commerce with foreign nations, and among the several states, and with the Indian tribes'; in fact, up until March 1871, when Congress legislated that 'Native American nations would no longer be recognized as independent nations or powers', relations between the government and Indian nation was conducted *via* treaties (Clinebell and Thomson, 1978, p.678).[29] While the U.S. constitution does not specify the exact nature of the relationship between the U.S. government and the first nation peoples of America, jurists nonetheless endorsed the notion of native title in the early nineteenth century (Palmer, 2001, p.207).

Alpheus Henry Snow notes that in *Johnson v. McIntosh* Marshall CJ characterised the relation between the Indian tribes and their 'European discoverers' as being principally grounded in the international rules governing 'conquest in war, as modified by the humanitarian instincts of the conquerors and the needs of the situation due to the mental and moral backwardness of those living in a tribal state' (Snow, 1919, pp.26–7). However,

Marshall CJ went on to state that the '"original inhabitants" should be recognised as having "a legal as well as just claim" to retain the occupancy of their traditional lands' (Brennan quoting Deane J in Bartlett, 1994, p.29). In the case of *The Cherokee Nation v. State of Georgia* in 1831, Marshall CJ famously defined the American Indian tribes as 'domestic, dependent nations' which, by virtue of being recognized in treaties and treated since settlement as 'sovereign and independent' states, possessed an 'exclusive right to their territory, and the exclusive right of self-government within that territory'. However, Marshall CJ also made it clear at the same time that the Indian nations could not be regarded as 'foreign nations'; rather, their relation with the United States was analogous to the relation of a 'ward to his guardian'.[30]

In the following year in *Worcester v. Georgia*, Marshall CJ gave fuller expression to this right of self-determination, finding that the Indian peoples had from the beginning been 'recognized as "distinct, independent, political communities"' and that their capacity for self-rule did not spring from 'any delegation of powers from the Federal Government, but by reason of their original tribal sovereignty' (Daes, 2004, p.8). Drawing on Vattel he stated:

> The settled doctrine of the law of nations is that a weaker power does not surrender its independence – its right to self-government – by associating with a stronger, and takings it protections. A weak state...may place itself under the protection of one more powerful, without stripping itself of the right of government, and ceasing to be a state (quoted in Daes, 2004, p.8).[31]

For Marshall CJ, both morality and prudence dictated that a conquered people should not be arbitrarily oppressed nor have its traditional way of life altered beyond that which was required by their incorporation, as 'subjects or citizens', into the state established by their conquerors (Balkin, 1988, pp.29–30). As subjects or citizens, conquered peoples were entitled to all those protections which are properly inherent to the sovereign power. Further to this, Marshall CJ suggested that a colonial state had a relationship with the nation or nations it had conquered which was of a different kind to that of the relationship it had with its non-indigenous subjects or citizens, precisely because conquest involved the forcible removal of a people from their traditional way of life and their amalgamation with an alien society. Marshall CJ stated:

> ...humanity demands, and a wise policy requires, that the rights of the conquered to property should remain unimpaired; that the new subjects should be governed as equitably as the old, and that confidence in their security should gradually banish the painful sense of being separated from their ancient connections, and united by force to strangers....[No

> conqueror can neglect these restraints] without injury to his fame, and hazard to his power (quoted in Balkin, 1988, p.30).[32]

Marshall CJ used the word sovereign to refer to the Indian nations, although he nonetheless understood that they had become a part of the wider constitutional arrangement of the United States. Domestic dependent nation status flowed from the recognition that before conquest, the Indians were an independent, self-governing people and that the proclamation of the sovereignty of the British Crown had not extinguished all their rights, even though recognition of this legal status necessarily was within the context of the sovereignty of the United States. For this reason, one can argue that the self-determination of Indian nations arises from the intersection of the historical reality of the Indian nations before colonisation and the subsequent and ongoing shaping and framing of that reality, first by Britain and then by the United States.

Thus, indigenous self-determination is neither wholly declaratory nor constitutive but combines elements of both qualities, albeit in a tensive way, such that the extent to which indigenous self-determination is seen as declaratory or constitutive depends on from whose perspective we are examining the issue and whether we are viewing it in formal legal terms or not. Formally, as stated by the U.S. Department of Justice, the 'sovereign powers' of the Indian tribes over 'their members and their territory' are subject to the 'plenary power' of Congress; thus, what is meant by sovereignty in this context is internal self-determination even if in the official rhetoric on Indian affairs these terms are used interchangeably (U.S. Department of Justice, 2004, pp.1–3).

Yet, some Native Americans insist that they were at the time of European settlement and remain in the present 'sovereign peoples', in the larger sense of that expression. In relation to this, it is argued that the fact that the U.S. government has imposed 'severe limitations on the exercise of that sovereignty...does not change the fact that natives are still entitled to their full sovereign rights' (Clinebell and Thomson, 1978, pp.669, 714). Further, while there is no constitutional guarantee of tribal sovereignty, the Supreme Court has repeatedly affirmed it. In *United States v. Wheeler* in 1978 Stewart J, sounding a declaratory note, stated that tribal sovereignty was not a 'congressional grant' but rather had its source in a 'retained sovereignty' (quoted in Brennan, Gunn and Williams, 2004, p.339). Nonetheless, he also explained that while the Indian nations were in possession of sovereignty or a right of autonomy, this had been limited through the tribes 'incorporation within the territory of the United States, and their acceptance of its protection; further, it was added that through 'specific treaty provisions' the tribes had 'yielded up other sovereign powers...[and]...by statute, in the exercise of its plenary control, Congress has removed still others' (quoted in Brennan, Gunn and Williams. 2004, p.339). From this it follows that the Indian tribes' right of self-determination exists, as stated by

Stewart J in *United States v. Wheeler*, at 'the sufferance of Congress and is subject to complete defeasance', however, 'until Congress acts, the tribes retain their existing sovereign powers' (quoted in Brennan, Gunn and Williams, 2004, p.339). Thus, the Indian tribes do not possess sovereignty but rather are recognised by various institutions of the American state as being in possession of a limited right of self-government derived from their independent status before colonisation. In the end, the constitutive dimension of indigenous sovereignty overwhelms the declaratory element, something that is also shown by the fact that while the American state is willing to accord a limited form of recognition to the Indian and Alaskan Native governments, such recognition does not extent to the native people of Hawai'i whose government was forcibly overthrown and whose land was seized by the U.S. government in 1893 (Trask, 2002, §57–60).

That the Supreme Court and the U.S. federal government would have little problem with the loose application of the word sovereignty is not surprising in a country where it is often claimed that there is no locus of sovereign authority because of its federal structure. Further, as McHugh writes, Americans are discomforted by the Hobbesian concept of absolute sovereignty because of their 'own colonial experience and the War of Independence' in the course of which the term sovereignty became associated with Crown sovereignty (McHugh, 2004, p.88). The contradiction between the common law's recognition of an inherent right of sovereignty, which can at the same time be derogated from by Congress, has led some indigenous advocates to question the adoption of sovereignty as a 'political objective'. Taiake Alfred, for example, argues that when Native Americans invoke sovereignty they are accepting the domestic dependent nation status accorded them by their supposed conquerors (Alfred, 2001, p.26).

Indigenous rights in Australia

Marshall CJ's characterisation of the legal relationship between colonising powers and those it colonised was well established in English law by 1774. English law governing the Crown's overseas holdings distinguished between territories acquired by conquest and those which had been settled. It held that where, in the case of conquered lands, there was an already existing system of law this system remained 'in force until...[it was]...altered by the conqueror' (Balkin, 1988, p.29). By contrast, settled territories were subject to the common law, that is, the common law became the 'law of the land' (Brennan in Bartlett, 1994, p.ix). It is also important to note here, as Richard H. Bartlett underlines, that while *terra nullius* is the international legal principle which authorised the British assumption of sovereignty over the Australian continent, this principle did not belong to the common law. In terms of the common law, 'settlement' is the 'analogous doctrine....to that of terra nullius' (Bartlett, 1994, p.ix).[33]

In the context of British law, Australia came to be viewed as a settled territory because its indigenous peoples were seen as 'barbarous or unsettled and without settled law' and therefore, as Lord Watson later put it, it was as if New South Wales were 'an uninhabited country...discovered and planted by English subjects' (Brennan in Bartlett, 1994, p.25). Importantly however, neither the concept of *terra nullius* nor that of settlement were ever viewed as a 'bar to native title in Australia or elsewhere', a point to which Westlake's remarks concerning the simpler rights which a native tribe might possess lends support (Bartlett, 1994, p.ix). Further, the notion that European states 'had a right to settle' in lands deemed to be in a barbarous condition did not preclude cession through 'negotiation or purchase', an approach which was firmly entrenched by the late eighteenth century and which was in fact reflected in the British Admiralty's instructions to Lieutenant James Cook in 1778 as he set out on his expedition. The instructions, drawing a clear distinction between the status of occupied and unoccupied territories, stated:

> You are likewise to observe the Genius, Temper, Disposition and Number of Natives, if there be any, and endeavour by all proper means to cultivate a Friendship and Alliance with them, making them presents of Trifles as they may Value, inviting them to Traffick, and Shewing them every kind of Civility and Regard; taking Care however not to suffer yourself to be surprised by them, but to be always upon your guard against any Accident.
>
> You are also with the Consent of the Natives to take possession of Convenient Situations in the Country in the Name of the King of Great Britain, or, if you find the Country uninhabited take Possession for His Majesty by setting up Proper Marks and Inscriptions as first discoverers and possessors (Beaglehole, 1988, p.cclxxxiii).

In the event, and in contrast with the method of colonisation employed in the United States, Canada and New Zealand, the consent of the 'natives' to the British claim to sovereignty was 'neither sought nor obtained' (Nettheim, 1993, p.223; see also Buchan, 2005, pp.2–3). Bruce Buchan writes that it was not that the British merely failed to 'acknowledge an Indigenous government with whom to negotiate. Rather, their perceptions of Indigenous people' as uncivilised and barbarous 'led them to deny the possibility (at an official level) of Indigenous government in Australia' (Buchan, 2005, pp.2–3).[34] Nor was any form of native title recognised along the south-east coast of Australia in 1788, despite it being recognised in other colonised parts of the world, something which Henry Reynolds suggests may have been because of a lack of colonial competition in that region (Reynolds, 1992, pp.52–3).

Yet, Reynolds also notes that the British Government recognised native title in Australia in the 1830s and 1840s while at the same time claiming sovereignty over the continent.[35] In 1836, the Full Supreme Court of New South Wales in *R v. Murrell* rejected the idea that the indigenous peoples of that state had a subordinate form of sovereignty (Nettheim, 1993, p.230).[36] The reasoning of Burton J was that the U.S. Supreme Court's position on tribal sovereignty did not apply in Australia because the Aborigines were not as politically or institutionally developed as the Indians of North America, although he added that while Aboriginal tribes could not be regarded as 'so many sovereign states governed by laws of their own', they were 'entitled to be regarded as a free and independent people' and as such were 'entitled to the possession of those rights which...are valuable to them' (quoted in Nettheim, 1993, p.230). Just over half a century later in *Cooper v. Stuart* in 1889 the Privy Council, hearing an appeal from the Supreme Court of New South Wales, found itself caught between legal principle and political imperatives in dealing with the question of whether Australia had been *terra nullius* before the British arrival, the upshot being a widened interpretation of Blackstone's definition of *terra nullius* (Simpson, 1993, p.200). Lord Watson stated therein that:

> There is a great difference between the case of a Colony acquired by conquest or cession, in which there is an established system of law, and that of a Colony which consisted of a tract of territory practically unoccupied, without settled inhabitants or settled law, at the time when it was peacefully annexed to the British dominions. The Colony of New South Wales belongs to the latter class (quoted in Bartlett, 1994, p.24).

As Simpson writes, the result of this highly 'artificial and purely formal' reconciliation of 'law, politics and history' was that the 'people that did inhabit the land were redefined as physically present but legally irrelevant and their history was obliterated' (Simpson, 1993, p.200). Gibbs J in *Coe v. Commonwealth* (1979) echoed Lord Watson's position in maintaining that occupation of a territory was permissible where that territory 'had no civilized inhabitants or settled law' according to '*European standards*.' However, Simpson argues that this further expansion of the meaning of *terra nullius* was necessary precisely because (as shown in *Milirrpum v. Nabalco Pty.* (1971) and by Justice Lionel Murphy's comments in *Coe v. Commonwealth*), the gap between the official story of the settlement of the Australian continent and the actual history of that event was proving increasingly difficult to bridge (Simpson, 1993, pp.200–1).

The High Court of Australia in *Mabo No.2 v. the State of Queensland* in 1992, began the process of addressing this problem in rejecting the idea that Australia was *terra nullius* at the time of European settlement and in recognising the native title of Australia's indigenous inhabitants.[37] The

High Court, drawing on English legal tradition, distinguished between the sovereignty or radical title of the Crown and beneficial ownership. This distinction had been somewhat unclear in English law because the Crown's sovereignty over England was based on the feudal idea, as expressed by Blackstone, 'that the king is the universal lord and original proprietor of all the lands in his kingdom', a notion which gave rise to subject obligations or 'feodal services' to the Crown under the tenure system (quoted in Bartlett, 1994, p.32). However, this blurring did not eliminate the understanding, as stated by Brennan J, that radical title largely concerned 'jurisdiction, involving questions of international and constitutional law, whereas...[title to land]...is a matter of proprietary rights, which depend for the most part on the municipal law of property' and that 'acquisition of one by the Crown would not necessarily involve acquisition of the other' (quoted in Reconciliation and Social Justice Library, p.1). Gummow J observed in *Wik Peoples v. Queensland* (1996), that the idea that the Crown owns 'all land is a modern one', noting that its acceptance in 'legal theory may have been related to Imperial expansion...well after the decline of feudalism' (quoted in Hepburn, 2005, p.70). It is modern because, as Samantha Hepburn points out, 'absolute ownership...[in Norman England]...only existed over alienated land and did not exist over land which was not the subject of a Crown grant'. However she adds, that 'under the colonial version of feudal tenure, Crown ownership was presumed to be absolute over all alienated *and* unalienated land' and this presumption, in turn, had its basis in the conviction that the native inhabitants were uncivilised and therefore unable to demonstrate legal title (Hepburn, 2005, pp.74–5).

Hepburn states that the colonial version of feudal tenure is more accurately called 'sovereignty tenure' because it rendered absolute beneficial ownership and sovereignty entirely 'coextensive', an idea which was not a 'necessary and enduring feature of feudal tenure' (Hepburn, 2005, pp.68–9).[38] The decision of the High Court in *Mabo* was a defeat for sovereignty tenure: the common law came to be seen as recognising and protecting a type of title, known as native title, based on pre-colonial customary laws (Patton, 2000, p.126).[39]

Some have expressed disappointment that the High Court declined to rule on the legitimacy of the sovereignty of the Australian state, holding that the fact of this sovereignty was 'not justiciable before municipal courts' (Brennan in Bartlett, 1994, p.20; see also Watson, 2002, §30). This might seem strange for, as some point out, if Australia were not '*terra nullius* in terms of land ownership, how could it have been *terra nullius* in terms of sovereignty?' (Nettheim, 1993, p.228; see also Reynolds, 1996, p.59).[40] The problem however, as Brennan J pointed out, is that there is simply no domestic legal arena in which the basis of the sovereignty of the Australian state can be addressed.[41] The Australian High Court, as with the U.S. Supreme Court, is wholly a creature of the sovereignty of the

Australia state and thus cannot pronounce on the legitimacy of that sovereignty without simultaneously silencing itself. Any such pronouncement could not stand as law insofar as it would necessarily involve a denial of the source of the authority of the Court. *Coe v. Commonwealth* concerned, in the words Jacobs J, a 'claim based on a sovereignty adverse to the Crown'. Such claims, Jacobs J maintained, were not a matter 'of municipal law but of the law of nations' and for this reason 'are not cognizable in a court exercising jurisdiction under that sovereignty which is sought to be challenged' (quoted in Nettheim, 1993, p.229).

When it came to the question of sovereignty the Court in *Mabo* argued, in accordance with the Court's reasoning in *Coe v. Commonwealth,* that 'the acquisition of sovereignty itself was an unchallengeable act of state' it being the ground on which the jurisdiction of the Court rested. Simpson states that while this position may be unsatisfactory from an indigenous perspective, 'this may be the only possible finding a court in Australia can make without undermining the very basis of its jurisdiction to hear the issue' (Simpson, 1993, p.206). That is, the notion of native title as determined by the Court and its protection by the common law presupposes the sovereign authority of the Australian state, a position that was reiterated once more by the Court in *Members of the Yorta Yorta Aboriginal Community v. The State of Victoria & Ors* in 1998. It was stated by the Court in that case that there can be 'no parallel law-making system' alongside that of the Australian state and thus, as Tom Calma notes, 'recognition of Indigenous sovereignty within the native title system' is precluded (Calma, 2006, p.7).

Such is the logic that unfolds given the legally unchallengeable fact, at least in domestic courts, of Crown sovereignty. However, even though the Court cannot adjudicate on the existence of the sovereignty of the Australian state it can, without endangering the Australian legal order, acknowledge that Australia was obtained by conquest.[42] Such an acknowledgement, Simpson argues, would not involve a challenge to the Australian legal order since conquest was 'a legitimate method of acquisition at international law prior to 1945 and, according to the doctrine of intertemporal law, the acquisition of Australia can be judged according to international law norms prevailing at the time' (Simpson, 1993, pp.208–9). The acknowledgement that the Australian state was established by a form of conquest might not only reconcile Australian law with its political history and with what has for two millennia been legal orthodoxy concerning the acquisition of territory, it would also be positive in terms of the further recognition of native title and indigenous customary law (Simpson, 1993, p.209). Thus, while it is true that after *Mabo* the colonial relationship between the Australian state and the Aboriginal people has not fundamentally changed but has only slightly shifted, it is also true that this case showed that modifications of the legal system can be made so as to better accommodate indigenous interests. There is no reason why, in this regard, accommodation cannot be made of an indigenous right of self-governance.

Paul Patton argues somewhat differently, stating that the *Mabo* case involved a momentary deterritorialisation or unbounding of the Australian state, precisely because it implicitly challenged the 'idea that Australia was settled rather than conquered' and that in doing so it raised questions about the 'legitimacy' of the British acquisition of sovereignty over Australia. The outcome of the case was also deterritorialising in that it saw a concept of title introduced into the domestic legal order the origins of which lay entirely elsewhere. Yet Patton also recognises that, in relation to native title, a simultaneous reterritorialisation took place in that this form of title does not stand on its own. As Brennan J observed, it exists through its incorporation within the common law. Thus native title, as Patton puts it, is a 'hybrid of indigenous and common law' involving 'a becoming-indigenous of the common law to the extent that it now protects a property right derived from indigenous law; and a becoming-common law of indigenous law to the extent that it now acquires the authority along with the jurisprudential limits of the common law doctrine of native title' (Patton, 2000, pp.129–30; see also Webber, 2000, p.63). Native title arises at the point where indigenous and common law perspectives converge, although a deeper engagement between these perspectives, both of which will nonetheless always remain in tension and somewhat mutually uncomprehending, would be required for a right of indigenous self-determination to be recognised. Indeed, until such a right is constitutionally entrenched the pattern will continue whereby political grants of self-determination are made only to be subsequently withdrawn and whereby native title, such as it is, will remain fragile and subject to extinguishment.[43] To the extent that this situation prevails the Australian state will remain an overtly imperialist structure in terms of its dealings with its indigenous inhabitants.

Indigenous rights in Canada

Although the indigenous peoples of Canada engaged in a struggle to assert their rights throughout the twentieth century, including making appeals to the League of Nations, it was only in 1970s that this struggle began to bear fruit (Niezen, 2000, p.119). James Tully notes that the transitional point in this regard is seen as the ruling of the Canadian Supreme Court in *R v. Calder* in 1973, a case which concerned the Nisga'a Nations 'assertion of their rights to collectively use and occupy their traditional lands' and which saw the Court acknowledge that 'Aboriginal rights existed at the time of contact' (Tully, 2000, pp.44–5). While this case did not settle the question of whether the rights of indigenous communities continued to exist, such rights have since been acknowledged in Canada's *Constitution Act* of 1982 (Tully, 2000, p.45). Section 35(1) of the *Constitution Act* recognised and affirmed the 'existing aboriginal and treaty rights of the aboriginal peoples of Canada', who are defined in Section 35(2) as including the 'Indian, Inuit, and Métis peoples of Canada' (Brennan, Gunn, Williams, 2004, p.331). Further, the Federal Policy Guide: Aboriginal Self-Government recognises the 'inherent Right of self-government' of Aboriginal peoples in Canada 'in relation to matters that are internal to their communities, integral to their unique cultures, identities, traditions, languages and institutions, and with respect to their special relationship to their land and resources' (Federal Policy Guide, 1995).

As should be clear, one important difference between the native American experience in the United States and Canada is that the Aboriginal right to self-government is not simply recognised at the sufferance of the state *via* statutory recognition but is now incorporated into the Canada's constitutional framework. The 1996 Report of the Royal Commission on Aboriginal Peoples stated that the treaties entered into by the Crown and nations of Aboriginal people 'are fundamental components of the constitution of Canada, analogous to the terms of the union under which provinces joined Confederation' and 'designed to embody the enduring features of the law of the country' (Report of the Royal Commission, 1996, 2.2.1).

Indeed, one may say that the Aboriginal tribes of Canada are among those instruments by which the sovereignty of the Canadian state is exercised. This characterisation is no doubt somewhat displeasing to Aboriginal peoples themselves since in the Canadian case, more so than in the case of the United States where the tribes have largely accepted their domestic dependent nation status, indigenous groups question the basis of the sovereignty of the Canadian state. The Royal Commission heard from indigenous representatives 'extensive presentations' to the effect that the Aboriginal 'nations were sovereign at the time of contact and continue to be so'. Precisely what the Aboriginal nations meant by sovereignty was not made clear by the Commission but it did comment that its assertion was 'often perceived as a threat to Canada as we know it' and that it could not find any 'rational way to bridge the gap between those who assert and those who deny the continuing sovereignty of Aboriginal nations'. These comments would indicate that the Commission's interpretation was that the Aboriginal nations were using the term sovereignty in a manner in keeping with its traditional legal meaning (Report of the Royal Commission, 1996, 2.1.3)

That sovereignty in its full sense is being asserted by Aboriginal nations is further supported by the fact that indigenous parties to what are known as the 'numbered treaties of "land surrenders"', insist that they did not in fact 'cede either their territories or their original juridical status as sovereigns' and that these treaties should be considered as akin to the earlier treaties of 'peace, friendship and alliance' (Martínez, 1999, §120). However, whether this assertion of sovereignty extends to a claim of sovereign status in respect to international affairs, something which a claim to juridical independence in respect to the Canadian state would logically entail, remains uncertain. In any case, the Federal Government of Canada, in its Federal Policy Guide on Aboriginal Self-Government, specifies that the 'inherent right of self-government does not include a right of sovereignty in the international law sense' and Canadian courts 'have accepted that it is not their role to question the legality' of the sovereignty of the Canadian state (Indian and Northern Affairs Canada, 1995 and Report of the Royal Commission, 1996, 2.1).

As indicated, the Commission could find no way to reconcile Aboriginal claims to sovereignty with the assertion of Crown sovereignty. Thus, it concluded that these '[d]ifferences in deep political beliefs' concerning sovereignty should be dealt with by fashioning a 'mutually satisfactory peaceful coexistence', although of course given the power imbalance which is a legacy of prior colonisation the degree of satisfaction achieved in any negotiation which always greater for the Crown (Report of the Royal Commission, 1996, 2.1.3). To illustrate these points, the example of the Nisga'a Final Agreement of 1998 can be cited. The Agreement recognises the Nisga'a Nations' right to self-determination, that is, its right to be 'different and apart' (O'Sullivan, 2006, p.4).[44] Yet the Agreement, even though it takes the form of a treaty between British Columbia and the Nisga'a Nation, does not and cannot resolve the question of where power is located satisfactorily from the point of view of indigenous communities as it seeks to reconcile the rights of the Nisga'a people with the title and sovereignty of the Crown.[45]

Indigenous rights in New Zealand

In New Zealand (Aotearoa), debate continues as to whether Māori surrendered sovereignty, retained it or agreed to exercise it in common with the Crown. Like the Canadian state, the New Zealand state avoids using the term sovereignty in relation to Māori, preferring instead to use the term self-determination. Māori however, like the indigenous people of Canada, 'do not accept that power lies solely with the Crown' (O'Sullivan, 2006, p.5). As in Canada peaceful coexistence, albeit similarly of more or less agonistic kind, is the way of dealing with competing ideas as to the location of sovereignty (see Maaka and Fleras, 2000, pp.90, 100). The divisions over the question of sovereignty in particular centre on the meaning of the Treaty of Waitangi of 1840 between Māori and the British Crown, divisions which first arose immediately after the negotiation of the Treaty and were initially resolved by war.[46] According to the English language version, Māori ceded sovereignty to the Crown. Article 1 of the British version of the Treaty states: 'The chiefs of the confederation of the united tribes of New Zealand, and the separate and independent chiefs who have not become members of the confederation, cede to Her Majesty the Queen of England...all the rights and powers of sovereignty' (quoted in Simpson, 1993, p.204n).

By contrast, according to Articles 1 and 2 of the Māori version, Māori chiefs granted the Crown 'kawanatanga' or 'complete government over their lands' while the Crown promised to 'protect the chiefs, the subtribes and all the people of New Zealand in the unqualified exercise of their tino rangatiratanga (chieftainship) over their lands, villages and all their taonga (treasures)' (Charters, 2003). Claire Charters notes that the term rangatiratanga is a better translation of the term sovereignty than kawanatanga. While both terms imply 'power, authority and jurisdiction', the former connotes 'chiefly power'. At the same time, Article 3 of the Māori version also holds that Māori 'have the same rights and duties of citizenship as British subjects', a provision which might be said to point in the direction of Crown sovereignty (Charters, 2003). Yet the question of whether there was a cession of sovereignty or not may be beside the point to the extent that the Māori chiefs envisaged their jurisdictions as existing alongside, rather than being either subordinate to or above, the jurisdiction of the Crown. Indeed, even if one were to adopt the position that a cession of sovereignty did take place it is certainly clear that from the Māori perspective a robust right of self-government was retained. Taking both the Māori and English language versions together, it would be hard to disagree with the suggestion of a 2001 report of Te Puni Kokiri (Ministry of Maori Development) that 'it seems likely that Maori felt that their tribal authority on the ground would be confirmed in return for a limited concession of power in the form of kawanatanga' (quoted in Charters, 2003).[47]

Andrew Sharp writes that some advocates of Māori sovereignty in the 1980s were able to construct a 'doctrine of sovereignty much like that of the modern nation state' through assimilating the concept of rangatiratanga with that of mana Māori motuhake, this last meaning the 'right-and duty...to be *separately and distinctly* Māori', adding that this permitted some to claim for the Māori 'coercive and legal sovereignty over the territory of Aotearoa'. However, he adds that most did not take this route and it was the idea of divided sovereignty, with the Crown and the Māori each having their own delimited sphere of jurisdiction, that was the notion most widely embraced in Māori circles. He notes that the 'assertion of Māori sovereignty was usually more a strategy of avoidance of Pākehā totalitarianism and the assertion of separate rights than the claim to rule everything' (Sharp, 1997, pp.249–51).[48] The appeal to sovereignty was thus a tactic used in order advance a less ambitious agenda. Even so, the New Zealand government must have felt challenged by Māori political rhetoric in that period since, in the course of renegotiating the status of the Māori, it felt the need to reaffirm the 'absolute sovereignty' of the New Zealand state (Sharp, 1997, p.266).

The translation of Māori sovereignty into reality would involve nothing less than the dismantling of New Zealand's established constitutional framework.

While this was obviously unacceptable from a non-Māori viewpoint, there was nonetheless an appreciation, as has been pointed out in relation to Canada, that the 'cost of "excluding Aboriginal peoples from the national agenda...[was]...unacceptably high in social, political and economic terms"' (O'Sullivan, 2006, p.9). There was recognition, Palmer argues, of the need to negotiate an appropriate balance between te tino rangatiratanga and kawanatanga with reference to contemporary conditions (Palmer, 2001, pp.208–9). The upshot was that Māori 'sovereignty' or self-government was reconciled with the sovereignty of the New Zealand state but in a way that rendered it an inextinguishable right to be protected and advanced by the state rather than a mere privilege granted at the state's discretion (Sharp, 1997, pp.251, 302).[49]

While the Treaty of Waitangi's implementation is not guaranteed under the 'largely unwritten Constitution' of New Zealand and requires statutory recognition, the legal reinvigoration of the Treaty over the last thirty years has seen it acquire a '"quasi constitutional" operation', such that it has an important influence on the shaping of legislation as well as informing judicial decision-making (Brennan, Gunn, Williams, 2004, p.343; see also McHugh, 2004, pp.91–2).[50] Conceptualised as a source of New Zealand's constitutional arrangements, the Treaty of Waitangi, as with the natural rights of New Zealanders in general, can be seen as a set of limits on the exercise of the sovereign power by the state.[51] The Waitangi Tribunal characterised the relationship in this way in 1983 in its *Motunui-Waitara Report* which stated: 'The Treaty represents the gift [by Māori] of the right to make laws in return for the promise to do so as to acknowledge and protect the interest of the indigenous inhabitants...That then represents the exchange of gifts that the Treaty represented. The gift of the right to make laws, and the promise to do so as to accord the Māori an appropriate priority' (quoted in Palmer, 2001, pp.208–9). Similarly, in its 1991 *Ngai Tahu Land Report* the Tribunal maintained that although 'legal sovereignty is exclusive and exhaustive' it is not 'absolute' since it was apparent that 'cession of sovereignty to the Crown by Māori was conditional' in that the Māori retained 'tino rangatiratanga' (quoted in Sharp, 1997, p.302). As Sharp argues, such a conception is not 'in itself inimical to the Crown's sovereignty'; rather, the exercise of Crown sovereignty should be seen as conditional on its fulfilling its obligations to Māori as well as to the wider society, and there is nothing in this notion at odds with traditional constitutional theory (Sharp, 1997, p.303).

The constitutional lawyer Paul McHugh managed to reconcile rangatiratanga with Crown sovereignty by drawing upon the Diceyan distinction between legal sovereignty, which according to British constitutional tradition resides in Parliament, and political sovereignty which resides with the community and is the source of the legal sovereignty of the state. Further, McHugh established that many past commentators on the British constitution have maintained that communal assent to the legal sovereignty of the state is contingent on the state's protection of the '"property" of its subjects', and in the case of New Zealand, since it was the 'legal custom of the British to obtain the consent of the sovereign nations whose sovereignty' they were seeking to absorb, it followed that the Crown had a duty to protect the interests of Māori just as Māori had a duty to uphold the sovereignty and laws of the Crown in exchange for such protection (Sharp, 1997, p.272). As Sharp expresses it:

> ...while "legal sovereignty". was lodged in the Parliament of New Zealand, "political sovereignty"...lodged not only in the ordinary people of New Zealand, but also, by virtue of the Treaty of Waitaingi and the rangatiratanga guaranteed them in it, the Māori tribes. This "political sovereignty" generated in the state of New Zealand, when it governed, an obligation to rule so as to protect the "property" of the people at large, and in particular the "rangatiratanga" of the Māori (Sharp, 1997, p.272).

The outcome of the revivification of the Treaty of Waitangi which took place in both the political and legal arenas, was a partial decolonisation of the sovereignty and law of the New Zealand state in that these have become to a lesser extent the tools of a dominant ethnic group. Beyond this, as Sharp notes, the arguments about sovereignty in New Zealand in relation to the revival of the Treaty of Waitangi raised, not only legal questions concerning the site at which sovereignty was located and how the sovereign powers were distributed among the various agents and institutions of the state, but also very important questions concerning the basis and legitimacy of the New Zealand state and why citizens ought to maintain a law-abiding attitude towards it (Sharp, 1997, p.268).

An inherent right

If indigenous peoples had not historically been treated, to borrow William James's words concerning the American intervention in the Philippines in 1899, so often as 'mere matter in ...[the colonialists]...way...to remote from...[them]...to be realized as they exist[ed] in their inwardness', then the issue of indigenous sovereignty might not be so prominent today (reproduced in Perry, 1935, p.311). Sovereignty in a legal sense, is relevant to a number of arguments mounted by indigenous groups. First, there is the question of the condition of pre-invasion indigenous societies which, as we have seen, some argue in the contemporary context were wholly sovereign entities. This does not amount to a claim that all such communities had developed state organs or that the European concept of sovereignty was a part of the indigenous conceptual environment, although this is not to deny that there were in many instances institutional and conceptual approximations. What it does mean, at least to begin with, is that these were societies with independent modes of existence and who, as their resistance to conquest showed, valued that independence. Taiaiake Alfred insists there was never any 'moral justification' for the assertion of sovereignty over the native peoples of North America, instead, there was 'only the gradual triumph of germs and numbers' and, based on this last point, he also suggestively denies that there was ever even a conquest (Alfred, 2001, p.29).[52]

It was partly in order to render comprehensible to European audiences, the serious injustice of denying free peoples their autonomy, their land and way of life, that earlier publicists sought to translate indigenous experience in terms of European notions such as dominion, *empire* and sovereignty. Indeed, they had no choice but to translate the autonomy of indigenous societies in this way as they were not in possession of the language and concepts appropriate to the indigenous experience. It is the element of incommensurability between indigenous and European experience that gives rise to such culturally hybrid notions as native title as well as to the ongoing translation of the indigenous relation to the land as sovereignty. As I have indicated, some think that the sovereignty paradigm is inappropriate when applied to indigenous people now and in the past because it fails to capture the particularity or character of indigenous nations. The concept of sovereignty, Alfred argues, to the extent that it is allied with the notion of dominion, obscures the expression of 'indigenous concepts of political relations – rooted in notions of freedom, respect and autonomy'; it denies us glimpses, he adds, of self-determining 'sovereignty-free regimes' with 'no absolute authority, no coercive enforcement of decisions, no hierarchy, and no separate ruling entity' (Alfred, 2001, pp.21, 27; see also McHugh, 1999, p.453).

He underlines the point that sovereignty is 'not Sioux, Salish or Iroquoian in origin' and questions how a European notion came to be so entrenched in and significant to the discourses of societies and cultures that had managed to establish their own political and legal systems 'since the time before the term sovereignty was invented.' Rather than being the path to freedom, Alfred views tribal sovereignty as a grant that indigenous nations have received in exchange for abandoning their autonomy and entering the state's legal political framework. Thus, he calls on scholars and activists to renounce the 'assimilative' pattern of thought that promotes the colonisation of indigenous nations 'beginning with the rejection of the term and notion of indigenous "sovereignty"' (Alfred, 2001, pp.26–7).

That aside, the claim to original sovereignty remains important because it adds significant moral and legal weight to demands for the recognition by the state of indigenous self-determination as well as other rights (Behrendt, 1999, p.99).

It is thus possible to designate two types of sovereignty in indigenous political discourse. The word sovereignty may be invoked in its full legal sense, as it was by the claimant in *Coe v. Commonwealth*. Yet as we have seen the term may be used in a political and a 'less confrontational' fashion, as it is widely used in the U.S. context, to mean the 'continuing though subordinate sovereignty of particular indigenous nations and peoples while acknowledging the ultimate sovereignty of the settler state' (Nettheim, 1993, p.228; see also Maaka and Fleras, 2000, p.93).[53] Some might argue where indigenous groups are not laying claim to sovereignty over the entire state in which they live or claiming a right of secession but only, as Frank Brennan puts it, autonomy 'within the life of the nation', then the expression self-determination is an appropriate description (Brennan, 1995, p.149). As we have also seen, in contrast with the concept of sovereignty, one can think of self-determination in terms of degrees. The term sovereignty is sometimes used in a relativised fashion, but it is much more commonly conceived as a legal status applying to states alone and one which is held absolutely. For this reason, when indigenous interests use the term sovereignty, even if they are using it only to indicate a limited form of self-determination, their opponents are able to portray their demands as a threat to the integrity of the state. As I have indicated, those who opposed the adoption of the Declaration on the Rights of Indigenous Peoples have cited this threat. Statist interpretations of self-determination have given further credence to such claims which is why some have suggested that indigenous groups stop using this word along with the word sovereignty (Pitty, 2001, pp.58–9).

However, claims that self-determination for indigenous peoples may result in the dismemberment of existing states have often been disingenuous at least when put forward by well-developed states. It has been made clear over many years, as Erica-Irene A. Daes as Chairperson of the UN Working Group has pointed out, that self-determination in the context of the UN Declaration is 'used in its internal character, that is short of any implications which might encourage the formation of independent states' (quoted in Watson, 2002, §44).[54] Indeed, Mayall writes that it is precisely because indigenous organizations have acted cautiously and requested only limited forms of self-government, rather than upsetting states by asserting their sovereign independence, that they have been moderately successful in 'establishing self-determination as one of their human rights' (Mayall, 1999, p.498). It should also be reiterated that international law, it being grounded in principles of territorial integrity and political unity, cannot permit an absolute right of secession; thus, full self-determination can generally only be attained where a people desirous of splitting from their state 'is capable and prepared politically, economically and militarily to fight for it' (Peang-Meth, 2002, p.111).

The opposition that the Declaration has encountered no doubt reflects an ideological commitment to the imperial state form.[55] Beyond this however, concern has been expressed about other aspects of the Declaration such as Article 19 which requests that government's consult with indigenous peoples and gain their consent before enacting legislation or pursuing policies that would impact on them, with Canada, Australia and New Zealand maintaining that this provision implies 'different classes of citizenship' (United Nations Department of Public Information, 2007). This Article is also problematic for South Africa which is 'both constitutionally and by treaty bound not to grant status to anyone on the basis of ethnic identity' (Corry and Suzman, 2003, p.5).

However, perhaps most important in explaining the opposition that the Declaration has encountered is the issue of land rights and the right to restitution of lands, rights which will be further internationalised now that the Declaration has been passed. I say further internationalised as the UN's 'Final Report on the study "Indigenous peoples' permanent sovereignty over natural resources"' states that as a result of a number of cases including the *Ogoni* decision by the African Commission on Human and Peoples' Rights concerning the Nigerian government and the *Ogoni* people, the *Case of the Mayagna (Sumo) Community of Awas Tigni v. the Republic of Nicaragua* of 2001 addressed by the OAS Inter-American Court of Human Rights and the case of the *Maya Indigenous Communities of the Toledo District* of 2004 which was addressed by the OAS Human Rights Commission, international law now 'protects the governmental or collective right' of indigenous communities rights to their land and resources (Daes, 2004, pp.9, 16).[56] For this reason, and because it has become clear that genuine self-determination is not possible without it, Daes, the Report's Special Rapporteur, argues that the Draft UN Declaration should have been 'amended to include express recognition of indigenous peoples' collective and 'permanent sovereignty over natural resources', a right which could only limited by 'the most urgent and compelling interest of the State' (Daes, 2004, pp.5, 15, 19).

Decolonisation in respect to indigenous peoples is a matter of ongoing and ceaseless negotiation. The outcome of negotiations between indigenous peoples and the society which encloses them will always be imperfect from the indigenous peoples' perspective because of the fact of prior dispossession and the inequalities of power flowing from that dispossession. Relations of inequality between indigenous peoples and the society which dominates them encompass the fact that in order that indigenous voices can be heard the indigenous experience must be translated into legal and political categories alien to the pre-colonial experience. Disputes over the applicability or otherwise of the term sovereignty to the indigenous social order before occupation reflect this difficulty in translation. To the extent that indigenous conditions and conceptual frameworks were not commensurable with those existing in Europe the application of the term sovereignty to these peoples, at least in its narrow legal sense, is misleading. Further, the crucial issue when it comes to the injustice of depriving them of their traditional lands and ancient privileges and enjoyments is not whether their societies were ordered along sovereign lines, but whether they were free and independent peoples. Yet, we have seen, past legal commentators had no problem characterising non-European peoples living independently of others as sovereign, even where such societies lacked the formal institution of the state. All these points suggest that there is more than an element of the metaphorical in the application of the term sovereignty to stateless societies and indeed, for this very reason, it is possible to see indigenous people in their early encounters with Europeans as both struggling to defend their sovereignty as well as struggling to defend themselves against the imposition of the sovereign state form.

As indicated, the insistence on an original sovereignty as well as the normative claim to its continuation can serve as a rhetorical means of securing recognition of the special status of indigenous peoples within the state as well as a greater share of the resources of the state. Further to this, the idea of an original sovereignty helps promote the view that the right of self-determination, along with rights to land, is an inherent right (see Curry, 2004, p.148). As one commentator puts it, it is a right that exists before the 'legal system of surrounding states' it having arisen '*sui generis* from the historical condition of indigenous peoples as distinctive societies with the aspiration to survive as such' (quoted in Marks, 2000, p.7). Conceived as such, an indigenous right to self-determination is something that commands recognition but is not something that can be 'given' (Zinsser, 2004, p.85; see also Martínez, 1999, §259). Rigorously applied, as Steven Curry suggests, the concept of an original indigenous sovereignty involves a reconceptualisation of the nature of relationship between indigenous peoples and settler societies such that non-indigenous societies come to think of their states as being founded upon 'indigenous possession': as if the 'settler societies had sought and been granted permission to enter indigenous lands on agreed terms' (Curry, 2004, pp.148–9). At the same time, we must also acknowledge that the legacy and perpetuation, however modified, of colonial rule means indigenous groups do not in fact exercise sovereignty and thus the realization of the rights they claim remains subject to the goodwill of settler societies (see Tully, 2000, p.57).

In the light of these considerations, one can conclude that the recognition of indigenous rights involves both declaratory and constitutive elements. Recognition involves a meeting of minds between a group which identifies itself as a rights bearing unit and a group on whose comprehension and empathy the status of their moral claims significantly depends. Because of the serious injustices that are the effect of the often large cleavages between the self-understanding of indigenous groups and the comprehension of them by their internal colonisers, the development and promotion of international normative instruments addressing the former's rights, especially where these have not been constitutionalised, remains vital.

6
The European Union: Sovereignty in the Twilight Zone

History and institutions

For some scholars the European Union (EU) offers the most compelling image at present of a post-sovereignty future as the EU, while not itself a sovereign body, is widely considered more than a 'complex' intergovernmental organisation (Eberlein and Grande, 2005, p.146).[1] Others however, argue that the EU's supranationalism is only superficial as its institutions ultimately function at the behest of its sovereign members. Differing conceptions of the EU's nature and destiny do not necessarily impinge on its diurnal activities. Indeed, assuming for the moment that the EU is some kind of institutional and legal hybrid, it could remain for a long time in a twilight zone as far as the question of its exact institutional and legal identity is concerned and without this having any bearing on its development and success. However, it might also be that such an unsettled situation will eventually prove intolerable and that the question of where final authority should lie will have to be addressed.

The EU was born of war. The calamity of the First World War, (as well as the pressure of American economic competition), gave rise to calls for a 'United States of Europe', its promotion being undertaken in particular by the French Foreign Minister, Aristide Briand in the late 1920s. Both he and Gustav Stresemann, the latter becoming head of the German Foreign Office in 1924, expressed support for a European Customs Union with common coins and stamps. Although the League established a Commission of Inquiry for European Union in 1931, the idea soon faded from view amidst rising nationalist and protectionist sentiment in Europe in the early 1930s (United Nations Library of Geneva, 1996, pp.140, 142).[2]

Then in 1943, in the midst of occupied France, the French public servant Jean Monnet set to thinking about the post-war situation in Europe. He determined that the errors committed at Versailles should not be repeated and conceived of a future in which Europeans ceased to think in terms of their 'national, limited responsibilities' but instead thought of their 'common, joint responsibilities' (quoted in Maitland, 2001, p.80). Donald Maitland notes that it was Monnet's 'vision' that stimulated the movement to integrate the states of Europe, the integration process commencing with the coming into force of the *Treaty Establishing the European Coal and Steel Community* or Paris Treaty in 1952, as established by Belgium, France, Italy, Luxembourg, the Netherlands and the Federal Republic of Germany. The name of this Community was prosaic but the thought behind it was profound: to place 'two basic industries which had provided the wherewithal to make war...under joint, rather than national, control' (Maitland, 2001, p.80). The European Economic Community was subsequently established by the same six states in 1957 with the signing of the *Treaty Establishing the European Community* otherwise known as the Rome Treaty. The remarkable transformation of intra-European relations which occurred over the following decades was heralded in the Preamble to this Treaty which stated a commitment to 'every closer union among the peoples of Europe' (Treaty Establishing the European Community, 1957).

The Treaties of Paris and Rome issued in a Council of Ministers. The Council is the EU's main decision-making organ and is composed of ministers from all Member States who have been elected to their national parliaments and who are nominated to represent the interests of their respective countries (Maitland, 2001, p.80). The Treaties also created a European Assembly which was later renamed the European Parliament. While at first, this body was composed of the nominees of the parliament's of Member States, in 1979 direct election replaced the system of nomination. While initially the Parliament was limited to an advisory role, its powers were later redefined under the *Treaty on European Union* or Maastricht Treaty and the *Treaty of Amsterdam Amending the Treaty of European Union*, which came into force in 1993 and 1999 respectively, in terms of '*consultation, cooperation* and *co-decision*.' The European Parliament is charged with approving the appointment of the members of the European Commission, this being the third institution created by the Treaties. The Commission performs functions similar to those of public services in Member States and although its members are nominated by the governments of Member States it is designed 'to serve the interests of...the Union, as a whole and not those of their own country' with Parliament being empowered to censure and demand the resignation of the Commission (Maitland, 2001, pp.80–1). The Commission is also responsible for ensuring compliance with EU Treaties and legislation through taking 'action to rectify breaches, including referring alleged violations to the European Court of Justice' (House of Commons Information Office, 2007, p.3).

The Commission alone is responsible for initiating legislation for enactment by the Council of Ministers although it is for the Council to determine whether proposed legislation is accepted, rejected or amended (Maitland, 2001, p.81). As a final measure the European Parliament is able to refuse any proposed legislation where it cannot reach any agreement with the Council of Ministers and since its inception 'all the laws and rules' of the EU have been established on the basis of negotiation and compromise, an approach to the making of law which Maitland considers to be without 'historical precedent' (Maitland, 2001, p.81).

This last point is crucial because some have argued that the EU's unique method of law-making, precisely because it involves consensual negotiation, renders EU law superior to the law issued by factionally controlled national parliaments.[3] This claim is analysed below in a discussion of the jurisprudence of the fourth principal EU institution: the ECJ. This body has been a significant force for the furthering of European integration, successfully establishing the legal groundwork so vital to this process (Gibson and Caldeira, 1998, pp.70–2).

The institutional progress of the European Union has been fitful (Caporaso, 1996, p.30). A period of relative inertia in the 1970s extending to the mid-1980s was followed by a flurry activity which resulted in two ground-breaking treaties. First, there was the Single European Act (SEA) which came into force in 1987 thereby creating a single European market. Second, there was the already mentioned Maastricht Treaty. The collapse of the Soviet empire in Eastern Europe and the subsequent reunification of Germany issued in 'challenges' and 'opportunities' that seemed to favour increased integration and it was in this context that Maastricht abandoned the title '"Community", conceived at Messina in 1955, in favour of the term "Union"' (Maitland, 2001, p.83). Maastricht also enhanced the powers of the European Parliament and, Joseph Grieco notes:

> ...established mechanisms whereby EC countries were to seek to improve policy coordination in such diverse areas as social affairs, high technology, border controls, immigration, and anti-crime efforts. It committed the EC members to work toward the establishment of a common foreign and security policy...[and]...laid out a path a timetable for qualified EC members to achieve Economic Monetary Union (EMU) by the end of the 1990s (Grieco, 1995, p.21).

In the early 1990s, such was the intensification of EU institutionalisation that it seemed as if this organisation was well on its way to becoming an authentic 'supranational authority' in the following century (Grieco, 1995, p.22). EU concerns extended to far more than the trade matters that early dominated it, coming to encompass public policy issues which historically were associated with the state alone (Grieco, 1995, p.21). In order to overcome the problem of legislative deadlock, the Single European Act and Maastricht also provided that in relation to some issues the Council of Ministers could operate on the basis of qualified majority voting: a method of voting requiring approval by approximately two-thirds of Council members for EU legislation (concerning issues such as the internal market, economic and social cohesion, research and development, the environment, and the coordination of national provisions on foreign nationals' right of establishment), to be adopted. Francis Campbell argues that the shift to qualified majority voting and its extension into an increasing number of policy areas, along with the doctrine of the supremacy of EU law, means that it is 'no longer tenable' to maintain that EU member states enjoy 'a monopoly of sovereignty' (Campbell, 2002, p.46). Indeed, the belief emerged that the transfer of competencies had gone so far down the path towards integration that the sovereignty of members, that is, their constitutionally independent status, had ceased 'to exist in more than purely nominal terms' (Sørensen, 1999, p.603).

Yet, by the mid-1990s the EU institutions appeared to be suffering from a crisis of confidence and legitimacy. Conflicts between Member States in respect to foreign and defence policy, the demise of a common enemy in the form of the Soviet Union, domestic social insecurity as well as the realisation that national identity was not about to be supplanted by a common European identity rendered doubtful the possibility that the EU would move towards supranationalism (Grieco, 1995, p.22). The question of identity, in relation to both culture and security, remains important, nonetheless, the early years of the twenty-first century saw further efforts to advance political and economic integration, most notably in form of the *Treaty Establishing a Constitution for Europe* which was signed in 2004. The rejection of this Treaty at referendum at France on 29 May 2005 was significant given that France was one of the Treaty's foremost and most powerful supporters. The result in France, along with the Treaty's subsequent defeat at referendum in the Netherlands on June 1 of that same year, brought to an end the ratification process throughout the rest of the Union. However, on October 19, 2007, Member States agreed on the *Treaty of Lisbon amending the Treaty on European Union and the Treaty establishing the European Community* (Reform Treaty) in lieu of the discarded *Treaty Establishing a Constitution*, and this was signed by the Heads of State and Government on December 13, 2007. Like its predecessor, the Reform Treaty is controversial among sections of the public as it contains much of the same text as or similar content to the treaty it replaces (openeurope, 2007, p.4). Nonetheless, it is important to add that however significant are the transfers of competencies and the extension of qualified majority voting under the Reform Treaty, it does not take the form, as was also the case with the *Treaty Establishing a Constitution* irrespective of its name, of a constitution. It does not involve a constituent act on the part of the peoples of Europe but is rather an inter-state agreement. It is also important to add here that under the Reform Treaty, unlike under previous EU instruments, clear terms are laid down for the voluntary withdrawal of Member States from the Union. This is not to suggest that Member States currently cannot legally withdraw from the EU, at least from the perspective of their own constitutions, a matter which is discussed below.

At this stage, the EU has a long way to go before it can be considered a centralised state. Certainly, the EU has some of the qualities of a state institution, such as common borders (with the exception of Britain and Ireland), and 'competences in the field of domestic security' (Walters, 2002, pp.97–8).[4] However, the supervision of the EU's frontiers is not undertaken by a single agency but is performed on a 'collective and cooperative basis by the national authorities of the various member states' (Walters, 2002, p.98). In addition to this, the EU is clearly lacking in centralised power when it comes to the taxation and budgetary activities traditionally associated with government, with member states having a near monopoly on these functions (Caporaso, 1996, p.39). While the EU is strong in the area of competition policy (with competition law giving the Commission wide powers in relation to member states), as well as in the area of technical policy, it lacks powers or is weaker in relation to such matters as social, labour and cultural policy and numerous other issues which deeply concern citizens (see Eberlein and Grande, 2005, p.155 and Pollack, 2005, p.371).

Further, because it is a decentralised institution the EU gives scope to 'nationally variable implementation' of its regulations and thus there is always the possibility that its regulations will be implemented in an uneven manner (Eberlein and Grande, 2005, p.157). From the point of view of the EU as a regulatory state, by which is meant that the EU is an ongoing rule-making institution, and given the EU's desire for a level-playing field, the best response to this problem would be further concentration of regulatory powers in the hands of EU institutions (Caporaso, 1996, pp.39–41). Yet as Eberlein and Grande write, because an increase in regulatory powers at the European level would encroach upon the 'highly sensitive, "close to state"' areas of economic policy, there is strong resistance to further centralisation in this area as well as in the area of social regulation (Eberlein and Grande, 2005, p.157). This gap, between the EU's drive for uniform standards in economic and other areas, and its limited powers of intervention to ensure such uniformity has led to what Michael Greven has called an '*informalization*' of transnational governance in the EU. He notes that the Commission published a White Paper entitled 'European Governance' in 2001 in which it announced a 'programmatic turn towards "a less top-down approach... complementing its policy tools more effectively non-legislative instruments"' (Greven, 2005, pp.262–3).

Thus, alongside the established and formal regulatory instruments, such as the European Court and European Parliament, which 'apply "hard" instruments of program implementation through the distribution of resources and penalties for rule breakers', are softer methods of policy implemenation involving negotiations and co-ordination with stakeholders (Greven, 2005, p.263). Greven argues that while such informal procedures of policy implementation may enhance the effectiveness of transnational governance they emphasise the 'executivism' of the EU, thus further detracting from its openness and accountability and hence also its democratic legitimacy (Greven, 2005, p.267).[5] Responses to the problems posed by informalization might involve a renewed reliance on formal regulatory mechanisms, the authority of which can only be diminished where they are increasingly eschewed in favour of indirect methods, and 'further empowerment of the European Parliament relative to Commission and Council' (Greven, 2005, p.265).

Yet these recommendations only once more bring into view the problem that led to informalisation in the first place: the refusal of states to relinquish key legal competencies. The phenomenon of informalisation is thus further evidence that the EU is not a state and that Member states continue to possess significant political and legal independence. At the same time, as the Union expands the problems intrinsic to co-regulation and the need for systemic reform are likely to become more pronounced (Maitland, 2001, p.85).

This legal autonomy is especially striking in the international domain. The deep divisions that emerged in Europe over the American decision to invade Iraq without the sanction of the Security Council in April 2003, reinforced the view that the EU is a long way from achieving the Common Foreign and Security Policy (CFSP) toward which Maastricht had committed Member States to working. This commitment was restated at the European Council meeting in Cologne in 1999 and the Reform Treaty, if it comes into force (something which is uncertain following its defeat at referendum by Irish voters on 12 June 2008), would see the institution of a High Representative of the Union for Foreign Affairs and Security Policy.[6] Some have expressed the concern that the creation of the High Representative position may weaken the control of Member States of their national foreign policies. Hence, at a EU Council meeting in Brussels in June 2007, it was stipulated that the legal powers of Member States as regards the development and conduct of their foreign policies would remain unaffected. Further, there is no suggestion that the CFSP, as also underlined at the Brussels meeting, will have any impact on the participation of states in international organisations including their membership of the UNSC.[7]

It was hoped that the euro, in addition to proving to be economically beneficial to euro-zone members and challenging the dominance of the US dollar, would cause the EU to embrace much greater political integration given the demands of currency management as well the symbolic power of a common currency (McNamara and Meunier, 2002, p.849). Kathleen R. McNamara and Sophie Meunier write that Member States, while having made the bold decision to renounce their national currencies, 'have not proved willing to relinquish their national sovereignty over its external face.' (McNamara and Meunier, 2002, p.850). This point is misleading as it implies that members of the euro-zone have relinquished some of their sovereignty in relation to the currency's internal face. As Jackson points out: 'The EU states that are opting to join the "euro" currency zone are deciding to exercise their sovereignty in that way. That is a matter of policy and not of sovereignty. Their sovereignty is being used to authorize certain common rules and activities in co-operation with other EU member states.' (Jackson, 1999, p.453)

In any case, McNamara and Meunier argue that although the euro needs a 'single voice' in order to maintain its position in currency markets and to 'influence decisions on a range of broader macroeconomic policy issues' states are wary of surrendering their 'freedom and flexibility' in respect to policy development and the pursuit of national priorities (McNamara and Meunier, 2002, p.851).[8] In general, the major European powers do not want to give up their independent presence in bodies such as the International Monetary Fund and the G7 because they believe this would diminish their influence (McNamara and Meunier, 2002, pp.857–9). The so-called pooling of sovereignty is thus selective, depending on how a state believes its priorities can best be served and on what it believes its domestic constituencies are prepared to accept (McNamara and Meunier, 2002, p.858).

We have seen that the EU does not qualify as a centralised state. While the level of integration in some areas is high, the level of integration in other areas is limited, weak or non-existent. From an institutional perspective, one would have to conclude that the EU remains a confederation of sovereign states. As Andrew Moravcsik remarks: 'The EU constitutional order is not only barely a federal state; it is barely recognizable as a state at all' (quoted in Pollack, 2005, p.371). Yet one would have to concede, that its confederalism, thus far, is of a centralising rather than decentralising kind, and indeed, this centralising tendency could propel it in the direction of a federal state, and it is worth adding that if this happens it would certainly not be the first state whose progress towards full integration has been long and fraught. However, this possibility is highly controversial for reasons of national identity and/or because of the concern that the EU is essentially a neo-liberal enterprise, a concern which is held by members of both the European right and left. This explains why moves to integrate macroeconomic policy-making in the interests of better management of the euro could prove politically costly to national governments.

The supremacy of EU law

So far, much of the discussion has centred on the institutional features of the EU and has explored both their reach and their limitations. What has been described manifests some of the features of a state properly speaking, yet also reveals significant deficiencies in this regard. The concept of the state is only rescued for the purpose of describing the EU where we sub-divide that category to encompass the concept of the regulatory state, which is something that both is and is not a state in the traditional sense (Caporaso, 1996, p.39). For some, the problem we have in understanding the EU arises from our attachment to statal models, something which causes analysts to search for hierarchical lines of authority that simply do not exist in the EU as a whole and which have greatly diminished in Member States. It is only when we reject the dichotomy which pictures the EU as either a federal super-state or as a collection of sovereign states engaged in intergovernmental arrangements that we can begin to appreciate its particularity as a multi-layered system of governance in which authority is distributed among a variety of public authorities at a variety of levels (Eberlein and Grande, 2005, pp.146–7). Such characterisations have led some to reject the description 'state' altogether in relation to the EU. One observer maintains that the EU 'is *not* a state, not even a federal state, it is *not* a traditional alliances of states, it is not a confederacy' but is rather, a 'political form which is dynamic, heterogeneous and non-hierarchical, and polycentric' (Preuss quoted in Prokhovnik, 1999, p.76).

Yet, if the status of the EU *qua* state is ambiguous, what is interesting is that the supremacy of EU law is not in question. As we have seen, legal supremacy is the principal mark of sovereignty. Thus, it would appear that we are presented with the seemingly curious situation in which a rather institutionally dispersed and to an extent, fractured body is nonetheless described as having a locus of supreme authority: EU law. If EU law is supreme one might expect that it is only a matter of time before European state-level political institutions begin to act in greater conformity with this legal reality. While the expression multi-level governance, an expression often used in relation to the EU, may simply denote particularly elaborate inter-governmental arrangements, it may also indicate, not some new political form, but rather a federal state in the making. Indeed, as Krasner notes, many European lawyers would argue 'that Europe is, in fact, a federal state, not a confederation of states' (Krasner, 1999, pp.236–7).

Ian Loveland regards EU Treaties as '"constituent" documents' as these set down and define the 'powers' of the Union's 'various lawmaking institutions', and he compares them in this regard to the constitution of the US which defines the powers of the federal and state governments and charges the Supreme Court with the responsibility for determining the legal significance of constitutional stipulations (Loveland, 1996, p.517). Article 164 of the Treaty of Rome accords the ECJ the role of ensuring that 'in the interpretation and application of this Treaty the law is observed' (*Treaty Establishing the European Community*, 25 March 1957). The common market and other economic objectives enshrined in the Treaty required that EU law 'have uniform impact throughout the community' and what this soon suggested was that national laws not consistent with EU law (whether in the form of treaties, regulations, directives or decisions) were invalid (Loveland,

1996, pp.518–19). Article 5 of the Treaty of Rome implicitly acknowledged that a breach could arise between domestic and EU law, insisting that Member States:

> ...shall take all appropriate measures, whether general or particular, to ensure fulfilment of the obligations arising out of this Treaty or resulting from action taken by the institutions of the Community. They shall facilitate the achievement of the Community's tasks. They shall abstain from any measure which could jeopardise the attainment of the objectives of this Treaty (*Treaty Establishing the European Community*, 25 March 1957).

However, the notion of the supremacy of EU law was nowhere openly asserted in the Treaty of Rome. Loveland notes that it was '"created" (or perhaps "found")' by the ECJ in the case *Costa v. ENEL* in 1964 (Loveland, 1996, p.518). In that case, the Court reached a conclusion that suggested it also viewed the EU treaties as constituent documents, not simply in the sense that they are basic to the functioning of this institution as would be the constitution of a social club, but that they had resulted in the creation of a wider constitutional order in which members of the EU were encompassed. The Court stated:

> By creating a Community of unlimited duration, having its own institutions, its own personality, its own legal capacity and capacity of representation on the international plane and, more particularly, real powers stemming from a limitation of sovereignty or a transfer of powers from the States to the Community, the Member States have limited their sovereign rights and have thus created a body of law which binds both their nationals and themselves...The law stemming from the Treaty, an independent source of law, could not because of its special and original nature, be overridden by domestic legal provisions, however framed, without being deprived of its character as Community law and without the legal basis of the Community itself being called into question. The transfer by the States from their domestic legal systems to the Community legal system of rights and obligations arising under the Treaty carries with it a permanent limitation on their sovereign rights, against which a subsequent unilateral act incompatible with the concept of the community cannot prevail (*Costa v. ENEL*, Case 6/64,15 July 1964).

In explaining the creation of the principle of the supremacy of EU law, Loveland underlines the Court's 'teleological' approach to legal interpretation, an approach inherited from the constitutional order of several of the EU's original members. This approach means that in making its decisions, the Court seeks to ensure the 'practical effectiveness' (*effet utile*) of EU law and hence domestic legislation is assessed in the light of the overall purpose of European integration (Loveland, 1996, p.519). A noted member of the court, Judge Federico Mancini, summed up this approach in stating:

> The preference for Europe is determined by the genetic code transmitted to the court by the founding fathers, who entrusted to it the task of ensuring that the law is observed in the application of a Treaty whose primary objective is an "ever closer union among the peoples of Europe" (quoted in Hartley, 1996, p.95).

Clearly, such a methodology leaves scope for creative interpretation and this approach contrasts starkly with the 'literal rule' of interpretation that British courts have employed in interpreting statutes (Loveland, 1996, p.520). As Trevor C. Hartley writes, it 'is becoming more and more widely recognised' that the European Court 'sometimes interprets provisions of the Treaties contrary to the natural meaning of the words used' (Hartley, 1996, p.95).

The doctrine of the supremacy of EU law is closely linked to the principle of direct effect or direct applicability which the Court also created or found *via* its teleological technique. The principle of direct effect simply means that EU law is directly applicable in the jurisdictions of member states and this 'irrespective of whether the Community provision came before, or after, the national provision' (Hartley, 1998, p.218). As Zenon Bankowski and Andrew Scott write in relation to this last point, in the context of the EU's legal order the principle of '"lex posterior derogat lex priori" does not apply...An earlier Community norm will always be superior' (Bankowski and Scott, 1997, p.83). The question of the means by which EU law could be rendered directly effective was addressed by the Court in its February 1963 ruling on the case of *Van Gend & Loos*. In its judgement, the Court found that the Treaty of Rome was 'more than an agreement which merely creates mutual obligations between the contracting states'. Rather, the Court concluded that the European Community constituted a 'new legal order of international law for the benefit of which the states have limited their sovereign rights, albeit within limited fields, and the subjects of which comprise not only the Member States but also their nationals' and that Community law had 'an authority which...[could]...be invoked' by the nationals of Member States in front of national courts and tribunals (*Van Gend & Loos*, Case 26–62, February, 1963).[9]

Direct effect operates in both a vertical direction, that is, not only between citizens and public authorities, but also in a horizontal direction between citizen and citizen. In the case of *Defrenne v. Sabeena* (1976), the ECJ found, based on the *effet utile* principle, that the Treaty of Rome's insistence on 'equal pay for equal work' was mandatory in both respects (Loveland, 1996, p.524). However, while the Court established the horizontal direct effect of

Treaty articles and regulations, according this function to directives was another matter. Even though under Article 189 of the Treaty of Rome Member States are bound by the directives addressed to them, it is left to the 'national authorities the choice of form and methods' as regards the 'result to be achieved', thus suggesting the effect of directives is simply vertical (*Treaty Establishing the European Community*, 25 March 1957; Loveland, 1996, p.524). The Court would later however, develop the principle of 'indirect direct effect' which insisted that '"loyalty" provisions' contained in Article 5 of the Treaty Rome compelled national courts 'to interpret domestic law in a manner that facilitated' the purposes of the EU 'in so far as they are given discretion to do so under national law' (Loveland, 1996, p.525).[10]

Constitutional considerations

Caporaso concurs that the effect of the Court's jurisprudence has been to constitutionalise the EU treaties and by the word constitutionalise he too means, not merely that they are the fundamental rules of this organisation, but also that they now approximate a constitutional document laying down the terms for the functioning of the state machinery. Thus, he writes that the Treaty of Rome and the Treaty of European Union have been 'converted from an agreement among sovereign states into a set of rules binding those states and at the same time conferring on EU citizens rights that are enforceable in national courts' (Caporaso, 1996, p.38). He sees this development as comparable in significance to the institution by the US Supreme Court of 'judicial review (1803), federal supremacy (1819), and federal regulation of interstate commerce (1824)' (Caporaso, 1996, p.37; see also Tsebelis and Garrett, 2001, p.358).

The view that the constitutional structure of the EU is now federal in scope is not shared by Member States. At the European Council meeting at Edinburgh on 12 December 1992, Member States underlined that the EU comprised 'independent sovereign States that have freely elected to exercise some of their competences jointly pursuant to the treaties in force' (quoted in Leben, 1998, p.298). On the 12 October of the following year the German Federal Constitutional Court or *Bundesverfassungsgericht*, ruled in *Manfred Brunner et al v. The European Union Treaty* that the European Union was, 'a federation of states ... and not a state based on the people of one European nation', adding that it was for the Federal [German] Constitutional Court to examine the 'legal instruments of European institutions and agencies to see whether they remain within the limits of the sovereign rights conferred on them or whether they transgress them' (Manfred Brunner and others, 1994).[11] Significantly also, the Court described the EU's Member States as '*Herren der Verträge*', that is, 'Masters of the Treaties' (Hartley, 1996, p.109; *Brunner et al*, 1994, p.259).

At the same time, the principle of the supremacy of EU law, whether created or found by the ECJ, has not been directly challenged by Member States thus implying their acceptance of it. This means that the disputed elements in EU law are now dealt with legally rather than politically: by the national courts with reference to the precedents set by the ECJ or, if needs be, by the ECJ itself. Section 3 (1) of Britain's European Communities of 1972 states:

> ...for the purposes of all legal proceedings any questions as to the meaning or effect of any treaties, or as to the validity, meaning or effect of any Community instrument, shall be treated as a question of law (and, if not referred to the European Court, be for determination as such in accordance with the principles laid down by and any relevant decision of the European Court) (quoted in Vaughan and Randolph, 1992, p.220).

Yet, it is important to add that while it is true that the principle of the supremacy of EU law is generally accepted by the national courts of Member States this principle does not extend in the case of 'most, if not all, national courts...to at least some of the provisions of their national constitutions' (Hartley, 1999, p.167). What this suggests is that despite the jurisdictional competence that has been transferred to the EU 'the basics of sovereignty remain unaffected'; in other words, transfers of jurisdictional competence do 'not entail shared or transferred sovereignty' (Loughlin, 2003, p.81).

Parliamentary sovereignty and the EU

As noted in Chapter 2, Austin maintained that the sovereign power cannot, logically, be subject to legal limitation and he further stated that despite the attempts by sovereigns to 'oblige themselves, or to oblige their successors' this principle holds 'universally or without exception' (Austin, 1906, p.156). As William Jethro Brown states, the notion that a Statute by Parliament can bind successor Parliaments must be rejected on logical grounds since the 'authority conferred upon a Statute by Parliament cannot be greater than parliament' and thus 'ought to be held withdrawable by Parliament' (Brown, 1906, pp.161n–2n).[12]

Some argue that in enacting the European Communities Act the British parliament knowingly and voluntarily legislated in contradiction to the Diceyan theory of parliamentary sovereignty. H.R.H. Wade, for example, sees a clear contradiction between the assurances given by ministers in 1972 to Parliament and the public, based on the orthodox view of the British constitution that insists that it is 'legally impossible to impair' the sovereignty of Parliament and that Parliament would remain unable to 'bind its successors', and the passing of the European Communities Act. The Act he states, provided 'in black and white that Community law was to prevail over common law and statute law alike' (Wade, 1991, p.3). He concludes that in passing this Act in 1972, Parliament had 'evidently succeeded in binding its successors, due to the necessity of honouring the Treaty', something which he describes as a 'constitutional revolution' (Wade, 1991, p.4).[13]

The British judiciary has come to gradually accept the principles, as articulated by the ECJ, underlying EU law. This acceptance is reflected in its deference to EU law. It has also embraced the ECJ's teleological technique when interpreting UK statutes which affect EU law. In *McCarthy v. Smith* (1979), Lord Denning held that one 'should not use literalist interpretative strategies in respect of domestic statutes which touched upon matters of EC law: such legislation had to be interpreted subject to the "overriding force" of the Treaty' (Loveland, 1996, p.527). Yet, the responsibility for these developments ultimately rests with Parliament. In relation to the question of interpretative strategies, Loveland writes that the 'rules of statutory interpretation are presumptively a matter of common law' and until Parliament chooses to enact 'legislation forbidding the courts from introducing teleological techniques, domestic courts...[are]...quite competent to reject the literalist approach and adopt new strategies' (Loveland, 1996, p.521). In relation to the question of judicial acceptance of the principle of the supremacy of EU law, in the case of *Factortame* 2 which was returned to the House of Lords for review by the ECJ, the House of Lords made it clear that it was fulfilling its legal obligation as legislated by Parliament to issue a corrective in favour of the recommendations of the ECJ. As Lord Bridge explained, there was nothing surprising in the House of Lord's judgement:

> If the supremacy within the European Community of Community law over the national law of member states was not always inherent in the EEC Treaty, it was certainly well established in the jurisprudence of the Court of Justice long before the United Kingdom joined the Community. Thus, whatever limitations of its sovereignty Parliament accepted when it enacted the European Communities Act of 1972 were voluntary. Under the terms of the 1972 Act it has always been clear that it was the duty of a United Kingdom court, when delivering final judgement, to override any rule of national law found to be in conflict with any directly enforceable rule of Community law. Similarly, when the Court of Justice have exposed areas of United Kingdom statute law which failed to implement Council directives, Parliament has always loyally accepted the obligations to make appropriate and prompt amendments. (quoted in Craig, 1997, p.202)

Contrary to Wade, T.R.S. Allan argues that the Court's ruling in *Factortame 2* did not represent a 'legal revolution' which imposed 'constraints on parliamentary sovereignty', rather what it involved was the House of Lords giving due recognition to Parliament's act of self-limitation in 1972. What the House of Lords was engaged in, Allan adds, was not the usurpation of the sovereignty of Parliament but a 'rational attempt to explore the boundaries of legislative sovereignty within the contemporary constitution' (Allan, 1997, pp.443, 450; see also Bankowski and Scott, 1996, p.82). Despite Wade's view of the case, *Factortame 2* can without any conceptual difficulty be treated in sovereignist terms. Lord Bridge acknowledged this when he remarked that Parliament had made a conscious choice to limit the exercise of its sovereignty through EU membership.

As we have seen, the effect of the passage of the European Communities Act is that Parliament can no longer legislate as it chooses as the national courts can 'disapply' domestic laws which contradict EU law (Loveland, 1996, p.531). In this way, the courts can be seen as playing a 'protective role', ensuring that Parliament does not 'unintentionally' breach its commitments under EU law (Loveland, 1996, p.527). Such a conception was foreshadowed in Blackstone who noted the law's role in correcting 'little inadvertencies' commanded by the king (Blackstone, 1973, p.98). Most importantly however, while British membership of the EU means that EU law must be accorded supremacy, something which has enhanced the role of the judiciary in relation to the legislature in terms of the British system of government, this situation only holds up until that point when Parliament either withdraws from the EU or '*explicitly derogates from this priority ranking of Community Law*' (MacCormick, 1993 pp.6–7; see also Craig, 1991, pp.251–3). As regards the latter prospect, MacCormick adds that on the sovereignist view:

> ...if Parliament did in future command something incompatible with Community obligations, while also commanding that this and subsequent commands should be deemed binding regardless of conflict with Community obligations or Community law, such a command would be obeyed by judges, officials and citizens in the UK, and would in that sense be valid law for us, regardless of anyone else's view. There is, of course, judicial authority for this. The practice, or habit, of obedience to Parliamentary enactment remains (according to this account) steady enough to justify the stated prediction in relation to the counterfactual condition. (MacCormick 1993, p.3).

Even Wade concedes that Parliament retains the 'ability to legislate in deliberate breach of the Treaty', although he regards it as a mere 'remnant of the old unqualified sovereignty' (Wade, 1991, p.3). His view can be contrasted with that of Brown who noted in his edition of Austin's *Jurisprudence* that 'even if the Courts declared that a Statute purporting to be unrepealable was binding until expressly repealed, the declaration would not involve no absolute limitation upon Parliament, since Parliament could at any moment effect such a repeal' (Brown, 1906, p.161n). This suggests that it is misleading to argue that the Parliament in 1972 acted in such a way as to bind its successors. The British Parliament can derogate from EU law, even though such derogation might mean the end of Britain's membership of the EU.[14]

Thus, it is arguably not sovereignty, which William Wallace rightly describes as 'formal, legal', that has been diminished, but rather state autonomy which, unlike sovereignty, is a 'relative' concept (Wallace, 1994, p.53). Autonomy has been diminished through the voluntary redefinition of the rights and duties of the British state in respect to the EU and the social and economic pressures it has submitted itself to as a result of its integration with the Union. Yet sovereignty has been preserved because Britain's submission to EU law is revocable without legal penalty, and one can contrast this with the situation of, for example, Québec which 'cannot legally withdraw from Canada without first obtaining the consent of Ottawa' (Jackson, 1999, p.453). Although he regards it as a 'monocular view', MacCormick concedes that on the surface one can give an account of the political and legal situation in contemporary Europe from an Austinian perspective centred on the principle of state sovereignty (MacCormick, 1993, p.4).

International law and direct effect

Austinian theory is of further relevance to this discussion in another and quite specific way. It should be recalled that Austin refused to classify international law as law properly so-called, although as we saw he accepted the English orthodoxy that the law of nations became the law of the land once it had been translated into statute by Parliament. The insistence that international law can have no effect in a municipal legal system until such time that its stipulations are enacted as national legislation is a feature of the dualist view of international law. The dualist maintains (although this interpretation of dualism is at variance with Kelsen's interpretation discussed in Chapter 3), that the municipal legal and order and the international legal order are entirely 'separate' and for this reason, 'there can be no question of international treaties ever having direct effect': they must be translated into national legislation to have effect. By contrast, the monistic theory of international law maintains that the international and municipal legal orders are 'ultimately part of one greater unity' and what this means is 'that direct effect is in principle possible' and that the provisions of international agreements 'can apply in the domestic legal system as international law' (Hartley, 1999, p.31n).[15]

As we have seen, EU law differs from general international law precisely because it has direct effect: there is in theory no need for secondary national legislation in order for it to be binding on the courts. Yet, it is important to note that in the UK the direct effect of EU law is the result of its previous incorporation 'by statute' which is necessary under UK law for the provisions of a treaty to take effect (Loveland, 1996, p.522). As Hartley writes, Britain is a 'strictly dualist country in its attitude to international treaties' and it follows from this that the Treaties of the European Union could only have effect in Britain by virtue of national legislation. He notes that this was clearly spelled out by Lord Denning in the case of *McWhirter v. Attorney-General* in 1972 wherein he stated: 'Even though the Treaty of Rome has been signed, it has no effect, so far as these Courts are concerned, until it is made an Act of Parliament. Once it is implemented by an Act of Parliament, these Courts must go by the Act of Parliament' (Hartley, 1999, p.169).

Yet as a matter of principle, it seems less than satisfactory that direct effect should not also apply in the case of conventional international law since ratification of a treaty creates an obligation to abide by its terms. The Advisory Opinion of the Permanent Court of International Justice in the Jurisdiction of the Courts of Danzig Case (1928) recognised the 'direct applicability of conventional norms' something which Leben notes was an 'exceptional occurrence' at the time but is now 'quite common' (Leben, 1998, p.297).[16] That a state can enter into certain international obligations yet not be obliged to act on those obligations domestically until they are enacted in the form of statutes is obviously logically problematic. This logical difficulty suggests that the origins of the dualist doctrine lie with politics rather than law. Certainly, this was the view of Krabbe who attributed to the rise of the dualistic doctrine to a form of state solipsism:

> And thus, under the stress of this theory, it has become the practice in some countries that a treaty imposing obligations upon the custodians of public or private interests must be re-enacted in the form of a statute before they are obliged to observe it. This perverted practice and artificial theory collapses as soon as one perceives the fallacy of a political doctrine which still adheres to an absolutist conception of the state, though it makes a distinction in terms by substituting a legal person for a personal sovereign as the natural ruler (Krabbe, 1930, pp.244–5).

In addition to being unsatisfying from a logical point of view, the dualist doctrine, as Charles Leben has more recently argued, holds back the 'existing potential in international law' (Leben, 1998, p.294). While tolerance and acceptance of this lack of coherence may be necessary if there is to be any coherence at all, the problem with this approach is that it comes close to reducing international obligation to a matter of individual volition, as was the case with some nineteenth century publicists who implied that international law was simply a matter of self-limitation and that this could be revoked at any time (Nussbaum, 1954, pp.137, 234–5). Such a view obviously cannot provide an adequate basis for the existence of international law. If treaty obligations hinged solely on acts of self-limitation, the obligation to uphold them would become a matter of caprice. As Leben argues, the 'primacy of international law...[is]...an "existential condition"' of the international legal order, something which is reflected in the fact that in 'an international court...a state cannot invoke domestic reasons to justify the non-performance of its obligations' and that 'different national constitutions themselves provide for the primacy of international norms' (Leben, 1998, p.297).[17]

Considering all these points, one would have to conclude with Leben that the EU is a highly successful and mature international legal order: compared to the wider international legal order, the EU's legal order is relatively centralised and it is this that facilitates the direct effect of EU law (Leben, 1998, p.298). And in this regard one can state that Member States have entered into the phase, to cite Neil Walker's description, of '*late sovereignty*' (Walker, 2003, p.19). At the same time, as indicated by the German Federal Constitutional Court in *Brunner* this level of centralisation and the accompanying acceptance of direct effect is not seen as undermining the sovereignty of Member States. Similarly to the German Court, the French Constitutional Court ruled in relation to the Maastricht Treaty on the 9 April 1992 that:

> ...nothing in the Constitution precluded France from concluding "subject to reciprocity, international commitments with a view to participating in the creation or development of a permanent *international organisation* endowed with legal personality and invested with decision-making power by the effect of transfer of competence consented by the Member States" (Leben, 1998, p.296).

Thus, we can say that the British, have legislated self-limitation in respect to this legal order although the basis of its obligation to self-limit rests on a promise that is normatively binding. Jackson concurs with this depiction supporting the view that the EU is fundamentally a 'union of sovereign states' with Member States authorizing 'all its basic rules, institutions, and organizations' *via* the negotiation of multilateral agreements instead of through the creation of a 'domestic constitution' (Jackson, 1999, p.451). He adds that a close examination of the constitutional foundations of the EU reveals that the supremacy of EU law has its basis in a 'familiar and traditional norm of a society of states, namely *pacta sunt servanda*' (Jackson, 1999, pp.451–2).

Unilateral revocability

Loveland argues that the undiluted sovereignty of parliament will continue to operate until that time when a constitutional crisis concerning the locus of sovereignty arises. Such a crisis could come about should Parliament enact legislation which openly contradicted EU law or 'sought to withdraw the United Kingdom from the Community and the UK courts then refused to enforce the Act' (Loveland, 1996, p.532). McCormick similarly insists that whether or not the unilateral enactment of legislation by Parliament 'directly revoking British membership of the European Community' would be 'generally obeyed in the UK' would be the 'ultimate test' of the sovereignty of the British Parliament (MacCormick, 1993, p.3). In this regard, he notes an inverted kind of sovereignist argument, equally as monocular in his view as its opposite, which sees the governments of Member States as 'mere delegates of the Euro-sovereign' (MacCormick 1993, p.4).

Framing this argument in Austinian terms, MacCormick suggests it is worthwhile asking whether the courts in responding to parliamentary statues 'have or have not a practice of habitual obedience' to EU law 'under...a certain consciousness of sanctions that would be incurred in the event of unilateral rather than amicably negotiated renunciation' (MacCormick, 1993, p.4). MacCormick notes a 'not very explicit threat of economic evil' which the UK might face in the event of unilateral renunciation which he describes as a 'sanction of a kind' (MacCormick, 1993, p.3). Yet, if one were to argue seriously that membership of the Union is not unilaterally revocable, then one must find a legal argument rather than simply highlight the practical difficulties of withdrawing from it. Thus, MacCormick sees as particularly pertinent the question of unilateral revocability, especially given the evolving interpretations of EU treaties, and adds that one must take into account, in this regard, the 'quite early holding of the Court, substantially affirmed and reaffirmed many times since, that the European Communities...constitute a new legal order co-ordinate with that of the Member States' (MacCormick, 1993, p.4).[18] In relation to any British attempt to withdraw from the Union, Loveland notes:

> The EC Treaties, of course, contain no express provisions for member state withdrawal. The only way that result can lawfully be achieved (as a matter of EC law, and hence, given the supremacy of EC law over contradictory domestic statutes, as a matter of domestic law) is if the EC treaties are amended to reconstitute the Community with one fewer member. That process, as specified in Article 236, requires the convening of an Inter-Governmental Conference, at which all existing member states must agree to alterations to the Treaty's provisions. As a matter of EC law (and of acute political irony), any one of the other 14 member states currently has a veto power over UK departure from the Community (Loveland, 1996, pp.532–3).

As indicated, a response to this point concerning Britain's rights and obligations under the EU treaties is that Britain's membership of the EU, with all that that implies, is predicated on the existence of a British statute due to the dualist nature of the treaty process. Hartley states that for Britain to leave the EU 'all that would be constitutionally required would be to repeal the European Communities Act of 1972. Community law would then cease to have effect in Britain: as far as British law was concerned, Britain would no longer be a member' and even though under EU law Britain would still retain membership 'the obligations resulting from this could not be enforced' (Hartley, 1999, p.164). From the perspective of the sovereignty of the British state (and as we have seen this holds for state sovereignty in general), no treaty could involve its irrevocable transfer. It is simply tautologically true that a sovereign power cannot bind itself because the sovereign power is defined as that legal capacity to make and unmake the law. Treaties are generally excluded from this rule because they are not in the way of a promise to oneself but a promise to others and, depending on the terms of that promise, cannot be renounced unilaterally. However, sovereignty itself cannot be renounced *via* a treaty precisely because the enactment of a treaty is itself an act of sovereignty and sovereignty, as Rousseau points out, cannot step outside of or annihilate itself without ceasing to be itself. A British Parliament which sought to bind itself in this fashion would not, by definition, be acting in a sovereign capacity. As Hartley states 'it is not something that Parliament itself could do; indeed, it is the only thing that *cannot* be done by Act of Parliament' (Hartley, 1999, p.172).

It follows from this that the restrictions on Parliament's sovereignty in respect to the supremacy of EU law do not exist at the legal level and that therefore there is no legal limit to the power of Parliament to withdraw from the Union. It also follows that should Parliament articulate the intention to renounce its sovereignty, this would be a purely political act. To articulate such an intention would be to simultaneously extinguish the sovereign voice, not because of any putative surrender to a higher authority, but because to make such a statement would be to speak outside the bounds of what sovereignty permits.

To uphold the view that Parliament has the sole right to decide where legislative competence should rest would be a perverse misreading of the significance of the concept of parliamentary sovereignty. Parliament is only sovereign on the basis that it is assumed to be, as Dicey insisted, the highest expression of the national will. This points to the normative dimension of the statement that Parliament cannot bind itself. Only those who have willed this power which is parliamentary sovereignty can rightfully make any decision concerning where legislative competence should reside. Further, any such decision would unavoidably be a political decision precisely because it would emanate from the collective power which is the source of the sovereignty of the state. Martin Loughlin notes that this point concerning the ultimately political basis of sovereignty was clearly articulated by the German Constitutional Court in *Brunner*. The Court stated, in noting the German constitution's guarantee of the people's 'right...to participate in the legitimation of state power', that the principle of democratic legitimation did not prevent the Federal Republic of Germany from being a member of a supranational organisation such as the EU. (Loughlin, 2003, p.82 and *Brunner et al*, 1994, p.254) Nonetheless, it added:

> ...it is a pre-condition for membership that a legitimation and an influence proceeding from the people is also secured inside the federation of States...If the peoples of the individual States provide democratic legitimation through the agency of their national parliaments (as at present) limits are then set by virtue of the democratic principle to the extension of the European Communities' functions and powers (*Brunner et al*, 1994, pp.256–7).

If the notion that the British parliament could bind its successors in respect to membership of the EU is unacceptable in terms of the logic of sovereignty, then also unacceptable is the idea that the courts, which are wholly emanations of the sovereignty of the British state, could bind Parliament through their interpretative processes. As indicated, any change in the location of the sovereignty of the British state cannot be made within the confines of the order of sovereignty. Change could result from the community exhibiting the belief that the deference of Parliament and the courts to EU law goes beyond mere toleration, but is in fact absolutely compelling because supreme authority is seen as being vested in its institutions and law.

Loveland touches on this issue in suggesting that EU law is a '"higher" form of law' in both a moral and legal sense, and he favourably contrasts it with the political factionalism that corrodes the British legislative process (Loveland, 1996, p.535). He states:

> The EC Treaties stand in marked contrast to our domestic lawmaking process. Their terms are not the product of majoritarian or even-majoritarian law-making. Their every provision has been arrived at through a consensual negotiatory process, demanding the unanimous approval of a growing number of nations – nations which themselves represent differing political philosophies and a multiplicity of cultural inheritances. And as the Treaties have been successively amended by the same protracted, negotiatory, consensual lawmaking process, so the innovative jurisprudence of the European Court and the member states' domestic courts have implicitly been granted a unanimous, cross-national legislative seal of approval. The prospect of EC law being narrowly majoritarian, and hence oppressive or irrational, has been reduced almost to vanishing point. It thus represents a modern manifestation of the ideal for which the seventeenth-century 'revolutionaries' strove. For

> the UK Courts to deny our modern Parliament the power either expressly to breach EC law, or to leave the Community altogether, would not therefore be to challenge the sovereignty of Parliament but to restore its original purpose (Loveland, 1996, p.535).

Loveland does not state openly that parliamentary sovereignty has been effectively conceded or displaced. Further, he appears to accept Wade's view, following Dicey, that 'efforts to find a legal route to remove the sovereignty of Parliament...[are]...futile' and that its removal demands 'not clever legal theorisation but another political "revolution"' of the nature of the 1688 English revolution (Loveland, 1996, p.522). However, he believes that in deferring to EU law British institutions are closer in spirit to the revolution of 1688 than they would be if they resisted it, in that the aim of the 1688 revolution was to create 'an anti-majoritarian source of sovereign legal authority' (Loveland, 1996, p. 534).

Citing Paul Craig's efforts to bring to light the normative roots of the British constitution, Loveland writes that the doctrine of parliamentary sovereignty triumphed in 1688 because it was the most 'broadly based mechanism for ensuring that laws enjoyed the consent of the people' that could be conceived. The sovereignty of Parliament was thus embraced for 'political or moral reasons – namely that it minimised the possibility that the English people would be subjected to factionally motivated legislation' (Loveland, 1996, p.534; Craig, 1991, pp.253–4). He thinks, however, that in contemporary times the British Parliament can no longer be assumed to be the highest expression of the national will since it is subject to the pressures of competitive party politics and open to domination by majorities and minority factions (Loveland, 1996, p.535).[19] Some might baulk at Loveland's characterisation of the way in which EU law is generated, even so, whether EU law is better law in the way Loveland describes it, is beside the point. Again, whether it is accepted as constitutionally superior to British law is a choice to be made by those who breathe life into Britain's constitutional arrangements: that number which Dicey referred to as the political sovereign.

As noted, from the point of view of the order of sovereignty it would be wholly acceptable that political communities within the EU came to view their legislatures as delegates of a European sovereign. However, as MacCormick points out, at this stage the EU simply does not possess sufficient political power or authority such that it could be regarded as anything like a sovereign super-state (MacCormick, 1993, p.16). Yet, he also contends that there may no longer be a locus of sovereign power and authority locatable anywhere in Europe. There is nothing theoretically objectionable about this line of argument, in contrast with the logically confused notion, one which effectively ends up in the same proposition, that sovereignty in Europe has been 'pooled, shared, divided, or split'. As

Walker points out, when used in this fashion sovereignty becomes a rather diffuse notion 'palpably incapable of filling the conceptual and discursive role it once did', and he adds that if we accept the view that sovereignty 'is now everywhere' it would seem that 'nowhere is it particularly important' (Walker, 2003, p.15). My view is that in the context of the EU the sovereign state form has been modified rather than transcended and that its fundamentals remain intact. However, I would also concede that as the set of obligations that membership entails continues to thicken, especially where this is accompanied by increasingly complex and evolving interpretations of the terms of that membership, the notion of derogating from EU law may well come to be widely seen as an 'antediluvian heresy': it may become increasingly difficult to view EU Member States through the prism of sovereignty (MacCormick, 1993, p.7). However, whatever form of polity might emerge as a consequence will almost inevitably be subject to the requirement of democratic legitimation: the consent of the governed.

7
The State and War

The origin of war

In the seventeenth century the idea of sovereignty, or at least notions approximating that idea, when applied beyond territorial boundaries was a way of ameliorating relations among distinct entities which were bound to collide and clash with each other in the course of their interactions. However, in the eighteenth century concerns arose that the construction and consolidation of a system of independent sovereignties was itself a cause of war. For Rousseau, the origins of war lay not with human nature but with the formation and necessary replication of the state form. Rousseau elaborated on this concern in a noted fragment later named 'The State of War': 'From the first formed society the formation of all the others necessarily follows. These must either become part of the first or unite to resist it; they must imitate it or be swallowed up by it. Thus the whole face of the earth is changed' (Rousseau, 1987a, p.238).[1] In Rousseau's account, the state of nature that exists among states is qualitatively different from the state of nature among individuals. While before the creation of the state there were 'incidental quarrels' and occasional murders, such collisions in no way matched the scale and intensity of the organised violence that states administered to each other (Rousseau, 1987a, p.237).

Just as the appearance of one state compelled the appearance of other states, so too were states compelled to keep growing, that is, if they were not to be gobbled up. Unlike human beings whose growth was subject to natural limits, states, as 'artificial' bodies, have 'no fixed measure' (Rousseau, 1987a, p.239). Yet no matter how strong they become, states never reach a sense of what should be their 'proper size' as there is always the possibility that other states can outgrow them. The power of states is thus not absolute but 'purely relative'; it is dependent on where a state stands in relation to other states (Rousseau, 1987a, p.239). Hence, states, or at least those states that aspire to power, lead a somewhat neurotic and in a sense insubstantial existence; their appreciation of their own strength and identity significantly rests on their perception of the strength and identity of surrounding states. As Rousseau wrote, the state 'is forced to compare itself ceaselessly in order to know itself' (Rousseau, 1971, p.383). States are driven to relentlessly expand even though such expansion might sap their vitality or reach the point where their relationship with other states tended 'towards...mutual destruction' (Rousseau, 1987a, p.240). The state of war among states and the level of violence in which this can issue, is the combined effect of the kind of artificiality that the state represents and the skewed logic of the state system itself. Rousseau fully appreciated this logic. As he noted in one of his delineations of the security dilemma, 'men are crazy, and...to be sane in a world of madmen', where madness denotes the constant quest for power, 'is in itself a kind of madness' (Rousseau, 1970a, p.156).[2]

Rousseau sought to protect human nature from that slur which he believed Hobbes had cast upon it, with his 'horrible' and 'insane system' specifying a 'natural war of every man against every man', through according human beings an innate passivity (Rousseau, 1987a, p.234). While the state is compelled, like Hobbes's natural man, to restlessly quest for power human beings themselves, according to Rousseau, typically recoil from aggression and bloodshed: 'Man', he wrote, 'is naturally peaceful and shy; at the slightest danger his first movement is to flee' and natural law, which is inscribed on the 'human heart...cries out to him that he may not sacrifice the life of his fellow man except to save his own'. Even where a man should find himself compelled to sacrifice another's life, he could not 'but feel a sense of horror at the sight of human blood' (Rousseau, 1987a, pp.236–7). At the same time, the formation of the state is only the 'permissive' cause of war; its 'root cause' lies with the oppressive and debased condition of civil society (Carter, 1987, p.98). Given human nature, and given that the systems of enslavement that have replaced natural liberty have not crushed the human spirit entirely, eternal peace remains a possibility provided that society is cleansed of corruption and inequality. For Rousseau there is no question of returning to that amoral condition where innocence is a gift of nature rather than a rational choice. Moral improvement involves 'the perfection of artifice' and indeed it is 'only within the state that man can achieve virtue' because it is only in the civil condition that we can come to understand the meaning of good and evil and thus emerge as moral agents (Carter, 1987, p.101).

Individuals are never enemies

It is precisely because the state and inter-state relations, even violent inter-state relations, are creations of reason that they can be recast in a way that better reflects humanity's natural inclinations. In particular, Rousseau emphasised that war is a relationship which can exist only between states along with their military instruments, and never between individuals. We are enemies, he observed, 'wholly by chance, not as men, not even as citizens, but only as soldiers; not as members of their country, but only as its defenders. In a word, a state can have as an enemy only another state, not men' (Rousseau, 1968, p.56). Since war is a relation between states alone, it cannot accord rights over the bodies of those who are outside of combat (Rousseau, 1968, p.55).

Grotius in Book III of his *Law of War and Peace* in discussing his *temperamenta belli,* quoted an exchange appearing in Seneca's *Trojan Woman* in which Pyrrhus tells the Greek commander Agamemnon: 'No law the captive spares, nor punishment restrains', to which Agamemnon replies: 'What law permits, this sense of shame forbids to do' (Grotius, 1925, p.716). Grotius made this distinction between what is legally permissible and morally impermissible in discussing things done in an unjust war, however he made much the same point when discussing things that can be done in just wars. As G.I.A.D. Draper argues, Grotius had in fact shifted closer to the view that *jus in bello,* as it was later called, is 'applicable irrespective of the justness or unjustness of a war' (Draper, 1992, p.193). Nonetheless, Draper concludes that Grotius's conception of *temperamenta belli* is of limited value because it is essentially a 'plea for moderation' and as such 'more a moral and prudential than a strictly legal idea' and he adds that Grotius's 'implicit concession that contemporary cruelties were permitted by the law of nations inevitably meant that much of the force of his passionate plea for the *temperamenta* was spent and wasted' (Draper, 1992, pp.198–9).[3] In the end, as Robert Kolb explains, the restraints on warfare which Grotius proposed were subsumed by his theory of the just war and for this reason it would be misleading to conflate Grotius's *temperamenta belli* with the modern notion of *jus in bello* which is a body of law distinct from but of equal legal status with the rules of *jus ad bellum.* Grotius was not alone in focussing on the latter at the expense of the former and it is for this reason that the expression *jus in bello* and the idea it signifies do not appear in 'classical' legal works (Kolb, 1997).

Rousseau's articulation of the principle of distinction gained favour in the context of eighteenth century cabinet wars, so-called because they concerned relations between governments rather than peoples and as such were undertaken by professional armies limited in size.[4] Yet, Rousseau's position was not a deduction from existing conditions but rather was based on an analytical distinction between the differing natures and capacities of states and individuals. The state can have no other identity than that of state, whereas citizens and citizen-soldiers have an identity as human beings which is inalienable and anterior to their membership of a particular state. War is an invention and an instrument of states alone. Only states can have the incentive and means for waging war. Individuals by contrast, simply do not have the moral or physical capacity to undertake war. It follows from his analysis that attacks directed against the society of an enemy state are always illegitimate.

This is one reason why public declarations of war are so important. A declaration of war not only gives one's enemy the opportunity to repair any injuries it has inflicted, it also serves as a warning to another society that it is about to be confronted by a hostile state, thus giving it the opportunity to prepare for a relation of belligerency. To attack another state without notice, even if the target of the attack is military, breaches the injunction against attacking society because it is not until a society has put itself on a war-footing that the enemy, speaking formally, comes into existence. To attack a state without notice is the act of a 'brigand' and 'not an enemy' (Rousseau, 1968, p.57). Further to this, war is an activity that must be freely chosen by all the parties to it: war can only be legitimate where it is mutually agreed upon. If a state attacks another state which has declined to enter into hostilities, then 'there is not a state of war but only violence and aggression' (quoted in Carter, 1987, p.118).[5]

By contrast, Vattel maintained that war takes place not just between states but also between societies. He stated that when the sovereign 'declares war against another sovereign, it is understood that the whole nation declares war against another nation; for the sovereign represents the nation, and acts in the name of the whole society...Hence, these two nations are enemies, and all the subjects of the one are enemies to all the subjects of the other. In this particular, custom and principle are in accord' (Vattel, 1863, p.321). For reasons of humanity, Vattel allowed that certain classes of enemy, such as women, children, the sick, the old and frail, should not be treated 'like men who bear arms, or are capable of bearing them' and indeed the same applied to all those 'whose mode of life is very remote from military affairs'. Further, Vattel insisted that 'quarter' must be given to those who have laid down their arms and he resolutely rejected, in terms similar to Montesquieu and Blackstone before and after him respectively, the Grotian claim which had its source in the *Digest* of Justinian: that a right of enslavement was among the rights of victory (Vattel, 1863, pp.321, 347–8, 351).[6] In general, Vattel's position can be summed up by his admonition that we must 'never forget that...[our]...enemies are men' (quoted in Carter, 1987, p.116).[7]

Christine Jane Carter contrasts Vattel's position with that of Rousseau, noting that for the latter 'human sacrifice' must be limited 'precisely because the enemies are not men, but states' (Carter, 1987, p.116). This is certainly a paramount and indefeasible principle for Rousseau and it holds good for all non-combatants. However, the issue becomes more ambiguous when it comes to combatants themselves. While the decision to wage war is an affair of state, at the same time, since states are notional entities warfare can only take material form through the deployment of human agents. To adapt Rousseau, while it is the 'sovereign that inflicts the harm' it is the soldier, as an instrument of the state, which 'receives it' (Rousseau, 1987a, p.244). In denouncing Grotius's interpretation of the law of nations,

Rousseau argues that 'as soon as they [soldiers] lay down their arms and surrender, they cease to be either enemies or instruments of the enemy; they become simply men once more, and no one has any longer the right to take their lives', a point which is logically entailed by the distinction that he draws between combatants and non-combatants (Rousseau, 1968, p.57; see also Rousseau, 1970b, pp.179–80).

Yet, in challenging the idea that a right of enslavement arises from a right to kill Rousseau maintains that: 'Men have the right to kill their enemies only when they cannot enslave them' (Rousseau, 1968, p.57). Such an injunction, one which parallels Vattel's insistence that the right to kill the enemy arises when 'gentler methods' prove 'insufficient to conquer their resistance', can only be based on a prior recognition of the fundamental humanity of soldiers which their status as enemy combatants, contingent and transient as it is, can never wholly absorb nor abolish (Vattel, 1863, p.347). Given all this, the figure of the soldier is bound to be highly problematic from the perspective of moral philosophy: it represents the human being become military instrument with the relation between these being both necessary and tensive. Soldiers can only serve as the kind of military instruments that they are because they are volitional human beings, yet precisely because they are volitional human beings they cannot be seen in purely instrumental terms, as is further discussed below in relation to Kant. Unfortunately, as long as states choose to resolve their disputes through military contests involving bloodshed, the problem represented by the figure of the soldier, due to the latter's dual and ambiguous nature, will continue to haunt us and in this context it is important to keep in mind Vattel's injunction to remember that our enemies are men and Rousseau's insistence that only states can be enemies. When considered in relation to the treatment of soldiers in combat, Vattel's and Rousseau's points concerning the treatment of enemy soldiers and their suggestion that there should be a certain bias in favour of their humanity amount to much the same thing. Nonetheless, Rousseau's argument concerning the different natures of states and individuals provides clear grounds for sharply distinguishing between those who are in and outside of combat and in this respect his analysis is superior to that of Vattel and that of Grotius before him.

While declarations of war and their acceptance are expressions of hostile intent, they are also a public commitment to conduct hostilities in accordance with the law. As we saw, war should only take place where there has been a mutual agreement to undertake it. This leads us to the conception of the state of belligerency as a legal relationship which states enter into at their choosing. This in turn gives rise to the idea of war as a rule governed activity. War is a contrivance of reason, and as such, it is subject from the outset to certain disciplines and there is no reason why it should not be amenable to further disciplines. Rousseau stated that war does not 'consist in several unpremeditated combats' nor in acts of 'homicide and murder' spurred by fits of anger; rather, it consists in the will to destroy the enemy because it has been determined that the 'existence of this enemy is incompatible with our well-being' and he added that this determination must be accompanied by a measure of '*sang-froid*' and 'reason' if a 'durable resolution' is to be produced (Rousseau, 1971, p.381). As Carter argues in relation to the necessity of a declaration of war and the functions that it serves, a crucial implication of Rousseau's argument is that war 'is the most artificial and "conscious" form of conflict, because calculated as an integral part of the policy of states. It must be recognised as such, and not viewed as the inevitable result of "human nature" at work, so that it might be more effectively proscribed or limited' (Carter, 1987, p.118).[8]

Rousseau's understanding of war as a public activity and instrument of state policy means not only that war can be regulated but that it *should* be regulated: its instrumental status implies moral limits to its deployment. Beyond these limits, war ceases to be tied to policy and becomes instead an expression of blood lust. As he stated: 'One kills in order to vanquish, but there is no man so bestial that he seeks victory in order to kill' (Rousseau, 1970a, p.178). One might question this to the extent that the desire to shed the blood of an enemy or indeed the desire for an enemy whose blood one can shed, may be part of the subconscious backdrop to or become a defining feature of any conflict. However, the principle still stands that war, as an instrument of state policy, can give 'no right to inflict any more destruction than is necessary for victory' and, indeed, where it is possible to destroy the social compact without taking a single life then there is an obligation to do so. On this last point, the principles of proportionality and distinction wholly converge as such a conclusion also follows from the strict insistence that only the state is the enemy and since the social compact is the essence of the state, its dissolution eliminates the enemy immediately and in its entirety (Rousseau, 1968, p.57; see also Rousseau, 1987a, p.244). Further to this, where the state is dissolved so too is the status of citizen: all that remains is a collection of individuals. These individuals must be afforded by their conqueror all the protection that their humanity warrants. As we have seen, for Rousseau our status as human beings is ultimately more significant than our citizenship because it is an intrinsic rather than accidental condition. As Montesquieu stated: 'the citizen may perish, and the man remain' (Montesquieu, 1949, p.135).

War as anti-law

The doctrine of the just war is widely seen to have held back the development of laws governing conduct in war. It denied to the enemy rights under the law of nations since it rendered enemies from the point of view of the just side, by definition, criminals deserving of punishment (Donelan, 1983, pp.233–43). Just war doctrine imposed a relationship of moral inequality on any two parties to a conflict and the material impact of this was worsened by the fact that every state involved in war, as one would expect, claimed to have justice on its side. As Vattel wrote, each party 'arrogate[s] to themselves all the rights of war, and maintains in war that its enemy has none', thereby rendering military conflicts 'more bloody, more calamitous', more devastating in their effects and more difficult to conclude (Vattel, 1863, p.381). Vattel despised war, yet he also recognised the need to contain the effects of military contests and he thus prescribed that '*regular war...is to be accounted just on both sides*' and, following from this, that '*whatever is permitted to the one in virtue of the state of war, is also permitted to the other*' (Vattel, 1863, p.382).

Like Rousseau, Kant understood that the mere presence of the other was sufficient for there to be war and he wrote in this regard that: 'Peoples who have grouped themselves into states may be judged in the same way as individual men living in the state of nature, independent of external laws; for they are a standing offence to one another by the very fact that they are neighbours' (Kant, 1970b, p.102). Yet Kant thought that such was the price exacted by the perpetuation of war even a world of 'devils' would be willing to submit to perpetual peace (Kant, 1970b, pp.103, 112). Kant presciently articulated the wholly commensurate and necessary relation between sovereignty and perpetual peace: if states are to enjoy their liberty and independence as *rights* rather than as a fortuitous circumstance, then peaceful behaviour is incumbent upon all. The idea that states have a right to wage war was absurd since the assertion of such a so-called right by any state would simultaneously deny the principles underwriting its international existence. As for those such as Vattel who proffered 'philosophically or diplomatically formulated codes' governing both the recourse to and conduct of war, codes which Kant dismissed as without 'the least *legal* force', they were 'sorry comforters'; the only rational path to take was to insist on an agreement among states 'to end *all* wars for good' (Kant, 1970b, p.103).

At the same time, Kant was not wholly at odds with Vattel in that he identified and distinguished between two categories of law relevant to warfare, the first concerning the legal justifications for war or '*Recht zum Krieg*' and the second concerning what was lawful in the course of war or '*Recht im Kriege*' (Kolb, 1997). He acknowledged the reality of war sufficiently enough to counsel against the use of 'dishonourable stratagems', insisting that in the midst of battle there must remain 'some sort of trust in the attitude of the enemy...otherwise peace could not be concluded, and the hostilities would turn into a war of extermination (*bellum internecinum*)' (Kant, 1970b, p.96).

Yet even though Kant joined attempts to place legal limits on the suffering war produced, the instrument itself remained for him 'inherently 'anti-law''' as general and eternal peace was the final aim of 'Law [*Rechtslehre*]' (Gallie, 1978, p.20; Kant, 1970d, p.257). Kant wrote that 'moral-practical reasons' inside us had issued an 'irresistible veto: *There shall be no war*', the moral-practical consideration at stake being that individuals and communities cannot grow and flourish amidst conditions of violence (Kant, 1970c, p.174). Further, war involves the conversion of citizens into both military targets and killing machines and thus is an extreme violation of the maxim that persons, including one's own person, since they are in possession of a 'rational nature', should never be used '*simply as a means, but always at the same time as an end*' (Kant, 2002, p.57).

Kant addressed the implication that this maxim had for the idea of the profession of arms in stating in *Perpetual Peace* that: 'the hiring of men to kill or be killed seems to mean using them as mere machines and instruments in the hand of someone else (the state), which cannot easily be reconciled with the rights of man in one's own person' (Kant, 1970b, p.95). This is another reason why Kant advocated the dismantling of standing armies and their replacement with a citizen's militia which would be used only for defensive purposes. Such a development would assist the cause of peace by reducing threat perceptions among states. However, the idea of a citizen's militia has an integrity of its own because it means that members of society must risk their own bodies in committing their state to war and not just the bodies of others. It was because war seldom came at a personal cost to rulers that they could 'never get enough of war'; acting with impunity they could indulge their warlike inclinations and 'order thousands of people to immolate themselves for a cause that does not truly concern them' (Kant, 1970b, p.103).

Kant perceived that war is less likely where the one who decides on this course of action is also the one who must shoulder some of its pain, which is one reason why Kant thought republican government, that is, a government which is accountable to its citizens, was an absolute precondition for perpetual peace. Yet, as Kant doubtlessly understood, even under republican government not all those, or even most of those, who choose to commit their state to armed conflict are likely to directly bear its costs. Only with a citizen's militia or mass conscription can this merger of society and the military arm of the state be achieved. States and societies, however, typically prefer to conduct hostilities by means of professional armies. Humanitarian and not just practical considerations render this choice understandable. For example, allocating the role of warrior to only certain members of society serves the same function that was served historically by the duel: it is a means of avoiding war between larger groupings, thus limiting the extent of the blood payment (Nys, 1912, p.293). Nonetheless, Kant's argument concerning how we should treat the persons of others demands that states and societies consider extremely carefully the question of the use of armed force as well as the make-up and source of the armed forces. It is one thing to expose our own person to severe physical and psychological hazards, it is quite another to demand that others be subject to such hazards on our behalf.

A dangerous instrument

Walzer maintains that Carl von Clausewitz underestimated 'the importance of the shift from diplomacy to force' and failed to 'recognize the problem that killing and being killed poses' (Walzer, 1977, p.79). Clausewitz was certainly unhesitating in his description of war as a 'real political instrument' and 'continuation of political intercourse', albeit mixed with 'other means' (Clausewitz, 1968, pp.119, 402). The concept of the just war had been under assault since the seventeenth century by the competing doctrine of *raison d'état* (see Kolb, 1997 and Draper, 1992, p.201). By the end of the eighteenth century (although clearly Rousseau, closer to the middle of that century, had a sharp grasp of the idea), the political conception of war, that is, the idea of war as a rational instrument of policy, had come to be accepted widely. However, it would be Clausewitz who would elaborate and expand on it (Smith, 1990, p.40). Clausewitz was also unhesitating in insisting that war, once commenced, should be pursued vigorously. He stated that in war one must use 'force unsparingly, without reference to the bloodshed involved' in order to obtain 'superiority', adding that 'in such dangerous things as War, the errors which proceed from the spirit of benevolence are the worst' (Clausewitz, 1968, pp.102, 119). While this point suggests a rather impassive attitude towards bloodshed, hardly surprising given his own battle-field experiences, it also suggests that Clausewitz in fact did have a significant appreciation of what was involved in the move from diplomacy to force and indeed, he might be interpreted here as saying that war should be waged energetically precisely because it is a dangerous undertaking involving very high stakes. It is true, as Hugh Smith notes, that Clausewitz came 'close' to exhibiting 'a certain relish in battle', nonetheless he was not one to endorse acts of 'barbarism' or vengeance; further, he thought that the aggressive prosecution of war would serve to limit its duration and the number of casualties produced (Smith, 1990, pp.55–6; see also Clausewitz, 1968, p.345).[9] Clausewitz thought that war should mainly be conducted by professional soldiers and that it generally should take place apart from society and this was exactly because he understood war to be a 'special activity' which, far from involving a suite of balletic manoeuvres, cannot 'be thought of without killing and bloodshed' (Smith, 1990, pp.53, 56; see also Clausewitz, 1968, pp.254–5).[10] Clausewitz's description of war as a 'duel on an extensive scale', recalling that the origins of the duel lie with the desire to limit bloodshed, gains added significance in this context (Clausewitz, 1968, p.101).

Nonetheless, and unlike Rousseau and Kant, Clausewitz saw war as a 'natural function of man' rather than an evil or irrationality that we should struggle to overcome (Clausewitz, 1968, p.197). While reason could and should regulate the conduct of war, it would not put an end to it. For Clausewitz the motives which led to war between 'civilized people' were not fundamentally different from the motives that led to war among 'savages', although he thought that over the course of time civilized peoples had learnt, through the application of intelligence to their feelings, to employ violence in a more economical and disciplined fashion (Clausewitz, 1968, pp.102–3).

Clausewitz categorised the motives for war into what he called '*hostile feelings*' and '*hostile intention*'. The former concerns the 'passion of hatred' for the enemy which can be of such intensity that it gives rise to a war of extermination. The latter, however, simply concerns the will to destroy the enemy and this need not be accompanied or dominated by hostility of feeling (Clausewitz, 1976, p.76). While Clausewitz thought hostile feeling was the predominant motive leading to war among 'savages' and hostile intention the predominant motive leading to war among 'civilized nations', he conceded that 'even the most civilized' of peoples 'may burn with passionate hatred of each other' (Clausewitz, 1968, pp.102–3).

Clausewitz, famously distinguished between absolute or extreme war and real war. The former he treated in part as an ideal type, a 'kind of logical chimera' which any particular war can at best only approximate because in reality war is limited. Thus, he wrote that real war 'is no such consistent effort tending to an extreme, as it should be according to the abstract idea, but a half-and-half thing' (Clausewitz, 1968, pp.105, 403). An important reason as to why war does not tend, at least not generally, towards the extreme concerns the political constraints which surround it. As he wrote, war is 'no mere passion for venturing and winning', 'no work of a free enthusiasm', rather, it is an element in a larger 'whole' which is state policy (Clausewitz, 1968, pp.118, 403). Yet absolute war also provides a template for actual wars, for if 'policy is grand and powerful, so also will be the War' (Clausewitz, 1968, p.403). The point here is that war moves between the poles of the real and the extreme depending on the circumstances and ends to be achieved. Clausewitz attributed the early military successes of Bonaparte to the 'fact that he planned his campaigns and battles in ways that approximated closely the idea of Absolute War' (Gallie, 1978, p.53). Yet, while Bonaparte's crushing victories over Prussia at Jena and Auerstedt justified a military 'strategy based on unlimited warfare and the decisive battle', his devastating defeats in Russia, Leipzig and finally at Waterloo suggested to Clausewitz that in most circumstances a more strategically conservative approach was warranted (Herberg-Rothe, 2001, pp.1–2, 5).

For Clausewitz, war was the state's ultimate reason for being: the state was made for war. As Clausewitz wrote, the 'main notion underlying the state is defense against the external enemy. All else can be, strictly speaking, regarded as *faux frais*' (quoted in Smith, 1990, p.44). Defending the state in a dangerous environment where there are always would-be conquerors may necessitate pre-emption, and indeed, Clausewitz states that the whole 'idea of war originates with the defense' (Clausewitz, 1976, p.377).

Defending the state and promoting its interests were the primary, although not the only functions served by war. Clausewitz, along with his compatriot and contemporary Hegel, thought that war served the additional purpose of re-awakening 'in people a respect for their state and with it a heightened awareness of citizenship' (Williams, 1992, p.114).[11]

For Clausewitz also, the modern state with its unified executive should function as a point of concentrated 'intelligence' which, while harnessing national feelings and exploiting the talents of generals and the army, should make decisions on foreign policy on a clear and logical basis (Smith, 1990, pp.45–6; see also Clausewitz, 1968, pp.121–2 and Clausewitz, 1976, pp.588–9). As he stated, no-one commences 'a war – or rather, no one in his sense ought to do so – without first being clear in his mind what he intends to achieve by that war and how he intends to conduct it' and these considerations, the former being political and the second operational, must be readdressed in the course of a conflict and not just at the outset (Clausewitz, 1976, p.579). As Clausewitz never tired of emphasising, war is an activity shrouded in swirling 'clouds of great uncertainty' (Clausewitz, 1968, p.140) Certainly, war's shifting tableau presents opportunities to warriors of boldness, courage and imagination, such as it did to the bold Bonaparte, who once stated: 'I never had a plan of operations' (quoted in Chandler, 1966, p.135; see also Clausewitz, 1968, pp.117, 217).[12] Yet war's volatility is what also makes it a dangerous and sometimes untrustworthy instrument: it can easily 'fall to pieces and bury us in its ruins' (Clausewitz, 1968, p.162). In the course of war, the relation between the object sought and the means deployed may change dramatically such that the value of the object recedes or even vanishes. Where war tends to the extreme there may cease to be any meaningful object whatsoever beyond survival itself. For these reasons, Clausewitz counselled that as soon as the 'required outlay becomes so great that the political object is no longer equal in value, the object must be given up, and peace will be the result' (Clausewitz, 1968, p.125).

While Clausewitz admired Bonaparte's dynamic campaigning style, unlike the 'dress-sword of obsolete and musty institutions' which he suggested characterised his own country's approach to military affairs, he also appreciated the fact that Bonaparte's imperial ambitions had not served the interest of the French nation.[13] Sound policy had given way to the personal politico-military ambition of someone who combined in himself the roles of head of state and military commander. Clausewitz acknowledged that there is no guarantee that policy will serve the commonweal and that it may be driven by greed and vanity, although he added that this is not the concern of the Art of War which simply assumes that policy represents 'the interests of the whole community' (Clausewitz, 1968, p.404). This is true since the Art of War refers to the military conduct of war and not to the policy which drives it. Yet Clausewitz does not confine himself to the

Art of War alone and, despite his evident enthusiasm for the activity of soldiering, *On War* can be seen as in part a hortatory tract, urging governments to be vigilant in ensuring that there is always a balance between the political goal sought and the 'measure of the sacrifices by which it is purchased' lest war is drained of any meaning beyond the Art of War itself (Clausewitz, 1968, p.125).

This exhortation is especially important in the light of the fact that absolute war also appears as a seed of potentiality: war contains within it a logic of escalation. Clausewitz described this logic in reference to the wars of the French revolution and especially to the campaigns of Bonaparte, stating that with these military operations the 'conduct of War attained to that unlimited degree of energy which we have represented as the natural law of the element' (Clausewitz, 1968, p.291). Clausewitz believed that the overall tendency of war in the period he observed (driven by political developments associated with the French revolution), was towards the pole of the absolute: the social impact of the revolution favoured the freeing up of the element. Most obviously, there were the phenomena of the French revolutionary army and the imperial *Grande Armée* of Bonaparte. The French revolutionary army was a mass conscript army (created following the enactment of a *levée en masse* on 23 August 1793), stirred by a sense of national purpose and, inspired by its own successes, exhibiting a high degree of 'martial elan'. For a period the *Grande Armée* would more than emulate its success and spiritedness (Rapaport in Clausewitz, 1968, pp.20–1; see also Woloch, 1994, p.385). However, it is important to note that there was considerable public resistance to the *levée en masse* in France at least up until the time of the Napoleonic regime, a regime that would extend conscription and succeed in rendering its avoidance 'futile' (Woloch, 1994, pp.432–43).

Clausewitz, knew that the *levée en masse* and the level of morale of the French revolutionary forces had been idealised, nonetheless, he saw in the idea of the nation in arms, something that the French revolutionary army represented, enormous military potential both in physical and psychological terms. The spectacular achievements of the imperial *Grande Armée* seemed to confirm this.[14] Given the threat that this new military phenomenon posed, Clausewitz believed it would have to be imitated by other countries and further, that this would see the intensity and scale of warfare increase (Clausewitz, 1968, pp.385–6). The intensity and scale of warfare was also likely to increase because of the spread of the very development which had made the French revolutionary army and the *Grande Armée* possible: the widening of the popular basis of the state. Extending the state's popular base, through establishing republican government or through at least constitutionalising the state, would allow the state to draw on much greater levels social power, thus significantly enhancing its capacity and will (Clausewitz, 1968, pp.384–6; see also Paret, 1966, pp.34–6).

For Clausewitz, it would appear that war becomes more real where it is tied to the vital interests of the totality of the nation, as in such circumstances it becomes readily apparent that war is an instrument of state and not a mere plaything of a narrow elite. Thus, Clausewitz stated that the French revolution had seen warfare emerge increasingly as an 'affair of the people...every one of whom regarded himself as a citizen of the State', adding that the 'whole power' of the nation was now amassed behind this 'great *affair of State*' (Clausewitz, 1968, pp.384, 386). At the same time, in becoming an affair of the people, war had also become more ideal: it began to approach the absolute, with the natural law of the element being matched in scope by the political interests and feelings involved. Clausewitz, echoing the sentiments he expressed concerning the wars of the French revolution and the campaigns of Bonaparte, announced that with the appearance of whole nations in arms the 'element of War, freed from all conventional restrictions, broke loose, with its natural force' (Clausewitz, 1968, p.386). Clausewitz was doubtful that all future wars in Europe would have the same 'grand character' as did the wars which took place in the wake of French revolution. He thought it might be that the barrier separating the interests of the government from the interests of the people would reappear (Clausewitz, 1968, pp.386–7). Nonetheless, he cautioned that:

> ...bounds, which to a certain extent existed only in an unconsciousness, of what is possible, when once thrown down, are not easily built up again; and...whenever great interests are in dispute, mutual hostility will discharge itself in the same manner as it has done in our times (Clausewitz, 1968, p.387).

This point is suggestive of the future direction of European politics and as such is also suggestive of a great danger: the possibility that the element of war, impelled by its own natural inclinations but also highly charged with social energies, might slip the chain of policy with devastating results. This is exactly what came to pass with the First World War, a war that saw, as Anatol Rapaport expressed it in his introduction to *On War*, 'massacres which transcended Napoleon's boldest dreams' and certainly also the imagination of a philosopher of war writing decades before the industrialisation of its means (Clausewitz, 1968, p.29).

Law and war in the late nineteenth century

The political conception of war that Clausewitz embraced and the accompanying notion that states possessed 'discretionary powers' to resort to war became 'entrenched', according to Robert Kolb, in the nineteenth century (Kolb, 1997).[15] Although it would remain of secondary importance to the insistence on the state's war powers, as suggested, the decline of the just war doctrine at least made it possible to see belligerents as legal equals and thus as possessing equal rights in terms of how war could be waged against them (see also Kolb, 1997). As W.E. Hall put it in 1880, reiterating the position of Vattel, given state practice at the time international law had 'no alternative but to accept war, independently of the justice of its origin, as a relation which the parties to it may set up if they choose, and to busy itself only in regulating the effects of the relation. Hence, both parties to every war are regarded as being in an identical legal position, and consequently as possessed of equal rights' (Hall, 1895, pp.64–5). Hall's comment indicates that in accepting war international law was acknowledging a political reality rather than a legal right, a political reality it sought to moderate.[16] That political will and not law lay behind the state's assertions of the right to wage war was obscured by the identification of this putative right with the sovereignty of the state, such that war was depicted as an expression of the sovereign will of the state. Treitschke, for example, stated that: 'War is politics *par excellence*...it is of the essence of the State that is should be able to enforce its will by physical force' (quoted in Emerson, 1928, pp.ix–x). In this context, Treitschke was treating sovereignty as power harnessed by will, rather than as legal phenomenon subject to prescribed limits. Sovereignty, in this regard, was stretched well beyond breaking-point.

Nonetheless, it should be underlined that the idea that war should be justified by no means faded away. Addressing Kelsen's 1940–41 lectures on the topic, Rigaux notes that even though aggressive war was not thought to be 'contrary to international law' before 1914 (a somewhat different proposition than claiming it was a legal right), in the nineteenth century and up until the time of the First World War the broad public view, both nationally and internationally, was that governments were not free to wage war 'without having a just cause.' This contention is supported by the fact that, as we saw in Chapter 3, a movement in support of the abolition of war made its appearance in the latter part of the nineteenth century. Yet it is also important to note that this view was reflected in the behaviour of states since governments sought to explain and justify why they were resorting to war and generally claimed that in this regard that their actions were 'defensive' (Rigaux, 1998, pp.340–1).[17] Bernhard Roscher, however, offers a contrary view stating that just before the First World War 'governments of the world, public opinion, and legal scholars agreed that every sovereign State could have recourse to war whenever it seemed advisable' (Roscher, 2002, p.294; see also Draper, 1992, p.201).[18] This observation begs the question as to why governments bothered to frame their actions, even where aggressive, as defensive. Clearly, they would not have troubled themselves in the absence of an audience holding expectations as regards just conduct. Nonetheless, in the absence of objective legal criteria, as von Martens had earlier conceded in insisting that 'sufficient legal reasons' should be given when resorting to war, it was up to 'each nation…to follow its own judgement regarding the justness of its cause' (Nussbaum, 1954, pp.182–3).[19]

Paths to peace

The American philosopher William James wrote his pacifist tract 'The Moral Equivalent of War' against the background of European war preparations in 1913. James's essay reflected the mood of the time to the extent that he noted that the peace party lacked the martial glamour and taste for the strong life exhibited by the war party. The peace party's image was 'mawkish' and 'dish-watery', he wrote, 'to people who still keep a sense for life's bitter flavours' (James, 1971, p.11). James revealed a certain ambivalence about war, or rather about the competitive and aggressive impulses which underscore it, noting that human beings have inherited the 'warlike type' and that it is to our 'cruel history' that we owe our capacity for nobility, bravery and self-sacrifice. James also thought that since our forebears had 'bred pugnacity into our bone and marrow' not even millennia of peace could 'breed it out of us' (James, 1971, p.5). Given these considerations, James urged the necessity of finding a substitute for war, something that would serve as an outlet for our aggressive energies while also ensuring the maintenance of that spirit of selflessness and sense of duty which are part of the culture of the warrior. James was well aware of the appetite for war shared by politicians and the public. War, he noted, can excite feelings of ecstasy; indeed, the policy of which war is supposedly an instrument may simply be a pretext behind which lies an unspoken desire for the pure spectacle of war. Indeed, this desire may not even be unspoken, for as James remarked: 'The popular imagination fairly fattens on the thought of wars' (James, 1971, p.5).

The presence of such potent feelings make the task of the peace party, with its appeals to reason in the form of what is good and useful, that much harder. A people or ruling elite infected with war fever cares little for such appeals since in such situations part of the reason for going to war is war. James noted that for those who took pleasure in contemplating war, 'its horror makes the thrill' (James, 1971, p.10). He was only being partly ironic in stating:

> [War's] Its horrors are a cheap price to pay for rescue from the only alternative supposed, of a world of clerks and teachers, of co-education and zo-ophily, of 'consumers' leagues' and 'associated charities', of industrialism unlimited, and feminism unabashed. No scorn, no hardness, no valour any more! Fie upon such a cattleyard of a planet! (James, 1971, p.7).

Like Clausewitz and Hegel, James appreciated that war had a wider social relevance in that it kept society from degenerating into a life of soulless ease and consumption. 'Militarism', he wrote, 'is the great preserver of our ideals of hardihood, and human life with no use for hardihood would be contemptible' (James, 1971, p.9). In the absence of war humanity, 'nursed in pain and fear' and having forsaken the strenuous life for a 'pleasure-economy', would descend into chaos. Indeed, he added, it is this fear of chaos that explains our '*fear of emancipation from the fear-régime*'; it is fear of the consequences of our own degeneracy that has replaced 'the ancient fear of the enemy' (James, 1971, pp.7, 9). He warned that a society which devotes itself to a life of comfort and pleasure would become vulnerable to attack by elements inside the state, that is, by elements that looked on their society with contempt, as well as by elements beyond the state: those looking for any opportunity to launch a military invasion. For this reason, he added: 'Martial virtues must be the enduring cement; intrepidity, contempt for softness, surrender of private interest; obedience to command, must still remain the rock upon which states are built' (James, 1971, p.12). As indicated, James's answer to the difficulty he posed consisted in harnessing martial virtues and channelling them into non-violent forms of public service. Such a response would also remove that injustice which condemned so many to a life of 'toil and pain and hardness', while allowing others to live in luxury, paying no 'blood-tax' at all and remaining utterly immune to the hardships that the planet required its human inhabitants to suffer in order to exist:

> If now...there were, instead of military conscription, a conscription of the whole youthful population to form for a certain number of years a part of the army enlisted against *Nature*, the injustice would tend to be evened out, and numerous other goods to the commonwealth would follow. The military ideals of hardihood and discipline would be wrought into the growing fibre of the people; no one would remain blind as the luxurious classes now are blind, to man's relations to the globe he lives on, and to the permanently sour and hard foundations of his higher life (James, 1971, pp.13–14).

Having proposed the redirection of those moral energies usually harnessed for military purposes towards socially constructive ends, James then went on to warn that with 'whole nations' effectively becoming armies, war would become 'absurd and impossible from its own monstrosity' (James, 1971, p.12).

While the First World War provided ample and bitter testimony to James's warnings concerning the monstrous nature of modern war, the effect of such warnings was muted such was the prevalence of war-loving sentiment and level of hypernationalism before its onset in 1914. Barbara Ehrenreich notes that in the early days of the war even Freud was 'swept up in the excitement' such that he was 'unable for weeks to work or think of anything else'; nonetheless, his feelings quickly sobered down and he reached the stark conclusion that the war was a manifestation of 'some dark flaw in the human psyche, a perverse desire to destroy, countering Eros and the will to live' (Ehrenreich, 1997, p.8; see also Stromberg, 1982, p.81). More specifically however, he condemned the state for orchestrating the conflict, a conflict that disdained the restraints of international law, was fought as though peace would never come again and severed all the ties binding humanity. Further, he noted that in the midst of the slaughter that was unleashed, the state demanded of citizens their unwavering allegiance. Thus, in a 1915 essay called 'Thoughts for the Times On War and Death' Freud wrote:

> Then the war in which we had refused to believe broke out, and it brought – disillusionment. Not only is it more bloody and more destructive than any war of other days, because of the enormously increased perfection of weapons of attack and defence; it is at least as cruel, as embittered, as implacable as any that has preceded it. It disregards all the restrictions known as International Law, which peace-time the states had bound themselves to observe; it ignores the prerogatives of the wounded and the medical service, the distinction between civil and military sections of the population, the claims of private property. It tramples in blind fury on all that comes in its way, as though there were to be no future and no peace among men after it is over. It cuts all the common bonds between the contending peoples, and threatens to leave a legacy of embitterment that will make any renewal of those bonds impossible for a long time to come...The state exacts the utmost degree of obedience and sacrifice from its citizens, but at the same time it treats them like children by an excess of secrecy...[it]...confesses shamelessly to its own rapacity and lust for power, which the private individual has then to sanction in the name of patriotism (Freud, 1985, pp.65–6).

The First World War was seen as violating the key Clausewitzian principle that policy should preside over the decision to wage war as well as its conduct. Raymond Aron wrote that with the First World War, war 'approached its absolute form insofar as the statesmen abdicated in favour of the army chiefs and substituted for political goals, which they were incapable of determining, a strictly military goal, the destruction of the enemy armies' (Aron, 1962, p.26). In a context in which war approached the absolute, another a crucial Clausewitizan element went missing: 'decisiveness'. Rapaport states that there 'was no decision' and as a result the 'nations were bled white' (Clausewitz, 1968, p.29). Gilbert Murray, who would play a prominent role in the activities of the League of Nations in the area of intellectual co-operation, likened the psychological condition of Europeans in the aftermath of the war to that of the Australian Aborigines who in certain portraits, he stated, had the look of 'human beings...beaten by forces they can neither resist or understand' (Murray, 1935, pp.18–20). Such was the trauma induced by this conflict that in its aftermath, the idea of war as a normal and recurring feature of international affairs would never again prevail in European political thinking in the way it did prior to 1914 (Rapaport in Clausewitz, 1968, p.29).[20]

The First World War was also seen, as Freud's comments indicate, as a violation of the social compact by the state itself. For many critics, it was the institution of the state with its putative sovereign right to wage war that was responsible for the senseless slaughter, something which was also sheeted home to theories which celebrated the strong state and glorified military sacrifice in its name.[21]

That the moral authority of the state had dissipated was reflected in the way the war was commemorated. Donald Horne observes that because it had been so 'full of horrors...all the victorious nations tempered their victory by developing compassionate cults of the fallen', most prominently in the form of what the British called in 1921 the tomb of the Unknown Warrior and the French, in the following year, the tomb of the *Soldat Inconnu* (Horne, 1981, p.37). The advent of this institution marked, according to Ehrenreich, the democratisation of military 'glory', democratised precisely because it is 'depersonalised' glory (Ehrenreich, 1997, p.192). Yet the honouring of the unknown soldier, especially given that as a symbol it conveys profound sorrow rather than a sense of triumph, may also be seen as a quiet form of penitence on the part of the state, even if it also symbolically served to obscure the war's appalling cost.[22]

Disillusionment with the state was also reflected in the rise of internationalist sentiment. For a period in the 1920s, the idea of international service at bodies such as the League of Nations had considerable allure. In terms of its representation, the League of Nations came bathed in the white light of science and modernity. The state, by contrast, frequently was portrayed as an archaic institution sustained by the primitive ideology of nationalism. Most importantly, the 1920s saw a vigorous reassertion of the role of international law and, in this regard, attempts to redefine the rights and duties of states.[23] Nicolas Politis in *Les nouvelles tendances du droit international* (1927) stated that: 'Sovereignty killed the theory of *justum bellum*. The pretension of States to not have to render any account of their acts has led them to demand the right to the force that they possess according to their purposes' (Politis, 1927, pp.100–1). The term sovereignty in this context referred to a self-referential '*pouvoir absolu*' rather than a complex of rights and obligations and it was this last understanding which the Covenant of the League of Nations upheld. The Covenant, Politis added, gave expression in a 'large measure' to the 'old idea that unjust wars must be proscribed' (Politis, 1927, p.101). Woodrow Wilson believed that Article 10 of the Covenant, an article designed to protect a state's political independence and territorial integrity, was 'the most vital feature of the whole Document' and that it was on adherence to Article

10 that international peace and security depended. That Wilson believed this was precisely because he understood, as Kant and others had understood before him, that a so-called right of war was utterly incompatible with the principle of sovereignty (Rappard, 1927, p.21; see also Gathorne-Hardy, 1950, p.16n).

The League Covenant did not explicitly outlaw war. Instead, 'members agreed to abstain from recourse to war while a dispute was in submittal to arbitration or inquiry by the Council and until three months after an award or report was made'. However, the Covenant clearly reflected the perception that sovereignty and the discretionary recourse to aggressive war were incompatible (Egerton, 1996, p.25). Sir John Fischer Williams maintained that 'on all the crucial questions that were problematic about the law as it stood in 1914 – the absence of a distinction between just and unjust war, concentration on the procedures of war and the absence of institutions for "peaceful change" – "the Covenant of the League offers a remedy, or the promise of a remedy"' (Koskenniemi, 2005, pp.40–1; see also Williams, 1929b, pp.70–1). Further, since the principle of sovereignty underwrote the whole international system and was the guarantor of each and every state's independence, it followed that aggression against any one state was a violation of the rights of all states. For this reason, the League Covenant enshrined the principle of collective security declaring 'that a member resort to war contrary to the Covenant should be deemed to have committed an act of war against all other members' (Nussbaum, 1954, p.267).

The contradiction within international law that saw it both recognise the independence of states yet permit violations of that independence, was further addressed by the Pact of Paris for the Renunciation of War in 1928. This Pact, in the words of the French foreign minister Aristide Briand, gave expression to the American notion that 'war is outside the law', a notion 'already familiar to the signatories of the League of Nations Covenant and the Treaties of Locarno' (quoted in Roscher, 2002, p.296).[24] Kolb points out that it was only at this time that the expressions *jus ad bellum* and *jus in bello* began to appear in legal discourse in order to refer to two distinct bodies of law, with the laws of armed conflict assuming an equal importance with the law concerning legitimate reasons for recourse to war. This development had been inhibited first, by the predominance of just war doctrine and second, by the currency of the belief that states had a right of discretionary recourse to war (Kolb, 1997).

With the advent of the UN Charter, the process of outlawing aggressive war appeared complete as importantly it included, unlike the Paris Peace Pact, a mechanism for punishing violators of its terms. Kelsen stated at the time: '…it is hardly possible to say any longer today that according to valid international law any state, unless it has obligated itself otherwise, may wage war against any other state for any reason without violating international law; it is hardly possible, in other words, to deny the general validity of the *bellum iustum* principle' (Kelsen, 1968, p.87). It was only at this point that we can say that thinking about sovereignty in respect to the question of war fully matured. As suggested earlier, that it took so long for the realisation that discretionary recourse to war and the principle of sovereignty were incompatible notions to sink in, can be put down, not only to backwardness in thinking, but also to the empirical conditions in which states found themselves: the only way of punishing aggressors was through responses in kind by other states. The powers accorded the United Nations Security Council (UNSC) under Chapter VII of the Charter have ameliorated this problem to some extent.

Wars of anticipation

To the extent that action on the part of the Security Council is subject to political bargaining and that it does not or cannot act as automatically and effectively as do domestic police authorities in well-ordered states, a degree of that former discretion maintains. Thus, the abuse of sovereignty remains a possibility when it comes to war as it does in other areas. Even if we view sovereignty as serving the function of constraining the behaviour of states, we would have to agree that it involves the acceptance of a measure of risk and while this risk can be reduced, it cannot be eliminated, at least within the constraints of a multipolar system. The price of a decentralised legal and political order and the freedom it affords is an international system subject to uncertainty and volatility. Acceptance of this is an implicit part of the sovereignty bargain as it stands today.

Grotius considered wars of anticipation to be an unfair and unreasonable response to the risks consequent upon membership of a state system. He wrote: 'But that the possibility of being attacked confers the right to attack is abhorrent to every principle of equity. Human life exists under such conditions that complete security is never guaranteed us' (Grotius, 1925, p.184). A war of anticipation is abhorrent to principles of equity because it involves a state claiming greater rights for itself than it would allow other members of the international system. It is to demand near complete security for oneself, a level of security that can only be achieved by denying security to others. It is an attempt to better enjoy one's sovereignty in a way that would deny the equal independence of others. As Calvo stated:

> ...usage of this right [of sovereignty] is subordinated to the exercise of the right which belongs to all. If it were otherwise, the unlimited right demanded by one would transform itself into a privilege and would destroy at the same time the principle of equality, the independence and even the sovereignty of other states (Calvo, 1887, p.268).

Yet, anticipatory wars have often been regarded as an acceptable means of preserving the balance of power. Walzer offers the example of the

Spanish War of Succession (1703–1712) which saw Britain lead an alliance of European states against an attempt to merge the crowns of France and Spain, something which was viewed by France's neighbours as part of Louis XIV's plan 'to dominate Europe' (Walzer, 1977, p.79). It was Louis XIV's behaviour in relation to his European neighbours that Vattel had in mind when he formulated criteria for 'legitimate prevention'. For Vattel, preventative wars maybe legitimate in cases where 'a state has given signs of injustice, rapacity, pride, ambition, or of an imperious thirst for rule...is on the point of receiving a formidable augmentation of power' and refuses to give guarantees of security when they are asked of it. Yet as Walzer notes, in relation to the Spanish War of Succession, Vattel concluded with the cautionary observation that since the end of the conflict it had become apparent that the 'policy [of the Allies] was too suspicious' (Walzer, 1977, pp.78–9).[25]

The 1842 *Caroline* formula, articulated by the US Secretary of State Daniel Webster in communication with Britain's Lord Ashburton, went much further than Vattel in clarifying the question of anticipation, specifying that while 'exceptions growing out of the law of self-defence do exist, those exceptions should be confined to cases in which the necessity of self-defence is instant, overwhelming, leaving no choice of means, and no moment of deliberation' (quoted in Colombos, 1928, p.95). Hosack was clearly alluding to it when he stated in relation to the right of intervention: 'There can be no doubt that the doctrine laid down by Grotius is the true one, although it has on many occasion been departed from in modern times..[it is]...now generally admitted that no state is justified in resorting to an armed intervention unless the danger to be apprehended is immediate and imminent.' Despite this endorsement, Hosack went on to add that as the dispositions of men are so varied and the 'circumstances in each case' so different, the question of intervention 'must ever remain a question of public policy and not of public law' (Hosack, 1882, pp.192–3).

However, whatever customary rights of anticipation existed in the past, they did not survive the creation of the UN Charter. In Article 2(4) the Charter stipulates that states must not use force or threaten to use it, although it is permissible under Article 51 to use force if 'an armed attack occurs'. Michael Bothe argues that it is significant that while Article 2(4) prohibits both aggression and threats of aggression, the exception to that rule only permits self-defence in response to an armed attack. He states: 'It is hard to conceive that it was merely due to a drafting oversight that the notion of threat was only mentioned in the rule and not the exception' (Bothe, 2003, p.229). Albrecht Randelzhofer similarly argues that Article 51 prohibits a right of anticipatory defence, stating that under Article 51 self-defence is 'permissible only after the armed attack has already been launched' (Randelzhofer, 1994, p.676).[26]

Political actors draw on legal discourse in order to justify their behaviour and the more generous is our understanding of self-defence then the more legal pretexts there are for opportunistic actions. To limit a state's recourse to legal justification is to place boundaries on what can plausibly be stated about one's actions. Where an action might test the limits of the available rhetoric of justification, actors may decide to undertake that action cautiously or to not undertake it at all. While one might want to qualify the strict understanding of the right of self-defence outlined above in certain circumstances, the important point here is that if states are allowed to play fast and loose with the legal meaning of self-defence, we could quickly be propelled back to the nineteenth century situation where 'war was not illegal' (Bothe, 2003, p.238).[27]

There are two other reasons reason why wars of anticipation have historically been regarded by legal publicists as illegitimate. As Grotius stated, for war to be 'lawful it must be necessary' and war only becomes necessary when we are 'certain' in respect to our neighbour's power and intention (Grotius, 1925, p.549). If we are not certain in this regard, then one is not engaged in a just war but in, as T.H. Green expressed it in echoing Rousseau, 'multitudinous murder' (Green, 1999, p.118). While Walzer argues that anticipation in certain instances may be legitimate, he nonetheless underlines the crucial point that war is killing and there is a 'great difference between killing and being killed by soldiers who can plausibly be described as the present instruments of an aggressive intention and, killing and being killed by soldiers who may or may not represent a distant danger to our country' (Walzer, 1977, p.80). In addition, as Kant urged, using other people's bodies in order to promote one's cause, especially where these bodies are deployed in violent and dangerous contexts, is always morally problematic. For this reason, the state in whose name soldiers serve, has an enormous burden of responsibility not to put soldiers in harm's way on ill-considered grounds.[28] Vattel eloquently described the twin evils which any war risks inflicting:

> Whoever entertains a true idea of war, – whoever considers its terrible effects, its destructive and unhappy consequences, will readily agree that it should never be undertaken without the most cogent reasons. Humanity revolts against a sovereign, who, without necessity or without very powerful reasons, lavishes the blood of his most faithful subjects, and his power to maintain them in the enjoyment of an honourable and salutary peace. And if to this imprudence, this want of love for his people, he moreover adds injustice towards those he attacks, – of how great a crime, or rather, of what a frightful series of crimes, does he not become guilty!...The violences, the crimes, the disorders of every kind, attendant on the tumult and licentiousness of war, pollute his conscience, are set down to his account, as he is the original author of them all. Unquestionable truths! Alarming ideas! which ought to affect the rulers of nations, and, in all their military enterprises, inspire them with

> a degree of circumspection proportionate to the importance of the subject! (Vattel, 1863, p.301).

The invasion of Iraq by the American-led 'Coalition of the Willing' in March 2003 and its aftermath, has given rise to a massive number of Iraqi causalities, including both soldiers and civilians. The war has also seen thousands of Coalition soldiers killed or maimed as well as placed in moral danger. When the *casus belli*, namely Iraq's possession of weapons of mass destruction in defiance of UNSC resolutions, proved to be falsely based the justification for the invasion shifted to regime change. However, as odious as the former Iraqi regime was, this shift is illegitimate from the point of view of international law since there is no generally recognised unilateral right of intervention in this regard and nor was any formal case made for regime change in the context of the UNSC. There is also the question of democratic legitimacy. As Ori Lev argues in relation to this consideration: 'Citizens through their representatives approved the invasion on specific grounds and if these grounds were wrong then in order to restore legitimacy the administration must either withdraw the military forces or ask for another authorization based on this new argument' (Lev, 2004, pp.3–4).[29]

In addition to the various legal violations that the invasion of Iraq has involved in relation to both *jus ad bellum* and *jus in bello*, and in the latter case horrific violations have been perpetrated on all sides, the exercise would seem to be a travesty of Clausewitz's emphatic insistence that one should only engage in war, at least if one is in one's right mind, where a proportionate relation between the cost of victory and the political goal to be achieved is maintained. In the case of the war in Iraq, these have not been kept in alignment. Indeed, the conflict is widely seen to have resulted in more insecurity than it sought to avert. Leaving aside the vagueness surrounding the political goals at stake now that weapons of mass destruction claims have been discounted, it is questionable whether the conflict is even militarily winnable given a relentless insurgency that has refused to accept the Coalition's initial military victory as decisive. Clausewitz urged that war is a 'serious means for a serious object' (Clausewitz, 1968, p.118). It should be pursued and prosecuted judiciously because it involves bloody slaughter, because it can have serious ramifications for third parties, and because it is an instrument which can viciously turn on the state which chooses to wield it For all these reasons, as Edmund Burke cautioned in relation to the English response to the American rebellion in 1777, one is entitled to expect that 'conscientious' leaders would be extremely careful in how they deal 'in blood'; one also is entitled to expect, as Burke went on to state, that they 'would feel some apprehension at being called to a tremendous account for engaging in so deep a play, without any sort of knowledge of the game' (Burke, 1872, p.13).

Carl Schmitt thought that the criminalisation of aggressive war under the Covenant of the League, Paris Peace Pact and the UN Charter eliminated the distinction between the 'legally recognized enemy' or '*justus hostis*' and the 'criminal'. States, armed with a *just causa* and unable to comprehend the notion of a *justus hostis* (just enemy), come to view their rivals (as Vattel pointed out in relation to earlier doctrines of the just war), as 'nothing more than...object[s] of violent measures' and thus the 'antithesis between the warring parties is increased exponentially' (Schmitt, 2003, pp.320–1). Schmitt did not see in the criminalisation of aggressive war a resurrection of the 'Christian-theological' doctrine of just war, rather he saw it as providing 'ideological' cover for the deployment of modern instruments of war, the ultimate end of such deployments being the 'nihilistic destruction of all law' (Schmitt, 2003, pp.187, 321). He argued that the deployment of modern weapons of destruction necessitated a just cause, since in the absence of such a cause people would be bound to ask themselves, 'if the foe was "not what they said he was – what were they?"' (Schmitt, 2003, p.322).

Koskenniemi thinks the contrast Schmitt draws between a past era during which inter-state conflict in Europe was regulated and contained under the Public Law of Europe and the post-League situation of 'hypocrisy and danger' is simplistic and open to question. Nonetheless, he finds Schmitt's analysis illuminating in the context of the so-called war on terror, a war which is both spatially and temporally unlimited, claims moral inspiration and 'in which the adversary is not treated as a *justus hostis*' (Koskenniemi, 2004, pp.493–5). I would argue that the fact that the invasion of Iraq was not given the imprimatur of the UNSC suggests that the wars of pacification of which Schmitt forewarned, are not authorised by the rules governing the use of force elaborated between 1920 and 1945 and indeed, arguably, may only be undertaken in violation of their terms. Further, I agree with Doehring that Schmitt underestimated the potential for adherence to the rules of *jus in bello* in the context of that legal framework (Doehring, 2002, p.376). Nonetheless, and following on from Koskenniemi, the rendering of Iraq as a theatre of war certainly bears all the hallmarks of a '*nihilistic* universalism' which Schmitt ascribed, wrongly in my view, to the new world orders instituted after the First and Second World Wars (Koskenniemi, 2004, p.501).

Whatever conscious motivations may explain the invasion, do we not also sense behind this ghastly spectacle a fascination with what the poet Charles Baudelaire called the '*joie de descendre*' towards hell, an impulsion which he described as the '*postulation*' of '*Satan*' or '*animalité*'? (Lagarde and Michaud, 1985, p.430). The former US Defence Secretary Donald Rumsfeld infamously quipped in relation to the looting of Baghdad on 11 April 2003 following the American invasion: 'Stuff happens' (CNN, 2003). One is tempted to believe, to adapt the ancient maxim, that embedded in the subconscious of some is the diabolical but stupid thought: let war be done, even if the world perish.

8
Conclusion

This study has traced the development of the concept of sovereignty and has explored its implications for both the domestic and international spheres of activity. In exploring the concept, I have tried to draw out what I believe to be the ethical imperatives contained within it and the political logic that is attendant upon these. In Chapter 2, I noted Toqueville's observation that resting at the base of nearly all social institutions is the idea of the sovereignty of the people and a study of the various theories of sovereignty over the centuries reveals an acute awareness of this perception. Even in the hands of some of its most absolutist exponents, it was well understood that sovereignty can have no other source but the minds of men and women: it was understood that sovereignty must be imagined and continue to be imagined by a community if it is to become real and endure.

That Toqueville's basic point receives so little attention is not surprising given, on the one side, public ignorance, laziness and fear and, on the other, the breath-taking claims of power, as well as power's own fear of the explosive significance of this very point. Thus, the problem is not simply one of power refusing to recognise or cleverly obscuring its origins: the problem also concerns the fact that a people fully apprised of the communal origins of sovereignty must, in all good faith, demand of itself nothing less than democratic vigilance, sometimes to the point of militancy.

In emphasising what I believe to be the ultimately and inescapably democratic logic of sovereignty, I have drawn attention to what I consider to be the natural alliance between sovereignty and self-determination. Indeed, the development of the concept of self-determination from the late eighteenth century onwards can be seen as a manifestation of sovereignty's downward thrust. My argument is that sovereignty's overall tendency is in the direction of the people, although this particular endpoint, given that sovereignty encapsulates a relationship of command and obedience, can never be fully reached: sovereignty can never dissolve into the people without dissolving itself. That said, the rise of the concept of self-determination reflects the belief that the gap between state and society, while impossible to eliminate in its entirety, can be bridged to a significant extent and indeed must be bridged. It is a gap that has to be bridged because the state and its sovereignty are merely instruments of the self-determination of peoples. State sovereignty is devoid of sense where it ceases to serve that function. The instrumental understanding of sovereignty means that those who wield the sovereign power can only operate within certain constitutional limits. Where they operate willfully outside these limits then the political nation has a right, and importantly a duty, to remove them.

There are many parts of the world where the struggle for self-determination is far from being realised: where the distance between state and society is so immense that it can only be bridged by the reconstitution or refounding of the state. Yet, the struggle for self-determination, which I have argued is ongoing (since although the institution of state sovereignty may be an important expression of the struggle for self-determination it is also simply a means through which it can continue), is still in question in democratic societies. It has been long appreciated that the interests of minorities and the socially disempowered may be overlooked by democratic majorities. This is why constitutional guarantees of rights (political, religious, cultural or economic), and institutions independent of political power to oversee these rights are essential. Such rights, in order to protect the identity and interests of minority cultures, may even take the form of a collective right self-determination within the framework of the state. The problem of majority tyranny also explains why, in democratic states, the people have somewhat distanced themselves from power *via* the mechanism of representation. Yet representation, coupled with the steady accretion of state power that sovereignty affords, holds out the danger that the gap between state and society may widen to the point where democracy becomes merely formal. It is thus important to repeatedly assert the power of the popular self and to look for and open up further avenues for the assertion of this power.

In respect to the international sphere, I have attempted to bring out what I believe to be the essentially pacific logic of sovereignty. To adapt Kant, properly conceived, sovereignty decrees that there shall be no war. For a long time, sovereignty, as practised by states, operated in alliance with war and conquest, serving to authorise and justify these activities. Yet, this alliance was bound to collapse as sovereignty, if one accepts what I have said about its relation to self-determination, is incompatible with aggression and conquest. Any state which engages in aggression, as Rousseau points out, denies the very basis of its being: it denounces all the rights of political independence and territorial integrity that it enjoys by virtue of its sovereignty. If states wish to enjoy their sovereignty as a recognised legal right rather than possess it as a mere reflex of their physical power (in which case, it would not be sovereignty at all), then aggressive war must be deemed illegal. The formal relation between sovereignty and aggression was gradually severed during the first half of the twentieth century, yet residues of the old idea that states have the option of waging war, should it appear advisable, remain. There is an undercurrent of this idea in current claims to a right of anticipation and in broad notions of self-defence. The task, as suggested in the previous chapter, is to rigorously police the existing limits imposed on the sovereign right of self-defence and to counter, in the name of the principle of sovereign equality, claims to privileged status by any state in this regard.

In explaining why for a long time the practice of sovereign by states was associated with war, I appealed to what Hans Kelsen called state solipsism. State solipsism reflects an understanding of sovereignty that would render the existence of other states and the international legal as projections of the will and ideas of whichever state gazed on the world in a solipsistic fashion. State solipsism is reflected well in a statement by a senior advisor to former President George W. Bush concerning the status of the United States: 'We're an empire now, and when we act, we create our own reality' (quoted in Suskind, 2004). Unfortunately for empires putative or otherwise, the world cannot be simply a projection of their own will and ideas. The world contains hard and resistant elements with which we may need to negotiate or around which we may need to navigate. These are the pragmatic reasons why in the past the practice of sovereignty had to be moderated. Yet, as I have also pointed out, recognition of and respect for the rights of others is the logical prerequisite for the recognition of and respect for one's own rights. The possession of significant stores of power may allow one to play fast and loose with the rules, but not on all occasions and only up to a point. Eliminating or ameliorating solipsistic thinking in regard to war meant that states had to accept that the rights they enjoyed were in an important sense co-productions. To adapt Balibar, such rights are trans-statal in the sense that through recognising each other, states 'co-constitute' their rights. I have made much of Mervyn Frost's constitutive theory of recognition because it explains well the sense in which rights are co-productions and why this means that states are compelled to respect them. Such respect cannot be a matter of will if there is to be any legal order at all.

Constitutive theory also provides an argument for extending and enriching international obligations: it highlights each state's existential-cum-ethical responsibility for the other. However, I have also argued following others, that the obligations that states owe each other ultimately spring from the obligations that exist among human beings. Humanity is currently organised into sovereign states. Yet, this has not always been the case and in the scheme of things, this mode of organisation may prove to be a temporary arrangement or juncture on the way to somewhere else. My argument has been throughout that the state is only valuable insofar as it serves as an instrument of human happiness. Should the state system fail large numbers of people – through casting them back into a state of nature whether for reasons of war, poverty or environmental collapse – then it may be discarded by parts of humanity or humanity as a whole and replaced by other modes of political organisation. Alternatively, we may attempt to further civilise this system through adding to and thickening the responsibilities of states to each other and to humanity in general.

Notes

'Tout Français en âge viril est citoyen politique, tout citoyen est électeur. Tout électeur est sourverain. Le droit est égal et absolu pour tous. Il n'y a pas un citoyen qui puisse dire à l'autre: "Tu es plus souverain que moi!" Contemplez votre puissance, préparez-vous à l'exercer et soyez dignes d'entrer en possession de votre règne.'
'Le règne du people s'appelle la République.'

'Every Frenchman of full age is a citizen, every citizen is an elector. Every elector is sovereign. The law is equal and absolute for all. There is no citizen who can say to another: "You are more sovereign than I!" Contemplate your power, prepare to exercise it and be worthy of entering into possession of your kingdom.'
'The kingdom of the people is called the Republic.'
Alphonse de Lamartine, Histoire de la révolution de 1848', Tome II, p.139.

Chapter 2 The Municipal Realm

1 Hinsley notes that 'African primitive states' were not always based on conquest but sometimes 'on the tradition of the first occupation of the land' (Hinsley, 1986, p.15).
2 As Rousseau counsels, the 'strongest man is never strong enough to be master all the time, unless he transforms force into right and obedience into duty' (Rousseau, 1968, p.52).
3 Resistance against the state is acceptable on the part of both individuals and groups in cases of 'atrocious cruelty' as long as what is preserved by such resistance is 'of greater importance' than obedience to the state's commands and where such resistance would not destroy 'a great many innocent people' (Grotius, 1925, pp.148–50). However, Grotius warns that liberty does not give to individuals any more than to states the 'right to war, just as if by nature and at all times liberty was adapted to all persons' (Grotius, 1925, p.551). Paul Christopher points out that if Grotius allowed 'disobedience to municipal law based on the subjective assessments of individuals' it would open the door to 'parallel applications in the international society of states' (Christopher, 2004, pp.72–3).
4 By determinate Austin means a 'body capable of corporate conduct' (Merriam, 1900, p.142).
5 Austin did not feel the necessity to inquire into the legitimacy of the sovereign power much beyond noting the outward evidence of it: habitual obedience. As Austin stated: 'I find governments to be established as a fact, to be considered useful, and to be supported by popular opinion. How these things came to be is a question that I, as a jurist, am not called upon to answer. If I *must* answer the question, I should say that the most important factor in the origin of society is a vague perception of the utility of society' (Austin, 1906, p.205n). Rousseau makes the same point in insisting that all law ultimately rests on 'belief', although he more clearly draws out the distinction between 'force of habit' and 'force of authority' (Rousseau, 1968, p.99).

6 Austin wrote that while the state 'would not and could not incur a legal pain or penalty' if it deviated from communal 'maxims' it 'might chance to meet with resistance' (Austin, 1906, pp.162–3).

7 Dicey insisted that representative government required that the 'legislature should represent or give effect to the will of the political sovereign, i.e., of the electoral body, or of the nation' (Dicey, 1908, p.425). However, Dicey thought that Austin's tendency to confuse legal with political sovereignty resulted in him treating Parliament as a body discharging a trust on behalf of the electorate: the political sovereign. Dicey insisted that such a notion was 'inconsistent with the language used by writers who have treated of the British constitution', as Austin himself conceded. Dicey denied that 'Parliament is in any legal sense a "trustee" for the electors', adding that the 'plain truth is that as a matter of law Parliament is the sovereign power in the state, and that the '"supposition" treated by Austin as inaccurate is the correct statement of a legal fact which forms the basis of our whole legislative and judicial system' (Dicey, 1908, pp.72–3). In response to Dicey's criticism, Manning points out that although Austin clearly appreciated the constitutional role of Parliament he did not bother to 'define legal sovereignty' and this was because for Austin sovereignty is that 'authority logically correlative to the prevalent attitude in a certain type of society.' In Austin's system this 'authority is logically *pre*-legal, as indeed almost everything, in his system, may be considered pre-legal, except the content of this or that separate command' (Manning, 1933, p.192). Note that a precedent for the distinction that Dicey makes can be found in early seventeenth century Holland and Germany with the doctrine of *majestas realis* and *majestas personalis*, with the former expression referring to the real or ultimate sovereignty of the people and the latter to the authority vested in the government, both of which were seen as coexisting side by side (see Merriam, 1900, p.20n).

8 Hinsley acknowledges that earlier kingdoms and empires such as the Kingdom of Macedon, the Empire of the Achaemenids and the Empire of Alexander had developed 'forms of state', yet he adds that they 'remained states in search of communities' (Hinsley, 1986, pp.30–1).

9 Ulpian 'laid it down as judicial doctrine that the imperium of the Emperor had absorbed the original *imperium populi Romani*' (Hinsley, 1986, p.42). He stated that a 'decision given by the emperor has the force of statute. This is because the populace commits to him and into him its own entire authority and power, doing this by the *lex regia* which is passed anent his authority' (Justinian, 1998, 1.4.1).

10 Telling of the papal grasp of the concept of legal supremacy is Jean Bodin's recollection that Innocent IV 'who understood best of all men the rights of sovereignty, and who had put under his feet the authority of almost all emperors and Christian princes, said that supreme power belongs to him who can take away from ordinary law' (quoted in Barker, 1915, p.109).

11 The Roman term *majestas* signifies the 'Supreme public dignity' (Bluntschli, 2000, p.389).

12 Charles Merriam writes that in that in the medieval period the theory was not well developed either in terms of the 'essential nature and attributes of the supreme power' or in relation to its 'location' (Merriam, 1900, p.13).

13 See D. Engster's and J.H. Elliott's discussion of the putative influence of Machiavelli on French politics (Engster, 1996, p.476; Elliott, 1968, pp.215–16). Franklin points out that in his *Methodus ad Facilem Historiarum Cognitionem* of 1566, Bodin hailed Machiavelli as 'the first of the moderns to revive the "civil science"

of the ancients', but Franklin also notes that in the *République* 'he is singled out as the arch atheist and destroyer of commonwealths'. Bodin adds that his 'poisonous teachings had been brought to France by Catherine de Medici along with her Italian counsellors. The crime of 1572 was thus the work, not only of a tyrant but of foreigners' (Franklin, 1973, p.49). Bodin writes in relation to commentators such as Machiavelli: 'This attitude is an unworthy betrayal of the sacred laws of nature, which requires not only that sceptres be wrested from the hands of the wicked, to be given to good and virtuous princes...but also that the good in the world at large be stronger and mightier than the evil.... It is, therefore, the grossest incongruity in matters of state, and of dangerous consequence, to teach princes the rules of injustice in order through tyranny to consolidate their power...This is the most likely means that may be imagined for the ruin of princes and their estate' (Bodin, 1606, p.A70).

14 Merriam reports that the term *Monarchomaque* was first used in a book published in 1600 called *De regno et regali potestate adversus Buchananum, Brutum, Boucherium et reliquos Monarcho machos libri sex* (Merriam, 1900, p.17). The word signifies those who combat the sovereign. The Calvinist reformists, Théodore de Bèze and François Hotman, were opposed to the royal power and sought to justify resistance, tyrannicide and even regicide, viewing rebellion against tyranny as being divinely ordained. Their doctrines ultimately led to the formulation of a theory of popular sovereignty. For example, the German Calvinist Johannes Althusius in his *Politica methodice digesta* (1609) maintained that '*majestas*' belonged to the people alone and therefore no prince was in possession of it (Althusius, 1995, p.54; see also Hinsley pp.132–3). Ernest Nys notes that Catholic writers were defending 'the thesis of tyrannicide' in the sixteenth century (Nys, 1896, p.230; see also Merriam, 1900, p.17).

15 Vincent observes that: 'Although Bodin himself was not a proponent of divine right, his notion of sovereignty was quickly adorned with robes of divinity by later thinkers' (Vincent, 1987, p.67).

16 That sovereignty inheres in the state rather than the royal person is evidenced by Bodin's observation that 'a state transcends a corporation by the fact that it embraces a multitude of citizens and towns within the protection of the majesty of its power' (quoted in Barker, 1915, p.109).

17 Bodin stated that: 'All the other attributes and rights of sovereignty are included in this power of making and unmaking law, so that strictly speaking this is the unique attribute of sovereign power' (Bodin, 1967, p.44).

18 Justinian declared, quoting Marcian, that 'Law is...a discovery and gift of God, and yet at the same time is a resolution of wise men' (Justinian, 1998, p.1.3.2).

19 Views of the relation between the two texts vary. Franklin sees the *Methodus* as being more in accordance with the 'French tradition of limited monarchy' (Franklin, 1973, p.38). However, in her introduction to her translation of the *Methodus,* Beatrice Reynolds argues that at least in respect to the question of the limits of government, the *République* does not mark as great a rupture with the *Methodus* as some have thought. She notes that in the preface to the 1608 edition of the *République* Bodin 'disclaimed any support for absolutism, quoting book and chapter to prove that he objected to the increase of royal power' and points to his prefatory comments to the first French addition concerning the evils of tyranny (Reynolds in Bodin, 1945, p.x). However, Preston King points to a number of weaknesses in Reynold's analysis and concludes that while both works are continuous with each other in the sense that both insist on 'unity and finality as the hallmark of sovereignty' and contain arguments

in favour of 'greater restraint on public power', the *République* 'argues more forcefully than the *Methodus* for unrestrained public power' (King, 1974, pp.301–2).

20 It is also important to note that Bodin did not believe that the laws of nature were without institutional protection (Franklin, 1973, p.79).

21 Similarly, rulers were not bound by the law of nations where that law ran contrary to the law of nature. Bodin notes in this context the continuing acceptance of slavery by states, something which the prince was required by natural law to ignore (Bodin, 1967, p.36).

22 See Croxton's discussion of the timing of the discovery of the Salic law (Croxton, 1999, p.587).

23 Bodin writes that 'many are of opinion that when a foreigner marries a queen, the rights and revenues of the kingdom belong to him, although the kingdom, and sovereign authority over it inheres in the queen...Such are the inconveniences and absurdities attendant on gynecocracy' (Bodin, 1967, p.204).

24 At the General Estates conference at Blois in 1576 and 1577 the Third-Estate, of which Bodin was a member, articulated this principle (Tooley in Bodin, 1967, p.xii).

25 Bodin also stated: 'Thus it was not in the power of the Emperors...to alienate any part of the public domain, and least of all the rights of sovereign majesty, without being always in the power of his successor to lay hands on it, just as a master may always retake his fugitive slave' (quoted in Franklin, 1973, p.76).

26 A similar point was made by the French National Assembly in its declaration of war against Austria on April 20 1792 in which it was stated: 'without doubt the French nation has distinctly proclaimed that sovereignty belongs to the people, who, limited in the exercise of their supreme will by the rights of posterity, cannot delegate a power which is irrevocable; it has recognised that no custom, no convention can submit a society of men to an authority which they have not the right to resume. Every nation has alone the power of making its law and the inalienable right of changing them. This right belongs to none, or it belongs to all' (quoted in Bluntschli, 2000, p.32).

27 Bodin writes that: 'And just as the cruellest tyranny does not make for so much wretchedness as anarchy...so the most fantastic superstition in the world is not nearly so detestable as atheism' (Bodin, 1967, p.142).

28 Andrew Norris writes that while 'it makes sense in one way to speak as I have of the sovereign overstepping the limits it lays down, in a deeper sense it is the limit, and hence carries the limit with it in its movement as it carries itself' (Norris, 2000).

29 Schmitt states that sovereignty 'must necessarily be unlimited' (Schmitt, 1986, p.12).

30 Vincent, rightly in my view, argues that while limitations are 'integral' to Bodin's 'idea of sovereignty' one should not overemphasise them such that Bodin is seen in a 'medieval constitutional context' (Vincent, 1987, p.59).

31 Ernest Nys points out that Suárez 'proclaimed that sovereignty did not reside in any particular man, but in the collection of men; that the people transmit the power to the prince and ...that the prince can be stripped [of power] if he degenerates into a tyrant' (Nys, 1896, p.230).

32 We might also consider here Bentham's remark in 1776 in *A Fragment on Government*: 'What difficulty, I say, there should be in conceiving a state of things to subsist in which the supreme authority is thus limited, – what greater difficulty

in conceiving it with this limitation, than without any, I cannot see. The two states are, I must confess, to me alike conceivable: whether alike expedient, – alike conducive to the happiness of the people, is another question' (Bentham, 1948, pp.99–100).

33 Franklin notes Bodin's view that: 'A sovereign monarch can and should be subject to the law; but a ruling people unfortunately cannot be except by moral self-restraint' (Franklin, 1973, p.36). In his *Methodus*, Bodin wrote that: 'those who praise the popular rule of the Romans seem not to have read their histories. What more tragic than the frequent secessions of the plebs from the patricians? What more shameful than that citizen with citizen so many times fought with stones, scythes, and swords, in the midst of the town, in the market place, in the camp, in the assemblies, in the senate, in the temple of Jupiter Capitolinus?' (Bodin, 1945, p.269).

34 Bodin wrote in relation to this: 'Though one can imagine a collective sovereign power, vested in a ruling class, or a whole people, there is no true subject nor true protector if there is not some head of the state in whom sovereign power is vested who can unite all the rest.' (Bodin, 1967, p.197).

35 See also *De Cive*, (1651): 'That he both judge what opinions and doctrines are enemies unto peace, and also that he forbid them to be taught' (Hobbes, 1651, VI.XI). Louis XIV also appreciated the inseparability of the various marks of sovereignty. He stated in his memoirs: 'As it is important for the public that it should be governed by only one man, it is also important to it that the man who performs this function should be so far above other men that no one could be mistaken for him or compared to him, and one cannot deprive the head of the state of the least mark of superiority which distinguishes him from the other members, without doing harm to the entire body of the state' (Louis XIV in Rowen, 1963, p.27).

36 Of sovereignty as the public soul Hobbes wrote in *De Cive*: 'They who compare a City and its Citizens, with a man and his members, almost all say, that he who hath the supreme power in the City, is in relation to the whole City, such as the head is to the whole man; But it appeares by what hath been already said, that he who is endued with such a power...hath a relation to the City, not as that of the head, but of the soule to the body. For it is the soule by which a man hath a will, that is, can either will, or nill; so by him who hath *the supreme power, and* no otherwise, the City hath a will, and can either will or nill. A Court of Counsellors is rather to be compared with the head, or one Counsellor, whose only Counsell...the chief Ruler makes use of in matters of greatest moment: for the office of the head is to counsell, as the soules is to command' (Hobbes, 1651, VI.XIX). Grotius, who also noted the similarity between the 'natural body' and such 'artificial bodies' as states, described the function of sovereignty, which he believed was the 'first product' of the 'spirit...in a people' and amounted to 'the full and perfect union of civic life', in like terms. Following Seneca, he claimed it was the 'breath of life which so many thousands breathe' (Grotius, 1925, p.310).

37 Hobbes stated that 'no man is so dull as to say, for example, the People of *Rome,* made a Covenant with the Romans, to hold the Sovereignty on such or such conditions; which not performed, the Romans might lawfully depose the Roman People'. 'Nor is it possible for any person to be bound to himselfe; because he that can bind, can release; and therefore he that is bound to himselfe onely, is not bound' (Hobbes, 1968, pp.213, 313). See also *De Cive*: 'Neither must we ascribe any action to the multitude, as it's one, but (if all, or more of them doe agree) it will not be an Action, but as many actions, as Men. For although in

some great Sedition it's commonly said, That the People of that City have taken up Armes; yet it is true of those onely who are in Armes, or who consent to them. For the City, which is one Person, cannot take up Armes against it selfe' (Hobbes, 1651, VI.I).

38 In *De Cive* Hobbes stated: 'if men could rule themselves, every man by his own command, that's to say, could they live according to the Lawes of Nature, there would be no need at all of a City, nor of a common coercive power' (Hobbes, 1651, VI.XIII).

39 In *De Cive* Hobbes wrote: 'every one of the Multitude...must agree with the rest, that in those matters which shall be propounded by any one in the Assembly, that be received for the will of all which the major part shall approve of; for otherwise there will be no will at all of a Multitude of Men, whose Wills and Votes differ so variously' (Hobbes, 1651, VI.XIII). Hegel argued similarly that the people can only be given a voice through representation. '*The many*, as single individuals – and this is a favourite interpretation of [the term] "the people" – do indeed live *together*, but only as a *crowd* i.e. a formless mass whose movement and activity can consequently only be elemental, irrational, barbarous, and terrifying. If we hear any further talk of "the people" as an unorganized whole, we know in advance that we can expect only generalities and one-sided declamations' (Hegel, 1991, p.344).

40 See also *De Cive*: 'a City is defined to be *one Person* made out of *many men*, whose will by their own contracts is to be esteemed as the wills of them all' (Hobbes, 1651, X.V). In *Leviathan* he stated: 'A Multitude of men, are made *One* Person, when they are by one man, or one Person, Represented....it is the *Unity* of the Representer, not the *Unity* of the Represented, that maketh the Person *One*' (Hobbes, 1968, p.220). According to Michael Oakeshott the 'agreement must be for each to transfer his right of willing in some specific respect, to a single artificial Representative, who is thenceforth authorized to will and to act in place of each individual. There is in this association no concord of wills, no common will, no common good; its unity lies solely in the singleness of the Representative, in the *substitution* of this one will for the many conflicting wills' (Oakeshott, 1991, p.282).

41 He wrote towards the end of *Leviathan*: 'And that which offendeth the People, is no other thing, but that they are governed, not as every one of them would himselfe, but as the Publicque Representant....thinks fit; that is, by an Arbitrary government: for which they give evill names to their Superiors; never knowing (till perhaps a little after a Civill warre) that without such Arbitrary government, such Warre must be perpetuall; and that it is Men, and Arms, not Words, and Promises, that make the Force and Power of the Laws' (Hobbes, 1968, p.699).

42 James R. Martel claims that there is 'ample evidence that Hobbes finds the sovereign to be a solipsistic and fairly random institution', a view with which he also credits Schmitt (Martel, 2004, n126). Oakeshott's notes that for Hobbes, 'Man is, by nature, the victim of solipsism, he is an *individua substantia* distinguished by incommunicability' (Oakeshott, 1991, p.279). However, Oakeshott points out that while the sovereign has a 'freedom' which transcends the bounds of reason and custom, Hobbes nonetheless 'conceives the Sovereign as a law-maker and his rule...the rule of law' (Oakeshott, 1991, p.282).

43 Hobbes wrote that the 'Common-peoples minds, unlesse they be tainted with dependance on the Potent, or scribbled over with the opinions of their Doctors, are like clean paper, fit to receive whatsoever by Publique Authority shall be imprinted in them' (Hobbes, 1968, p.379).

44 Vincent, however, writes that under Louis XIV the divination of the king only served to render both the sovereign person 'more abstract and impersonal'. He adds that the growing complexity of government, aided by office theory which viewed the prince as simply 'another servant of the State', also rendered the institution of the state more abstract and impersonal. He thus adds, that there is 'complex and subtle' thread linking the '"State as monarch" and the "State as standing over and above the monarch" and the "imperial abstract State."' (Vincent, 1987, pp.65, 74) Louis XIV well understood the distinction between the interest of the state and the personal interests of the monarch and of these, he stated: 'The interest of the state must come first. One must constrain one's inclinations and not put oneself in the position of berating oneself because one could have done better some important affair but did not because of some private interest, because one was distracted from the attention one should have for the greatness, the good and the power of the state' (Louis XIV in Rowen, 1963, p.28) Louis HIV's apocryphal pronouncement *'l'état c'est moi'* can thus be seen as signalling the monarch's deference to the state.

45 Toqueville also explained the structure of the US system by reference to the idea of divided sovereignty. In the US he wrote, there are 'two governments completely separate and almost independent, the one fulfilling the ordinary duties and responding to the daily indefinite calls of a community, the other circumscribed within certain limits, and only exercising an exceptional authority over the general interests of the country. In short there are twenty-four small sovereign nations, whose agglomeration constitutes the body of the Union.' Yet, Toqueville, as should already be apparent, appreciated that the people were the ultimate and singular source of the sovereignty of the American state. He wrote: 'The people reign in the American political world as the Deity does in the universe. They are the cause and the aim of all things; everything comes from them, and everything is absorbed in them' (Toqueville, 1945, pp.55, 59).

46 Vattel's understanding of the nation can be seen as similarly ambiguous.

47 Althusius had similarly maintained that the sovereignty of the people was inalienable and thus the people, understood as a corporate 'whole' and not as individuals, is 'superior to the administration' (Merriam, 1900, p.19). Althusius writes that 'as long as this right thrives in the realm and rules the political body, so long does the realm live and prosper. But if this right is taken away, the entire symbiotic life perishes, or becomes a band of robbers and a gang of evil men, or disintegrates into many different realms or provinces' (Althusius, 1995, p.54).

48 Rousseau is referring to a situation where the 'established order is bad' (Rousseau, 1968, p.99).

49 Article 3 of the 1789 *Declaration of the Rights of Man and the Citizen* states: 'The principle of all sovereignty resides essentially in the Nation; no body, no individual can exercise any authority that does not expressly emanate from it.' However, the *Declaration* also insists 'to the contrary, on the guarantee of natural rights pre-existing the institution of politics' (Balibar, 2004, p.264).

50 See n34 above.

51 Rousseau added, however, that the people in their decisions may be 'misled' and thus 'may will what is bad' (Rousseau, 1968, p.72; see also Green, 1999, p.62).

52 As well as in his statement that the people are not being bound by the social contract, it is implicit in his explanation of why the laws of the majority can bind the minority: that the 'law of majority-voting itself rests on a covenant, and implies that there has been on at least one occasion unanimity'. Rousseau also speaks of a people being 'bound together by some original association,

interests or agreement' but who have 'not yet borne the yoke of law' (Rousseau, 1968, pp.59, 95).

53 Hence the saying: 'The law wills, the king does' (quoted in Bluntschli, 2000, p.409).

54 Both Kant and Hegel articulate versions of this argument (Kant, 1970c, p.158; Hegel, 1991, p.126).

55 Bluntschli noted that publicists writing in French typically defined the nation in this fashion and distinguished it in this sense from a mere multitude (Bluntschli, 2000, p.393).

56 Vattel asks: 'Could the society make such use of its authority as irrevocably to surrender itself and all its members to the discretion of a cruel tyrant? No, certainly, since it would no longer possess any right itself, if it were disposed to oppress a part of the citizens. When, therefore, it confers the supreme and absolute government, without an express reserve, it is necessarily with the tacit reserve that the sovereign shall use it for the safety of the people, and not for their ruin' (Vattel, 1863, p.18).

57 Rousseau had earlier observed that states needed sound constitutions if they were to survive in a competitive international environment (Rousseau, 1968, p.92).

58 It does not follow from this that sovereignty in Austin is a non-normative phenomenon as some suggest. As Austin stated, the sovereign body is 'obliged or restrained morally: that is to say, it is controlled by opinions and sentiments in the given community' (Austin, 1906, p.172). MacCormick is right to note that Austin's treatment of sovereignty as simply a political fact is deficient, as this, in conjunction with his narrow command theory of law and emphasis on sanctions, prevents him from conceiving of a sovereign power which is properly constitutionally, and not simply morally, constrained. MacCormick writes that on the Diceyean view, sovereignty is a 'normative power defined by the common law. It is a doctrine of the common law that whatever Parliament enacts must be respected as law, save if Parliament should seek to bind its successors, and to be a sovereign is to have exactly this legally conferred but legally unlimited normative power of law-making'. The advantage of this outlook is that it shows that while sovereignty, here understood legally, 'may be a central feature of some constitutions and is central to the British constitution...[it]...is not a necessary element or presupposition of law's existence at all' and further, that where we understand sovereignty as being 'conferred by constitutional law, there is (as Dicey expressly recognised) no reason why you cannot devise forms of constitutional law in which none of the legislative powers conferred by law is near absolute' (MacCormick, 1993, p.12).

59 Balibar takes this notion from Herman Van Gestern.

Chapter 3 The International Arena

1 See Sections LXX and LXXIV of the Latin, German and French versions of the agreement. The Treaty between the Empire and France states that no other power can bring a challenge against the *'Droit de Souveraineté'* of the Crown of France (Die Westfälischen Friedensverträge, 1648).

2 The Latin and German texts of 1648 translate territorial right as *'libero iuris territorialis'* and *'freyen Gebrach ihres Juris Territorialis'* respectively. See Section LXII of the Treaty of Peace between France and the Empire (Die Westfälischen Friedensverträge, 1648). Note that the Treaty of Peace between the Empire, Sweden

and France recalls the principle of *cuijus regio, ejus religio* as established by the Peace of Augsburg in 1555 (Parry, 1969a, p.214). Bluntschli writes that the term sovereignty, then new to Germany, was used in a draft of the agreement instead of the older expression *Landeshoheit* or territorial right in order to relax the bonds of empire, although he adds that the German princes 'were already almost "sovereign"'. He quotes this draft as follows: 'que tous les Princes et Estats seront maintenus dans tous les autres droits de *souveraineté*, qui leur appartiennent' (Bluntschli, 2000, p.480).

3 Philpott, however, argues that while the Holy Roman Empire 'still enjoyed codified constitutional powers after 1648...the empire did not practice sovereignty in any meaningful way' (Philpott, 2001, p.23).

4 Maurice Keens-Soper claims that the overall language of the Treaty of Utrecht indicates that the states of Europe were conscious of themselves as members of an inter-state system by the early eighteenth century (Keens-Soper, 1978, p.28).

5 See Fénelon's anonymous 'Lettre à Louis XIV' which he sent towards the end of 1694. In *Les Aventures de Télémaque* (1699) Fénelon warned that 'kings ought to take care in the wars that they undertake. They should be just but this is not enough; they must be necessary for the public good. The blood of a people should only be shed to save the people in extreme necessity' (Fénelon, 1861, p.277).

6 Walzer points out that while states 'went to war on behalf of the balance, they thought they were defending, not national interest alone, but an international order that made liberty possible throughout Europe' (Walzer, 1977, p.76).

7 The decree of 22 May 1790 was incorporated into the 1791 constitution under Title VI, while non-intervention was incorporated into the Constitution of 1793 (Nussbaum, 1954, p.332).

8 See also the 1801 edition in which he continues to condemn the disdain of the French revolutionaries for the 'positive law of nations of Europe' and the 'old diplomacy' and warns of the danger to the government of Europe posed by their promise to assist all those 'who would raise the flag of rebellion' (Martens, 1801, p.xiv). Linda Frey and Marsha Frey write that Martens accepted that the modern law of nations 'had its blemishes and imperfections and violations' but he thought that 'it was still preferable to the new law of war and peace established in the first years of the revolution, which scorned basic principles' (Frey and Frey, 2006, p.3).

9 Brandli notes that in 1793, the 'militant Jacobinism of certain diplomats...[was]...perceived badly by the governments which still received them' and adds that the 'reflux of French diplomatic representation' was the 'outcome of the enlightenment critique of the organisation of the external politics of kings' (Brandli, 2007).

10 At the same time, the Congress also reflected the view that the five great powers had the right to govern 'European affairs, and to exercise a veritable hegemony over the minor states' in the form of what was called the 'Pentarchy'. However, Fiore adds that more sophisticated legal reasoning, as well as the 'progress of civilization', soon rendered this view outdated. As he states: 'The principle of the legal equality of states is inconsistent with the preponderance of certain states over others' (Fiore, 1918, p.53).

11 Martens insisted that any intervention in the internal affairs of the state could only be justified where it was approved by all the powers in situations calling for counter-intervention or where internal revolution gave rise to threats against other states. As an example of such a threat, he cited the statement of the French

politician Alphonse de Lamartine in 1849 that the French republic 'was not tied to the treaties of 1815' (Martens, 1883, pp.396–7).

12 Remec writes that the Spanish theologians and Grotius saw the law of nations as 'personally binding sovereign princes and other persons participating in international intercourse'. He adds that Samuel Pufendorf was the first to apply 'the theory of the juristic person to the state' and make a 'clear-cut analogy from individual to state in order to explain the latter's inherent subjective position under the law of nature' (Remec, 1960, pp.23, 170). Pufendorf stated in *De Jure Naturae et Gentium* (1688) that the state was a 'single person with intelligence and will, performing other actions peculiar to itself and separate from those of individuals' (Pufendorf, 1934, p.983). It is also worth noting that Pufendorf ascribed sovereignty to monarchies and republics alike: 'And, in the first place, we cannot admit, that he should ascribe Majesty to Kings alone, and utterly deny to free States and Democracies. It's true, the Custom of Speech, during the last Ages, seems to have appropriated the Term of Majesty to Kings, by placing it amongst their Royal Titles. Yet, this doth not hinder but that the same Word may be used to denote the Supreme Authority under any Form of Government....*The chief Power everywhere over the State*' (Pufendorf, 1729, p.656).

13 Nussbaum notes that the principle of *rebus sic stantibus* arose from canon law 'which tended to temper with considerations of equity the rigor of Roman private law' (Nussbaum, 1954, p.96).

14 As John Crawford puts it: 'There are rules which are preconditions for meaningful international activity – for example, *pacta sunt servanda*. To abrogate that rule is not possible: a treaty providing that *pacta sunt servanda* is mere reaffirmation; a treaty denying it is an absurdity. The point is that the very activity of treaty-making assumes the general rule' (Crawford, 1978, p.146).

15 Passerin D'Entrèves observes of this formulation: 'Of course, since it cannot secure confirmation from a higher or "sovereign" power, it has to be ultimately warranted, according to Grotius, by justice or natural law, by the rule of *pacta sunt servanda*. But, insofar as it is positive law, it is valid, and can be laid down with certainty, to the extent to which States in fact regard themselves as bound by it and respect it, uniformly regulating their behaviour and their mutual relations according to its rules: in short, in as far as *pacta sunt servata*' (Passerin D'Entrèves, 1967, pp.126–7).

16 Vattel rejected the way in which Grotius's 'exclusively' appropriated the 'name "Law of Nations" to those maxims which have been established by the common consent of mankind' since it suggested that 'observance' of these maxims was at 'the 'discretion of...[the states']...consciences.' He stated that Grotius's assumptions, namely that nations 'live, with respect to each other, in a reciprocal independence, in the state of nature...and...subject to the natural law', should have led him to realise that there is among nations 'an *external* obligation wholly independent of their will; and that the common consent of mankind is only the foundation and source of a particular kind of law, called the *Arbitrary Law of Nations*' (Vattel, 1863, p.ix; see also Rabkin, 1997, p.302). Pufendorf, as a natural law exponent, had earlier criticised Grotius for 'basing all international law on the consent of states'; indeed, it was his emphasis on consent that made Grotius influential among legal positivists (Hinsley, 1986, p.190).

17 Wolff wrote that in *civitas maxima* or 'supreme state the nations as a whole have a right to coerce the individual nations, if they should be unwilling to perform their obligation' (Wolff, 1934, p.14). Yet he also insisted on the principle of non-intervention, arguing that since 'sovereignty is originally a thing belonging to

the people' any trespass on the sovereignty of the state is a denial of the 'natural liberty of nations' (Wolff, 1934, pp.130–1). Note also that while the *civitas maxima* was '"naturalist" in original thinking...its actual creation and realization would also require the positive pacts of communities' (Jianming, 2000, p.20).

18 Wolff had written 'just as the tallest man is no more a man than the dwarf, so also nation, however small, is no less a nation than the greatest nation (Wolff, 1934, p.15). Bodin had earlier made the same point in stating: 'a little King is as well a Sovereign as the greatest Monarch in the world' and this had as its corollary a prohibition on wars of conquest (quoted in D'Entrèves, 1967, p.100).

19 The 'kingdom is forfeited if a king sets out with a truly hostile intent to destroy a whole people...For the will to govern and the will to destroy cannot coexist in the same person' (Grotius, 1925, pp.157–8).

20 Vattel also stated, citing the example set by Hercules as did Grotius before him, that 'those monsters who, under the title of sovereigns, render themselves the scourges and horror of the human race,,,[are]...savage beasts' and that 'every brave man may justly exterminate...[them]...from the face of the earth' (Vattel, 1863, p.156).

21 Vattel stated: 'Since nations ought to perform these duties and offices of humanity towards each other, according as one stands in need, and the other can reasonably comply with them, – every nation being free, independent, and sole arbitress of her own actions, it belongs to each to consider whether her situation warrants her in asking or granting any thing on this head' (Vattel, 1863, p.137). Wolff similarly stated: 'the right to those things which one nation naturally owes to another is an imperfect right' (Wolff, 1934, p.85).

22 Nussbaum writes, however, that due to his 'lack of legal training', the work was defective and it was not greeted with 'much praise' by the 'legally learned' (Nussbaum, pp.159–60).

23 Mirkine-Guetzévitch points to some eighteenth century treaties which bore witness to the 'penetration of the idea of juridical universalism' such as the treaties of the peace between France, England and Spain in 1762 and between England and France in 1783, although he adds that the practice of states continued to be characterised by reason of state (Mirkine-Guetzévitch, 1928, p.307).

24 Bentham pointed out that the expression law of nations, 'were it not for the force of custom', seemed to 'refer to internal jurisprudence'. He noted that this observation had been presaged by Henri-Francois D'Aguesseau who, as Chancellor of France during the reign of Louis XIV, maintained that 'what is commonly called *droit des gens*, ought rather be termed *droit entre les gens*' (Bentham, 1970, p.296). Etienne Dumont, who translated Bentham's writings into French, 'introduced the word "international" into the French language in 1802' (Nys, 1911, p.872n).

25 Between 1786 and 1789, Bentham had been privately studying international law, although his 'first clear and formal statement' on this subject matter did not appear until 1802 (Nys, 1911, p.876).

26 Nussbaum asserts the relation between Vattel's thought and that of Grégoire. (Nussbaum, 1954, p.158).

27 The final article of the *Déclaration* stated that 'treaties between peoples are sacred and inviolable' (quoted in Nys, 1896, p.396).

28 Grégoire explained the grounds for its rejection in his *Mémoires*: 'It is perhaps the first declaration of the law of nations, which has been made. It was greeted with applause; I had consecrated therein the eternal principles of the liberty of nations. The Committee of Public Safety thought that these principles pro-

claimed in the face of Europe, would irritate the despots with whom it was intended to enter into negotiations, and on the following day, in the name of the Committee, [Philippe-Antoine] Merlin [de Douai], although bestowing high eulogies on the work, declared that the tranquillity of Europe demanded that the decree which ordered the printing thereof be revoked' (quoted in Nys, 1911, p.893; see also Chevally, 1912, p.50).

29 On the 21 April 1793 Maximilien Robespierre told the Convention that the person 'who oppresses a nation...declares himself the enemy of all. Those who make war against a people in order to stop the progress of liberty and annihilate the rights of man, must be pursued by all, not as ordinary enemies but as assassins and rebellious brigands. The kings, the aristocrats, the tyrants whatever they be are slaves revolting against the sovereign of the earth which is the human race, and against the legislator of the universe which is Nature' (quoted in Nys, 1896, p.394). Mirkine-Guetzévitch, however, claims that this was only tactical on Robespierre's part since at this time revolutionary intervention was 'popular' (Mirkine-Guetzévitch, 1928, p.314).

30 Volney presented his project, which was not adopted by the National Assembly, 18 May 1790. Mirkine-Guetzévitch notes, that it came to exercise 'a certain influence' on the proposal of Grégoire. Volney insisted on the 'universality of the human race' and that it 'formed a society the object of which was peace and happiness for all its members.' He further proclaimed that 'peoples and States' enjoyed the 'same natural rights' as individuals in society and were equally subject to the rules of justice'. Invasion of another state's territory was prohibited as was the 'deprivation of a people of their liberty and natural advantages'. Only wars in defence of a 'just right' were permissible (Mirkine-Guetzévitch, 1928, pp.308–9).

31 Frey and Frey write that Martens regarded Article 5 as 'specious, theoretically unlimited, and in practice unenforceable' (Frey and Frey, 2006, p.3).

32 Lawyers of both a positivist and natural law persuasion invoked the term science. For example, Fiore referred to *'la scienza'* of international law, however, this included both *'naturale o razionale'* law, deduced from *'principii della giustizia naturale'*, and law *'positivo.'* His concept of science in relation to international law is consistent with that of Giambattista Vico in his 1725 booklet called *Principii di una scienza nuova intorno alla natura delle nazioni, per li quali si ritrovano altri principii del Diritto naturale delle genti* (Fiore, 1909, pp.31, 97–8).

33 Nussbaum argues that Martens 'relegated' natural law to the domain of morality, even though he often used it to make 'a point of legal argument'. He goes on to note that the significance of the law of nature for Martens concerns the natural rights, 'rather than "obligations"', of states. Nussbaum maintains that Martens's emphasis on the rights of states unmistakably reflects the influence of Grégoire's *Déclaration* and he suggests that this is why he 'inveighed, in one of his most brilliant and spirited discourses, against the vulnerable and unsuccessful pronouncement of the French revolutionary leader, from whom he very definitely wanted to dissociate himself' (Nussbaum, 1954, pp.182–3).

34 H.B. Jacobini notes that it was James Mill who argued that 'international law is true law because it rests on the sanction of public opinion' (Jacobini, 1948, p.415).

35 Hegel wrote that it is the *'right of heroes'* to make concrete the 'Idea', that is, to 'establish states' and that this same consideration '...entitles civilized nations... to regard and treat as barbarians other nations which are less advanced than they are in the substantial moments of the state (as with pastoralists in relation

to hunters, and agriculturalists in relation to both of these), in the consciousness that the rights of these other nations are not equal to theirs and their independence is merely formal' (Hegel, 1991, p.376).

36 Tomuschat agrees that the term 'äußeres Staatsrecht' suggests that 'international law is dependent on unilateral decisions of an individual State' but he adds that this description may have resulted from a 'misperception by Hegel' since other commentators at that time 'translated *droit des gens* correctly as "äußeres Staatenrecht" (external law of States), a term which does not invite criticism and which was intended to denote the character of the discipline as *jus inter gentes*' (Tomuschat, 1999, p.167).

37 Such views of international law were not peculiar to German commentators. The British neo-Hegelian Bernard Bosanquet, in his *Philosophical Theory of the State* [originally published in 1899], 'voiced with almost convincing eloquence the...principle of the absence of law between states' (Lauterpacht, 1927, p.106; see also Hinsley, 1986, p.209). In the aftermath of World War One, adopting a somewhat defensive tone, Bosanquet stated that while he believed 'in the League of Nations as the hope and refuge of mankind' he did 'not believe that any moral being can divest itself of moral responsibility , or limit that responsibility's *ultima ratio'*. He stated that while a state can be morally criticised for brutal acts in the name of the public interest a 'public act which inflicts loss, such as war...is wholly different from murder or theft. It is not the act of a private person. It is not a violation of law' (Bosanquet, 1920, pp.l, 303–4).

38 Bara thought that only states which were 'ruled internally by law' were capable of respecting international law and thus he excluded autocratic states and colonies, where people lived 'in tutelage', from participation in the international legal order (Cooper, 1972, p.13).

39 Koskenniemi notes that in September 1873 eleven European lawyers, rejecting the 'old doctrines of "European public law" which they identified with the 'post-Napoleonic Concert', adopted the 'Statute of the *Institut de droit international'*, an association which they designated the 'organ of the juridical conscience of the civilised world'. The *Institut*, he adds, was highly effective in promoting international law and encouraging 'liberal progress' in Europe in the late nineteenth and early twentieth centuries. According to Koskenniemi, by the close of the nineteenth century, 'the profession had been organised. University chairs of international law had been created all over Europe. Thick, many volumed textbooks and international law journals had started to appear in several languages. Arbitration was understood as an effective cure for inter-European rivalries and relations with the "Orient" were formalised by annexation and colonial government. The Hague Peace Conferences of 1899 and 1907 inaugurated the era of international legislation as part of the mass politics of industrial societies' (Koskenniemi, 2005, pp.2–3, 10).

40 Koskenniemi notes that in Article 1 of the Statute of the *Institut* members described themselves as the 'juridical conscience of the civilized world' (Koskenniemi, 2005, p.120). The original motto of the Institute was '*Verité, Justice à tous, Indépendance de tous les peoples, Garantie des faibles contre les abus de la force*' (quoted in Cooper, 1972, p.10).

41 Fiore added that he did not think such an outcome was possible 'because civilization is constantly describing its parabolas and is subject to the law of ebb and flow' (Fiore, 1918, p.102).

42 In their introduction to Treitschke's theory of the state M.G. Forsyth, H.M.A. Keens-Soper and P. Savigear note that his work was attacked during

World War One in England for 'exaggerated devotion to the nation-state, and...[for]...inciting the Germans to militarism in the years before 1914', although they add that more recent work on Treitschke has examined 'the development of his thought as a German nineteenth century liberal' (Treitschke, 1970, p.325).

43 Mirkine-Guetzévitch argues, in contrast to Kelsen, that the supremacy of international law should found itself on the 'unity of the juridical conscience and on the empirical unity of historical evolution' (Mirkine-Guetzévitch, 1928, p.321).

44 Charles Leben notes that Article 55 of the French constitution allows for the 'superiority, under certain circumstances, of treaties over legislation, even when enacted subsequently' (Leben, 1998, p.297).

45 Zolo notes that this agnosticism as regards the two forms of monism was adopted in the second edition of *Reine Rechtslehre in die rechtswissenschaftliche Problematik* (1960) which was translated into English as the *Pure Theory of Law*. He adds however, that in the 1934 edition he presented the idea of the primacy of international law and 'the dissolution of the "dogma of sovereignty"' as the 'technical outcome of the pure theory of law' (Zolo, 1998, p.308n).

46 Zolo observes that Kelsen's science of the law is based, following Kant, in a 'universal objective reason' of which both states and individuals are subordinate parts (quoted in Zolo, 1998, p.307). Kelsen wrote that '...the subjects who know and will are really only ephemeral and temporary phenomenal forms, the spirits of which are co-ordinated and related only insofar as they are integral parts of the universal world spirit, the knowing reason of which is merely an emanation of the supreme universal reason...For objectivism the individual is a mere appearance. And the legal theory that takes the objectivity of law to its ultimate consequences and therefore affirms the primacy of international law, must not only remove the idea that individual state subjects are definitive and supreme entities, but ultimately must, to be consistent, reduce the "physical" person too – the "natural" legal subject – to its substrate, that is, to an element of the objective legal system' (quoted in Zolo, 1998, p.308).

47 According to Rigaux, Kelsen dispensed with the idea of an orginary norm because this 'term conveys a time element' and for Kelsen it 'is of the utmost importance for the status of international law...[that]...no argument whatsoever must be sought in the historical process which brought preexisting states into the framework of an international community' (Rigaux, 1998, pp.327–8).

48 While it cannot be proved, it is a necessary 'hypothesis that international custom is a law-creating fact. This hypothesis may be called the basic norm. It is not a norm of positive law; it is not created by acts of will of human beings; it is presupposed by the jurist interpreting legally the conduct of states' (Kelsen, 1952, p.314). Remec contrasts the ethical conception of the basic norm with Kelsen's conception which he describes as 'formal' and 'colorless' (Remec, 1960, p.35). Lauterpacht, by contrast, treated the fundamental norm as a 'rational and ethical' phenomenon possessing an 'external and imperative character' and necessitated by 'the fact of the existence of international society', adding that the need to find a basis for international law 'other than the will of states' had been appreciated for a long time (Lauterpacht, 1937, p.151).

49 Koskenniemi states that for Kelsen and those who followed him, the state was viewed 'not as something preceding or standing over the law but as something *constructed* by the law. It was the sum total of the rights, powers and competencies that State officials possessed. To think otherwise was to believe in "sovereignty" as a metaphysical or mythical quality in statehood that was inadmissible for a scientific approach to the matter. For this approach, "sovereignty" was often simply an

expression of an ideological nationalism that it opposed. Whether coming from positivists or natural lawyers, the methodological critique was accompanied by a unitary, cosmopolitan view of law' (Koskenniemi, 2005, p.36).

50 Hedley Bull writes that this is the Grotian view of the international legal order, adding that Kelsen is 'clearly within the Grotian tradition of international law' (Bull, 1986, p.323).

51 Kelsen stated: '...just as for an objectivist conception of life the ethical conception of man is humanity, so for the objectivist theory of law the concept of law is identified with that of international law and for that very reason is at the same time a moral concept' (quoted in Zolo, 1998, p.310).

52 It is international law, according to Kelsen, which 'determines the sphere and reason of validity of national law' (Kelsen, 1946, p.384).

53 Kelsen wrote in the *Pure Theory of Law* that 'the tendency of [contemporary] international law to lay down direct rules of obligation and authorisation of individuals must necessarily be reinforced to the same degree as it increasingly extends to subjects of areas that were previously governed by state law alone' (quoted in Leben, 1998, p.304).

54 In fact, Leben suggests that the idea of a 'universal' state may have meant for Kelsen 'simply a more developed and peace-loving international legal order, which does not imply the disappearance of nation-states' (Leben, 1998, p.295). Mirkine-Guetzévitch also argues that the idea of a world state in Kelsen is not something that can actually be realised but rather reflects the 'development of international law' to the point where we reach the *civitas maxima* (Mirkine-Guetzévitch, 1928, p.319). Fiore announced in 1887, revealing the influence of Wolff, that the ultimate destination of international law was a *Magna civitas*. He wrote in the conclusion of the second, third and fourth Italian editions of his *Diritto Internazionale Codificato e la sua Sanzione Giruidica*: 'The primitive legal society was the family; the final society will be the juridical union of civilized peoples' (Fiore, 1909, pp.700, 704).

55 James maintains that even states under authoritarian rule may be said to possess constitutions to the extent that there is a common understanding about how the state should be governed (James, 1940, p.40).

56 As Bleckmann states, the notions of 'internal and external sovereignty are also closely related from a political perspective, as there can be no internal sovereignty without external sovereignty' (Bleckmann, 1994, p.80).

57 Balibar similarly points out that statehood depends on a 'reciprocity of perspectives' as a 'state that was not treated as an independent power by other states would never be recognized as having unshared power over its own territory and vice versa' (Balibar, 2004, p.158).

58 The principle that Derrida is citing is drawn from Hannah Arendt's *The Origins of Totalitarianism* (1951).

59 The conception of humanity as forming in some sense a single polity has long been entertained in writings on the law of nations. Francisco de Vitoria stated in *De potestate civili* (1528), in explaining why the law of nations had the force of positive law, that the 'whole world, which is in a sense a commonwealth, has the power to enact laws which are just and convenient to all men; and make up the law of nations' (Vitoria, 1991, p.40). Suárez in *De legibus, ac Deo legislatore* (1612) wrote that 'the human race, howsoever many different peoples and kingdoms it may be divided, always preserves a certain unity, not only as a species, but also a moral and political unity (as it were) enjoined by the natural precept of mutual love and mercy; a precept which applies to

all, event o strangers of every nation' (Suárez, 1944, p.348). Christian Wolff noted in his *Jus Genitum Methodo Scientific Pertactatum* (1764) that 'nature herself has established society among all nations and compels them to preserve it, for the purpose of promoting the common good by their combined powers' (Wolff, 1934, p.12). Grotius stated in *De iure praedae commentarius* (1604) that one finds in the mutual need for security the basis of 'that brotherhood of man, that world state' of which the Stoics spoke and which existed prior to international society and still subsists, not simply in an ideal sense, because it actually manifests itself at certain times. He added that states were not formed 'with the intention of abolishing the society which links all men as a whole, but rather in order to fortify that universal society by a more dependable means of protection' (Grotius, 1950, pp.13, 19). Seneca had stated: 'All this world that you see and which contains everything that is divine and human, is one...We are the members of a great body. Nowhere is man a stranger...The universe is his true country' (quoted in Fiore, 1918, p.13).

60 Concerning their mystification, Balibar rightly states, the 'task of democratizing borders' necessitates 'their representation be desacralized' (Balibar, 2004, p.113).

Chapter 4 From Imperial to Post-Imperial Sovereignty

1 Mill did not, however, extend this principle to 'uncivilized' peoples. He stated that 'to suppose that the same international customs, and the same rules of international morality, can obtain between one civilized nation and another, and between civilized nations and barbarians, is a grave error' (Mill, 1963, p.377).

2 Kant stated that it is permissible to assist in a situation where a state had 'split into two parts' and where 'each of which, while constituting a separate state...[laid]...claim to the whole' (Kant, 1987, p.69).

3 See Bull and Watson's discussion of the complexity of these and other non-European political systems (Bull and Watson, 1985, p.2).

4 The General Act of the Berlin Congress authorised the dismemberment of Africa.

5 It was on this basis that many European publicists rejected conquest as a legitimate means of acquiring territory (Korman, 1996, p.94).

6 Gentile made a remark that might sum up the positions of Grotius and Vattel: 'But if the unjust man gain the victory, neither in a contention in arms nor in the strife carried on in the garb of peace is there any help for it. Yet it is not the law which is at fault, but the execution of the law' (quoted in Wight, 1977, p.164).

7 Yasuaki Onuma writes that while Alexandrowicz 'made a great contribution by uncovering a wide-range of "treaty" practice between Europeans and political entities in Asia and Africa from the sixteenth to the eighteenth century' he failed to account for how 'the treaty practice was *perceived, understood and explained by Asians or Africans* during those periods' (Onuma, 2000, p.61).

8 James Mayall similarly notes that even by the start of the nineteenth century, 'formal relations between European and African "states" were still conducted on the basis of theoretical equality on the grounds that whatever paramount political authority existed in the non-Western world constituted a "sovereign state"' (Mayall, 1978, p.128).

9 Wheaton had earlier responded to the question: 'Is there a uniform law of nations?', in stating that there 'certainly is not the same one for all the nations and states of the world. The public law, with slight exceptions, has always been, and still is, limited to the civilised and Christian people of Europe or to those of European origin' (Wheaton, 1936, p.15). However, Nicholas Onuf argues that in using the terms 'Christian' and 'civilized' Wheaton was simply pointing to the specifically European 'ancestry and reach of international law...without the lofty pretensions of superiority which, later in the century, their use all too typically conveyed' (Onuf, 2000, p.7).

10 Rougier wrote that the theory of humanitarian intervention was only placed on juridical footing in the nineteenth century. He added that earlier articulations of this theory by figures such as Grotius and Vattel had a 'character more moral than juridical'. Rougier allowed for both collective and unilateral intervention in any state which engaged in activities which were 'contrary to the laws of humanity' (Rougier, 1910, p.472). Martens argued however that this right could only be exercised against barbarous nations in order to protect co-religionists and out of 'considerations of humanity' and he mentions Turkey, China and Japan in this context (Martens, 1883, p.397). Bluntschli discussed intervention in the name of human rights in relation to nationalities which had not yet organised themselves politically since they lacked the protection of the state. However, he also supported intervention against governments which were oppressing a particular nationality. The fact that there were no legal guarantees in this regard, he put down to an exaggerated emphasis on sovereignty. The instances of human rights abuses contrary to international law that he mentions in this context are the 'violent extirpation' of the indigenous inhabitants in European colonies and North America and the persecution of Jews in certain European countries (Bluntschli, 1874, pp.69–70).

11 Onuma notes that there was a range of 'independent human groups' in the region and these groups did not at all times accept the Sinocentric normative framework. He adds that this was particularly the case 'for nomads in Central Asia, who were regarded by China as northern or western barbarians'. Such groups would pay obeisance to China when it was strong and 'exploit it when it was weak'. Indeed, he adds that when 'the Nomads were exceptionally strong, they succeeded in concluding a treaty with China on the basis of equality, or even characterizing their leader as superior to the Chinese emperor...Such an image was common to many human groups, including....the Japanese and the Vietnamese. They sought to have relations with China based on equality, and to develop their relations with non-Chinese neighbours on the premise of their superiority' (Onuma, 2000, p.13).

12 The twentieth century Chinese philosopher Feng Youlan wrote that 'what the Chinese were always concerned about was the continuation and integrity of the Chinese culture and civilization...from the early Qin dynasty onwards, Chinese had clearly made a distinction between the "China", or "Huaxia", with the "Barbarians (Yidi)"' (quoted in Chen, 2005, p.36). Gerrit W. Gong notes that Chinese superiority was at significant moments bolstered by military force but he adds that tributary states, as well as certain nomadic peoples, generally regarded this superiority as 'historically proven, and thereby acceptably prescriptive' (Gong, 1985, p.174).

13 It is important to note that Chinese 'culturalism did not regard the boundary between the Chinese and barbarians as static or fixed. Once the '"barbarians" adopted Chinese culture, they became Chinese' (Chen, 2005, p.37).

14 Ogden notes that the Chinese Bureau of Rites informed Korea that its peoples could come and go in and out of China as long as this tributary state ruled 'in conformity with the Will of heaven' and created 'no strife on...[China's]...borders' (Ogden, 1975, pp.26–8; see also Krasner, 2001, p.178).
15 Up until the nineteenth century British trading relations with China 'was carried out within the framework of the Chinese tribute system' (Onuma, 2000, p.27).
16 Onuma notes that according to Alain Peyrefitte the 'prevalent image of McCartney's rejection of kowtow was exaggerated' (Onuma, 2000, p.28n).
17 The treaties were unequal in the sense that they arose out of unequal power relationship and because they 'embodied unequal obligations' (Anghie, 1999, p.41).
18 Ogden writes that the Qing dynasty 'did not believe these treaties permanently sacrificed part of China's "sovereignty"' but rather saw them as a 'means of controlling and confining Westerners' (Ogden, 1975, p.4). Onuma concurs, stating that the Qing dynasty was unable to appreciate that its 'defeat in the Opium War was fundamentally different from' earlier periods of retrogression in its relations with its neighbours (Onuma, 2000, p.31).
19 The Asian tradition of hospitality often meant allowing 'community of traders settling in a foreign country.... to govern itself by its own law and enjoyed a measure of autonomy under the control of its own heads of a quasi-consular character' (Alexandrowicz, 1969, p.470).
20 Onuma adds that the expectation of the Europeans was that China would rigorously adhere to the treaties in accordance with 'the general rules and principles of European international law. The European states expected that China abide not only by specific provisions of the treaties, but also by customary rules and principles of European international law when they dealt with matters relating to the treaties. For China, to abide by the treaties meant to abide by their explicit provisions. Rules and principles not explicitly stipulated in the treaties had nothing to do with them, even if these rules and principles were assumptions or inevitable consequences of the explicit provisions in the eyes of the Europeans. It was thus inevitable that both parties clashed with each other. In 1856, they rushed into the Second Opium War. The result was a miserable defeat on the part of the Ch'ing dynasty'. The Second Opium War concluded with the Treaty of Tianjin which obliged the Qing dynasty to receive foreign representatives in accordance with European protocols. This stipulation was acceded to in 1873 but 'only in accordance with tributary practice including the kowtow... It was as late as in 1894 that the emperor began to receive foreign envoys...in accordance with the European way of reception' (Onuma, 2000, pp. 31–2).
21 In relation to China, Immanuel Chung-yueh Hsü notes that it was only in the wake of the industrial revolution that the Europeans possessed 'power sufficient to make a vigorous and sustained effort to reach China' and adds that it was not an 'accident that England, as the cradle of the Industrial Revolution, took the lead in this drive' (Hsü, 1995, p.7).
22 My translation. Onuma writes that Article 7 prepared the ground for Articles 8 and 9 which were concerned with forestalling interference by 'Russia or any other power' in the Ottoman Empire and was not concerned with the 'international legal status' of the Empire '*per se*' (Onuma, 2000, p.37).
23 Dr. Peter Parker, an American medical missionary, undertook the translation on the request of the Imperial Commissioner Lin Tse-hsü (Ogden, 1974, p.5n; Ogden, 1975, p.37).
24 See also Chen's discussion of the Chinese transition from cultural universalism to nationalism. Liang Qichao argued at the time that 'we Chinese are not by

nature an unpatriotic people. The reason the Chinese do not know patriotism is because they do not know that China is a state' (quoted in Chen, 2005, p.37).

25 A. Pearce Higgins noted that the 'mere fact that the Chinese Government was invited to send representatives' to the 1907 Hague Peace Conference could be 'taken as an acknowledgement of its international status' (Hall, 1924, p.49).

26 Tomuschat argues that the descriptions barbarian and savage, since these denoted human beings of inferior 'rank', had a 'decisive impact on the treatment meted out to any adversary' in the context of colonial wars (Tomuschat, 1999, p.32).

27 Chen notes that before 1931 'under the nationalism anti-imperialism banner of Chiang Kai-shek's KMT government' these privileges were in fact reduced thus 'winning unprecedented diplomatic status for China' (Chen, 2005, p.40).

28 Georg Sørensen writes that following the Congress of Vienna in 1815, the 'rules of recognition became clearer, but were still subject to exemptions which reflected the specific interests of the European great powers' (Sørensen, 1999, p.596). Bull notes that the doctrine of constitutive recognition 'is widely viewed today as having been simply an instrument of European dominance' but he adds, albeit without addressing the issue of imperial conquest itself, that 'it could hardly have been expected that European states could have extended the full benefits of membership of the society of states to political entities that were in no position to enter into relationships on a basis of reciprocity' (Bull, 1985, pp.121–2).

29 Crawford notes that Kelsen had earlier been declaratist. He wrote in the *Revue de droit international* in 1929 that: 'In the presence of the incontestable, positive rules of international law, one can not deny that the new State has some international rights and obligations even before being recognized by the older States' (quoted in Crawford, 1978, p.102n).

30 Pasquale Fiore maintained that the Treaty of Berlin acknowledged 'that man may find the basis of his rights in international law' (Fiore, 1918, p.109).

31 Alfred Cobban notes that similar protests greeted the earlier Genoese sale of Corsica to the French (Cobban, 1969, p.32). In an essay in the *Annual Register* in 1768, Edmund Burke stated of this sale: 'Thus was a nation disposed of without its consent, like the trees on an estate' (Burke, 1768, p.2).

32 Gilbert Murray claimed that the expression is 'clearly German in origin', noting that August Bebel complained 'in the 'nineties of last century that there was no *Selbstbestimmungsrecht* in Germany' and that the expression appeared in the writings of the 'Radical German philosophers of 1848' in relation to nationalities (Murray, 1922, p.6). Guenter Weissberg observes, however, that the expression was 'initially employed by the First International in its 1865 Proclamation on the Polish Question' (Weissberg, 1965, p.181).

33 Simon Bolivar maintained correspondence with Bentham and Francisco Miranda was a personal acquaintance (Nys, 1911, pp.893–5). The historian Gervinius observed that: 'After 1820 it was thought by the Latin American races that the study of Bentham's works was an absolute essential for every educated man. They, as well as the Spanish, honoured this writer as the oracle of the century and the lawgiver of the world' (quoted in Nys, 1911, p.895). Calvo offered the pragmatic advice that modern history had shown that such acquisitions frequently proved costly and were a source of 'weakness...[and]...complications of all sorts' for the colonising power (Calvo, 1887, p.208). As well as being translated into French in 1887, Calvo's work was translated into Chinese (Nussbaum, 1954, p.245).

34 Bluntschli wrote that he was in accord with Mancini to the extent that human nature and not the will of states was the 'fundamental reason for being' of inter-

national law. However, he added that 'if the law of nations really rested on the elastic base of nationality and not on the solid terrain of the state, it would lose every point of application and would become incapable of being recognised and respected' (Bluntschli, 1874, p.70). Calvo noted that for the majority of Italian publicists the 'principle of nationality would seem to be the vital source of the law of nations' (Calvo, 1887, p.277).

35 Mirkine-Guetzévitch writes that the 'syllogism of nation' was for the French in the late eighteenth century: 'we are free, thus, we are a nation' (Mirkine-Guetzévitch, 1928, p.312).

36 However, even Renan's definition has been criticised for being 'historical and not rationalist' (Mirkine-Guetzévitch, 1928, p.312).

37 The idea was also very much in the air at the Zimmerwald Conference of international socialists in 1915 and was a noted feature of liberal rhetoric towards the end of the First World War. Murray supplies the example of the Inter-Allied Labour Conference in London in February 1918 which laid down that: 'It is the supreme principle of the *Right of Each People to Determine its own Destiny that must now decide*" the steps to be taken for settlement.' (Murray, 1922, p.6).

38 Lindley notes that in Roman law a defining aspect of a mandatory 'contract... was that the mandatory undertook its performance gratuitously' and he adds that this principle was reiterated in relation to the League's mandate system at the Paris Peace Conference (Lindley, 1926, p.248).

39 Note that under this system there was no assurance of any protection for minorities once sovereignty had been achieved. Kedourie writes that shortly after achieving independence the 'Iraqi Army carried out a massacre of Assyrians in Mosul' and adds that Britain, the mandatory state, which had assured the Permanent Mandates Commission of Iraq's readiness for independence felt under no obligation 'to protect minorities in Iraq' (Kedourie, 1966, p.138).

40 As Michla Pomerance writes, 'if "consent" was to be given continuously, rather than as a one-time exercise, the form of government chosen would probably have to be *democratic*' (Pomerance, 1969, p.1).

41 Wilson spoke of his aspiration for the League of Nations in a speech delivered at Oakland, California, on 18 September 1919: 'One of the interesting provisions of the Covenant of the League of Nations is that no nation can be a member of that League which is not a self-governing nation. *No autocratic government can come into its membership; no government which is not controlled by the will and vote of its people.*' Gathorne-Hardy states that the American President appeared to be the sole advocate of this interpretation of the Covenant (quoted Gathorne-Hardy, 1950, p.148).

42 The *Greco-Bulgarian Communities* Case of 1930 referred to a minority as a 'group of people living on a delimited territory, possessing distinct religious, racial, linguistic, or other cultural attributes and desiring to preserve its special characteristics' (Doehring, 1994, p.64). Minorities Treaties were signed by the following states: Albania, Austria, Bulgaria, Czechoslovakia, Estonia, Hungary, Iraq, Latvia, Lithuania, Poland, Turkey and Yugoslavia.

43 Pomerance notes that Wilson thought that the 'special minorities regimes' were only needed 'in the absence of true self-government' (Pomerance, 1969, p.3).

44 Heyking also argued that since Peace Treaty of Versailles 'proscribed' the persecution of 'humanity for race or religion', minorities, even though not 'constituted...as independent sovereign States', should be recognised as 'subjects' of international, or better still, 'Universal law' (Heyking, 1924, pp.149–50).

45 The Arbitral Tribunal stated in relation to the new Polish state: '...the recognition of a State is not constitutive but merely declaratory. The State exists by itself and the recognition is nothing else than a declaration of this existence, recognized by the States from which it emanates' (quoted in Crawford, 1978, p.104).
46 Article 1 of the Montevideo Convention specifies the following empirical prerequisites: 'The State as a person of international law should possess the following qualifications: (a) A permanent population; (b) a defined territory (c) government; and (d) capacity to enter into relations with other States' (quoted in Crawford, 1978, p.111). Thomas D. Grant notes that there were many nineteenth century legal publicists who anticipated the criteria laid down by this Convention including, most notably, Hall (Grant, 1999, p.7).
47 Thornberry states that at the San Francisco Conference 'the opinions of statesmen... towards minorities were largely negative in character' (Thornberry, 1989, pp.871–2).
48 Crawford adds that a right of a people to 'choose its own form of government irrespective of the wishes of the rest of the State of which it is...[a]...part' while 'not mentioned...is implicit' in Articles 73 [b] and 76 [b], yet it is to go beyond the 'terms of the Charter' to proclaim a 'general right of self-determination' (Crawford, 1978, p.152). Pomerance also notes that the principle of self-determination 'is *not* referred to as a legal "right"' or that 'its scope is in any case limited to "non-self-governing territories"' (Pomerance, 1982, p.69).
49 Ogden writes that 'as far back as 1950 the Chinese insisted that regional autonomy granted by the Chinese government to the national minorities inside the country is an autonomy within the confines of Chinese sovereignty'. Consequently, the People's Liberation Army was entitled to 'enter Tibet to liberate the Tibetan peoples and defend the frontiers of China' (Ogden, pp.217–18). The 1982 Constitution, continuous with the previous constitutions, states in Article 4: 'Regional autonomy is practised in areas where people of minority nationalities live in compact communities; in these areas organs of self-government are established for the exercise of the right of autonomy. All the national autonomous areas are inalienable parts of the People's Republic of China' (Constitution of the People's Republic of China, 1982). Christopher Hughes notes that today there is concern in China that 'political stability' might be threatened if minority calls for cultural autonomy grow into a demand for political independence (Hughes, 1997, pp.104, 115)
50 The 'cultural pluralism' argument is highly contentious for those concerned with setting human rights standards (Loh, 1995, pp.154–5). However, Clapham considers that moving the 'defence of state power...out of the universalistic sphere of state sovereignty...into the particularist realm of "culture"', is an acknowledgement of the limits of the sovereignty defence. However, he notes that China continues to uphold the sovereignty defence (Clapham, 1999, p.535).
51 Concerns as regards legitimacy in the face of the disintegrating forces of globalisation also explain why the Chinese state places so much emphasis, as Wang Huning puts it, on 'cultural sovereignty' (quoted in Hughes, 1997, p.115). Chester C. Tan notes that Liang Chin Chao, a Chinese political thinker and actor of the early twentieth century said that: 'To lose one's character is to lose one's essence. The same is true of a nation....Without its own character, a nation cannot begin to exist'. (Tan, 1971, p.37).
52 Chen argues that Chinese nationalism, as reflected in its foreign policy, has become less virulent than it was throughout the twentieth century and has, since the

1980s, been shaped in a 'positive' way such that it can 'accommodate both the Chinese desire for a national rejuvenation, and the general welfare of the world community' (Chen, 2005, p.36).

53 Clapham also believes that exposure to global economic forces can play a role in the reform of quasi-states and in fact he notes that the post-war sovereignty regime that served to protect corrupt, despotic and ineffective governments has been unravelling since the 1980s in the wake of the Third World debt crisis. The subsequent pressure on ineffective states to improve their quality of governance and human rights standards, Clapham describes as 'one of the most significant instruments in the assault on sovereignty'. Confronted with such pressure, he notes, Third World states and their advocates began to articulate a more circumscribed and reasonable version of the doctrine of state sovereignty, a version that was more legally nuanced and less politically opportunistic than that put forward in the 1970s when the post-colonial sovereignty regime was at its peak (Clapham, 1999, pp.532–5).

Chapter 5 Sovereignty, Self-Determination and the Rights of Indigenous Peoples

1 Although as James Tully argues, this second understanding of the right of self-determination remains highly relevant as indigenous peoples are 'peoples in the clear meaning of the term as it is used in the Charter and the General Assembly Declaration on the Granting of Independence to Colonial Countries and Peoples, and thus the principle of self-determination enunciated in the Declaration applies to them' (Tully, 2000, p.55).

2 Hitchcock notes that indigenous peoples 'range from the highly urbanized Maori of New Zealand to small, mobile groups of Aqua foragers in the rain forests of central Africa, from sizable Indian peasant communities in South and Central America to pastoral nomads in the mountains of Pakistan and Afghanistan' (Hitchcock, 1994, p.2).

3 This definition is, however, problematic from the point of view of urbanised indigenous peoples (Eruetie, 2006, p.4).

4 Sharp makes this comment in relation to Māori assertions of sovereignty in New Zealand.

5 While I do not discuss the example of Nicaragua at length, it is worth noting that the Constitution of Nicaragua recognises 'indigenous forms of social organization as well as the right of indigenous peoples to manage their local affairs, maintain their communal forms of ownership, and their right to the use and enjoyment of their lands' (Daes, 2004, p.10). See Articles 5, 89, 180 of the Political Constitution of Nicaragua (1987) as reformed in 1995 and 2000. See also Autonomy Statute of the Regions of the Atlantic Coast of Nicaragua, Law No.28, *Gaceta Oficial*, No.238, 30 October, 1987 and Law 445 (*Ley del Régimen de la Propiedad Communal de los Pueblos Indígenas y Communidades Étnicas de las regiones Autónomasde la Costa Atlántica y de los Ríos Coco, Bocay, Indio y Maíz*), published in *La Gaceta Diario Oficial*, No.16 , 23 January 2003 (cited in Daes, 2004, pp.24–5).

6 The Declaration was supported by 143 states, with four opposed (Australia, Canada, New Zealand and the United States otherwise known as the CANZUS states). Eleven states abstained from the vote (Azerbaijan, Bangladesh, Bhutan, Burundi, Colombia, Georgia, Kenya, Nigeria, Russian Federation, Samoa and Ukraine). There were also 34 states absent from the vote including the African

states of Eritrea, Ethiopia, Somalia, Uganda and Rwanda and also Israel (United Nations Department of Public Information, 2007). Botswana, which had as late as November 2006 opposed the Declaration in alliance with the CANZUS state, voted for the Declaration probably because the indigenous San people of the Kalahari Desert had scored a significant legal victory at the Botswanan High Court in December of that same year concerning their eviction from the Kalahari Game Reserve (Mutume, 2007, p.1).

7 While some commentators question the assumption that sovereignty, in the internal sense, can only be associated with developed governmental institutions, it is certainly 'questionable' that societies would come to think of themselves as having a 'right of self-government' in the absence of outside claimants (Webber, 2000, p.65).

8 According to Nys, the first treatise on the question of the liberty of the indigenous people of South America was by Jean Lopez de Palacios Rubios, a professor of civil and canonical law at Salamanca, royal judge at Valladolid and member of the supreme council of justice, under the title of *Tractatus insularum maris oceani* (Nys, 1896, p.225).

9 S. James Anaya notes that Las Casas especially condemned the 'Spanish *encomienda* system, which granted Spanish conquerors and colonists parcels of lands and the right to labor of the Indians living on them' (Anaya, 1996, p.10).

10 Greg Marks interprets Las Casas as follows: 'having criticised the usual grounds by which the Spanish justified their subjugation of the Indians, Vitoria needed to find some grounds to justify Spain's continued presence in the Americas' (Marks, 2000, p.9).

11 The *jus gentium* was defined by Ulpian as that law which 'all human peoples observe' and in this regard it is different from natural law which Ulpian defines as the law which is observed by all living creatures (Justinian, 1998, 1.1.1).

12 Brennan J. writes that while Blackstone approved of 'sending colonies [of settlers] to find out new habitations' he also expressed doubts about its consequences. Blackstone stated: 'so long as it was confined to the stocking and cultivation of desert and uninhabited countries, it kept strictly within the limits of the law of nature. But how far the seising on countries already peopled, and driving out or massacring the innocent and defenceless natives, merely because they differed from their invaders in language, in religion, in customs, in government, or in colour; how far such a conduct was consonant to nature, to reason, or to Christianity, deserved well to be considered by those, who have rendered their names immortal by thus civilising mankind' (quoted by Brennan in Bartlett, 1994, pp.22–3).

13 This framing of the Inca state in terms of the principle of sovereignty is understandable given the claim that the Sopa Inca of Peru, before Spanish conquest, 'exercised sovereign power to a degree that has no parallel in native American history. He is pictured as an independent and almost absolute ruler, rarely in consultation with his subordinates' (Gibson, 1948, p.9).

14 On the right of occupation Wolff stated: 'Since separate families dwelling together in a certain territory own the lands which they have occupied, but the other places are the property of nobody; if in a district in which separate families hold their own lands there are still other lands the use of which can be private or individual, those lands can be occupied by anybody...All the earth is open to every body as long as sovereignty over it has been assumed by no one, and every one who needs them can occupy things in it which have no owner' (Wolff, 1934, pp.158–9).

15 It is worth noting that in the original French version of his *Law of Nations*, Vattel stated that independent families are '*sans Empire*' in the sense of being without sovereignty, however, he then went on to state, in denying that these people can be subjected against their will, that no-one can seize the '*Empire*' of that country (Vattel, 1768, pp.325–36). Note that the word *empire* translates as sovereign authority and dominion.

16 Grotius and Hobbes presaged Vattel in respect to the question of the acquisition of territory which is surplus to a group's requirements. Grotius wrote: 'Again, if within the territory of a people there is any deserted and unproductive soil, this also ought to be granted to foreigners if they ask for it. Or it is right for foreigners even to take possession of such ground, for the reason that uncultivated land ought not to be considered as occupied', although he qualifies his point in adding, 'except in respect to sovereignty, which remains unimpaired in favour of the original people' (Grotius, 1925, p.202). Hobbes similarly wrote: 'The multitude of poor, and yet strong people still increasing, they are to be transplanted into countries not sufficiently inhabited; where nevertheless, they are not to exterminate those they find there; but constrain them to inhabit closer together, and not range a great deal of ground to snatch what they find, but to court each little Plot with art and labour, to give them their sustenance in due season.' Hobbes also maintains that should the native inhabitants oppose themselves to this transplantation' for things superfluous...[they are]...guilty of the warre that thereupon is to follow' (Hobbes, 1968, pp.210, 387).

17 Locke stated in regard to American Indians chiefs that they are '...little more than *Generals of their Armies*; and though they command absolutely in War, yet at home and in time of Peace they exercise very little Dominion, and have but very moderate Sovereignty, the Resolutions of Peace and War, being ordinarily either in the People, or in a Council' (Locke, 1967, pp.357–8).

18 Austin, however, then adds the qualification that an independent political society 'must not fall short of a number which may be called considerable' (Austin, 1906, p.110). On the question of Austin's attitude towards the source of political obedience, see n5 Chapter 2.

19 Grotius stated: 'whatever was originally occupied by the people, and has not since been distributed, must be considered the property of the people' (Grotius, 1925, p.300).

20 An anti-slavery movement, inspired by philosophical and humanitarian ideals, had appeared in France before the revolution. A *Société des amis des noirs* was formed in Paris in 1788 headed by Brissot, Mirabeau, the Abbé Grégoire, le duc de La Rochefoucauld, Clavière and Pétion.

21 For Fiore, whose concern lay not with existing law but with law as it should be, the only means of acquiring the territory of 'uncivilised' tribes without violating international law was through cession accompanied by the payment of an 'indemnity' to them. However, it was lawful to entice the tribal society to free land from which they were not profiting in order that others could colonise it. Fiore argued that 'savage tribes ruled by their chief elected in their manner and according to their constitution' were to be regarded as 'invested with the power of sovereignty and could not be regarded as territory vacant of a master', adding that 'however praiseworthy' might be the objective of spreading civilisation 'one could not admit that the civil state could be brought to the uncivilised at the point of a bayonet and with the terror of the cannons' (Fiore, 1909, pp.416–17). However, while 'independent tribes are not to be considered as outside the law of humanity' they do not have the same status under international law as

'civilised states' (Fiore, 1909, p.122). This same view was also proffered by a Commission appointed by colonial powers at the African Conference of Berlin (Lindley, 1926, p.46).

22 Louis Renault had written of the 'essential rights which derive from the existence of a human society...[and] from its establishment on a determinate territory.' He complained that too often so-called civilised nations had 'abused of their power' in declaring 'unjustifiable wars' on the 'so-called barbarians' and violating 'the most elementary rules of the law of nations' (Renault, 1879, p.22).

23 Martens excepted 'districts simply held by nomadic tribes' from this prescription (Lindley, 1926, p.17). Heffter stated that 'no power on earth has the right to impose its laws on a people even if they are erratic or savage' (quoted in Bonfils, 1912, p.360). However, Heffter conceded that in the interest of conserving the human race, nations could unite to force open another nation's doors to trade (Jèze, 1896, p.109). Worthy of mention here is Moser's view that while positive international law was confined to Europe, it was important to accept that Asia and Africa existed under the protection of natural law (Jianming, 2000, p.21).

24 In noting the requirement that for a society to have international legal rights it must be sufficiently durable such that it can guarantee the 'fulfilment of obligations', Hall also observed that there 'is no reason' why in theory 'even a wandering tribe or society should not feel itself bound as stringently as a settled community by definite rules of conduct towards other communities' even though there 'might be difficulty in subjecting such societies to restraint, or in some cases in being sure of their identity' (Hall, 1895, p.20).

25 Crawford notes that the exceptions were Australia, the South Island of New Zealand, some 'scattered islands or totally uninhabited tracts' (Crawford, 1979, p.180). In terms of the understanding of a political society, Crawford argues that it 'had long been established that the only necessary pre-condition was a degree of governmental authority sufficient for the general maintenance of order, and subsequent practice was not sufficiently consistent or coherent to change that position' (Crawford, 1979, p.176). In its *Advisory Opinion on Western Sahara* (1975) the International Court of Justice stated in relation to the late nineteenth century situation that: 'Whatever differences of opinion there may have been among jurists, the State practice of the relevant period indicates that territories inhabited by tribes or peoples having a social and political organization were not regarded as terrae nullius. It shows that in the case of such territories the acquisition of sovereignty was...considered as effected...through agreements concluded with local rulers...such agreements with local rulers, whether or not considered as an actual "cession" of the territory, were regarded as derivative roots of title, and not original titles obtained by occupation of terrae nullius' (quoted by Brennan in Bartlett, 1994, pp.27–8). According to Lindley, however, state practice allowed that territory could be acquired by occupation where it was inhabited by a 'number of individuals who do not form a political society' (Lindley, 1926, p.45).

26 Article 34 of the Declaration stipulated that any power annexing such land or assuming a 'protectorate there, shall accompany the respective act with a notification.' Article 35 stipulated that signatories were obliged to 'insure the establishment of authority in the regions occupied by them on the coasts of the African continent, sufficient to protect existing rights and...freedom of trade and of transit' (quoted in Westlake, 1910, p.108).

27 Despagnet argued that even though the need to respect the sovereignty of all peoples, civilised or uncivilised, was not inserted in the agreement issuing from the Berlin Conference this view prevailed at the Conference as reflected in all the declarations made in the course of it (Despagnet, 1910, p.398). The Institute of International Law in 1888 had rejected a proposed definition of *territorium nullius* as 'any region not effectively under the sovereignty or protectorate of one of the States forming the community of international law, whether inhabited or not' (Lindley, 1926, p.16). In the same year, it endorsed a statement concerning the securing of 'good title to occupied territory', one of its stipulations being, in line with Article VI of the General Act of the Berlin Conference, 'the duty of watching over the conservation of the aboriginal populations' (Anaya, 1996, p.25).

28 However, there remains disagreement among scholars as to 'whether the Royal Proclamation recognized or undermined tribal sovereignty' (Calloway, 2006, p.96).

29 The act of March 3, 1871 stipulated that from that date relations with the tribes would be governed by acts of Congress: 'No Indian nation or tribe, within the territory of the United States, shall be acknowledged as recognised as independent nation, tribe, or power, with whom the United States may contract by treaty'. This act, however, did not impair the treaties made before this act (Snow, 1919, p.32).

30 See *Cherokee Nation vs. the State of Georgia,* 30 (5 Peters), (1831), 4,17 (quoted in Snow, p.28). See also Daes's reference to this case (Daes, 2004, p.9). As Webber notes, it is unimaginable that indigenous societies would have considered themselves domestic dependent nations 'except perhaps for those peoples who acknowledged the suzerainty of another indigenous people' (Webber, 2000, p.64).

31 Note, however, that Vattel also stated a version of the principle of prescription, thus suggesting that independence is in fact surrendered in this context. He stated that when 'a people...has passed under the rule of another, [it] is no longer a State, and does not come directly under the Law of Nations (quoted in Anaya, 1996, p.16). Anaya suggests that Marshall went further in respect to native self-determination in *Worcester v. Georgia* than he did in *Johnson v. MacIntosh* because the case involved the Cherokee Nation, the leaders of which had been 'educated in Christian missionary schools' and 'had adopted Western forms of governance and land use, and had otherwise borrowed heavily from Anglo-American or European ways' (Anaya, 1996, p.18).

32 In *The U.S. v. Percheman* in 1833 Marshall CJ again followed Vattel in stating that when 'people change their alliance; their relation to their ancient sovereign is dissolved, but their relations to each other, and their rights of property remain undisturbed' (quoted in Reynolds, 1992, p.38).

33 Buchan argues that the 'application' of the doctrine of *terra nullius* 'belongs to a period in Australian history long after initial colonization' (Buchan, 2005, p.2).

34 In this regard, it is worth noting the comments of Joseph Banks before a committee in England in 1785 inquiring as to whether the land within Australia was to be obtained from the Aborigines 'by Cession or Purchase'. Banks stated that he did not know of anything that the Aborigines would take in exchange for their land. He stated that he had also observed the nomadic habits of the natives and that he believed that they would quickly abandon their land (Atkinson, 1997, p.71).

35 Imperial law decreed in three provisions 'the establishment of reserves, the recognition of rights of use and occupancy on Crown land and the provision for compensation to provide for education and welfare' (Reynolds, 1992, p.125).

36 In 1837, a Select Committee on Aborigines told the House of Commons 'that the state of the Australian Aborigines was "barbarous" and "so entirely destitute...of the rudest forms of civil polity, that their claims, whether as sovereigns or proprietors of the soil, have been utterly disregarded"' (quoted by Brennan in Bartlett, 1994, p.27).

37 Eddie Koiko Mabo initiated 'a common law land claim in 1982' which was decided by the Australian High Court 'after the death of three of the five Murray Island Plaintiffs including Mabo himself' (Nettheim, 1993, p.223). Bartlett argues that although the concept of *terra nullius* was addressed in the case it was 'essentially irrelevant to native title at common law', since, as we have also seen, it is a principle pertaining to international and not municipal law and, as we have seen, the concept does not necessitate 'a denial of native title'. He writes that the 'real question put before the court...was whether or not native title was part of the common law of a settled territory such as Australia. Every other relevant jurisdiction, in particular, the United States, Canada and New Zealand, had held that it was, and the High Court determined that Australia was no different' (Bartlett, 1994, p.ix).

38 Hepburn notes that in *Lansen v. Olney* in 1999 the Federal Court observed: '...territorial sovereignty may not equate, even under the common law doctrine of tenure, to absolute beneficial ownership, the latter being arguably alien to the medieval cast of mind' (Hepburn, 2005, p.70).

39 Brennan J stated in *Mabo* that native title had '...its origin in and is given its content by the traditional laws acknowledged by and the traditional customs observed by the indigenous inhabitants of a territory. The nature and incidents of native title must be ascertained in fact by reference to those laws and customs' (quoted in Calma, 2006, p.5).

40 Bartlett notes that although the Court's assertion that 'sovereignty was acquired by "settlement"' would seem to negate the idea of an 'original sovereignty' its citation, 'with approval', of Blackburn J's 'finding of the original legal system, and implicitly, the original sovereignty, of Aboriginal peoples in *Milirrpum v. Nabalco*' suggests otherwise. He adds that the real importance of the 'rejection of the concept of terra nullius' is that it involved the rejection of the idea that the 'Aboriginal people were "without laws, without a sovereign and primitive in their social organisation"' (Bartlett, 1994, p.x).

41 Marshall CJ stated in *Johnson v. McIntosh* that: 'However extravagant the pretension of converting the discovery of an inhabited country into conquest may appear, if the principle has been asserted in the first instance and afterwards sustained; if a country has been acquired and held under it; if the property of the great mass of the community originates in it, it becomes the law of the land and can not be questioned' (quoted in Snow, 1919, p.27).

42 While such an acknowledgement might be beneficial in certain respects it is also problematic given that, as Brennan J noted in the *Mabo* case, indigenous lands were never 'taken as a result of an overt conquest', a fact which raises further questions concerning the nature and legitimacy of the British acquisition of sovereignty from an international perspective (Hepburn, 2005, p.76). In the case of the *Mabo* decision, the Court simply reaffirmed that 'sovereignty was acquired by "settlement"' (Bartlett, 1994, p.x).

43 Calma notes that the 'compatibility' between the 1998 amendments to the *Native Title Act* of 1993 and Australia's human rights obligations has been a matter of ongoing concern for the UN's Committee on the Elimination of Racial Discrimination (Calma, 2006, p.5).

44 Brennan, Gunn and Williams note that the Nisga'a Final Agreement of 1998 'recognised the legislative, executive and judicial power of the Nisga'a Nation and the responsibility of the Nisga'a Lisims Government for intergovernmental relations with the provincial and federal governments' (Brennan, Gunn and Williams, 2004, p.332).

45 Tully views the Agreement as an example of the Canadian state's strategy of 'extinguishment' of the rights of indigenous communities by 'incorporation by agreement' (Tully, 2000, p.50).

46 Snow sourced the dispute over the meaning of the Treaty Waitangi which took place between the 1840s and the 1860s to the fact that the Treaty was 'so unfortunately worded as to give ground for the claim that Great Britain had recognized the tribes as an independent State, having the title in fee to all the land of that part of New Zealand.' As a result, he adds: 'Incessant trouble arose between the home government and the colonial government on the one side, and the Maori Tribes and the Europeans claiming under them on the other. Twice the matter was considered by parliamentary committees – in 1840 and 1844 – both of which insisted that Great Britain had not intended to make any such admission, upholding its full sovereignty and recommending a compromise adjustment. Finally, in the sixties, the matter was settled by a war with the Maoris' (Snow, 1919, pp.119–20).

47 In relation to the Treaty's interpretation, McHugh writes that the term *kawanatanga* means in English 'governership' (McHugh, 2004, p.89). McHugh also notes that 'Māori tribalism' was forcefully subjugated during the New Zealand Wars and this was judicially confirmed in *Wi Parata v. the Bishop of Wellington* in 1877. He adds that the 'wars had revealed the fragility of the Anglo-settler state's self-styled absolute and indivisible "sovereignty" – its uneasy claim to be the "Leviathan" of the New Zealand islands...and so the Crown's courts could not afford to be generous' (McHugh, 1999, p.447).

48 McHugh writes that it was during the 1980s 'that sovereignty talk began again to raise its profile in Māori discourse...Extreme subjection tends to produce extreme dogma, and that was one of the more notable produces of a new, young breed of Māori activist' (McHugh, 1999, p.457).

49 Sharp notes that the idea that ' native peoples retain an inextinguishable separate status in constitutions, and that all other authorities are disabled from infringing them...[was]...comparatively new in New Zealand, though not elsewhere' (Sharp, 1997, p.302).

50 McHugh notes that in 1995 the New Zealand Court of Appeal 'reaffirmed the orthodoxy that treaty rights, including those associated with the one concluded at Waitangi in 1840, required statutory incorporation and took effect only and subject to that manner of recognition' (McHugh, 2004, pp.91–2).

51 As J.G.A. Pocock states: 'The Treaty is not used to delegitimise sovereignty, but as a reminder of its conditionality and put in its mind claims to which it is urgently concerned to attend' (Pocock, 2000, p.26).

52 Alfred states that until '"sovereignty" as a concept shifts from the dominant "state sovereignty" construct and comes to reflect more of the sense embodied in western notions such as personal sovereignty or popular sovereignty, it will remain problematic if integrated within indigenous political struggles' (Alfred, 2001, p.28).

53 Paul Coe has stated that 'despite the fact that Europeans have taken our land and "legitimised" this theft, we are still a sovereign people and nation' (Coe, 1988, p.142).

54 Watson views this latter understanding as a continuing form of colonialism (Watson, 2002, §44).
55 As Roderic Pitty argues in relation to Australia and New Zealand, such an ideological commitment reflects the identification of 'citizenship...with a dominant idea of a culturally uniform nation, rather than with effective political participation'. If indigenous claims are to be advanced it is essential that society constructs a 'shared framework for differentiated citizenship' (Pitty, 2001, pp.4, 15).
56 Eruetie discusses the Mayan Case (Eruetie, 2006, p.4).

Chapter 6 The European Union: Sovereignty in the Twilight Zone

1 The expression European Union (EU) denotes herein both the Union itself as well as the European Community, the latter being one of the three pillars of the European Union as established by the Maastricht Treaty. Should the Reform Treaty come into force in 2009, the European Community will be wholly incorporated into the EU.
2 See 'European Federal Union: Text of the British Reply', August 1930. 'His Majesty's Government in the United Kingdom understand from the memorandum that the fundamental purpose which the French Government have in view is to divert the attention of the peoples of Europe from the hostilities of the past and from the conflicts of interest between them...and to fix their attention instead upon the more important common interests which to-day they share. The French Government hope that by their proposals they may promote closer cooperation among the nations and Governments of Europe, and thus strengthen the safeguards against another European war' (United Nations Library at Geneva, 1996, p.142).
3 By contrast, as Adam Jan Cygan writes, it is often argued that because the EU's legislative process is undertaken 'not by an elected Parliament but by the Council of Ministers behind closed doors...the legislation is devoid of any democratic legitimacy. No national parliament has any involvement in the final legislative stage' (Cygan, 1998, p.3).
4 However, despite the existence of common borders it remains the case that the 'national state undoubtedly remains the only authority that can confer the status of European citizen through nationality law' (Schnapper, 1997, p.205).
5 The democratic deficit refers to the fact that EU treaties make no allowance for the direct involvement of parliament in the legislative process.
6 The European Council decided at Cologne that in order to realise the aims of the Common Foreign and Security Policy the EU must acquire 'the capacity for nomous action, backed by credible military forces, the means to decide to use them, and a readiness to do so, in order to respond to international crises without prejudice to actions by NATO' (quoted in Maitland, 2001, p.84). In 2004, Member States agreed on the formation of a European Rapid Reaction Force, an agreement which provided for, not a standing army, but a '"virtual army" of nationally available forces'. These forces were 'in theory, "ready for deployment" for a period of up to one year' as of January, 2007 (Glover, 2007).
7 The Reform Treaty endows the EU with full legal personality thus enabling it to sign international agreements concerning all three policy areas on which the EU was based under Maastricht: European Communities; Common Foreign and Security Policy and Police and Judicial Co-operation in Criminal Matters.

Previously, legal competence in this regard was possessed only by the European Community. Note, however, that Member States are able to deny the EU competence in a number of the policy areas that come under these three headings.

8 Dealings between the states which are members of the Euro-zone and the EU states which are not members, are particularly 'sensitive' with Britain being especially cautious about 'allowing a process of policy formulation on topics of fiscal policy and international monetary affairs to deepen among the euro-zone states' (McNamara and Meunier, 2002, p.853).

9 Loveland adds that the courts act to protect citizens against 'underhand or deceptive parliamentary efforts' to eliminate or reduce their rights and duties under EU law. In this way the courts have informed the operations of Parliament because if Parliament now sought to remove a 'citizen's EC entitlements or obligations it would have to do so in the most candid and transparent of ways' (Loveland, 1996, p.527).

10 Krasner notes that in 1971 the ECJ 'promulgated the doctrine of implied powers which holds that the community has the right to make treaties, because otherwise it could not efficiently carry out its assigned tasks...During the same period the court also ruled that there were certain areas, such as trade, where the community had exclusive powers. Individual states were prohibited from taking any unilateral action in these areas, even actions that did not contradict European union rules' (Krasner, 1999, p.235).

11 Hartley writes that the Danish Supreme Court, in ruling on the Danish Maastricht case, 'expressly said that the Community cannot be given the power to adopt legislation that would be contrary to the Danish constitution'. Similarly, the *Bundesverfassungsgericht* has made it clear that a transfer of powers to the Community cannot affect the basic framework of the constitutional order in Germany. The '*Corte Costituzionale* (Italian Constitutional Court) considers that Community law cannot prevail over the fundamental principles of the Italian Constitution' and a comparable outlook is 'implicit in decisions of the French *Conseil Constitutionnel* and would almost certainly be taken by courts in other Member States' (Hartley, 1999, pp.167–8).

12 It is nonetheless possible to argue, in the tradition of Bodin, that '[r]ules of fundamental constitutional laws stand on a different footing. They appear at times to impose an absolute limitation upon the supreme organization' (Brown, 1906, p.161n).

13 Wade maintains that when in the second *Factorame* case, the House of Lords 'disapplied' a 1988 Act of Parliament deemed incompatible with EU law it was clear that 'something drastic had happened to the traditional doctrine of Parliamentary sovereignty' (Wade, 1996, p.568).

14 There are certain statutory requirements governing British and EU relations that support the view that Britain retains its sovereignty. Richard Rawlings insists that the British Parliament maintains its sovereignty expressly through section 6 of the European Parliamentary Elections Act 1978 which states that: 'No treaty which provides for an increase in the powers of the European Parliament shall be ratified by the United Kingdom unless it has been approved by an Act of Parliament' (quoted in Rawlings, 1994, p.259).

15 The '"dualistic" doctrine of international law' was also articulated by Heinrich Triepel in 1899 under the heading *Völkerrecht und Landesrecht* or *International and Municipal Law*. Therein he argued that: 'In order to give the international rule affect in municipal law, especially for the courts, it must be transformed into a

rule of municipal law by an act of national legislation; only thereafter are the courts bound to apply it' (Nussbaum, 1954, p.235).

16 The PCIJ stated: '...the very object of an international agreement, according to the intention of the contracting Parties, may be the adoption by the Parties of some definite rules creating individual rights and obligations and enforceable by the national courts' (quoted in Leben, 1998, p.294).

17 Article 55 of the French Constitution stipulates 'the superiority, under certain circumstances, of treaties over legislation, even when enacted subsequently' (see Leben, 1998, p.294).

18 See also Georg Sørensen who writes: 'The counterargument is that constitutional independence remains intact; countries dissatisfied with EU-developments can, should they so wish, discontinue their membership. I support this counter-argument, but the discussion indicates how far-reaching modifications of sovereignty's regulative rules raises new debates about the institution. Sovereignty becomes a contested concept' (Sørensen, 1999 , pp.603–4).

19 Craig points to the domination of Parliament by the executive (Craig, 1991, p.238).

Chapter 7 The State and War

1 As Rousseau stated, 'we have taken all kinds of precautions against private wars only to kindle national wars a thousand times more terrible? And that, in joining a particular group of men, we have really declared ourselves the enemies of the whole race?' (Rousseau, 1970a, p.132). In the *Social Contract* he developed a similar argument, stating that collectivities 'generate a kind of centrifugal force, by which they brush continuously against one another, and they all attempt to expand at the expense of their neighbours, like the vortices of Descartes. Thus the weak are always in danger of being swallowed up, and indeed no people can well preserve itself except by achieving a kind of equilibrium with all the others which makes the pressure everywhere the same for all' (Rousseau 1968, p.92).

2 Rousseau makes a similar point in remarking that since 'reason without an assured guide, in matters of doubt...[is]...always biased towards personal considerations, war would still be inevitable, even when everyone wished to be just' (Rousseau, 1987b, p.45).

3 In the Prolegmona to *De Jure Belli ac Pacis* Grotius maintained that for wars to 'be justified, they must be carried out with not less scrupulousness than judicial processes are wont to be', nonetheless the overall effect of the *temperamenta* was to render such scrupulousness a discretionary matter (Grotius, 1925, p.18).

4 According to Nussbaum, the principle of distinction articulated by Rousseau, was generally embraced by nineteenth century 'public opinion, statecraft, and legal theory' and as a result, it exercised a restraining influence on the conduct of war. In 1870, at the outset of the Franco-German War, William I of Prussia issued a war Manifesto that stated that war was to be fought against 'the French soldier and not with the French citizens' (Nussbaum, 1954, p.139). However, and possibly because of this commitment to the distinction between combatant and non-combatant, when the French population participated in the war against the Germans, having been roused by the republican government of Léon Gambotta, the reprisals against them were harsh (Schmitt, 2004, p.24).

5 My translation.

6 Montesquieu also criticised the position of Grotius in this regard. He wrote that the 'authors of our public law...have fallen into very great errors. They have adopted tyrannical and arbitrary principles, by supposing the conquerors to be invested with I know not what right to kill...from the right of killing in the case of conquest, politicians have drawn that of reducing to slavery – a consequence as ill grounded as the principle (Montesquieu, 1949, p.135). Vattel argued similarly, stating that the conqueror can have no right to enslave the conquered in exchange for sparing their lives. He stated that 'he who makes such an assertion is ignorant that war gives no right to take away the life of an enemy who has laid down his arms and submitted' (Vattel, 1863, p.389). Vattel stated that it was 'monstrous' to think that slavery could be legitimised through 'a kind of compact by which the conqueror consents to spare the lives of the vanquished, on condition that they acknowledge themselves his slaves'; such an argument shows an ignorance of the fact that 'war gives no right to take away the life of an enemy who has laid down his arms and submitted' (Vattel, 1863, pp.388–9). Blackstone in his *Commentaries on the Laws of England* (1765) also denied a right of enslavement under the law of nations: 'The conqueror, say the civilians, has a right to deal with him as he pleases. But it is an untrue position, when taken generally, that, by the law of nature or nations, a man may kill his enemy: he has only a right to kill him, in particular cases; in cases of absolute necessity, for self-defence; and it is plain this absolute necessity did not subsist, since the victor did not actually kill him, but made him a prisoner. War is itself justifiable only on principles of self-preservation; and therefore it gives no other right over prisoners but merely to disable them from doing harm to us, by confining their persons: much less can it give a right to kill, torture, abuse, plunder, or even to enslave, an enemy, when the war is over. Since therefore the right of *making* slaves by captivity, depends on a supposed right of slaughter, that foundation failing, the consequence drawn from it must fail likewise' (Blackstone, 1973, p.115). In fairness, one should note that Grotius's argument is that since life is of 'greater value than liberty' it is right, as well as prudent, for a conquered people to prefer enslavement to death (Grotius, 1925, pp.573–4). Justinian notes that slaves '(*servi*) are so-called, because generals have a custom of selling their prisoners and thereby *preserving* rather than killing them' (Justinian, 1998, 1.5.4)

7 Rousseau states that the principles governing warfare are 'derived from the nature of things; they are based on reason' (Rousseau, 1968, p.57).

8 My translation.

9 Gallie writes that as stoical as Clausewitz the professional soldier was, through his long acquaintance with danger, was unable to let go of the ghastly image of the retreat of the *Grande Armée* of Bonaparte following the 1812 campaign, a campaign which resulted in horrendous levels of casualties on both the French and Russian sides (Gallie, 1978, p.39). Of the slaughter of trapped French forces by Cossacks near the Beresina River, he later reported to his wife: 'If my feelings had not been hardened it would have sent me mad' (quoted in Keegan, 1991, p.8). Clausewitz's appreciation of the horror of war is also reflected in *On War* wherein he notes how the 'moral power' of soldiers could dissolve in the face of the 'heartrending sight of the bloody sacrifice' (Clausewitz, 1968, p.145).

10 At the same time, Clausewitz was also enamoured of the idea of armed popular resistance against a foreign invader. Indeed, he stated that a war 'conducted by a people in its own fields [*Fluren*] on behalf of their freedom and independence' was 'the most beautiful of all wars' (quoted in Schmitt, 2004, p.31). Clausewitz had been greatly impressed by the efforts of the Spanish *guerilleros* during the

Spanish Guerilla War who, despite the defeat of regular Spanish forces, managed to hold up the invading French army in 1808 (Schmitt, 2004, p.4) He, and other reforming members of the Prussian general staff, pressed for a similar war of resistance, which they referred to as the 'nation armed', during the French occupation of Prussia between 1808 and 1813 although to no avail (Schmitt, 2004, p.40). The Prussian government, as was also the case with the Spanish government in response to the French invasion, showed little leadership on the issue of popular armed insurrection, seemingly not knowing 'who the real enemy was' (Schmitt, 2004, p.4). Schmitt notes that according to a Prussian royal edict of April 1813, all citizens, were 'obliged to resist the intruding enemy with weapons of whatever kind. Axes, pitchforks, scythes, and shotguns are explicitly recommended. Every Prussian is charged to obey *no* order from the enemy, but to harm him with whatever means are at hand'. Schmitt adds that the edict was completely altered three months later and 'purged of every partisan danger' (Schmitt, 2004, pp.29–30). As Anatol Rapaport pointedly expresses it, Clausewitz's opponents feared 'armed citizens' more than 'foreign invasions' since 'a peasant with a gun may get ideas about his own place in society' (Rapaport in Clausewitz, 1968, p.24).

11 Hegel had written in relation to the 'ethical *moment of war*' that it was the 'condition in which the vanity of temporal things [*Dinge*] and temporal goods...takes on a serious significance, and it is accordingly the moment in which the ideality of *the particular attains its right* and becomes actuality. The higher significance of war is that, through its agency..."the ethical health of nations [*Völker*] is preserved in their indifference towards the permanence of finite determinacies, just as the movement of the winds preserves the sea from that stagnation which a lasting calm would produce – a stagnation which a lasting, not to say perpetual, peace would also produce among nations"' (Hegel, 1991, p.361). He added that 'sacrifice for the individuality of the state is the substantial relation of everyone and therefore a *universal duty*, it itself becomes, as *one* aspect of the ideality...of particular subsistence [*Bestehen*], at the same time particular relation with an estate of its own – the *estate of valour* – attached to it' (Hegel, 1991, p.363).

12 '*Je n'ai jamais eu un plan d'opérations.*' David G. Chandler writes that the 'real implication' of this statement is that Bonaparte was 'never dominated by a hard and fast plan worked out in advance' (Chandler, 1966, p.134).

13 However, it would appear that for Clausewitz what is most interesting about Bonaparte is the change he wrought in the nature of military campaigning not whether or not his campaigns were politically wise. Thus, he concedes, before going on to urge the pursuit of decisive battle victories: 'Perhaps, by-and-by, Bonaparte's campaigns and battles will be looked upon as mere acts of barbarism and stupidity' (Clausewitz, 1968, pp.344–5). In explaining Clausewitz's attitude towards Bonaparte, Paret writes that while Metternich found it difficult, to 'recognize that Napoleon might pursue a course of action that obviously conflicted with the interests of France', Clausewitz did not since he 'expected the Emperor to obey his demon, whatever the consequences'. Paret adds that in any case, Clausewitz thought Bonaparte, precisely because of the 'conflict of personal and national interests' he represented, had been able to impart to the French nation a legend and in doing so he ultimately psychologically strengthened it (Paret, 1966, pp.34–5).

14 Paret writes that Clausewitz understood that among France's revolutionary armies the 'republican spirit was less than universal, that the *levée en masse* remained an ideal' and that theses armies 'suffered far more from desertion than their professional opponents, who fought not for principles but for a few cents

a day; but the extent to which the idea was actually fulfilled seemed less significant to him than the new possibility that men – if they wished – could now make the cause of the state their own' (Paret, 1966, p.35).

15 Smith writes that by the time of the Congress of Vienna 'the tradition of the just war that had developed before 1789 was defunct' (Smith, 1990, pp.46–7).

16 Draper observes in relation to Hall's point that it was the centrality of war in the international system that informed the 'traditional scepticism of statesmen and jurists towards international law', although this is somewhat ironic in the case of the former given that it was state practice rather than law that was the problem (Draper, 1992, p.201).

17 Rigaux explains that in 1914 the Kaiser was keen to emphasise 'Germany's 'defensive position (Einkreisungstheorie)' before the Reichstag 'in order to have the war credits voted by [it]' (Rigaux, 1998, pp.340–1).

18 Draper claims that by the end of the nineteenth century, states 'had the right in international law to resort to war for the national policy of the moment' and adds that it was seen as an 'essential part of their inherent sovereignty' (Draper, 1992, pp.201–2).

19 Martens also held that wars '"between nations" must be considered as just on both sides with respect to the treatment of enemies, military arrangements, and peace' (Nussbaum, 1954, pp.182–3).

20 Roland A. Stromberg similarly writes that after the conclusion of the conflict 'a revulsion against war took place, quite as powerful as the welcoming of it in 1914' (Stromberg, 1982, p.178).

21 In the last year of the war, L.T. Hobhouse wrote that in the hands of some, Hegelian idealism had been transformed into a 'naked doctrine of power', a doctrine which elevated 'the state above men' and which had thus contributed enormously to the 'abomination of desolation, as seen at Ypres or on the Somme' (Hobhouse, 1918, pp.134, 136). Hobhouse may well have been thinking of Treitschke who had written: 'One must say in the most decided manner: "War is the only remedy for ailing nations!" The moment the State calls, "myself and my existence are at stake!" social self-seeking must fall back and every party hate be silent. The individual must forget his own ego and feel himself a member of the whole...In that very point lies the loftiness of war, that the small man disappears entirely before the great thought of the State' (quoted in Ehrenreich, 1997, p.202).

22 I owe this point to Gregory Pemberton.

23 Koskenniemi notes that in the wake of the First World War, lawyers considered it naïve and dangerous to think that the progress of civilisation naturally culminated in peace. They felt strongly, he adds, that they 'could not assume that their nationalism would lay down peacefully with their internationalism'. For them, the 'sense of automatic progress that the Victorian generation had linked to modernity was lost...Peace and development had to be artificially created, just like the State had created peace among warring tribes or religions in the domestic realm' (Koskenniemi, 2005, pp.41–2).

24 My translation. The Preamble to the Paris Pact states: 'Deeply sensible of their solemn duty to promote the welfare of mankind; persuaded that the time has come when a frank renunciation of war as an instrument of national policy should be made, to the end that the peaceful and friendly relations now existing between their peoples may be perpetuated.' Article 1 states: 'The High Contracting Parties solemnly declare, in the names of their respective peoples, that they condemn recourse to war for the solution of international controversies,

and renounce it as an instrument of national policy in their relations with one another' (quoted in Colombos, 1928, pp.98–9).

25 Vattel, in discussing this matter in his *Law of Nations*, stated that 'on occasions where it is impossible or too dangerous to wait for an absolute certainty, we may justly act on a reasonable presumption' (Vattel, 1863, p.309).

26 Randelzhofer argues that 'recourse to traditional customary law does not lead to a broadening of the narrow right of self-defence laid down in Art. 51' (Randelzhofer, 1994, pp.675–6).

27 Such a restrictionist approach is not a recipe for inaction in the face of threats to which the ordinary meaning of self-defence would seem to deny a response. In cases where the ordinary meaning of self-defence is inadequate, for example in dealing with terrorist threats or states in possession of weapons of mass destruction, then the correct procedure, both in terms of 'law and policy' according to Michael Bothe, (and this is also the case when it comes to military responses to humanitarian crises), is to seek a Security Council mandate (Bothe, 2003, p.240).

28 Fiore wrote, citing Fénelon, that the state must 'consider seriously and profoundly that the exercise of its right of war is the most grave, the most terrible, the most formidable of its responsibilities' (Fiore, 1909, p.522). For Fénelon's views on this matter, see Chap. 2, n.5.

29 The US also justified the invasion because there was an ongoing-armed conflict dating from the Persian Gulf War of 1991 which continued into 2003. Bothe argues however that the 'various bombing periods constituted separate periods of armed conflict, each of which has to be assessed separately in the light of the *ius ad bellum*. The notion of continuous armed conflict is a dangerous one, open to abuse.' As to whether the action was authorised by UNSC Resolution 678 of 29 November 1990, it was 'for the Security Council, not for individual states, to determine the consequences to be drawn from the breach of its resolutions. Such breach could not automatically re-establish the situation as it was before the resolutions' (Bothe, 2003, pp.235–6).

Bibliography

Alexandrowicz, C.H. 'New and Original States', *International Affairs* (1969), XLV (1969), 465–79.

Alfred, T. 'From Sovereignty to Freedom Toward an Indigenous Political Discourse', *Indigenous Affairs*, III (2001), 22–9.

Allan, T.R.S. 'Parliamentary Sovereignty: Law, Politics, and Revolution', *Law Quarterly Review*, CXIII (1997), 443–52.

Althusius, J. *Politica,* trans. and ed., F.S. Carney (Indianapolis: Liberty Fund, 1995).

Anaya, S.J. *Indigenous Peoples in International Law* (New York: Oxford University Press, 1996).

Anderson, M.S. *Europe in the Eighteenth Century* (London: Longmans, 1961).

Anghie, A. 'Francisco de Vitoria and the Colonial Origins of International Law', *Social & Legal Studies,* V (1996), 321–36.

Anghie, A. 'Find the Peripheries: Sovereignty and Colonialism in Nineteenth-Century International Law', *Harvard International Law Journal,* XL (1999), 1–80.

Aron, R. *Peace and War: A Theory of International Relations,* trans. R. Howard and A.B. Fox (London: Weidenfeld and Nicolson, 1962).

Atkinson, A. *The Europeans in Australia: A History* (Melbourne: Oxford University Press, 1997).

Austin, J. *'Jurisprudence'* in W.G. Brown, *The Austinian Theory of Law: Being an Edition of Lectures I, V, and VI of Austin's 'Jurisprudence,' and of Austin's 'Essay on the Uses of the Study of Jurisprudence' with Critical Notes and Excursus* (London: John Murray, 1906).

Balibar, E. *We, The People of Europe: Reflections on Transnational Citizenship,* trans. James Swenson (Princeton: Princeton University Press, 2004).

Balkin, R. 'International Law and Sovereign Rights of Indigenous Peoples' in B. Hocking, ed., *International Law and Aboriginal and Human Rights* (Sydney: Law Book Co., 1988).

Bankowski, Z. and A. Scott, 'The European Union?' in R. Bellamy, ed., *Constitutionalism, Democracy and Sovereignty: American and European Perspectives* (Aldershot: Avebury, 1996).

Bara, L. *La Science de la Paix,* C. Potvin, ed. (New York: Garland Publishing, Inc., 1972).

Barker, E. 'The Discredited State', *Political Quarterly,* February, (1915), 101–21.

Bartlett, R.H. *The Mabo Decision: Commentary by R.H. Bartlett and the Full Text of the Decision in Mabo and Others v State of Queensland* (Sydney: Butterworth, 1994).

Beaglehole, J.C., ed., *The Journals of Captain James Cook on His Voyages of Discovery,* Vol. I, *Voyage of the Endeavour 1768–1771,* Vol. I, Part 1 (New York: Kraus Reprint, 1988).

Behrendt, L. Achieving Social Justice: Indigenous Rights and Australia's Future (Annandale: Federation Press, 1999).

Bentham, J. *A Fragment on Government and an Introduction to the Principles of Morals and Legislation* (Oxford: Basil Blackwell, 1948).

Bentham, J. 'Plan for an Universal and Perpetual Peace' in *Peace Classics,* Vol. VI (London: Peace Book Company, 1968).

Bentham, J. *An Introduction to the Principles of Morals and Legislation*, J.H. Burns and H.L.A. Hart, eds (London: Althone Press, 1970).

Bentwich, N. 'The League of Nations and Racial Persecution in Germany', *Transactions of the Grotius Society*, XIX (1933), 75–88.

Blackstone, W. *The Sovereignty of the Law*, ed., G. Jones (London: Macmillan, 1973).

Blaney, D.L. and N. Inayatullah, 'The Third World and a Problem with Borders' in M. E. Denham and M.O. Lombardi, eds, *Perspectives on Third-World Sovereignty: A Post-Modern Paradox* (London: Macmillan Press, 1996).

Bleckmann, A. 'Article 2(1)' in B. Simma, ed., *The Charter of the United Nations: A Commentary* (Oxford: Oxford University Press, 1994).

Bluntschli, J.C. *Droit International Codifié* (Paris: Librarie de Guillaumin, 1874).

Bluntschli, J.C. *The Theory of the State*, Authorised English trans. [1875] (Kitchener: Batoche Books, 2000).

Bodin, J. *Method for the Easy Comprehension of History*, trans., Beatrice Reynolds, (New York: Columbia University Press, 1945).

Bodin, J. *The Six Bookes of a Commonweale*, trans. Richard Knolle [1606], ed. K.D. McRae (Cambridge: Harvard University Press, 1962).

Bodin, J. *Six Books of the Commonwealth*, Abridged and trans., M.J. Tooley (London: Basil Blackwell, 1967).

Bonfils, H. *Manuel de Droit International Public*, 6th ed. (Paris: Libraries Nouvelle de droit et de jurisprudential, 1912).

Bosanquet, B. *The Philosophical Theory of the State*, 2nd edn (London: Macmillan, [1899] 1920).

Bothe, M. 'Terrorism and the Legality of Pre-emptive Force', *European Journal of International Law*, XIV (2003), 227–40.

Bowden, B. 'The Colonial Origins of International Law: European Expansion and the Classical Standard of Civilization', *Journal of the History of International Law*, VII (2005), 1–23.

Brandli, F. 'La Révolution boulevards la diplomatie française', *Le Courier* (24 Avril 2007).

Brennan, F. *One Land One Nation: Mabo – Towards 2001* (St. Lucia: University of Queensland Press, 1995).

Brennan, S., Gunn B. and G. Williams, '"Sovereignty" and its Relevance to Treaty-Making Between Indigenous Peoples and Australian Governments', *Sydney Law Review*, XXVI (2004), 307–52.

Broglie, Duc de, *Memoirs of the Prince de Talleyrand*, ed., R.L. de Beaufort (New York: G.P. Putnam's Sons, 1891).

Brown, W.G. *The Austinian Theory of Law: Being an Edition of Lectures I, V, and VI of Austin's 'Jurisprudence,' and of Austin's 'Essay on the Uses of the Study of Jurisprudence' with Critical Notes and Excursus* (London: John Murray, 1906).

Brunner et al. v. The European Union Treaty (Cases 2 BvR 2134/92 & 2159/92), *Bundesverfassungsgericht*, Judgement of 12 October 1993, *Common Market Law Review*, XXXI (1994), 251–62.

Buchan, B. 'The Empire of Political Thought: Civilization, Savagery and Perceptions of Indigenous Government', *History of the Human Sciences*, XVIII (2005), 1–22.

Bull, H. and A. Watson, 'Introduction' and 'Conclusion' in *The Expansion of International Society* (Oxford: Clarendon Press, 1985).

Bull, H. 'The Emergence of a Universal International Society' in H. Bull and A. Watson, eds, *The Expansion of International Society* (Oxford: Clarendon Press, 1985).

Bull, H. 'Hans Kelsen and International Law' in R. Tur and W. Twining, eds, *Essays on Kelsen* (Oxford: Clarendon Press, 1986).

Burke, E. 'A Letter to John Farr and John Harris, Esquires., Sheriffs of the City of Bristol, On the Affairs of America' in *The Works of the Right Honourable Edmund Burke*, Vol. II (London: Bell & Daldy, 1872).

Burke, E. 'The History of Europe', *The Annual Register*, XI (1768), 1–84. <http://www.bodley.ox.ac.uk/cgi-bin/ilej/image1.p?item=page&se> (19 July 2007).

Butler, P.F. 'Legitimacy in a States-System: Vattel's Law of Nations' in M. Donelan, ed., *The Reason of States: A Study in International Political Theory* (London: George Allen & Unwin, 1978).

Calhoun, J.C. *A Discourse on the Constitution and Government of the United States* (1851), available at <http://www.constitution.org/jcc/dcgus:text> (26 December 2006).

Calhoun, J.C. *The Works of John C. Calhoun*, Vol. II (New York: D. Appleton & Company, 1853).

Calloway, C. The Scratch of a Pen: 1763 and the Transformation of North America (Oxford: Oxford University Press, 2006).

Calma, T. Aboriginal and Torres Strait Islander Social Justice Commissioner, Human Rights and Equal Opportunity Commission of Australia, 'Examples of Arrangements to Accommodate Indigenous Peoples' Rights over Natural Resources – Native Title and Land Rights in Australia', *Expert Seminar on Indigenous Peoples' Permanent Sovereignty Over Natural Resources and on their Relationship to Land'* (25, 26 and 27 January, 2006), Palais des Nations, HR/Geneva?IP/SEM/2006/BP.6 <http://www.ohchr.org/english/issues/indigenous/sovereignty.htm> (6 June 2006).

Calvo, C. *Droit International Théorique et Pratique: Précédé d'un Exposé Historique des Progress et la Science du Droit des Gens* (Paris: Rousseau, 1887).

Campbell, F. 'Federalism Arrangements, Negarchy, and International Security: The Philadelphia System and the European Union' in Andreas Heinemann-Grüder, ed., *Federalism Doomed? European Federalism Between Integration and Separation* (New York: Berghahn Books, 2002).

Caporaso, J. 'The European Union and Forms of State: Westphalian, Regulatory or Post-Modern?', *Journal of Common Market Studies*, XXXIV, 1996), 29–52.

Carlson, A. 'Constructing the Dragon's Scales: China's Approach to Territorial Sovereignty and Border Relations in the 1980s and 1990s', *Journal of Contemporary China*, XII (2003), 677–98.

Carlson, A. 'Helping to Keep the Peace (Albeit Reluctantly): China's Recent Stand on Sovereignty and Multilateral Intervention', *Pacific Affairs*, LXXVII (2004), 9–27.

Carter, C.J. *Rousseau and the Problem of War* (New York: Garland Publishing Inc., 1987).

Chandler, D.G. *The Campaigns of Napoleon* (London: Weidenfeld & Nicolson, 1966).

Chang, M.H. 'Chinese Irredentist Nationalism: The Magician's Last Trick', *Comparative Strategy*, XVII (1998), 83–100.

Charters, C. 'Report on the Treaty of Waitangi 1840 Between Maori and the British Crown', Background Paper Prepared for Expert Seminar on Treaties, Agreements and Other Constructive Arrangements Between States and Indigenous Peoples, Geneva, 15–17 December 2003, HR/GENEVA/TSIP/SEM/2003/BP.15: <http://www.unhchr.ch/indigenous/charters-BP15.doc.htm> (29 November 2004).

Chen, Z. 'Nationalism, Internationalism and Chinese Foreign Policy', *Journal of Contemporary China*, XIV (2005), 35–53.

Chevally, L. *La Déclaration de droit des gens de L'Abbé Grégoire 1793–1795: Etude sur le droit international public intermédiaire*, Thèse pour la Doctorat (Paris: Université de Paris – Faculté de Droit, 1912).

Choi, C. 'Party Hints European Socialism will not Influence Reform Agenda', *South China Morning Post* (26 September 2007).

Christopher, P. *The Ethics of War & Peace: An Introduction to the Legal and Moral Issues*, 3rd edn (New Jersey: Pearson, 2004).

Clapham, C. 'Degrees of statehood', *Review of International Studies*, XXIV (1998), 143–57.

Clapham, C. 'Sovereignty and the Third World State', *Political Studies*, XLVIII (1999) 522–37.

Clausewitz, C. von, *On War*, trans. J.J. Graham (London: Penguin, 1968).

Clausewitz, C. von, *On War*, trans. M. Howard and P. Paret (Princeton: Princeton University Press, 1976).

Clinebell, J.H. and J. Thomson, 'Sovereignty and Self-Determination: The Rights of Native Americans Under International Law', *Buffalo Law Review*, XXVII (1978), 669–714.

CNN.com <http://www.CNN.com/2003/US/o4/11/sprj.irqpentagon/> (26 July 2007).

Cobban, A. *The Nation State and National Self-Determination* (London: Collins, 1969).

Coe, P. 'Laws of the Black People – 1985 (c) Sovereignty' in B. Hocking, ed., *International Law and Aboriginal and Human Rights* (Sydney: Law Book Co., 1988).

Colombos, J.C. 'The Paris Pact, Otherwise Called the Kellogg Pact', *Transactions of the Grotius Society*, XXIV (1928), 87–101.

Connolly, W.E. *Political Theory and Modernity* (Ithaca: Cornell University Press, 1993).

Cooper, S. 'Introduction' in L. Bara, *La Science de la Paix*, C. Potvin, ed. (New York: Garland Publishing, Inc., 1972).

Constitution of the People's Republic of China, 1982: http://english.peopledaily.com.cn/constitution/constitution.html (13 March 2008).

Corry, S. and J. Suzman, 'News – reactions and interactions, Kalahari Conundrums, James Suzan Before Farming 2002/3 (4)', *Before Farming*, Issue 2, No. 14 (2003), 1–10: http://www.wespress.co.uk/journals/beforefarming (28 November 2007).

Costa v. ENEL, Case 6/64, Judgement of the Court of Justice (15 July 1964): http://www.ena.lu/ (20 November 2007).

Craig, P.P. 'Sovereignty of the United Kingdom Parliament after *Factor tame*', *European Yearbook of International Law* (1991).

Craig, P.P. 'Report on the United Kingdom' in A. Slaughter, A.S. Sweet and J.H.H. Weiler, eds, *The European Court and National Courts – Doctrine and Jurisprudence: Legal Change in its Social Context* (Oxford: Hart Publishing, 1997).

Crawford, J. 'The Criteria for Statehood in International Law', *British Year Book of International Law: 1976–1977* (Oxford: Clarendon Press, 1978).

Crawford, J. *The Creation of States in International Law* (Oxford: Clarendon Press, 1979).

Croxton, D. 'The Peace of Westphalia of 1648 and the Origins of Sovereignty', *International History Review*, XXXI (1999), 569–91.

Curry, S. *Indigenous Sovereignty and the Democratic Project* (Aldershot: Ashgate Publishing, 2004).

Cygan, A.J. *The United Kingdom Parliament and European Union Legislation: Doctrine and Jurisprudence* (The Hague: Kluwer Law International, 1998).

Daes, E.A. United Nations Economic and Social Council, Commission on Human Rights, Sub-Commission on the Promotion and Protection of Human Rights, 56th Session Item 5 (b) of the Provisional Agenda, *Prevention of Discrimination: Prevention of Discrimination and Protection of Indigenous Peoples: Indigenous Peoples' Permanent Sovereignty over Natural Resources*, Final Report of the Special Rapporteur, E/CN.4/Sub.2/2004/30 (13 July, 2004).

Davis, M.C. 'Chinese Perspectives on Human Rights', in M.C. Davis, ed., *Human Rights and Chinese Values: Legal, Philosophical and Political Perspectives* (New York: Oxford University Press, 1995).

Declaration of Independence: The Unanimous Declaration of the thirteen United States of America. In Congress, July 4, 1776: <http://www.ushistory.org/declaration/document/> (21 July 2007).

Declaration on the Granting of Independence to Colonial Countries and Peoples, adopted by General Assembly Resolution 1514 (XV) of 14 December, 1960: http://www.unhchr.ch/html/menu3/b/c_coloni.htm> (10 January 2008).

Declaration on Principles of International Law, Friendly Relations and Co-operation Among States in Accordance with the Charter of the United Nations, 1 May 1970 <http://www/hku.ed/law/conlaw/outline/Outline4/2825.htm> (20 January 2008).

Degan, V-D. 'L'Affirmation des Principes du Droit Naturel par la Révolution Française: Le Projet de Déclaration Droit des Gens de l'abbé Grégoire', *Annuaire Française de Droit International,* XXXV (1989), 99–116.

Denham, M.E. and M. O. Lombardi, 'Perspectives on Third-World Sovereignty: Problems With(out) Borders' in M.E. Denham and M.O. Lombardi, eds, *Perspectives on Third World Sovereignty: A Post-Modern Paradox* (London: Macmillan Press, 1996).

D'Entrèves, A.P. *The Notion of the State: An Introduction to Political Theory* (Oxford: Clarendon Press, 1967).

Derrida, J. *On Cosmopolitanism and Forgiveness,* Trans. M. Dooley and M. Hughes (London: Routledge, 2001).

Despagnet, F. *Cours de Droit International Public* (Paris: Refuel Sire, 1910).

Dessauer, F.E.E. 'The Constitutional Decision: A German Theory of Constitutional Law and Politics', *Ethics,* LVII (1946), 14–37.

Dicey, A.V. *Introduction to the Study of the Law of the Constitution,* 8th edn (London: Macmillan, 1908).

Die Westfälischen Friedensverträge vom 24 Oktober 1648. Texte und Übersetzungen (Acta Pacis Westphalicae. Supplementa electronica, 1): <URL: http://www.pax-westphalica.de/ipmipo/> (25 July 2007).

Doehring, K. 'Self-Determination', in B. Simma, ed., *The Charter of the United Nations: A Commentary* (Oxford: Oxford University Press, 1994).

Doehring, K. 'Carl Schmitt. Le Nomos de la Terre dans le Droit des Gens du Jus Publicum Euopaeum. 1950 (Translation 2001)', *Journal of the History of International Law,* IV (2002), 374–6.

Donelan, M. 'Grotius and the Image of War', *Millennium,* XII (1983), 236–7.

Donnelly, J. 'Human Rights: Impact of International Action', *International Journal,* XLIII (1988), 241–63.

Donnelly, J. 'Human Rights: A New Standard of Civilization?', *International Affairs,* LXXIV (1998), 1–24.

Doppelt, G. 'Walzer's Theory of Morality in International Relations', *Philosophy & Public Affairs,* VIII (1978), 3–26.

Doubleday, N. 'Aboriginal Subsistence Whaling: the right of Inuit to Hunt Whales and Implications for International Environmental Law', *Denver Journal of International Law and Policy,* XVII (1989), 373–93.

Doyle, M. *Empires* (Ithaca: Cornell University Press, 1986).

Draper, G.I.A.D. 'Grotius' Place in the Development of Legal Ideas about War', in H. Bull *et al,* eds, *Hugo Grotius and International Relations* (Oxford: Clarendon Press, 1992).

Eberlein, B. and E. Grande, 'Reconstituting Political Authority in Europe: National Regulatory Networks and the Informalization of Governance in the EU' in E. Grande and L.W. Pauly, eds, *Complex Sovereignty: Reconstituting Political Authority in the Twenty-first Century* (Toronto: University of Toronto Press, 2005).

Egerton, G. 'The League of Nations: An Outline History 1920–1946' in *The League of Nations 1920–1946: Organization and Accomplishments: A Retrospective of the First Organization for the Establishment of World Peace* (Geneva: United Nations Library at Geneva, 1996).

Ehrenreich, B. *Blood Rites: Origins and History of the Passions of War* (New York, Henry Holt & Co., 1997).

Elliott, J.H. *Europe Divided: 1559–1598* (London: Collins, 1968).

Emerson, R. *State and Sovereignty in Modern Germany* (New Haven: Yale University Press, 1928).

Engster, D. 'Jean Bodin, Scepticism and Absolute Sovereignty', *History of Political Thought*, XIVII (1996), 469–99.

Eruetie, A. 'Indigenous Peoples' Ownership, Use and Responsibility for Lands and Resources', *Expert Seminar on Indigenous Peoples' Permanent Sovereignty over Natural Resources and on their Relationship to Land*. 25, 26 and 27 January, 2006, Palais des Nations, HR/Geneva/IP/Sem/2006/BP.4.

Eulau, H.H.F. 'The Depersonalization of the Concept of Sovereignty', *Journal of Politics*, IV (1942), 3–19.

Eyre, E.J. *Journals of Expeditions of Discovery*, Vol. II (London: T. and W. Boone, 1845).

Federal Policy Guide: Aboriginal Self-Government: The Government of Canada's Approach to Implementation of the Inherent Right and the Negotiation of Aboriginal Self-Government (1995) <www.ainc-inac.gc.ca/pr/pub/sg/plcy_e.html> (13 October 2004).

Federalist No. 39 'The Conformity of the Plan to Republican Principles': <http://www.constitution.org/fed/federa47.htm> (26 December 2006).

Fénelon, F. 'Lettre à Louis XIV' (1694): <http://www.gutenberg.org/etext/13914> (25 September 2007).

Fénelon, F. *Les Aventures de Télémaque* [1699] (Paris: Didier et Cie, 1861): <http://www.archive.org/details/lesaventuresdet00fnuoxx> (8 August 2007).

Fénelon, F. 'Essay on the Balance of Europe' in *A Collection of Scarce and Valuable Tracts on the Most Interesting and Entertaining Subjects*, 2nd edn (London: Cadell, Davis etc., 1815, 766).

Fiore, P. *Diritto Internazionale Codificato e la sua Sanzione Giruidica* [1890] (Torino: Union Tipografico-Editrice Torinese, 1909).

Fiore, P. *International Law Codified and its Legal Sanction or the Legal Organization of the Society of States* [1890] E.M. Borchard (New York: Baker, Voorhis and Company, 1918).

Fitzpatrick, J. 'The Stars on China's Flag: Appropriating the Universe for the Nation', J.A. Camilleri, A.P. Jarvis, A.J. Paolini, eds, *The State in Transition: Reimagining Political Space* (Boulder: Lynne Rienner, Boulder, 1995).

Fitzpatrick, P. '"Terminal Legality": Imperialism and the (De)composition of Legal Culture' in D. Kirby and C. Coleborne, eds, *Law, History, Colonialism: The Reach of Empire* (Manchester: Manchester University Press, 2001).

Follett, M.P. *The New State: Group Organization the Solution of Popular Government* (New York: Longmans, Green and Co., 1918).

Franklin, J. *Jean Bodin and the Rise of Absolutist Theory* (London: Cambridge, 1973).

Freud, S. 'On Narcissism: An Introduction' in *Collected Papers*, Vol. IV (London: Hogarth Press, 1957).

Freud, S. 'Thoughts for the Times on War and Death' in *Civilization, Society and Religion: Group Psychology, Civilisation and its Discontents and Other Works* (Harmondsworth: Penguin, 1985).

Frey, L. and M. Frey, 'The Rhetoric of Fraternity, The Reality of Conquest: The French Revolutionary Empire': <http://www.bu.edu/historic/06conf_papers/Freys.pdf> (19 July 2007).

Frost, M. *Ethics in International Relations: A Constitutive Theory* (Cambridge: Cambridge University Press, 1996).

Gallie, W.B. *Philosophers of Peace and War* (Cambridge: Cambridge University Press, Cambridge, 1978).

Garrison, J.A. 'China's Prudent Cultivation of "Soft" Power and Implications for U.S. Policy in East Asia', *Asian Affairs*, March (2005), 25–30.

Gathorne-Hardy, G.M. *A Short History of International Affairs*, 1920–1939, Fourth edn (London: Oxford, 1950).

Gentile, A. *De Iure Belli Tres*, trans. J.C. Rolfe [1612] (Oxford: Clarendon Press, 1933).

Gibson, C. *The Inca Concept of Sovereignty and the Spanish Administration in Peru* (New York: Greenwood Press, 1948).

Gibson, J.L. and G.A. Caldeira 'Changes in the Legitimacy of the European Court of Justice: A Post-Maastricht Analysis', *British Journal of Political Science*, XXVIII (1998), 63–91.

Glover, P.C. 'Merkel's European Army: More Than a Paper Tiger?', *World Politics Review*, 25 April 2007: <http://www.worldpoliticsreview.com/article.aspx?id=727> (20 November, 2007).

Gong, G.W. 'China's Entry into International Society' in H. Bull and A. Watson, eds, *The Expansion of International Society* (Oxford: Clarendon Press, 1985).

Grant, T.D. *The Recognition of States: Law and Practice in Debate and Evolution* (Westport: Praeger, 1999).

Green, T.H. *Lectures on the Principles of Political Obligation* (Kitchener: Batoche Books, 1999). First published as part of the *Works of T.H. Green*, ed., R.L. Nettleship, 3 Vols (London: Longmans Green, 1885–8).

Greven, M.T. 'Informalization of Transnational Governance – A Threat to Democratic Government' in E. Grande and L.W. Pauly, eds, *Complex Sovereignty: Reconstituting Political Authority in the Twenty-first Century* (Toronto: University of Toronto Press, 2005).

Grieco, J.M. 'The Maastricht Treaty, Economic and Monetary Union and the Neorealist Research Programme', *Review of International Studies*, XXI (1995), 21–40.

Grotius, H. *The Freedom of the Seas* (New York: Oxford University Press, 1916).

Grotius, H. *The Law of War and Peace*, F.W. Kelsey (Indianapolis: Bobbs-Merrill, 1925).

Grotius, H. *De iure Praedae Commentarius* (Oxford: Clarendon Press, 1950).

Hall, W.E. *A Treatise on International Law* [1880] 3rd edn (Oxford: Clarendon Press, 1895).

Hall, W.E. *A Treatise on International Law*, ed. A.P. Higgins (Oxford: Clarendon Press, 1924).

Hannum, H. *Autonomy, Sovereignty, and Self-Determination: The Accommodation of Conflicting Rights* (Philadelphia: University of Pennsylvania Press, 1990).

Hanson, D. 'Hobbes's Highway to Peace', *International Organization*, XXXVIII, (1984), 329–54.

Hartley, T.C. 'The European Court, Judicial Objectivity and the Constitution of the European Union', *Law Quarterly Review*, CXII (1996), 95–109.

Hartley, T.C. *The Foundations of European Community Law*, 4th edn (Oxford: Oxford University Press, 1998).

Hartley, T.C. *Constitutional Problems of the European Union* (Portland, Oregon: Hart Publishing, 1999).

Hegel, G.W.F. *Elements of the Philosophy of Right,* ed., A.W. Wood and trans. H.B. Nisbet (Cambridge: Cambridge University Press, 1991).

Henkin, L. 'The Human Rights Idea in China' in R.R. Edwards, L. Henkin and A.J. Nathan, eds, *Human Rights in Contemporary China* (New York: Columbia University Press, 1986).

Hepburn, S. 'Feudal Tenure and Native Title: Revising and Enduring Fiction', *Sydney Law Review,* XXVII (2005), 49–86.

Herberg-Rothe, A. 'Primacy of "Culture" over War in a Modern World?: John Keegan's Critique Demands a Sophisticated Interpretation of Clausewitz', *Defense Analysis,* II (2001): <htttp://www.clausewitz.com/CWZHOME/Herberg-Rothe/Keeggan2.htm> (30 October 2002).

Herman, J. 'The League of Nations and its Minority Protection Programme in Eastern Europe: Revolutionary, Unequalled and Underestimated' in the United Nations Library of Geneva: The League of Nations Archives, *The League of Nations 1920–1946: Organization and Accomplishments: A Retrospective of the First Organization for the Establishment of World Peace* (Geneva: United Nations, 1996).

Heuser, R. 'China and Developments in International Law: Wang Tieya as a Contemporary', *Journal of the History of International Law,* IV (2002), 142–58.

Heyking, A. Baron 'Some Defects in the Protection of Racial and Religious Minorities', *Transactions of the Grotius Society,* X (1924), 143–57.

Heyking, A. Baron 'The International Protection of Minorities – The Achilles' Heel of the League of Nations', *Transactions of the Grotius Society,* XIII (1927), 31–51.

Hinsley, F.H. *Sovereignty* (London: C.A. Watts & Co. Ltd, 1986).

Hitchcock, R. 'International Human Rights, the Environment, and Indigenous Peoples', *Colorado Journal of International Environmental Law and Policy,* V (1994), 1–22.

Ho, P-T. 'The Significance of the Ch'ing Period in Chinese History', *Journal of Asian Studies,* XXVI (1967), 189–95.

Hobbes, T. *Leviathan* (London: Penguin, 1968).

Hobbes, T. *De Cive* [1651]: <http://www.consitution.org/th/decive06.htm> (11 June 2006).

Hobbes, *Behemoth,* [1682]: <http://oll.libertyfund.org/Texts/Hobbes/0123/Works/HTMLs?Vol06/005106_Pt02_Behemoth.html#hd_lf051.06.head.005> (28 December 2006).

Hobhouse, L.T. *The Metaphysical Theory of the State* (London: Macmillan, 1918).

Holy Alliance: http://www.russianobility.org/Default.asp?Page=24 (7 August 2007).

Horne, D. 'A Challenge to the Legend of Anzac', *Sydney Morning Herald* (25 April, 1981).

Hornung, J. 'Civilisés et Barbares', *Revue de Droit International et de Législation Comparée,* XVI1 (1885), 447–70.

Hornung, J. 'Civilisés et Barbares', *Revue de Droit International et de Législation Comparée,* XVIII (1886), 188–206.

Hosack, J. *The Rise and Growth of the Law of Nations, As Established by General Usage and Treaties, From the Earliest Time to the Treaty of Utrecht* (London: John Murray, 1882).

House of Commons Information Office, *EU Legislation and Scrutiny Procedures,* Factsheet L11, Revised May 2007: <http://www.parliament.uk.factsheets> (22 November 2007).

Howard, R.C. 'Introduction', *The Journal of Politics,* XXIX (1969), 7–14.

Hrissimova, O. 'The League of Nations and the Problems of Minorities in the United Nations Library of Geneva: The League of Nations Archives', *The League of Nations 1920–1946: Organization and Accomplishments: A Retrospective of the First Organization for the Establishment of World Peace* (Geneva: United Nations, 1996).

Hsü, I.C. *The Rise of Modern China* (New York: Oxford, 1995).

Hughes, C. 'Globalisation and Nationalism: Squaring the Circle in Chinese International Relations Theory', *Millennium*, XXVI (1997), 103–24.

Indian and Northern Affairs Canada, *Federal Policy Guide: Aboriginal Self-Government*, (1995): < http://www.ainc-inac.gc.ca/pr/pub/sg/plcy_e.html> (20 July 2007).

Jackson, R. 'Sovereignty in World Politics: A Glance at the Conceptual and Historical Landscape', *Political Studies*, XLVII (1999), 431–56.

Jackson, R.H.J. 'Surrogate Sovereignty? Great Power Responsibility and "Failed States"', *Working Paper No. 25*, November (1998): <http://www.ipu.purdue.edu/failed_states/1999/papers/Jackson.html> (18 July 2003).

Jackson, R.H. *Quasi-States: Sovereignty, International Relations and the Third World* (Cambridge: Cambridge University Press, 1990).

Jacobini, H.B. 'Some Observations Concerning Jeremy Bentham's Concept of International Law', *American Journal of International Law*, XLII (1948), 415–17.

James, W. *The Moral Equivalent of War and Other Essays*, J.K. Roth, ed. (New York: Harper & Row, 1971).

James, A. *Sovereign Statehood: The Basis of International Society* (London: Basil Blackwell, 1986).

Jèze, G. *Étude Théorique et Pratique sur l'Occupation Comme Mode d'acquérir les Territoires en Droit International* (Paris: V. Giard & E. Brière, 1896).

Jianming S. 'The Elements of International Law', *International Legal Theory*, VI (2000) 15–34.

Jones, G., ed., *The Sovereignty of the Law: Selections from Blackstone's Commentaries on the Laws of England* (London: Macmillan, 1973).

Jones, W.T. *Masters of Political Thought: Machiavelli to Bentham*, Vol. II (London: Harrap, 1975).

Justinian, *The Digest of Justinian*, trans. A. Watson, Vol. 1 (Philadelphia: University of Pennsylvania Press, 1998).

Kant, I. *Religion within the Limits of Reason Alone*, trans. T.M. Greene and H.H. Hudson (New York: Harper & Brothers, 1960).

Kant, I. 'Perpetual Peace' in *Kant on History*, Lewis White Beck, ed. (Indianapolis: Bobbs-Merrill, 1963).

Kant, I. *Contest of the Faculties* in H. Reiss, ed., *Kant's Political Writings* (Cambridge: Cambridge University Press, 1970a).

Kant, I. *Perpetual Peace* in H. Reiss, ed., *Kant's Political Writings* (Cambridge: Cambridge University Press, 1970b).

Kant, I. *Metaphysics of Morals*, in H. Reiss, ed., *Kant's Political Writings* (Cambridge: Cambridge University Press, 1970c).

Kant, I. 'The Metaphysical Elements of Justice' in M.G. Forsyth, H.M.A. Keens-Soper and P. Savigear, *Theories of International Relations* (London: George Allen and Unwin, 1970d).

Kant, I. 'Eternal Peace' in H.P. Kainz, ed., *Philosophical Perspectives on Peace: An Anthology of Classical and Modern Sources* (Basingstoke: Macmillan, 1987).

Kant, I. in L. Pasternack, ed., *Immanuel Kant: Groundwork of the Metaphysic of Morals in Focus* (London: Routledge, 2002).

Keal, P. *European Conquest and the Rights of Indigenous Peoples: The Moral Backwardness of International Society* (Cambridge: Cambridge University Press, 2003).

Keal, P. 'Indigenous Self-Determination and the Legitimacy of Sovereign States', *International Politics*, XLIV (2007), 287–305: <http://www.palgrave-journals.com/ip/journal/v44/n2/full/8800189> (14 November 2007).

Kedourie, E. *Nationalism*, 3rd edn (London: Hutchinson, 1966).

Keegan, J. *A History of Warfare* (London: Random House, 1991).

Keens-Soper, M. 'The Practice of a States-System' in M. Donelan, ed., *The Reason of States: A Study in International Political Theory* (London: George Allen & Unwin, 1978).
Kelsen, H. 'Théorie Générale du Droit International Public', *Recueil des Cours*, LXII.IV (1932), 121–349.
Kelsen, H. 'Recognition in International Law: Theoretical Observations', *American Journal of International Law*, XXXV (1941), 605–17.
Kelsen, H. *General Theory of Law and State*, trans. Anders Wedberg (New York: Russell & Russell, 1946).
Kelsen, H. *Principles of International Law* (New York: Rinehart and Co., 1952).
Kelsen, H. *The Pure Theory of Law*, trans. M. Knight (Cambridge: Harvard University Press, 1967).
Kelsen, H. 'The Essence of International Law' in K.W. Deutsch and S. Hoffmann, eds, *The Relevance of International Law: Essays in Honor of Leo Gross* (Cambridge, MA: Schenkman Publishing Company, 1968).
King, P. *The Ideology of Order: A Comparative Analysis of Jean Bodin and Thomas Hobbes* (London: George Allen & Unwin, 1974).
Kirby, W.C. 'Traditions of Centrality, Authority and Management in Modern China's Foreign Relations' in T.W. Robinson and D. Shambaugh eds, *Chinese Foreign Policy: Theory and Practice* (London: Clarendon Press, 1994).
Klüber, J.L. *Droits des Gens Moderne de l'Europe*, reviewed, annotated and completed by A. Ott, 2nd edn (Paris: Guillaumin, 1874).
Kolb, R. 'Origin of the Twin Terms jus ad bellum/jus in bello', *International Review of the Red Cross*, no. 320 (1997), 553–62: <http://www.icrc.org/Web/eng/siteeng0.nsf/html/57JNUU> (20 July 2007).
Korman, S. *The Right of Conquest: The Acquisition of Territory by Force in International Law and Practice* (Oxford: Clarendon Press, 1996).
Koskenniemi, M. 'International Law as Political Theology: How to Read *Nomos der Erde?*', *Constellations*, XI (2004), 492–511.
Koskenniemi, M. 'Nationalism, Universalism, Empire: International Law in 1871 and 1919', Draft paper for the Conference 'Whose international Community? Universalism and the Legacies of Empire' (Columbia University, April 29–30, 2005).
Koskenniemi, M. 'International Law in Europe: Between Tradition and Renewal', *European Journal of International Law*, XVI (2005), 113–24.
Koskenniemi, M. 'Georg Friedrich von Martens (1756–1821) and the Origins of Modern International Law', *History and Theory of International Law Series*, IILJ Working Paper 2006/1, 1–24: <www.iilj.org> (24 July 2006).
Krabbe, H. *The Modern Idea of the State* (New York: D. Appleton and Company, 1930).
Krasner, S. *Sovereignty: Organized Hypocrisy* (Princeton: Princeton University Press, 1999).
Krasner, S. 'Organized Hypocrisy in Nineteenth-century East Asia', *International Relations of the Asia-Pacific*, I (2001), 173–97.
Lagarde, A. and L. Michaud, *Dixneuviemme Siécle: Les Grands Auteurs Français du Programme Anthologie et Histoire Littéraire*, XIX (Paris: Bordas Paris, 1985).
Las Casas, B. de, *In Defense of the Indians: The Defence of the Most Reverend Lord, Don Fray Bartolomé de Las Casas, of the Order of Preachers Late Bishop of Chiapa, Again the Persecutors and Slanderers of the Peoples of the New world Discovered Across the Seas*, trans. S. Poole (DeKalb: Northern Illinois University Press, 1974).
Lâm, M. *At the Edge of the State: Indigenous Peoples and Self-Determination* (New York: Transnational Publishers, 2000).
Laski, H.J. 'The Apotheosis of the State', *New Republic* (22 July 1919), 302–4.
Laski, H.J. *A Grammar of Politics* (London: Macmillan, 1925).

Laski, H.J. *Studies in the Problem of Sovereignty* (London: Allen & Unwin, 1968).

Lauterpacht, H. 'Spinoza and International Law', *British Yearbook of International Law*, VIII (1927), 89–107.

Lauterpacht, H. 'Règles générale du droit de la paix', *Recueil des Cours*, LXII.IV (1937), 62–416.

Leben, C. 'Hans Kelsen and the Advancement of International Law, *European Journal of International Law*, IX (1998) 287–305: <http://www.ejil.org/journal/Vol9/No2/index.html> (19 July 2007).

Lenin, V.I. 'The Right of Nations to Self-Determination' [1914] in *Lenin Collected Works* Vol. XX (Moscow: Progress Publishers, 1972): <http://www.marxists.org/archive/lenin//works/1914/self-det/index.htm> (23 July 2002).

Lesaffer, R. 'Emmannuelle Jouannet. Emer de Vattel et l'Émergence Doctrinale du Droit International Classique', *Journal of the History of International Law*, IV (2002), 384–6.

Lev, O. Review of Michael Walzer's Arguing about War, *Logos*, 3.4, Fall (2004), 3–4: <http://www.logosjournal.com/lev_walzer.htm> (19 July 2007).

Lindley, M.F. *The Acquisition of Government of Backward Territory in International Law* (London: Longmans Green, 1926).

Locke, J. *Two Treatises of Government*, ed., P. Laslett (Cambridge: Cambridge University Press, 1967).

Loh, C. 'The Vienna Process and the Importance of Universal Standards in Asia' in M.C. Davis, ed., *Human Rights and Chinese Values: Legal, Philosophical and Political Perspectives* (New York: Oxford University Press, 1995).

Loughlin, M. 'Ten Tenets of Sovereignty' in N. Walker, ed., *Sovereignty in Transition*, (Oxford: Hart Publishing, 2003).

Louis, W.R. 'The Era of the Mandates System and the Non-European World' in H. Bull and A. Watson, *The Expansion of International Society* (Oxford: Clarendon Press, 1985).

Loveland, I. 'Parliamentary Sovereignty and the European Community: The Unfinished Revolution?', *Parliamentary Affairs* , XLIV (1996), 517–35.

Maaka, R. and A. Fleras, 'Engaging with Indigenity: Tino Rangatiratanga in Aotearoa' in D. Ivison, P. Patton and W. Sanders, *Political Theory and the Rights of Indigenous Peoples* (Melbourne: Cambridge University Press, 2000).

MacCormick, N. 'Beyond the Sovereign State', *The Modern Law Review*, LVI (1993), 1–18.

McHugh, P. 'From Sovereignty Talk to Settlement Time: The Constitutional Setting of Māori Claims in the 1990s' in P. Havemann, ed., *Indigenous Peoples' Rights in Australia, Canada, & New Zealand* (Auckland: Oxford University Press, 1999).

McHugh, P. 'What a Difference a Treaty Makes – The Pathway of Aboriginal Rights Jurisprudence in New Zealand Public Law', *Public Law Review*, XV (2004), 87–102.

McIlwain, C.H. 'A Fragment on Sovereignty', *Political Science Quarterly*, XLVIII (1933), 94–106.

McNamara, K.R. and S. Meunier, 'Between National Sovereignty and International Power: What External Voice for the Euro?', *International Affairs*, LXXVIII (2002), 849–68.

Madison, J. 'The Conformity of the Plan to Republican Principles', *Federalist*, No. 39 (1788): <http://www.constitution.org/fed/federa47.htm> (21 July 2007).

Madison, J. 'Restrictions on the Authority of the Several States', *Federalist*, No. 44 (1788): <http://www.constitution.org/fed/federa47.htm> (21 July 2007).

Madison, J. 'The Particular Structure of the New Government and the Distribution of Power Among its Different Parts', *Federalist,* No. 47 (1788): <http://www.constitution.org/fed/federa47.htm> (21 July 2007).

Maiguashca, B. 'The National Indigenous Movement in a Changing World' in U. Sakamoto, ed., *Global Transformation: Challenges to the State System* (Tokyo: United Nations University Press, 1994).

Maitland, D. 'The European Union: The Way Ahead', *International Relations,* XV (2001), 79–85.

Manisty, H.F. 'The Right of Immigration', *Transactions of the Grotius Society,* XII (1926), 1–5.

Manfred Brunner and others v. The European Union Treaty, CMLR 1 (1994) 57: <http://www.unizar.es/euroconstitution/Library/BrunnerSentence.pdf> (17 June 2008).

Manning, C.A.W. 'Austin To-Day: Or "The Province of Jurisprudence Re-examined"', *Modern Theories of Law* (Oxford: Oxford University Press, 1933).

Marks, G. 'Sovereign States vs Peoples: Indigenous Rights and the Origins of International Law', *Australian Indigenous Law Reporter,* I (2000) 1–10: <http://www.austlii.edu.au/au/journals/AILR/2000/14.html> (5 June 2007).

Martel, J.R. 'Strong Sovereign, Weak Messiah: Thomas Hobbes on Scriptural Interpretation, Rhetoric and the Holy Spirit', *Theory & Event,* VII (2004): <http://muse.jhu.edu/journals/theory_and_event/v007/7.4martel.html> (10 February 2007).

Martens, G.F. von *Précis du Droit des Gens Moderne de l'Europe* (Göttingen: Librairie de Dieterich, 1801).

Martens, F. de *Traité de Droit International,* translated from the Russian by A. Léo (Paris: Libraire Marescq Aine, 1893).

Martínez, M.A. 'Study on Treaties, Agreements and Other Constructive Arrangements Between States and Indigenous Populations', Final Report, E/CN.4/Sub.2/ 1999/20, 22 June (1999): <http://www.puebloindio.org/study.htm> (21 July 2007).

Mayall, J. 'International Society and International Theory' in M. Donelan, ed., *The Reason of States: A Study in International Relations Theory* (London: George Allen & Unwin, 1978).

Mayall, J. 'Sovereignty, Nationalism, and Self-determination', *Political Studies,* IV (1999), 474–502.

Merriam, C.E. *History of the Theory of Sovereignty since Rousseau* (New York: Columbia University Press, 1900).

Mettam, R. *Power and Faction in Louis XIV's France* (London: Basil Blackwell, 1988).

Metzger, T.A. and R.H. Myers, 'Chinese Nationalism and American Policy', *Orbis* XLII (1998), 21–36.

Mill, J.S. 'A Few Words on Non-Intervention' in *Essays on Politics and Culture,* (New York: Doubleday, 1963).

Mirkine-Guetzévitch, B. 'L'Influence de la Révolution Française sur le Développement du Droit International sans l'Europe Orientale', *Recueil des Cours,* XXII: II (1928), 299–350.

Montesquieu, Baron de, *The Spirit of the Laws,* [1748] Vol. I, trans. T. Nugent (New York: Hafner Publishing Company, 1949).

Murray, G. 'Self-Determination of Nationalities', *Journal of the British Institute of International Affairs,* I (1922), 6–13.

Murray, G. *Then and Now* (Oxford: Oxford University Press, 1935).

Mutume, G. 'Indigenous People Fight for Inclusion: Press for an End to Discrimination and Marginalization', *Africa Renewal,* XXI (2007): <www.un.org/ecosocdev/geninfo/afrec/vol21no1/211-indigenous-rights.html> (28 November 2007).

Nettheim, G. '"The Consent of Natives": Mabo and Indigenous Political Rights', *Sydney Law Review*, XV (1993), 223–38.

Neuberger, B. 'National Self-determination: Dilemmas of a Concept', *Nations and Nationalism*, I (1995), 297–325.

Niezen, R. 'Recognizing Indigenism: Canadian Unity and the International Movement of Indigenous Peoples', *Comparative Studies in Society and History* (2000), 119–48.

Norris, A. 'Carl Schmitt's Political Metaphysics: On the Secularization of "The Outermost Sphere"', *Theory and Event*, IV (2000): <http://info.library.unsw.edu.au/cgi-bin/local/access/ej-access.cgi?url=http://muse.jhu.edu/cgi-bin/resolve_openurl.cgi?genre=&issn=1092-311X&volume=7&issue=1&date=2004> (5 February 2007).

Nussbaum, N. *A Concise History of the Law of Nations* (New York: Macmillan, 1954).

Nys, E. *Études de Droit International et de Droit Politique* (Brussels: Alfred Castaigne, 1896).

Nys, E. 'The Codification of International Law', *American Journal of International Law*, V (1911), 871–900.

Nys, E. 'The Development and Formation of International Law', *American Journal of International Law*, VI (1912), 279–315.

Oakeshott, M. 'Introduction to Leviathan' in M. Oakeshott, *Rationalism in Politics and Other Essays*, ed., T. Fuller (Indianapolis: Liberty Funds, 1991).

Ogden, S. 'Sovereignty and International Law: The Perspective of the People's Republic of China', *Journal of International Law and Politics*, II (1974), 1–32.

Ogden, S.P. *Chinese Concepts of the Nation, State, and Sovereignty*, Brown University, PhD (Ann Arbor: Xerox University Microfilms, 1975).

Ogden, S. 'The Approach of the Chinese Communists to the Study of International Law, State Sovereignty and the International System', *The China Quarterly*, LXX (1977), 315–37.

Ong, A. 'The Chinese Axis: Zoning Technologies and Variegated Sovereignty', *Journal of East Asian Studies*, IV (2004), 69–96.

Onuf, N. 'Henry Wheaton and "The Golden Age of International Law"', *International Legal Theory*, VI (2000), 2–9.

Onuma, Y. 'When was the Law of International Society Born? – An Inquiry of the History of International Law from an Intercivilizational Perspective', *Journal of the History of International Law*, II (2000), 1–66.

Openeurope, *A Guide to the Constitutional Treaty*, August 2007: <www.openeurope.org.uk> (20 November 2007).

Oppenheim, L. *International Law: A Treatise*, Vol. I, 2nd edn (London: Longmans, Green, and Co., 1912).

Österud, O. 'The Narrow Gate: Entry to the Club of Sovereign States', *Review of International Studies*, XXIII (1997), 167–84.

O'Sullivan, D. 'Needs, Rights, Nationhood, and the Politics of Indigeneity', *MAI Review*, I (2006), 1–12.

Palmer, M. 'The Treaty of Waitangi in Legislation', *New Zealand Law Journal* (June 2001), 207–11.

Paret, P. 'Clausewitz and the Nineteenth Century' in M. Howard, ed., *The Theory and Practice of War* (New York: Frederick A. Praeger, 1966).

Parry, C., ed. *Consolidated Treaty Series*, Vol. I, 1648–49 (New York: Oceana, 1969a).

Parry, C., ed. *Consolidated Treaty Series*, Vol. XXVIII, 1713 (New York: Oceana, 1969b).

Parry, C., ed. *Consolidated Treaty Series*, Vol. CXIV, 1855–56 (New York: Oceana, 1969c).

Patton, P. *Deleuze and the Political* (London: Routledge, 2000).

Peang-Meth, A. 'The Rights of Indigenous Peoples and their Fight for Self-Determination', *World Affairs*, CLXIV (2002), 101–14.

Pemberton, J. 'James and the Early Laski: The Ambiguous Legacy of Pragmatism', *History of Political Thought* (1998), 264–92.

Perry, W.J. *The Thought and Character of William James*, Vol. I (Boston: Little, Brown and Company, 1935).

Philpott, D. *Revolutions in Sovereignty: How Ideas Shaped Modern International Relations* (Princeton: Princeton University Press, 2001).

Pillet, A. 'Sur les Droits Fondamentaux des États', *Revue Générale de Droit International Public*, VI (1899), 503–32.

Pitty, R. 'Indigenous Peoples, Self-Determination and International Law', *International Journal of Human Rights*, V (2001), 44–71.

Pocock, J.J. 'Waitangi as Mystery of State: Consequences of the Ascription of Federative Capacity to the M_ori', in D. Ivison, P. Patton and W. Sanders, *Political Theory and the Rights of Indigenous Peoples* (Melbourne: Cambridge University Press, 2000).

Pogge, T., ed., *Freedom from Poverty as a Human Right: Who Owes What to the Very Poor?* (Paris and Oxford: UNESCO and Oxford University Press, 2007).

Politis, N. *Les Nouvellles Tendances du Droit International* (Paris: Hachette, 1927).

Pollack, M.A. 'Theorizing the European Union: International Organization, Domestic Polity, or Experiment in New Governance?', *Annual Review of Political Science*, VIII (2005), 357–98.

Pomerance, M. *Self-determination in Law and Practice: The New Doctrine in the United Nations* (The Hague: Martinus Nijhoff, 1982).

Prokhovnik, R. 'The State of Liberal Sovereignty', *British Journal Politics and International Relations*, I (1999), 63–83.

Pufendorf, S. *Of the Law of Nations and Nations: Eight Books*, trans. Basil Kennet (London: J. Walthoe, R. Wilkin *et al*, 1729).

Pufendorf, S. *De Jure Naturae et Gentium Libri Octo*, [1688] trans. C.H. and W.A. Oldfather (Oxford: Clarendon Press, 1934).

Qian, W. 'The United Nations and State Sovereignty in the Post-Cold War Era', *Pacifica Review*, VII (1995), 135–46.

Rabkin, J. 'Grotius, Vattel, and Locke: An Older View of Liberalism and Nationality', *The Review of Politics*, LIX (1997), 293–322.

Raič, D. *Statehood and the Law of Self-Determination* (The Hague: Kluwer Law International, 2002).

Randelzhofer, A. 'Article 51' in B. Simma, ed., *The Charter of the United Nations: A Commentary* (Oxford: Oxford University Press 1994).

Rappard, W. 'The League of Nations as an Historical Fact' in Geneva Institute of International Relations, *The Problem of Peace* (London: Oxford, 1927).

Rawlings, R. 'The United Kingdom: Legal Union and Ratification of the Treaty on European Union (part one)', *Public Law*, CCLV (1994), 254–78.

Rayneval, G. de *Institutions du droit de la nature et des gens* (Paris: Rey et Gravier, 1803).

Remec, P.P. *The Position of the Individual in Individual Law according to Grotius and Vattel* (The Hague: Martinus Nijhoff, 1960).

Renan, E. *Qu'est ce Qu'une Nation?* (Paris: Calman Levy, 1882).

Renan E. *Qu'est ce Qu'une Nation?:* <http://ourworld.compuserve.com/homepages/bib_lisieux> (15 March 2007).

Renault, L. *Introduction à l'Étude du Droit International* (Paris: L. Larose, 1879).

Report of the Royal Commission on Aboriginal Peoples (1996). Vol. II – Restructuring the Relationship, < <http://www.ainc-inac.gc.ca/ch/rcap/sg/sh3_e.html#1.3 > (20 July 2007).

Reynolds, H. *The Law of the Land* (Ringwood: Penguin 1992).

Reynolds, H. *Aboriginal Sovereignty* (St. Leonards: Allen & Unwin, 1996).

Riesenberg, P.N. *Inalienability of Sovereignty in Medieval Political Thought* (New York: Columbia University Press, 1956).

Rigaux, F. 'Hans Kelsen on International Law', *European Journal of International Law*, IX (1998) 325–43 <http://www.ejil.org/journal/Vol9/No2/index.html> (19 July 2007).

Roscher, B. 'The Renunciation of War as an Instrument of National Policy', *Journal of the History of International Law*, IV (2002), 293–309.

Rougier, A. 'La Théorie de l'Intervention d'Humanité', *Revue Générale de Droit International Public*, XVII (1910), 468–526.

Rousseau, J.J. *Considerations on the Government of Poland* (1762): <http://www.constitution.org/jjr/Poland> (15 April 2008).

Rousseau, J.J. *The Social Contract*, trans. M. Cranston (Harmondsworth: Penguin, 1968).

Rousseau, J.J. 'Abstract of the Abbé de Saint-Pierre's Project for Perpetual Peace' in M.G. Forsyth, H.M.A. Keens-Soper and P. Savigear, *Theories of International Relations* (London: George Allen and Unwin, 1970a).

Rousseau, J.J. 'Fragments on War' in M.G. Forsyth, H.M.A. Keens-Soper and P. Savigear, *Theories of International Relations* (London: George Allen and Unwin, 1970b).

Rousseau, J.J. 'Que l'État de Guerre Naît de l'État Social' in *Oeuvres Complètes*, Vol. 2 (Paris: Aux Éditions du Seuil, 1971).

Rousseau, J.J. *A Discourse on Inequality*, trans. M. Cranston (London: Penguin, 1984).

Rousseau, J.J. 'The State of War' in G.G. Roosevelt, 'A Reconstruction of Rousseau's Fragments on the State of War', *History of Political Thought*, VIII (1987a) 225–44.

Rousseau, J.J. 'Project for Perpetual Peace', in H.P. Kainz, ed., *Philosophical Perspectives on Peace: An Anthology of Classical and Modern Sources* (Basingstoke, Macmillan 1987b).

Rowen, H.H. *From Absolutism to Revolution 1648–1848* (New York: Macmillan New York, 1963).

Royal Proclamation of October 7, 1763, Virtual Law Office: <http://www.bloorstreet.com/200block/rp1763.htm> (5 March 2008).

Salomon, C. *De l'Occupation des Territoires sans Maître: Étude de Droit International* (Paris, A. Giard, 1889).

Sanders, D. 'Self-Determination and Indigenous Peoples' in C. Tomuschat, ed., *Modern Law of Self-Determination* (Dordrecht: Martinus Nijhoff, 1993).

Schmitt, C. *Political Theology: Four Chapters on the Concept of Sovereignty*, trans. G. Schwab (Cambridge, Mass: MIT Press, 1985).

Schmitt, C. *The Nomos of the Earth in the International Law of the Jus Publican Europium*, trans. G.L. Ulmen (New York: Telos Press, 2003).

Schmitt, C. *The Concept of the Political*, trans. G. Schwab (Chicago: University of Chicago Press, 2004).

Schmitt, C. 'The Theory of the Partisan', *The New Centennial Review*, IV (2004) 1–78: <http://www.msupress.msu.edu/journals/cr/schmitt.pdf> (19 July 2007).

Schnapper, D. 'The European Debate on Citizenship', *Daedalus*, CXXV (1997), 199–222.

Seaman, L.C.B. *From Vienna to Versailles* (London: Methuen & Co. Ltd, 1964).

Shambaugh, D. 'Containment or Engagement of China? Calculating Beijing's Responses', *International Security*, XXI (1996), 180–209.

Sharp, A. *Justice and the Māori: The Philosophy and Practice of Māori Claims in New Zealand since the 1970s*, 2nd edn (Auckland: Oxford University Press, 1997).

Simpson, G. 'Mabo, International Law, Terra Nullius and the Stories of Settlement: An Unresolved Jurisprudence', *Melbourne University Law Review*, XIX (1993), 195–210.

Smith, H. 'The Womb of War: Clausewitz and International Politics', *Review of International Studies*, XVI (1990), 39–58.

Snow, A.H. *The Question of Aborigines in the Law and Practice of Nations*, [1919] reproduced in *The Inquiry Handbooks*, XX (Wilmington: Scholarly Resources Inc., 1974).

Sørensen, G. 'Sovereignty: Change and Continuity in a Fundamental Institution', *Political Studies*, XLVII (1999), 590–604.

Sorley, W.R. 'The State and Morality' in *The International Crisis: The Theory of the State*, Lectures Delivered in February and March 1916 by Louise Creighton, W.R. Sorely *et al* (London: Oxford University Press, 1916).

Stromberg, R.N. *Redemption by War: The Intellectuals and 1914* (Lawrence: Regents Press of Kansas, 1982).

Suárez, F. *Selections from Three Works*, Vol. II (Oxford: Clarendon Press, 1944).

Suskind, R. 'Without a Doubt', *The New York Times* (17 October 2004). <http://www.cs.umass.edu/'immerman/play/opinionO5/WithoutADoubt.html> (10 January 2008).

Temperley, H.W.V. *Life of Canning* [1905] (New York: Haskell House, 1968).

Tan, C.C. *Chinese Political Thought in the Twentieth Century* (New York: Doubleday, 1971).

Thornberry, P. 'Self-determination, Minorities, Human Rights: A Review of International Instruments', *International and Comparative Law Quarterly*, XXXVIII (1989), 867–89.

Tomuschat, C. 'International Law: Ensuring the Survival of Mankind on the Eve of a New Century', *Recueil des Cours*, CCLXXXI (1999), 1–438.

Toqueville, A. de. *Democracy in America*, Vol. I, trans. H. Reeve (New York: Alfred Knopf, 1945).

Trask, H. K. 'Restitution as a Precondition of Reconciliation', *Borderlands: e-journal*, I (2002).

Treaty Establishing the European Community as Amended by Subsequent Treaties (25 March 1957): <http://www.hri.org/docs/Rome57/Part1.html> (10 January 2008).

Treitschke, H. von, *Die Freiheit* in M.G. Forsyth, H.M.A. Keens-Soper and P. Savigear, *Theories of International Relations* (London: George Allen and Unwin, 1970).

Tsebelis, G. and G. Garrett, 'The Institutional Foundations of Governmentalism and Supranationalism in the European Union', *International Organization*, LV (2001), 503–21.

Tully, J. 'The Struggle of Indigenous Peoples for and of Freedom' in D. Ivison, P. Patton and W. Sanders, *Political Theory and the Rights of Indigenous Peoples* (Melbourne: Cambridge University Press, 2000).

United Nations Library of Geneva: The League of Nations Archives, 'The Mandate System' in *The League of Nations 1920–1946: Organization and Accomplishments: A Retrospective of the First Organization for the Establishment of World Peace* (Geneva: United Nations, 1996).

United Nations Department of Public Information (New York: News and Media Division, 2007), '13 September, 2007 – General Assembly GA/10612 – General Assembly Adopts Declaration on Rights of Indigenous Peoples: "Major Step Forward" Towards Human Rights for All, Says President': <http://www.un.org/News/Press/docs/2007/ga10612.doc.html> (23 November 2007).

United Nations General Assembly (2007), 'United Nations Declaration on the Rights of Indigenous Peoples', December 2006 – Press Conference on Declaration of Indigenous Peoples' Rights':<http://www.un.org/esa/socdev/unpfii/en/declaration.html> (23 November 2007).

U.S. Department of Justice, Office of Tribal Justice, Department of Justice Policy on Indian Sovereignty and Government-to-Government Relations with Indian Tribes: <http://www.usdoj.gov/otj/sovtrb.htm> (13 October 2004).

Van Gend & Loos, Judgement of the Court of Justice, Case 26-62 (5 February 1963): <http://www.ema.lu> (5 March 2008).

Vattel, E. de *Les Droit des Nations ou Principes de la Loi Naturelle, Appliqué a la Conduite & Aux Affaires des Nations & des Souvereigns*, Tome I (Londre: 1768): <oll.libertyfund.org/index.php?option=com_staticxt&staticfile=show.php%3Ftitle=105> (25 September 2007).

Vattel, E. de *The Law of Nations; or, Principles of the Law of Nature Applied to the Conduct and Affairs of Nations and Sovereigns* (Philadelphia: T. & J.W. Johnson, 1863).

Vaughan, D. and F. Randolph, 'The Interface between Community Law and National Law: The United Kingdom Experience', in D. Curtin and D. O'Keeffe, eds, *Constitutional Adjudication in European Community Law and National Law* (Dublin: Butterworth, 1992.)

Victoria, F. de, *De indis et de Ivre Belli Relectiones* (William S. Hein & Co., 1995).

Vincent, A. *Theories of the State* (London: Basil Blackwell, 1987).

Vitoria, F. de *Political Writings*, A. Pagden and J. Lawrance, eds (Cambridge: Cambridge University Press, 1991).

Wachman, A. 'The China-Taiwan Relationship: A Cold War of Words', *Orbis*, XLVI (2002), 695–711.

Wade, H.R.H. 'What has Happened to the Sovereignty of Parliament', *Law Quarterly Review*, CVII (1991), 1–14.

Wade, H.W.R. 'Sovereignty – Revolution or Evolution?', *Law Quarterly Review*, CXII (1996), 568–75.

Wakeman, F. *Policing Shanghai 1927–1935* (Los Angeles: University of California Press, 1995).

Waldren, A. 'China's Coming Constitutional Challenges', *Orbis*, XXXIX (1995), 19–35.

Walker, N. 'Late Sovereignty in the European Union', *Sovereignty in Transition* (Oxford: Hart Publishing, 2003).

Wallace, W. 'Rescue or Retreat? The Nation State in Western Europe, 1945–93', *Political Studies*, XXXXII (1994), 52–76.

Walters, W. 'The Power of Inscription: Beyond Social Construction and Deconstruction in European Integration Studies', *Millennium* XXXI (2002), 83–108.

Walzer, M. *Just and Unjust Wars: A Moral Argument with Historical Illustrations* (New York: Basic Books, 1977).

Watson, I. 'Aboriginal Laws and the Sovereignty of Terra Nullius', I (2002), *Borderlands: e-journal*: <http://www.borderlandsejournal.adelaide.edu.au/issues/index.html> (19 July 2007).

Webber, J. 'Beyond Regret: Mabo's Implications for Australian Constitutionalism' in D. Ivison, P. Patton and W. Sanders, *Political Theory and the Rights of Indigenous Peoples* (Melbourne: Cambridge University Press, 2000).

Weissberg, G. 'Reviewed Work: *Das Selbstbestimmungsrecht der Volker*, by Kurt Rabl', *American Journal of International Law*, LIX (1965), 181–2.

Westlake, J. *International Law*, 2nd edn. Part 1 Peace (Cambridge: Cambridge University Press, 1910).

Weyland, I. 'Idealism and Realism in Kelsen's Treatment of Norm Conflicts' in R. Tur and W. Twining, eds, *Essays on Kelsen* (Oxford: Clarendon Press, 1986).

Wheaton, H. *Elements of International Law* [1836] G. Graft, ed. (Oxford: Clarendon Press, 1936).

Wight, M. *Systems of States* (Leicester: Leicester University Press, 1977).

Williams, J.F. *Chapters on Current International Law and the League of Nations* (London, Longmans, Green and Co., 1929a).

Williams J.F. 'Recogntion', *Transactions of the Grotius Society,* XV (1929b), 53–81.

Williams, J.F. 'The New Doctrine of "Recognition"', *Transactions of the Grotius Society,* XVIII (1932), 109–29.

Williams, H. *Kant's Political Philosophy* (Oxford: Basil Blackwell, 1983).

Williams, H. Clausewitz: 'The Strategic Dimension' in *International Relations in Political Theory* (Milton Keynes: Open University Press, 1992).

Wolff, C. *Jus Gentium Methodo Scientifica Pertractatum* [1764] J.J. Drake (Oxford: Clarendon Press, 1934).

Woloch, I. *The New Regime: Transformations of the French Civic Order, 1789–1820s,* (New York: W.W. Norton & Co., 1994).

Wu, E. 'Human Rights: China's Historical Perspectives in Context', *Journal of the History of International Law,* IV (2002), 335–73.

Wu, G. 'Identity, Sovereignty, and Economic Penetration: Beijing's Responses to Offshore Chinese Democracies', *Journal of Contemporary China,* XVI (2007), 295–313.

Zinsser, J.P. 'A New Partnership: Indigenous Peoples and the United Nations System', *Museum International,* LVI (2004), 76–88.

Zolo, D. 'H. Kelsen: International Peace through International Law', *European Journal of International Law,* IX (1998), 306–24: <http://www.ejil.org/journal/Vol9/No2/index.html> (19 July 2007).

Zolo D. and N. Bobbio, 'Hans Kelsen, the Theory of Law and the International Legal System – A Talk', *European Journal of International Law* IX (1998), 355–67 <http://www.ejil.org/journal/Vol9/No2/index.html> (19 July 2007).

Index